INSIDE
JAPAN'S
POWER
HOUSES

INSIDE JAPAN'S POWER HOUSES

The Culture, Mystique
and Future of
Japan's Greatest Corporations

KEVIN RAFFERTY

Weidenfeld & Nicolson
London

A catalogue record for this book is available
from the British Library.

Weidenfeld & Nicolson
The Orion Publishing Group Ltd
Orion House
5 Upper Saint Martin's Lane
London WC2H 9EA

Printed in Great Britain by Butler & Tanner Ltd,
Frome and London

Contents

Illustrations

(These pictures are all copyright of Kevin Rafferty)

Preface

Much has changed since this book was first mooted. Back in late 1989, it seemed that Japan was about to become the owner of the whole world, or at least the most valuable areas of it. Its industrial companies had earned international envy and, from steel and motorcars to electronics, were confounding all rivals. In those heady days, Shintaro Ishihara, the maverick member of parliament from the ruling Liberal Democratic Party, summed up an increasingly assertive mood by boasting that without Japanese technology in ceramics and electronics neither US satellites nor US missiles would ever get off the ground. The Pentagon had to admit its dependence. With Japan piling up huge surpluses on its trade and current accounts and massive net external assets, where would it all end? Under foreign pressure, Japan was setting up factories in the USA and Europe as well as in Asia, so that some economists saw the possibility of a handful of big Japanese companies owning all the productive parts of the world.

The less gullible would have seen the warning signs. It was surely hubris not to see the flimsy foundations on which the skyscraper of cards was built. In spring 1990 I remember a conversation with Yoshihisa Tabuchi, president of Nomura Securities, who predicted that the Nikkei Index of the Tokyo Stock Exchange would be at new record levels by the end of the year, beating the level of almost 40,000 set in December 1989. Japanese stocks were the most expensive in the world. But then so was so much else, including ludicrous land prices. There is the often quoted fact that Tokyo's Imperial Palace gardens were worth more than the whole of California; on a more homely scale, we calculated out that a friend's modest plot just outside Tokyo's Yamanote line (which is similar to London Underground's Circle line, although the Tokyo circle is bigger) was worth about $10 million in mid-1990 (when one dollar was worth 150 yen), this for a small, flimsy two-storey house in the equivalent of Shepherds Bush or Holloway. At the height of the boom rich Japanese, both corporate and individual, splashed huge sums of money on land, works of art, even slices of the 'Great American Dream' when Mitsubishi Estate bought New York's Rockefeller Center, and Sony and Matsushita paid billions for Hollywood film studios.

It could not go on. It did not go on. Plummeting prices for stocks and land on top of recession have damaged Japan's self-confidence. In a real sense, the 1995 Great Hanshin Earthquake that devastated Kobe marked the other extreme and showed not just the country's vulnerability to natural disaster but also exposed the flaws and failures of Japan Inc. These make the story more interesting and more urgent for examination.

I was lucky to have Jennifer Kavanagh as my agent. She was concerned to find a publisher who was in the mainstream but had a broad view of the world and could see the important forces beyond misty Britain that are shaping our lives and opportunities. Anthony Cheetham, who had recently bought the established house of Weidenfeld and Nicolson to be part of his Orion group, offered exactly the right sort of commitment to old values within a fresh and radical approach. He expressed fascination at the contrasts of old and new, the blend of tradition and modern technology that distinguish Japan. He advised me at our very first meeting that a story often comes alive by being told through the personalities. He chose Benjamin Buchan to oversee the project, a job he has done with great sympathy as his author struggled with a computer that was felled by the dreaded Barcelona telephone virus and then with the treacly world of bureaucracies that are the bane of Japan from Big Brother State to most big companies.

In Tokyo I was fortunate to have the support of Yoh Kurosawa, president of Industrial Bank of Japan, whom I had met in the 1980s when he was a managing director. He has always been generous with his time and prepared to handle any question I have thrown at him. When this book was a mere idea, he invited me for lunch, listened, made some helpful suggestions and promised his help. Whenever I was feeling gloomy about running into yet another bolted bureaucratic door, I knew that I could always take the book another few paragraphs forward by going to talk to Kurosawa-san. My only regret is that I have never played tennis with (or against) him.

Any journalist anywhere knows the pain of bureaucracies and public relations departments that all too often see their jobs as preventing the leakage of any useful, helpful or even amusing information, let alone damaging secrets. They exist annoyingly in the West: you know that the executive in question can answer illuminatingly in half a minute but his secretary insists that you go through the PR department and that can take days. The disinformation department wants to know all the questions you can possibly ask even on those occasions when the idea is to get the senior executive talking and take it from there, or when the issue is so confidential that the last thing you want is to blab it to lowly PR flacks.

In Japan the system is worse simply because of the confusion in any organisation about how to handle strangers. Any elementary business guide to Japan will instruct a foreigner not to expect to make any serious progress for at least several meetings, which will be spent exchanging the all-important *meishi* (name-cards), drinking Japanese green tea (or, increasingly, coffee), making strained attempts at polite conversation while the Japanese try to discover whether they feel comfortable with the people opposite and where they would fit in the network of business dealings *if* they decide to do business. Every organisation in every country has to employ such filters, but the Japanese have developed it into an art form.

When it comes to dealing with reporters, Japanese nervousness is the greater because PR people don't know what damage the alien might do, but fear the worst. Even the press division of the Foreign Ministry, which has probably more experience than most organisations in handling the foreign press, as well as being able to get information from Japanese diplomats abroad, asked for what was in effect a curriculum vitae of *The Guardian* (along with my own CV) before a lunch I was due to attend with the next ambassador to the UK. Even Toyota, which has the most professional of all the PR departments, with a mixture of Japanese and foreign staff, tried to tell me not to ask president Tatsuro Toyoda the vexing question about whether he had got the chief executive's job because of his family connections, although he had publicly addressed that issue himself.

The seemingly easier option of using a contact inside an organisation was not so easy for a project like this where I wanted to get a broad sweep and ask a wide range of questions of a wide range of people. So apart from IBJ, where Kurosawa-san and his personal assistants Mari Nishijima, Koichi Shimazu and Yasuhiro Sato were helpfulness personified in providing me with managers, directors and managing directors to see, and the Ministry of Finance, where I had a wide range of contacts and some friends and where the PR department was hopeless, the only option was to tread the treacle and try not to get stuck as the demands came for CV, book outline and synopsis, translated into Japanese please, what do you want to discuss, detailed questions in Japanese please, which other companies and who precisely in those companies are you going to see, and please clarify this and that and the other. One PR department even held up progress for a few months while it got its London office to check that Weidenfeld & Nicolson was a respectable publisher (and having reassured itself was thereafter most helpful).

In the end, the efforts were worth it. I got to see the chief executive of every company in this book. There were just one and a half failures. The failure, surprisingly, was Sony, whose co-founder Akio Morita I had twice met while working for *Institutional Investor* and where I had previously had extensive interviews with senior executives, although they had by this time left. I wanted to talk to Sony because it has factories in the UK and it would have been a useful counterpoint to Matsushita (though, as Matsushita people were quick to point out, their company is twice as big as Sony). But several years on, I am still waiting for a response to my requests for interviews. These were sent by fax, followed by telephone calls, re-sent and chased with telephone calls, but the Englishman in the

Sony PR department has not managed to get back to me. The half failure was with the Keidanren (federation of economic organisations) whose secretary-general Masaya Miyoshi agreed to see me but then had to call off twice because of business trips.

In selecting the powerhouses, I sought the biggest and strongest companies with an international outlook. In the case of the banks, IBJ is not the biggest, but it has played a key role both before and after the war in building up Japanese industry. Other city banks are bigger in terms of assets and capital, but the clinching factor was that none of them has a personality like Yoh Kurosawa round whom to build the story. Among the trading companies I chose Mitsubishi because the *keiretsu* links are strongest between Mitsubishi companies. When it came to the electrical concerns, I opted for Toshiba over Hitachi because Hitachi was close to IBJ, and over NEC because of the variety of Toshiba's operations straddling heavy industry and electronics. Because I did not want this to be a purely 'business' book and wanted to set the industrial and economic factors into the wider social and political framework, I also included reviews of education, bureaucracy and politics.

Wherever possible I have tried to make my own reporting the basis of this work. Most of the quotations from chief executives or leading figures were either from personal interviews or from public occasions which I attended or, in the case of the very biggest political events, watched on television. Japan's daily newspapers, besides leading the world in terms of sales,* offer sustained and serious coverage which in its quality makes the so-called 'quality' British press look luridly downmarket.

This makes the mainstream press good for keeping up with the public statements of politicians and other leaders of Japan Inc. and what they want you to know through careful leaks. The problem is that these reporters hunt in packs, known as 'kisha clubs', and pursue a dedicated quarry – a single ministry or leading politician. An acquaintance who was once a leading bureaucrat complained that one pack camped outside his house each night, demanded to be let in for drinks and would not go unless they had been fed with a good story. Such misbehaviour is intolerable, but it may be a small price to pay for domesticating the reporter. The existence of these clubs of reporters – and the determination on both sides to exclude intruders who might question the cosy system – means that the club reporters are effectively in the pocket of the people they cover. You have to read magazines, such as *AERA*, *Shukan Bunshun*, *Shukan Asahi* and

---

* *Yomiuri Shimbun* leads with 9.88 million copies a day for its morning edition and another 4.5 million in the evening, followed by *Asahi* with 8.2 million morning, 4.5 million evening, and *Mainichi* with 4 million, and 2 million in the evening; *Nihon Keizai Shimbun*, the *Financial Times* or *Wall Street Journal* of Japan, even sells 2.9 million copies in the morning plus 1.7 million in the evening.

Shukan Shincho and even gossipy ones like *Shukan Gendai* and trendy ones like *SPA!* among the weeklies, and the monthly *Bungei Shunju*, to get new slants on the news or the examination of controversial issues.

Of the people whom I saw and quoted in the book, I owe much to Yoh Kurosawa, to Toyoo Gyohten, previously of the MoF, and now chairman of Bank of Tokyo, and to Isao Kubota of the MoF, all of whom have over the years allowed me to call them at work or at home and seek their views on a variety of issues. Osamu Ebihara, auditor of Mitsubishi Corporation, offered me insights into the business world far beyond his own company. I came to like and respect Satsuki Eda, even though his political punch is less than he deserves. Shijuro Ogata, former deputy governor of the Bank of Japan and now adviser to Yamaichi Securities and on the board of Barclays Bank, only gets a small quoted part in this book but he has always been fun to talk to and a fount of commonsense. Atsuko Toyama, head of the cultural affairs agency, was most stimulating to talk to.

I have made my complaints about PR departments, but Nobuya Etoh of Toyota, and indeed the whole Toyota PR team, must be excepted from such strictures. Etoh-san took great care to understand what I wanted and then fixed visits to Toyota City, tours of several factories and interviews with all the top executives and senior managers I wanted, including chairman and president Shoichiro and Tatsuro Toyoda and honorary chairman Eiji Toyoda (though I fear I greatly upset the old man when I asked him which non-Toyota car he admired: he looked at me as if I were mad and the interview went cold). When I visited Toyota's Kentucky plant, Kaz Sato was an invaluable guide not only to the plant but also to cars in America. At Burnaston, Jinny McDonald arranged first-class briefings and a tour, and my only regret was that she would not allow a single photograph to be taken, a restriction not applied in Japan or the USA or indeed at the Nissan UK plant.

At Toshiba, I had three people to attend to my needs, Tetsuo Kadoya, Yuichi Takano and Makoto Ueda, who doggedly demanded details of the questions for interviews but delivered the goods in the form of the factory visits and leading executives and graciously gave me dinner after I had pestered them to let me into the clean room at Ome. At Matsushita, Toshiyuki Nakahara and his assistant Akihiro Tanii managed to find a gap in president Yoichi Morishita's busy schedule. Nippon Steel's general manager Toshio Yonezawa was quietly efficient in supplying information and fixing an interview with president Takashi Imai at short notice.

It has been a difficult book to write, not least because my wife Michelle remained in London concluding her studies to become a solicitor. Even in the middle of her taxing examinations she found time to keep me supplied with details of what the rest of the British press was saying about Japan and Asia, for which my undying gratitude. And when I made flying visits back, she found time to check my work and make often uncomfortably pertinent criticisms.

To my regret and continuing puzzlement, British coverage of East Asia and particularly Japan remains meagre. The *Financial Times* is an honourable exception. It has lots of space, though it does not always use it discriminatingly and rarely offers enlightenment on wider social issues. For the rest of the so-called 'quality newspapers' Japan evokes little interest. *The Guardian* was sometimes surprisingly better than the rest, and confounded me by showing an unexpected interest in Japan. But most Tokyo reporters for British 'quality' papers say they can hear the groans from their news desks when they suggest a political story, an important scandal, an emerging Japanese social trend, an achievement in science or technology or vital economic numbers. Foreign news desks are attracted by blood and gore and understand wars and disasters and death-tolls but find it hard to handle more sophisticated or subtle developments. Other departments of newspapers – education, health, law, women's affairs ('We have had enough foreign women for some time', was how I was once put in my place without getting a hearing), sport – are firmly in the hands of editors with a domestic agenda and perhaps an occasional glimpse at Europe. City pages fill with the UK first, then the UK implications of foreign stories, then let's-see-what-space-is-left.

This is a pity for a variety of reasons. For all its problems, Japan remains a great economic power with billions of dollars of net external assets – $640 billion as of March 1994. Its former economic dominance is now under threat, from a US revival, from the soaring yen and from the failure of the Japanese government to realise or take measures to arrest the decline, but the great Japanese industrial companies are stronger than wishful-thinking critics wish. And in Britain's case, the Japanese are playing a role in reviving industry that Margaret Thatcher's free market revolution squashed in domestic entrepreneurs. Why?

A story that will always get space in the British press is one that screams: aren't the Japanese weird, quaint, out of this world ha-ha-ha. This is an even greater pity. Not only is it demeaning, but it misses a great debate that is going on in Japan as to whether it wants to join Western civilisation with its commitment to democracy and liberal values or whether it should embrace the 'Asian values' that Lee Kuan Yew of Singapore and China advocate, which gives pre-eminence to the bureaucracy and the State.

The emphasis on the crash-bang-wallop and the weird creates gaps in our understanding of the Japanese, which is surely stupid for a country, the UK, that still has pretensions of being an international trading and financial player. To quote Jonathan Rauch, whose *The Outnation: A Search for the Soul of Japan* (Harvard Business School Press, 1992) is one of the few sparkling general books to have been published about Japan in the last few years: 'I was just a sociological tourist in Japan. I took notes and drew maps, looking about me as only the outsider can do. I did not find The System, a capitalized entity weaving its web around the hapless common man. I found, in the end, just systems. There was no dark secret. The Japanese are precisely as mysterious and unique as my aunt in Hackensack.'

Within an hour in Tokyo, I ran into two aspects of the dreaded bureaucracy. I was on Shinjuku station at morning rush-hour observing the peculiar rituals of the 300 per cent packed trains. Along the platform, station staff in uniform, cap and white gloves, one man every ten yards, played the amateur chorus line waving their right hands, index finger extended, along the platform as the train arrived, conducting passengers when to start their rush for space, pushing them in, then finishing the ballet with a synchronised wave to the departing train. I took my camera out, but no sooner had I taken a shot than one Japan Rail employee broke ranks and shoved his white-gloved hands in an X a few inches from my face. He shouted angrily through his face mask in English: 'No, no picture. Passport. Office.' He was not threatening me with crucifixion, but using the Japanese gesture for forbidden and telling me I had to get written permission and a pass to take pictures. He remains to me the epitome of the jumped-up bureaucrat.

I then went to the Imperial Palace and tried to take a picture of the policeman by his box beside the scenic spot of the double arched bridge. 'No,' he said, 'Wait'. I feared that after Shinjuku station, he might pull his gun. No, all he wanted to do was make himself presentable for having his picture taken, by putting his white gloves on first.

This is inevitably a moving story, which set off again at a gallop in March and April 1995. No one was prepared for the terrorist attack on the Tokyo subway system at the height of the morning rush-hour on 20 March. Containers of the deadly sarin nerve gas developed in Nazi Germany were left in five places, including three trains. More than 5,500 people were rushed to hospital, of whom twelve died and three were still in a coma a month later from inhaling the gas which swiftly paralyses the nervous system.

The confidence of the greater Tokyo population in the authorities was hardly enhanced when two further gas attacks, although with a milder form, were made in the centre of the adjacent port-city of Yokohama in April. All the while the media regaled the public with stories of daily police raids on a doomsday Buddhist cult Aum Shinrikyo (the Way of Divine Truth). The police went in wearing full combat gear against chemical and germ warfare and carrying caged canaries to warn them of possible gas leaks, and came out with several tons of chemicals comprising all the ingredients for sarin gas as well as for production of cyanide, dynamite and cultures for germs and bacteria. In addition, they found millions of yen in cash, gold bars, a Russian military helicopter, gun parts, precision lathes for making rifles, and books and documents suggesting that Aum was seeking nuclear and laser technology, nuclear warheads and tanks from Russia, where it has 30,000 members (three times as many as in Japan). The police also took 53 children aged between three and fourteen into care, most of them dirty and malnourished and many of them complaining of headaches from having to wear electronic headgear for hours at a time to tune into the thoughts of Aum guru and founder Shoko Asahara.

The story of Asahara was scary enough. He styled himself 'the Emperor' at the head of a network of 'government ministries' and predicted that the world as we know it would end in 1997 after clashes between Buddhists and Christians had triggered a third world war. By that time Aum would have taken over the government of Japan. One policeman commented that he seemed to be building an arsenal to destroy the world single-handed. When Asahara predicted that the weekend of 15–16 April (Easter in the West) would see a terrible disaster in Tokyo, more than 100,000 police were on guard and many of the jittery population went away for the weekend or filled their bathtubs with clean water for fear that the mains supply would be poisoned.

A month after the Tokyo subway terror, more than 100 Aum leaders had been arrested, but all for offences such as trespassing, traffic violations and using a false name at an hotel. Asahara had gone into hiding, but continued to give video performances for his followers. Some lawyers were afraid that the police raids were illegal – since they were supposedly conducted in pursuit of investigations into a kidnapping of which Aum was suspected. Meanwhile Aum protested its innocence of the sarin gas attack and claimed that its chemicals were for peaceful purposes, such as making fertilisers, plastic and toothpaste.

Public faith in the politicians was at such an all-time low that in the Tokyo and Osaka gubernatorial elections of April 1995, the voters rejected former senior bureaucrats who had the backing of most of the major political parties. In Tokyo, they chose Yukio Aoshima, a writer and trans-vestite actor who had starred as 'Nasty Grandma' in a television series; and in Osaka they opted for a comedian, 'Nokku Knock' Yokohama. In the face of this competition, maverick MP Shintaro Ishihara resigned his parliamentary seat, saying that politicians had become eunuchs.

Meanwhile the yen was rising at its own pace, soaring by 20 per cent in the first three and a half months of 1995 and touching 79.75 against the dollar at one point, in spite of the best efforts of the bank of Japan to buy dollars and the government to talk it down before it could damage cor-porate Japan irreparably. In the kingdom of lies, damned lies and statistics, Japan is clearly emperor. With the yen at 80 to the dollar, per capita income in Japan had risen to $48,000. The unbelievably rich included stewardesses on Japan Airlines, whose eight million yen income translated into $100,000, a princess's ransom (unless you have to buy at Japanese prices). More to the point, if the yen rises to 69.75 or higher against the dollar, then Japan will take over from the USA as the world's biggest economy in *absolute terms*.

In the end, Anthony Cheetham is right, and it is the people who count, make the story come alive and worthwhile, and this is an additional reason why Japan's riches are worth unwrapping and describing. On a very personal level, I owe wider debts of gratitude. Kenjiro and Kiyoko Hashimoto offered me the warmest hospitality on my first visit to Tokyo many years ago, showed me the richness and generosity of Japan, answered my naïve questions on almost every topic under the sun, from politics and banking to Buddhism, *kabuki* and the imperial family, and ensured that my ignorance was not so apparent to the outside world. I cherish the memory of their help and the fascination about Japan that it left with me.

Keiko Atsumi and Keiko Akatani, owners of the proudly all-female conference and translation agency InfoPlus, instructed me in the finer aspects of politics and the bureaucracy, introduced me to Eda, former prime ministers Takeo Fukuda and Kiichi Miyazawa and other interesting pillars of bureaucracy and business, and gave me comments on many other leading lights. Professor Shigeto Tsuru, former head of Hitotsubashi University, spared valuable time for tuition about the importance of introducing a more human and environmentally friendly form of economy. Novelists Shusaku Endo and Kenzaburo Oe made it worthwhile being a journalist in Tokyo with two stimulating, but different, afternoon sessions in which we talked about Japan – past, present and future.

But my greatest debt is to my assistant who fixed interviews, translated articles into English and questions into Japanese, and calmed me down when there was another mountain of questions to be answered before I could get entry into one of the powerhouses. She found Sumio Baba for me, who has developed and printed all the photographs in this book as well as the pictures I have taken for *The Guardian* and *The Observer*, frequently in a matter of hours, a service that is rarely available in the West.

It was a lesson in the Japanese language in itself to listen to my assistant sweet-talking an important person or a low-ranking PR official, then switching to English to tell me what she really thought. She was Takemura-san to most of the people to whom she talked, though sometimes Matsumoto or Fukuda. She is unwilling to reveal her real name because neither I nor *The Guardian* could afford to pay a full-time wage and her regular employers might object. Her ability to understand and jump between Japanese and foreign culture is impressive, as is her grasp of politics and her incisive judgement of politicians and bureaucrats, both the individuals and the issues. I find it hard to accept her protests that 'I am just a country girl' and I hope that one day I shall have time to see the chestnut village from which she comes.

Note on yen/dollar conversion. In this book the yen has been converted into dollars at 100 yen to $1, the rate prevailing in early 1995. By April 1995, then yen had risen to the 80–84 range.

Note on Japanese names. When writing in Japanese, the Japanese put their family names first, given names second. But when using *Romaji* or Roman forms and addressing Westerners, they invariably follow Western practice of given names first, followed by family names. For this reason, I have followed the same practice (given name, followed by family name), thinking it pretentious to reverse the order for a book written in English.

INSIDE
JAPAN'S
POWER
HOUSES

1

Introduction:

Japan, the Once and Future Superpower

In Osaka, Japan's second city, residents were roughly shaken from sleep or tossed from their beds. In Kobe, 25 miles away, it was worse, like the roar of an exploding bomb. In a matter of seconds just before dawn at 5.46 on Tuesday 17 January 1995 the cosmopolitan port-city of Kobe (meaning literally 'God's Door') was transformed into a devastated burning third world wasteland by Japan's worst earthquake for 70 years. The disaster did more than kill 5,100 people, create 300,000 homeless refugees, destroy 100,000 buildings and wreck a large part of the country's economy. It ruined the myth of Japan Inc. as a confident well-organised country ready to meet any unexpected challenge. It exposed major deficiencies in the way in which the Tokyo-centred political and bureaucratic rulers run the country and – most important of all for the outside world – it showed that Japan still has little idea of itself as part of the international community.

The Great Hanshin Earthquake (as it was later officially named) came with a sudden fury. It split houses open and scattered their occupants and contents or crushed them almost to dust; it ripped up electricity cables and gas and water pipes in an orgy of destruction of modern man's best-laid infrastructure; it removed the fifth floor of a seven-storey hospital, tumbled a ten-storey apartment building into an instant roadblock, took bites out of roads and railway lines, toppled supposedly earthquake-resistant highways on their sides, left buses and trains dangling in mid-air, twisted the cranes and gantries and mockingly reduced the world's sixth busiest container port to a waterlogged morass.

If it laughed at modern science and technology, it was no respecter of religion either. It sent out one large Shinto shrine crashing on its face, as if caught in a kowtow, and obliterated several small, almost household, shrines. A small Roman Catholic church in the worst-hit area of Kobe was burned to the ground, but a life-sized statue of the Sacred Heart remained untouched in the ashes with its arms outstretched. As far as 60 miles away from the epicentre, temples in Kyoto and Nara were shaken, priceless statues of Buddha fell and one had its fingers broken.

That was just the initial impact. The quake also triggered hundreds of fires which the emergency services could not get near, especially as gas and water pipes burst, so that the gas fed the fires and there was no water to put them out. Michael Miller of the Kobe Institute said the city 'exploded in flames in front of us'. At the end of the first night the only lights in Kobe were of the flames from the fires. Apocalyptic images epitomised the earthquake. 'I felt I was being thrown into a deep pit like hell,' said one resident near Kobe. 'I had reconciled myself to going to heaven,' said one old man who was pulled out after thirteen hours. That was by no means the record for survival. The human spirit can be tough: on Sunday, six days after the earthquake, a 66-year-old woman and a 79-year-old man were miraculously rescued after being buried alive for 128 hours without food or water. They had to have their faces covered with blankets to keep out the light when they returned to face the world.

No one who saw the damage can ever take lightly expressions such as 'the force of Nature'. Yet within the destructiveness there was a random savagery. It is not easy to explain why one house was spilled in rubble across the road, while its neighbour was only split in two; why others down the street merely had their tiles tossed onto the street like discarded dominoes, while yet others were apparently untouched. The most congested part of Kobe, where the poorest people live along with a large community of *burakumin** and foreigners like Koreans, Chinese and Vietnamese, was burned to ashes. Though Nature was democratic and hit rich as well as poor areas, it was frequently the poorer people's homes that collapsed and buried them, while the rich escaped with a lowered standard of living: from Mercedes to motor scooter, chinaware to crockery, hot baths to cold ones.

Days after the disaster, 300,000 homeless refugees were crowded into congested emergency shelters or shivering round fires in the open air, some of them burning the remains of their houses in the attempt to ward off the chill winter air. Those inside the shelters were not much better off, occupying about a grave space each, with no heating and without enough blankets, with scarce food supplies and no running water for bathing or flushing toilets. The dead were not far away either, attended by offerings of fruit and sake to aid their journey to the next life, but unburied because many had not been identified, undertakers had also been hit by the quake and crematoria had not had their gas supplies restored.

The resourceful media again managed to show the rescue services the way to the scene of the disaster. As in the case of the 1985 crash of a Japan Airlines Boeing 747 – when the press had helicopters over the site the night before the rescue services staggered up the mountain – the Japanese media were quickly organised to bring pictures of the horror and interviews with the victims. At one stage, angry Kobe people, still sitting in their

* The untouchables whom self-respecting Japanese pretend do not exist, though they go to great pains to make sure that their children do not marry one.

nightclothes waiting for food and water, yelled at the media to go away and let their helicopters bring in supplies instead.

The failures of the authorities were caused by a variety of factors. Japan constantly lives with the fear of earthquake – and the Meteorological Agency has been spending more than 10 billion yen ($100 million) a year observing the behaviour of catfish and how they twitch as a clue to earthquake prediction, for which it won the Massachusetts Institute of Technology Ignoble Prize (along with a church in Alabama which claims to have discovered a mathematical formula to determine the number of souls destined to spend eternity burning in Hell). But Kobe and the Hanshin region, of which it and Osaka are twin centres, were not considered to be particularly earthquake-prone because they had not suffered one for 399 years, a strange view given that all of Japan is crisscrossed by major fault lines and has as many minor ones as hairs on a man's forearm.

Japan's rulers in Tokyo slept peacefully in their beds through the earthquake, not even feeling a tremble let alone a tremor. This helped explain the initial reaction in the capital that since it had not happened there, it was not a big event. Prime minister Tomiichi Murayama heard the news first on television and had to wait 90 minutes for an official report. Several economists claimed in the first few days that the disaster might even be mildly beneficial to the country because of the boost it would give to the construction industry. At this stage, damage from the earthquake was being put at $20 billion, but estimates have since risen to $150 billion or more. Not until the first evening when the media brought blazing pictures of the aftermath into every living-room did people wake up to the fact that this was a major tragedy. Kobe's earthquake also shattered the myths of Japan's marvellous engineering and of its sophisticated disaster organisation. There was a four-hour delay before soldiers from the Self-Defence Forces (Japan's equivalent of armed forces, which it does not have because the constitution forbids them) were called out because the governor of Hyogo prefecture, of which Kobe is the capital, did not realise that his go-ahead was necessary. This contrasts with the fifteen minutes it took to get the National Guard out after the Los Angeles Northridge earthquake in January 1994.

Even when they got moving, the performance of the Japanese authorities left much to be desired. Training of officials in precision small-scale drills left them clearly unprepared for the widespread chaos of the real thing. For example, on day 4 the Kobe relief co-ordinator claimed he was 'delighted, delighted' with the response and his supplies of blankets, tins of food, packets of instant noodles and bags of rice. But when pressed he admitted that tin-openers had not been supplied with the tins and that many supplies had not got to the relief centres because he lacked drivers and the roads were congested. Meanwhile at the overflowing evacuation centres, just one blanket had been distributed for every five people and they were sitting on packets of instant noodles and rice with no water in which to cook them. Water was a problem. On day 4 there were 80 lorries going round carrying supplies, but not enough tanks to put the water into. To get a perspective, one area alone (with 60 of several hundred refugee centres) said it needed 100 lorry-loads of water a day to satisfy the urgent needs for drinking and washing. Sadly, but not surprisingly, thirsty refugees were bending down to scoop water from broken mains on the street.

The whole of the first week the rescue and relief effort was an object lesson of too little too late. Rescue efforts were still continuing on day 6 when the relief operation should have been in full swing. The relief operation was running late – as illustrated by plans by day 7 to build 11,000 emergency housing units over the next few weeks when there were more than 310,000 homeless and in the constant grumbles from refugees that they had not had a bath since the earthquake struck. It was hard to believe that this was Japan, the richest country in the world with income of more than $41,000 a head and not able to provide basic living standards for a disaster-struck medium-sized town.

Japan's building standards are obviously not as earthquake-proof as its engineers had believed, even gloated, when California was hit. Lurking under the surface, given the frequent corruption in the Japanese construction business, are questions about how many corners were cut and standards disregarded. Sure enough, bits of wood were discovered in some road pilings and it was revealed that standards had been relaxed on safety measures against vertical shaking, which is what distinguished the Kobe earthquake.

Japan's leaders were slow to get a proper relief and rescue operation into gear, to grasp all the help available, or to set priorities, such as getting roads clear and giving relief supplies safe passage, organising helicopter drops of essential items, planning comfortable encampments to house several hundred thousand refugees for months until housing could be repaired or rebuilt, and even shifting refugees to Osaka in the east or Himeji or Hiroshima in the west where the common luxuries of life continued to run freely. There was little use of helicopters to speed operations. Worse still, the whole exercise exposed the flaws in Japan's bureaucracy, ultracareful and anxious to explore all the options before acting, divided by the narrow tribal lines of their ministries and agencies – too bad for anyone suffocating under rubble and needing sniffer dogs to find them, or heavy lifting gear to get them out or urgent medical treatment to patch them up.

All this help was available if there had been anyone to organise it: France and Switzerland offered dogs trained to find people buried under avalanches; the UK volunteered a team with special sensing equipment; the USA had medical evacuation teams, heavy lifting gear, tent cities on standby; doctors offered their help from Japan and around the world;

there were Japanese who have experience of earthquake aid elsewhere in the world; the self-defence forces have considerable emergency capacity, including, said Kazuhisa Ogawa, president of Crisis Management Research Institute, a private think tank, the ability to make 300,000 hot meals a day. But officials dithered and continued to tie red tape round critical decisions. The European dogs were initially refused, then accepted, then delayed while the Ministry of Agriculture had to be persuaded to waive quarantine rules, so that the first critical days were lost; US troops sat kicking their heels in Okinawa; doctors from outside the area were discouraged from going; the self-defence forces never were fully deployed.

The performance of prime minister Tomiichi Murayama was particularly discouraging. He waited until day 3 before dropping in to Kobe, expressing his horror at the devastation and urging refugees, '*Gambatte* [Keep your chin up]', then flying back to Tokyo. Clearly, a Socialist prime minister was unhappy about calling for a mass mobilisation of troops, let alone seeking the assistance of foreign soldiers. The minister whom he appointed to co-ordinate the relief operations was not one of the heavyweights with political clout nor known for his management abilities. Some leading Japanese even made a virtue out of chaos. Kazutoshi Ito, director of the National Land Agency's disaster prevention co-ordination division, raised the spectre of pre-war militarism. 'In an emergency like this, if you are referring to the central government having the power to suppress and suffocate the will on the part of the local municipalities, it reminds me of the rebirth of Japanese militarism,' he claimed at a press conference ten days after the quake. 'In the name of the state of emergency, our country restricted the rights of people and even trampled on the rights of people ... I am firmly resolved we shall never, ever return to the state of affairs that we were in 50 years ago.'

Weeks after the earthquake, bureaucrats were again arguing over the prime minister's demands for a new law to bring special relief to the victims. The officials claimed that no new measures were needed nor was there any reason to set up a reconstruction agency. Some officials noted that the cabinet-level emergency taskforce had no legal basis. Such sentiments hardly offered much hope to the refugees who faced months in temporary shelters, but who were bravely making the best of wretched circumstances.*

The Great Hanshin Earthquake brought some worrying lessons with it, not all of which were recognised by the ruling élite. Kobe was visited with terrible loss of life even though the earthquake occurred before the

---

* Unlike Los Angeles, where there was an orgy of looting, there was very little theft in Kobe and inhabitants who went back to their houses after several days were able to pick working electronic items as well as clothes and furniture from the rubble where the quake had tossed them.

morning rushhour when the trains, subways and buses would have been packed and the roads jammed. Although it was undoubtedly a big earth-quake, it was not 'the Big One' that everyone fears, another big Tokyo earthquake. Tokyo has its share of wooden houses, narrow lanes, vul-nerable apartment blocks. It has a greater concentration of tall tower-blocks. Most important is the sheer number of people in Tokyo, about 12 million in the city and 30 million in the immediate conurbation. None of the regular safety drills, normally lighthearted affairs where people gather once a year as if going on a picnic with their emergency equipment, takes account of the mass devastation of communications and utilities as happened in Kobe nor of the months of dislocation that will continue after the earthquake has passed.*

But the disorganisation also pointed to problems in the normal life of Japan Inc. One was that the bureaucratic machine may work wonderfully when it has time to plan and consider carefully all the aspects of a problem, but finds it hard to adapt to a crisis. Another is that the bureaucracy is not a seamless and smooth machine, but is comprised of different, sometimes antagonistic parts, which can be aggressively tribal.

Equally important as Japan moves towards the twenty-first century and aspires to a seat at the top table internationally is its failure to see itself as part of a world community. The way in which officials dealt with offers of foreign help was tragic and may have caused hundreds of deaths and hundreds of thousands of needless cases of hardship. Kitao Abe, a professor of psychology at Sei Gakuin University, commented, 'For Japanese, it is appropriate to make their own efforts before turning to outsiders' help.' This is true of other countries too, but other countries in crisis, for example the Netherlands under the January 1995 floods, recognised their limi-tations and asked for help. Hardpressed Japanese officials could reasonably be sceptical about whether Greek thoracic surgeons or Bangladesh nurses who can't speak Japanese would be much help. But sniffer dogs don't have to speak Japanese to find people in the rubble; the foreign doctors who were told that they were not licensed to practice or give injections had Japanese interpreters; and the US troops had vital equipment in the country which was left idle.

In their distress, the Japanese victims wanted help from wherever it was offered. One old man lamented: 'Chinese leader Deng Xiaoping said it does not matter whether the cat is black or white as long as it catches mice. I don't care what the colour of soldiers' eyes – if only they could have pulled my wife out in time. But it is too late.' It is hard to think of

---

* About 140,000 people died in the Great Kanto Earthquake of 1923 which hit Tokyo. Many of them were killed by the fires that consumed much of the city after the earthquake. Some people were even killed as they leapt into rivers which were boiling with the heat of the flames.

any leader in any other country who would try to make a triumphant nationalistic statement out of tragedy. Yet former construction minister Taku Yamasaki claimed that Japan's uniqueness, its single race and language had helped it to pull it through. 'I may be nationalistic ... but the state of Japan as one race, one country and one language is an identity that has created this sort of national power after the war,' he said after the earthquake (quoted by the Kyodo news agency), forgetting the Koreans and Chinese who also died. In the fiftieth anniversary year of the dropping of the atomic bombs and the end of the war, it was a reassertion of the view that Japan sees itself as victim, both of the war and of the angry forces of nature, and is alone and unique – a dangerous view, but one that is often encountered.

Japan's claims to be unique and its uneasiness in dealing with the outside world are quickly apparent to any visitor. The Boeing 747–400 airliner, the biggest, latest model of the jumbo, sleek epitome of the jet age, equipped with sophisticated computer navigation systems, touched down smoothly after a flight of 13 hours and 52 minutes from the other side of the world. It then began a journey to the third world. First it had to stop and wait while another aircraft pulled out in front of it, then it taxied for twenty minutes before halting and making a slow detour round a small piece of farmland, slap in the middle of the apron on the direct route to the shining new terminal. 'Sorry, nothing we can do. The farmers insisted on retaining their land right in the middle of the airport; sometimes aircraft are delayed while they go across to farm,' said the pilot afterwards.

The terminal was bright and new, but the immigration procedures were shufflingly slow, almost as bad as New York. Customs was worse: everyone without exception had to wait in line, even in the green channel, hand over their passport, answer questions about where they had been, what their occupation was, why they had come, how long they were staying, what their luggage contained and what duty-free goods they had, and some were asked to open a bag for the official to prod and poke and riffle through – time-consuming procedures which third world countries like India and Bangladesh have abandoned in favour of spot checks. But there was no point in rushing. Trains to the city were available, but booked full for two hours; buses were taking three hours thanks to traffic jams; taxis cost almost a prince's ransom, $250 to $300 to downtown. The prices, nearly $30 on the train, were the giveaway that this was not the third world. Welcome to Japan (though no one said it)!

Narita airport, the main gateway to Tokyo, 66 kilometres (44 miles) away, reflects the ambivalence of Japan, especially towards foreigners. The airport was built far far away from the city, poorly served by public transport for the numbers of people using it. Worse for a country which prides itself on consensus and consultation, the arrogant planners antagonised local farmers, who protested so ferociously against their land being taken that the airport today lives under a constant state of siege, ringed with fences and barbed wire, guarded round the clock by security police, with armoured personnel carriers, water cannon and tear gas at the ready. Its single runway is totally inadequate for the present traffic, but the farmers have prevented the building of the second one. Part of each end has been built, but then the tarmac peters into farmland, so that it is like two jigsaws that have got mixed up, one revealing the urgent lines of a modern airport, the other, unhurried mucky edges of pastoral life that is governed by the sun and seasons not the clock.*

This new terminal opened in late 1992, easing check-in congestion for the airlines and passengers lucky enough to use it, principally the Japanese carriers, but doing nothing about the queues for the runway. Meanwhile at the old terminal, airlines stuck there have had to make do with the same cramped old space since one wing was boarded up 'for renovation', which will take eight years or more, longer than most countries take to build a brand new airport. At busy times, the old terminal resembles an evacuation by prosperous refugees, so cluttered with bodies and suitcases that it is impossible to get through without shoving people out of the way.

A government with any understanding of the feelings of passengers, many of whom travel from twelve to twenty-four hours to get to Tokyo, would not have built its international gateway in such a faraway spot, or would have laid the domestic transport connections first, and would have provided smoother, faster processing formalities.† A government concerned about the feelings of its own people would have tried to reach an accommodation with the farmers first. A government less arrogant would have taken steps sooner to improve the situation; after all, Narita opened back in May 1978.

As with the New (but somewhat tarnished) Tokyo International Airport, as Narita is formally called, so with Japan. Ichiro Ozawa, the most forceful and controversial of the country's leading politicians, wrote recently that Japan is today so strong economically that it accounts for 16 per cent of the world's total gross domestic product, second only to the USA. This

---

* In 1994 the government and farmers reached a truce, with the government dropping plans for the new runway and promising fresh negotiations, but these have so far been fruitless.

† The opening in 1994 of the new Kansai International Airport on a man-made island near Osaka makes it easier for passengers travelling to that area to reach Japan. But it has done nothing to relieve the strains of people who live or have business to do in Tokyo, which after all is the capital and main financial and commercial centre. And the horrendous landing fees and rents have produced new world records at the airport, such as the $20 cup of coffee.

means, he asserted, that 'Japan's slightest move has an impact that reaches every corner of the globe.' This is true, yet Japan has critical flaws, most crucially – and potentially tragically – in its own failure to understand the outside world or its place in it. Japan's economy is by classic indicators the strongest in the world; yet it has to depend on other countries for almost all its energy needs and for essential supplies of food to stay alive, as well as for most of the raw materials it makes into steel, clothes, housing, household products, sophisticated electronics and other exports. It lives by trading; yet it has faced, with growing resentment, increasingly strident complaints from its industrial partners that its practices are unfair. It has used much of its money from the trade surpluses to buy US Treasury bills and bonds, which are of diminishing worth given the policies that have seen the yen increase in value. By some calculations, Japan's actions have been equivalent to throwing away 25 per cent of its savings. Increasingly, Japan has been demanding a permanent seat at the top table for international political decisions, but it regularly does not seem to know or care how its neighbours are harmed by its actions and comments.

Many of these problems have deep historical roots going back to the Second World War and before that. After the dropping of the atomic bombs on Hiroshima and Nagasaki, and its surrender in August 1945, Japan was reduced to dust and ashes, both metaphorically and literally. The first Australian civilian to go to Japan after the war described central Tokyo as a burnt-out desert. 'Ashes from central Tokyo to Yokohama,' he said. American B-29 aircraft, dropping firebombs, had laid waste much of the old wooden-built city. Other major cities had fared badly in air attacks and 66 of them, with the notable exception of historic Kyoto, had been largely destroyed; half the housing in Japan's cities had been lost, destroyed directly by bombs or in the fires that followed; more than half the commercial and industrial property had been badly damaged and was unusable; there were no exports and Japan's merchant fleet consisted of a few coastal ships. Food was scarce. The few factories left standing had no fuel to run on. The harvest in 1945 had been disrupted. In all, industrial production was only 30 per cent of its pre-war levels. The conquering allies had promised to make Japan pay reparations, but there was virtually no equipment left to be stripped and sent abroad. This gloomy situation was exacerbated by the return of about 3.5 million Japanese troops and an equal number of civilians from abroad to swell an already poverty-stricken population and put further pressures on a near-starving, threadbare economy.

What Japan did have was a functioning government, unlike defeated Germany. The Allies conducted purges of militarist politicians, most of the military establishment, rightiest teachers and 2,000 business leaders in their determination to destroy the pre-war military–economic combine and smash the old *zaibatsu* (conglomerates). Altogether, by May 1946,

210,288 Japanese had been purged and ultranationalist organisations dissolved. Later seven Japanese leaders were condemned to death and hanged in 1948 as part of controversial war trials, including the former prime minister, General Hideki Tojo. There was much argument about the wisdom and still more about the justice of these trials. This was especially so since Japan's ruler and supposed living god, Emperor Hirohito, was many foreigners' favourite scapegoat for the war, but was not brought to book. 'The first gentleman of Japan' was what the Supreme Commander for the Allied Powers (SCAP) General Douglas MacArthur called Hirohito after he had renounced his divinity and agreed to be a constitutional monarch.

Most damagingly, the procedures at the trial evidently did not follow accepted legal precedents. The only judge with experience of international law, the Indian Radhabinod Pal, found all the defendants not guilty. The main charge against the trials was that they constituted vindictive victor's justice. This created a feeling of bad blood on both sides, with Japanese leaders feeling resentful about show trials and many of them determined to wipe out the shame of defeat, while many non-Japanese felt that justice had not been done because Hirohito (or Emperor Showa as he is posthumously known) had been let off without a trial. In spite of this, Japan's bureaucracy was left more or less functioning and the main economic ministries saw their powers enhanced rather than diminished, given the magnitude of the task of putting the country on its feet again and the inability of the Americans to understand a complex society.

The first years were tough, not just because of the immediate problems of putting the country back together after the war. Food was extremely scarce and people from the cities went to the countryside to try to buy black market food. One of the memorable news pictures of the time is of a train, composed partly of passenger carriages and partly of open goods cars, but with every available millimetre packed with people, including many perched precariously on the carriage roofs, going to the countryside to get sweet potatoes. Family treasures were sold on a large scale. Many Japanese lived under improvised accommodation, using tarpaulins, or even found shelter under bridges. Farmers used human manure for fertilisers.

For the first three years, the government had to rely on American food aid even to survive. The crusading democrat SCAP MacArthur, who came to be regarded almost as a substitute emperor by the Japanese, pushed through a new democratic constitution. Article 9 famously committed Japan to renounce war and to promise not to keep land, sea or air forces, or war potential of any sort. The constitution and article 9 were part of a compromise deal, allowing the emperor to continue on Japan's Chrysanthemum Throne as, in the words of the constitution, 'the symbol of the state'. Under the constitution, promulgated in November 1946 and effective from 3 May 1947, the emperor has no role in the business of government. But this constitution was very much an American creation, pressed on the Japanese after the committee under Joji Matsumoto appointed by the prime minister had offered simply a rewording of the old nineteenth-century Meiji constitution. It was accepted at the time by a defeated country, but has come to be resented by some vociferous political leaders as a foreign imposition.

Getting Japan on its feet again proved to be a more difficult task. MacArthur's brief was not to assume any obligation for the standard of living in Japan, since the Japanese were regarded as responsible for their own plight. But he became impatient with the government's sluggish and ineffectual policies. The supremo's own camp was divided at the very top: MacArthur's two most important immediate subordinates were loyal, arrogant, hard working and vehemently opposed to each other in their views. The government section under Major-General Courtney Whitney was headed by a lawyer and liberal idealist; whereas the intelligence section was run by Major-General Charles Willoughby, a vigorous anti-Communist whom MacArthur called 'my lovable fascist'. Apart from the contradictions between the two men, the other problems were that the Japanese government itself was unstable and its policies proved not to be very practical. In consequence, the economy plunged from bad to worse, with the economic problems generating labour unrest, political crisis and stagflation.

Japan was rescued by the changing tides of history. First came the Cold War, which changed Washington's priorities and made it important to enlist Japan as a bulwark against Communism and again to become 'the workshop of Asia'. Responsibility for economic policy was taken out of the hands of MacArthur, and a Detroit banker, Joseph Dodge, was sent to Tokyo. He proposed harsh measures to tackle inflation, and fixed the exchange rate for the currency at 360 yen to the dollar. The Dodge Plan wiped out inflation. Japan was then rescued from the recession that this created by the Korean War, which boosted production as the country became a frontline base for the war effort. Equally important, the war and Japan's regaining of its independence through the San Francisco peace treaty (effective in April 1952) had an important rejuvenating effect on business and government. Japan was assisted by the infusion of funds from bilateral and multilateral agencies, including the World Bank, one of whose triumphs was to lend money for the first *Shinkansen* bullet train line. Shinkansen (which literally means 'new trunk line') trains started running on 1 October 1964, just ten days before the opening of the Tokyo Olympic Games, so they became twin symbols of the successful conclusion of the first stage of Japan's struggle back to economic maturity.

The country was helped by its high education levels, the industrial tradition developed since the Meiji era – since Japan would not have been able to wage the war without a strong industry – the dedication and determination of its people, and its smooth organisation under the triumvirate of bureaucrats, businessmen and politicians, in which the politicians played a decidedly subservient role. Bureaucrats under the old Meiji Restoration of 1868* had always regarded themselves as the servants of the emperor, superior to the money-grabbing politicians, and they very much continued this attitude. The Ministry of International Trade and Industry (Miti, previously the Ministry of Commerce and Industry and before that the powerful pre-war Ministry of Munitions, following the same ministerial tradition), laid down the guidelines for industrial development, while the Ministry of Finance, through its supervision and direction of the banks, controlled the flow of funds to make sure they went to the right purposes.

Japan was also helped by its social as well as its economic practices. Unlike in Anglo-Saxon countries, where shareholders demand an improving financial performance every quarter – an attitude famously criticised by Sony co-founder Akio Morita, who claimed that western companies have an attention span of only ten minutes – the Japanese traditionally take a longer view, counting market share as more important than immediate profits. In the West, the desire for profits in the next quarter has often led to American and British industrial companies coming under the control of accountants and financial experts, rather than the engineers and executives responsible for making a quality product. Japanese companies rarely hire mercenary Masters of Business Administration or PhDs, but take on fresh graduates and steep them in the company culture before perhaps sending them away for a couple of years to acquire an advanced foreign degree at company expense.

The existence for most companies of a stable group of controlling shareholders, with the leading bank playing an important role as shareholder, provider of funds and, sometimes, general nanny, has helped to insulate corporate Japan from the immediate pressures of a fickle stock market. With a few notable exceptions, Japan's antipathy towards predatory mergers and acquisitions has also curbed the growth of financial whizkids, and has concentrated attention on the business in hand, making a

---

* The young Mutsuhito became Japan's emperor in 1867 at the age of 15 when the Tokugawa *Bakufu* still ruled the country. But the shogunate and its policy of *sakoku* or 'the closed country' had been weakened by the arrival of Commodore Matthew Perry and other westerners. On 3 January 1868 anti-shogunate forces led by southern lords from Satsuma and Choshu seized the imperial palace in Kyoto and announced the reversion of political power from the shogun to the emperor who later that year assumed the name Meiji (or enlightened government). In the narrow sense, this was a coup shifting rule from one clique to another, but over the period of the emperor's reign up to 1912 radical political, social and economic changes transformed Japan from a feudal into a modern unified state.

good product. This cultural climate has offered Japanese manufacturers stability and the chance to get well established, spreading the costs of a new product over a period of time long enough to pay off its investment. In any industry there has always been plenty of ultrasharp domestic competition. Indeed, John Loughran, the able and well-connected head of Morgan Guaranty Trust in Tokyo in the 1980s, commented that 'Japanese manufacturers are so honed to sharpness by competition at home, that put them in any foreign market and they will go through it like a hot knife through butter.'

The Japanese were undoubtedly greatly helped by the building up of immense protective walls about them. Foreign car makers had dominated the Japanese market, and indeed had local plants until the 1930s when the militarists shut them out. Those doors were not opened again until the Japanese manufacturers were firmly established and becoming exporting powers themselves. Indeed, right until the 1990s, there were complaints from foreign car makers – and from foreign manufacturers in other areas – that Japanese bureaucrats typically twist, bend and extend the rules, via administrative guidance or inspections or any other excuse, effectively to shut foreigners out of the market. Thus in the case of cars, small suppliers to the Japanese market not only faced stringent safety rules different from those in their home country, but also had to pay for lengthy inspections of each individual car to make sure that it met the peculiar and usually highly particular rules and regulations of the Japanese market, all of this adding expensive cost and time to selling to Japan.

In a typical example of how Japanese inspectors did their best to kill a market, imports of Dutch flowers faced quarantine inspections to such detail, sometimes with individual flowers being handled, that the products were virtually dead before they could be sold. Apples offered another classic case of protection: Japan's agriculture ministry for years refused to approve the test and pest control procedures of the USA, Australia and New Zealand, which had been proved by practice over many years, but insisted on its own more exacting standards. In another famous case, Philips of the Netherlands was first into Japan with a coffee-making machine, but then was beaten out of sight when Japanese manufacturers made a similar version and used their Mom 'n' Pop corner shops to make sure that the foreign intruder found it near-impossible to sell. By such means, markets that are formally open – as 'proved' by the fact that Japan has the fewest and the lowest formal tariff barriers of any rich country – can quickly be closed as the bureaucracy shows its might by lengthy and costly tests, inspections and checks.

Japanese business and economic practices differ considerably from those commonly seen in the West, quite apart from seeking market share and profitable long-term business rather than shortsightedly chasing immediate profits. There is not the 'them and us' mentality between management and workers in Japanese business that is commonly seen in the West. Japanese frequently express amazement at the differences in pay between the ordinary workers and the bosses in the USA, and even more so at the antics of American businesspeople who award themselves vast sums in bonuses and share options even when their companies are hardly making profits or are on the verge of collapsing. Japanese bosses are certainly well treated, enjoying substantial pay plus all possible perks, including cars, entertainment and golf club memberships. But the pay differentials are not as ocean-wide as between workers and management in the West. In the early 1990s, the average pay difference between the president and his shop floor workers in Japan was eighteen times; in the USA it was 119 times.

In the office or factory, Japanese managers normally have modest offices, and in some companies only the top few have their own personal offices. In Mitsubishi Corporation, the giant trading company, board-level directors work in the same big room along with other managers, although they have a privileged vantage point. It would be unthinkable for a Japanese boss to be installed in palatial isolation from the rest of his workers, as Roger Smith was in the 1980s, lording it over General Motors. More important, Japanese are expected not to flaunt their financial superiority ostentatiously, as western bosses often do. Equally telling, in the West, recession or bad fortunes of a company are frequently followed by massive lay-offs. In the British utility companies in the early 1990s, a new form of lay-off was practised as privatised electricity, gas and water companies made more and more money, and their chief executives took fatter and fatter pay cheques home, while large numbers of workers were sacked in the interests of creating a lean and efficient machine. Japan's prevailing philosophy has been that the company is an enterprise of management and workers and shareholders together, and that the workers also have rights. Since the company has obligations to its workers, lay-offs should come last.

It is easy to exaggerate the influence of 'lifetime employment', which in its purest form is practised only by the very biggest companies. Toyota and Toshiba can afford to offer lifetime employment to their workers because the daily and yearly fluctuations of recession and economic tides are borne by a large number of supplier companies. If you work as a supplier directly for Toyota, that is probably all right because Toyota also has obligations to you, but if you are supplying the widgets or tiny small parts at the end of a chain of many links to Toyota, then you will run the risk of going bankrupt when the economy is hit by recession. Such companies are small, typically with just a handful of workers, and do not have the luxury of a 'them and us' mentality. Even during the gloomy height of the 1992–4 recession, the biggest companies were still refusing to lay people off, instead preferring to limit new recruitment – and there was an outcry when the electrical company Pioneer at the end of 1992 gave thirty-five middle-ranking managers in their early fifties the choice of accepting redundancy or being sacked.

'Consensus' management has often been overrated, but it still plays an important part in Japanese business life.* Japanese companies, like those elsewhere in the world, have to reach decisions, and sometimes top management has to make difficult choices. But generally speaking, the Japanese make more of an effort to undertake as wide a consultation as possible. Another way of looking at it is to say that most Japanese companies go to great lengths to discover and analyse the possible pitfalls and problems in any course of action *before* proceeding. Big industrial concerns like Toyota go to extraordinary lengths to smooth out the production process, to make it as efficient and easy as possible. Normally great pains are taken to involve the line workers in decisions and to ask for their suggestions. It is almost impossible to imagine a situation similar to that which happened in the USA, where bored, antagonised General Motors autoworkers were deliberately trying to damage the cars they were making as they went along the production line.

The Japanese have also avoided the common British affliction of infights between different labour unions working within the same company over pay and skill differentials. Most Japanese companies have one union. Wage negotiations are done annually in spring, in groups of companies. The main guides to the pay levels are what increases the path-breaking negotiators, normally the engineers or steel workers, have achieved, and what is the state of the economy. In the early 1990s, pay increases were extremely modest at only a couple of per cent, reflecting Japan's troubled times. Strikes over the spring wage offensive became increasingly token, with only the private rail unions coming out on strike, for a matter of hours only.

Of course, there has been a price to pay for this kind of success. The emphasis on consensus imposes obligations on workers – and indeed everyone at every stage of life – to fit in. Employers in the difficult economic conditions of the early 1990s began to make noises suggesting that they were not sure how long the 'lifetime employment' system could last if economic stringency continued. But lifetime employment is a two-way obligation. It also imposes restrictions on workers that would not be tolerated in a western environment, such as the commitment to stay with one firm for life, and to tolerate the seniority system, which sees progress by a series of slow steps, and the long working hours. Sometimes the latter

* Emphasis on consensus and conformity has deep roots, say sociologists, going back to farming practices and the rice culture which required that villagers work together in a disciplined way to produce the crop.

is carried to ludicrous lengths, with workers dragging out the day just to be seen still at their desks or to keep company with the slowest person. A European friend who went on secondment to the Japanese parent company was appalled to find that 'In the afternoons, my Japanese colleagues were larking around, reading comics, doing anything to fill in time so that they could stay late. It was not done to cost the company money, since they did not receive overtime, but was part of a corporate binding process. On evenings when work did not drag on there was corporate drinking, with the company picking up the tab for a lot of it. Curiously, young workers could get very rude about their bosses: people who would not dare say "boo" in the office, in the bar would let their hair down and be downright insulting to the boss's face, and yet no one held it against them because they were in their cups.'

The slow pace of pay rises makes it difficult financially for a young man with a family – and socially for his wife.* In 1994 a report from a Tokyo housing agent said that for the first time housing was in reach of young newly marrieds. The fall in house prices meant that it was possible to buy a flat on the outskirts of Tokyo, perhaps an hour's sardine commute from work, for 'only' 40 million yen ($400,000); for this trifling sum the lucky young couple would get three rooms – in fact, a basic living room, a bedroom and a combined kitchen-diner – plus a bathroom and a lavatory separate from the bathroom. (Japanese find it hard to accept the frequent British practice of having the lavatory in the same room as the bathroom.) Equally tough for any young spirited person working for a Japanese company is the limited room for initiative – but then this is a lesson learned over many years from early schooldays. Any foreigner staying for any length of time in Japan gets easily tired of hearing a piece of folk wisdom that has become a cliché: 'the nail that sticks up will get hammered down'.

Japan's rapid economic progress brought an increasing assertion of national identity. This became vigorous in the mid- to late 1980s, as Japanese contrasted what they had achieved with all too obvious American and western failings, especially as the West increasingly began to bleat about Japan's unfair trade practices. The then prime minister, Yasuhiro Nakasone, started a big stir in 1986 when he claimed that Japan's successes

---

* This is why some big companies provide basic accommodation for their male employees. Young women on the whole are expected to live with their families until they get married, and it is not uncommon for young women to be investigated for marriage – a common practice in Japan – and turned down because they are not living at home but have their own flat. Hypocrisy also being rife in Japan, both factors (the dormitories for men and the women living at home) help encourage a flourishing 'love-hotel' industry, renting rooms in two-hourly stints. Only a few very rich companies, like the Industrial Bank of Japan, provide accommodation for young married couples.

were the result of its racial homogeneity. Conveniently forgetting the Ainu, the dwindling band of original inhabitants of the country squeezed out by the majority Japanese, and the underclass *burakumin*, similar to the untouchables in India, he presented Japan as having a unique special race, unlike the USA where blacks, Hispanics and other immigrants helped dilute IQ levels and the pursuit of excellence. This was not a particularly new idea in Japan, where belief in the special purity and superiority of the Yamato race was still strong and whole forests have been chewed up to produce books expressing the view that Japan is unique, alone, inimitable and unfathomable to outsiders.* The new factor was that the head of government had dared to give public expression to these arrogant claims.

A more threatening version of the same theme came in the late 1980s, particularly in the book originally written in Japanese by maverick ruling Liberal Democratic Party MP Shintaro Ishihara and Sony's Akio Morita, entitled *No to ieru Nihon*. By the time that the English version, *The Japan that Can Say No: Why Japan Will Be First Among Equals*, was published in 1991, Morita had regretted his involvement with Ishihara's more out-spoken comments, so the politician's views were published alone. Basic-ally, Ishihara's thesis was that it was time for Japan to stand up to the bullying USA. We do not have to take these threats from a declining power, was the essence of his work. Explosively, Ishihara pointed out that Japan supplied the key parts that made American intercontinental missiles and spaceships take off and function properly. 'America wants to steal Japanese know-how. It cannot manufacture the most technologically advanced fighters without advanced ceramic and carbon fibre technology from Japan.' He added, 'The time has come for Japan to tell the US that we do not need American protection.' Just to drive the message home, he suggested that it was open to Japan to sell its technology to the Soviet Union. He made it clear that he knew what he was saying when he added, 'This would change the military balance entirely.' Pentagon officials scurried round and had to admit that the USA no longer made some of the parts needed to get its most advanced weapons systems in the air.

Ishihara's political timing was unfortunate to say the least, given that the English version of the book was hardly in print before the Berlin Wall was down, the Soviet Union was crumbling and the Cold War was at an end. The collapse of the Soviet Union and Japan's own economic diffi-culties helped to quieten such cries, but under the surface there was still the claim that Japan was being pushed around too much by a USA that

---

* Special variations on this theme, enunciated at various times by politicians, are that Japanese intestines are special and different from those in the West, so that Japanese cannot eat beef; that Japanese snow is different and needs special Japanese skis; and that the Japanese brain has special qualities, making it impossible for any foreigner really to penetrate or understand.

was responsible for most of its own problems. Japanese claimed with justification that they had had to take on the American market the hard way, learn its particular requirements, and build up contacts and people who would distribute their products. The Americans, they said, wanted to be offered entry to Japan on a plate. The 'big three' American car giants, for example, did not even take the precaution of putting the steering wheel of their cars on the right hand side to sell in Japan, which, like Britain, drives on the left. Japanese car companies had quickly realised back in the 1960s that they had to build left-hand-drive cars if they wanted to sell in the USA. To rub in their complaint, the Japanese pointed out that, even with left-hand-drive cars, Mercedes and BMW had taken the trouble to understand the Japanese market and were taking the lion's share of car imports. These began to rise rapidly in the early 1990s as the rising yen made imports more attractive.

Western experience in penetrating the Japanese market was mixed. A small number of companies had found their niche and discovered that the Japanese market was profitable like few others in the world. Coca-Cola was *the* soft drink and had Japan virtually to itself. McDonald's, followed a good way behind by Kentucky Fried Chicken and Burger King, captured the fast-food market so convincingly that the story was told of Japanese children visiting the USA, seeing the golden arches of the McDonald's M and saying, 'Oh look, Daddy, they have *Makudonarudo* in America too.' Other companies like Nescafé in the instant coffee market, Procter and Gamble soap powders, and Wella shampoos and beauty products also have a strong hold on the market. Some Americans, not just the big successful companies, have grumbled that their compatriots just do not try hard enough to penetrate a market that is difficult, full of its own quirks, but not impossible to make profits from.

There has also been a price to pay for the particular shape of the Japanese economic miracle. Manufactured goods, with some notable exceptions, are in good supply, and thanks to the cut-throat competition among Japanese industrialists, are reasonably priced. Although foreign critics made a fuss, claiming that Japan was producing televisions, radios, hi-fi, cameras, other electronic items and cars, and selling them at cheap export prices, growth of discount stores and increasingly keen Japanese ability to shop around mean that most gadgets can be bought almost as cheaply in Tokyo as abroad. One notable exception is a laptop computer with English software, which costs 50 per cent more in Tokyo than in New York, even though made by Toshiba. Part of the reason for the difference is that there is little demand in Tokyo for computers with English software. The popularity of discounting is such that some imported goods can also be bought more cheaply in Japan than outside. For example, bottles of Scotch whisky, although subject to higher duty than locally distilled *shochu* (in defiance of GATT international trade rulings that domestic and foreign distilled liquor should be treated equally) were available for about 1,600 yen ($16 or £10.39), which was cheaper than the price in the UK.

On the other hand, basic everyday items of food and clothing are much more expensive in Japan than outside. Of a common basket of regular family purchases in 1993, only toilet paper and eggs were cheaper in Tokyo than in London or Paris, though the eggs were more expensive than in New York. Rice cost twice as much in Tokyo as in the other major cities; beef was three times as expensive; milk was more than twice the price; so was beer; a suit, shirt or jeans cost about 75 per cent of the Tokyo price. Overall, in 1993 Tokyo prices were 48 per cent higher than those in New York or London, against only 31 per cent higher the previous year. The widening gap was caused by the appreciation of the yen, according to economists.

Again Japanese were finding ways around some of the expensive prices, other than by travelling to Paris and London and buying up the branded clothing stores. The fashionable answer was to buy by mail order, ordering goods directly from abroad, and thus bypassing Japan's complicated and expensive distribution network. Discount stores, particularly for men's clothing, were also becoming popular, and Isao Nakauchi, founder of the leading supermarket chain Daiei, also began discounting and selling cheap, unbranded everyday goods. In glaring contrast to the super-efficient manufacturing sector, where prices are honed by competition, the services sector is inefficient, overstaffed, padded by extra layers of distribution and cosseted by government protection. Featherbedded agriculture is even worse, using political leverage to the full.

Housing is also notorious, caught by idiosyncratic land zoning laws and ownership patterns, and the corrupt Japanese construction industry – a triple whammy with vicious implications. American construction companies reckoned that, if allowed access to Japan, they would be able to build superior houses at between a third and a half of the cost. But of course the day of such international competition was remote. One enterprising company did try to import materials for a Japanese house, but it fell foul of bureaucratic regulations on top of the cost of using local workers to put it up. The net result was that the house was more than twice as expensive to put up as it had been in the USA, and hardly worthy the hassle.

The society that the economic miracle has produced is a strange one. Some visitors from the USA have been quick to see similarities between Japanese and American towns. But that is a highly superficial view, based on the profusion of signs in the English language, often advertising products that are familiar the world over, such as McDonald's, Kentucky Fried Chicken – replete with models of Colonel Sanders, who is dressed in a Father Christmas outfit towards the end of the year – Nescafé and Coca-Cola, and on baseball games on television almost every night in the season. From a distance too, the skyscrapers of Shinjuku or Osaka, or those springing up along Tokyo Bay, might remind you of Chicago or Dallas or Houston, or any other booming American city. But anyone who says, as some visitors from America have, that 'Japan is just like home' must have switched their brains off. To match the superficial with the superficial, Japanese cars drive on the left-hand side, not the right. Although Japan is the birthplace of so many of them and Tokyo always seems traffic jammed, the automobile is not the master in Japan as it is in the USA. The inner twenty-three wards of Tokyo have a ratio of roads to land of about 15 per cent, far less than the 25 to 40 per cent of most international major cities. Tokyo's central business area of Marunouchi-Otemachi has its tower blocks, but they have been pruned short of true skyscrapers because of their closeness to the Imperial Palace and official reluctance to permit really tall buildings peeping into the back garden (for the same reason of not disturbing the Imperial family's peace, no subway lines run under the palace land).

Once clear of these business areas, even the capital takes on a different shape. It might be called homely, but few westerners can feel comfortable with the odd shapes and sizes, twists in the road, crazy shapes of housing, tiny plots of land. No two houses are alike: a few old wooden traditional structures, no higher than two storeys because of fire and earthquake regulations concerning wooden constructions, mix with contorted modern shapes. Perhaps because of the small packages of land, or perhaps because owners have a myriad private fantasies to fulfil, here you have a new block with clean lines but bubble glass windows like a dentist's waiting room; there is an L-shaped building with two storeys at the front, rising to four at the back; two blocks away is a grand miniaturised copy of a Texan ranch, next to a decrepit wooden house that still preserves grace in its weather-beaten age; elsewhere is a white-tiled house whose walls could have come from any public lavatory, but which are covered in ivy; just around the corner, hidden by greedy greenery of house plants, is something that looks like mock-British Edwardian, down to the mock pebble-dash prefabricated sheets in the front. Tokyo, even in its prosperity, has not produced any of the magnificent buildings that still adorn British or some American cities. There are no gorgeous classical terraces, probably because it is too much of an effort to get neighbours to agree to have common walls or a common design. Nor is there any noble imagination at work in designing the houses. They all look flimsy too, as if the next wind might tear them down; certainly the next earthquake would account for them. Perhaps that is the idea: not to build substantially and tempt fate.

Japan's fine modern buildings are dominated by temples to commerce, bridges and some new public buildings. They include a few strange constructions like the Tokyo headquarters of Wacoal, the underwear maker, which looks as if it were a stray spare part of a spaceship programme. Many of the so-called 'intelligent' buildings are unremarkable to look at – straight lines in stone, steel and plate glass. Collectively, the Shinjuku skyscrapers offer a magnificent contrast to the humble lanes and homes which they tower over, but closer to they lack individual distinction, apart perhaps from the metropolitan government headquarters in Shinjuku. With its twin towers in steel and glass, it is almost like a belated oriental attempt to build a western-style cathedral. The disappointment of this modern Tokyo is that it does not offer the unexpected surprises you can encounter in any walk round an ordinary neighbourhood in the capital. The clinically boring modern lines have no pleasant surprises hidden behind them.

In contrast, the higgledy-piggledy areas of Tokyo and Osaka offer constant serendipitous presents that delight the eye and mind. In smaller towns that have any history and did not suffer wartime bombing, they crop up even more frequently. Inevitably, there is a Buddhist temple or Shinto shrine, many of which, disappointingly, have modern, most often ugly, main structures. But most have some redeeming feature, an old wooden gate gnarled and creaking with age, an ancient bell that no longer rings true, images of Inari the fox god, or an old Buddha statue, usually worn and freshly wet with scrubbing by devotees. Occasionally there is a refreshing garden of bamboo groves and running water, and always there is a graveyard attached to temples.

Japanese graveyards are more compact and packed than western cemeteries because they are the reposing places not of whole bodies, but only of cremated bones and ashes. Often there are family graves, regularly cleaned and washed and with incense sticks burning before them. Such is the pressure on space that some areas are considering building multistorey parking lots for the bones of the dead. Most touching of all, in each cemetery are small images usually wearing a baby's bonnet and red bib: called *jizo*, they are sad memorials to aborted babies and occasional stillbirths. Japan has a high abortion rate, but evidently mothers cannot shrug off their responsibility to the being that was growing inside them, so they erect these memorials. Some of them are accompanied by tiny pots of water, flowers, miniature children's windmills and other childish trinkets to keep the spirits of the dead amused.*

Here and there, even in the cities, old shops still flourish – woodenfloored rice merchants, builders' yards with wooden beams and planks

---

* The Japanese are eclectic as far as religions go, with 109 million of the 123 million people professing Shintoism and 96 million calling themselves Buddhist. Typically, a baby may be received and blessed at a Shinto shrine and be given Buddhist rites before cremation. It is fashionable among the young to be married according to a Christian ceremony, although baptised Christians number only 1.5 million.

chained up outside, a store selling kimonos or traditional paper, an occasional old communal bath house, a reminder of the times when the neighbourhood bath was the place to catch up with the local gossip at the end of the day. In some places, the town bath is still popular because household plumbing in much of Japan still lags behind that of the West. Though Japan's cities lack wide green spaces – Tokyo, for example, has 2.5 square metres of park space per inhabitant, a tiny patch compared to Paris's 12.2, Chicago's 23.9 and London's 30.4 square metres – there are small patches of green where old men gather to play *shogi* or *go*, and grandmothers gossip while minding their children's offspring. Most of all, Japan is full of surprise gardens. On a busy Tokyo railway station, for example, there was a miniature garden laid out, neat with rocks and gravel, and small, not quite bonsai trees. Almost anywhere in the country it is possible to see the Japanese affection for the small things of nature. In one superurban part of Tokyo, a family plants a small pot of tiny paddy seedlings each year outside its home, and tends their growth into a handful of rice grains as if sighing for green fields instead of constant concrete.

Along with this display of infinite care and attention for the small and particular comes, frankly, a rank carelessness about fundamentals of beauty when it comes to town planning. The clash of housing styles is one example: all elbows out individuality. The screaming garish neon in any town of size is another. Equally appalling is the spaghetti-like profusion of wires hanging from almost every pole in any city. Only the tangles in old Dhaka in Bangladesh, or the spider's webs of wires in Hong Kong's Walled City (pulled down in the early 1990s), can match this. You would not think it possible to pack so many dark strands on to a single lump of concrete. A journey into the countryside is an exhibition of the ugly hand of Man, from the ever-dammed rivers to the criss-crossing electricity pylons and wires, to the thoughtless suburban architecture and the mindless signs advertising modern life. If you travel on the road from Kyoto to Nara, two old capitals full of historic treasures, you see a landscape scarred by wires, such that it is almost impossible to take a picture of an ancient pagoda without corporate or household wires intruding. It is as if the Japanese are shortsightedly paying minute attention to the works of nature close at hand and not bothering to lift their eyes to the communal ugliness they have created.

Japan's is a very safe society. The statistics say so. Japan is by no means crime-free, but in the late 1980s it had 1.1 homicides per 100,000 population, only one-ninth of the numbers in the USA or UK. Rapes were 1.3 per 100,000, against 38.1 in the USA and 12.1 in the UK. In robbery statistics Japan was even better: again 1.3 compared with 65.8 in the UK and 233 in the USA. In my apartment block late one night, there was a yell. Within ten minutes, three policemen were knocking on every door to check that all the inhabitants were safe and well. The *koban*, or corner police box, is ubiquitous in Japan, and policemen still take their beat seriously, riding round not in cars, which are mainly used by women police checking on traffic offences, but on bicycles. There is a downside to this too, of course, that everyone knows what is going on in everyone else's life. Foreigners in particular complain that they are more liable to be stopped by police to be asked for their papers. With recent changes in the law, it is a criminal offence now for foreigners not to carry their alien registration card. This is obtained from the local ward office by handing over a fingerprint, something which is extracted from Japanese only when they are convicted criminals.

There is a good deal of violence, however, beneath the surface of this apparently law-abiding, pacific society. One worrying aspect is the rise of *boryokudan* criminal gangs, normally known in the West as *yakuza*.* The passing of the Organised Crime Law in spring 1992 was supposed to mark a police crackdown on the gangs because it made extortion and violent debt collection, two main yakuza activities, criminal. Recession also put the gangs under pressure, and the National Police Agency estimates that by November 1993, the number of active boryokudan had fallen by 10,000 to 53,000. But the curbs have made the gangsters more determined and desperate. They have also been able to build on years of cosy relationships with business, politicians and the police. The revelations in the Sagawa scandal, which brought the downfall of political godfather and kingmaker Shin Kanemaru, revealed a few tasty details of the way that leading politicians trusted leading mobsters to do their essential dirty work (see Chapter 11). Some big corporations, especially the leading stockbrokers, were no strangers to the gangs. Leading companies paid off gangsters rather than have awkward questions raised at their annual meetings, and the head of Nomura Securities was forced to resign after revelations of links between the brokerage and underworld figures. The squeezes have meant that the gangs are breaking out in three dangerous ways: they are becoming more prepared to use violence, cases involving guns doubling in 1994; they are becoming more sophisticated; and their empire is growing offshore.

Yamaguchi-gumi, the biggest of the gangs, has gone hi-tech, equipped its members with computers and set up a 'financial research association' with the intention of indulging in corporate blackmail. Secret instructions went out to Yamaguchi gangs telling them to collect dirt on financial institutions in their area and then get to know the executives involved in the scandals. The yakuza have considerable financial resources at their disposal: estimates of their annual income range from a low of 1,000 billion yen a year to a high of 7,000 billion yen ($70 billion), according

* *Boryokudan* means 'violent group'; *yakuza* comes from slang in a gambling game and roughly translated means 'good for nothing'.

to Takatsugu Nato, professor at Tokyo International University. This is big money by international corporate standards. The most recent development is the international spreading of the yakuza's wings. Police in places as far distant as the USA, Brazil and Russia have become concerned about the growing activities of Japanese gangs. But at a United Nations conference on organised crime in Naples in November 1994, Japan's senior civil servant in the Justice Ministry warned that any attempts at international controls could conflict with national cultures. Kunihisa Hama added: 'That would be undue infringement of fundamental human rights or excessive control of normal economic activities.' At home in Japan, Takaji Kunimatsu, head of the National Police Agency, had just warned that growing crime was threatening the 'foundation of public order'.

But repressed violence is not far away even in ordinary life. You have only to peer over the shoulders of male passengers on commuter trains to wonder what is really going through the minds of the soberly suited and booted *sararimen*. The chances are that several will be reading comics, most of which seem to glory in sexual violence of the extreme kind, in which women are the playthings of men. Although until recently photographs of pubic hair were absolutely forbidden in publications, and importers of girlie magazines like *Playboy* employed elderly women to scratch out the unsightly hair, in the comics anything goes, and rape and thrashings are common and graphically depicted.

In real life, women receive as good an education as men at least until high school, but fall behind as the competitive struggle for the best jobs hots up. Women are only 15 per cent of the students at Tokyo University, though some of the professors say that women are the brightest students. Many of the best jobs are closed to women because employers believe that it is a waste of time taking them on since they will – and should – leave on marriage or at least on becoming pregnant. Some leading companies have traditionally employed large numbers of 'OLs' (office ladies), as they are called, just to impress visitors and serve gracious cups of tea. In western terms, this is an enormous waste of talent and any feminist would be appalled.

There is a contrary argument from some men that women have *too much* power. In the 'rabbit hutch' home (an expression that many Japanese now use because they recognise their cramped conditions), the woman is sovereign, responsible for the household budget, from which she will dole out pocket money to her husband, and for the education of the children. A husband who strays into the kitchen will be called *gokiburi* (cockroach) or, worse, *sodaigomi* (oversize garbage) or *nureochiba* (wet fallen leaves) because he is in the way. Some critical Japanese women claim that what is wrong with the country is that the most powerful men in the Ministry of Finance and other leading institutions are still tied to their mother's apron strings and that Japan suffers from a *mazacon* (mother complex).

Foreigners especially have a tough time, apart from the small number of pampered white expatriates sent to work in Japan by rich western companies. The privileged few are mainly bankers and financiers, but also include some journalists, who have housing benefits of up to 1.5 million yen ($15,000) a month, plus school fees allowing their children to be taught in English, and an assortment of other perks, including cars and membership of exclusive clubs. Frequently, such cosseting causes resentment among Japanese employees of the companies. 'Latter-day colonialism,' grumbled one worker at an English financial firm, complaining that the expatriate boss's housing allowance alone was more than twice the salary of the ordinary Japanese employee. 'Japanese companies do not permit such a gulf between the bosses and the workers.' By the mid-1990s, even some of the wealthy companies were beginning to complain about the cost of doing business in Japan.

Such expatriates, however, are few and live in a world of their own, occasionally visiting ordinary Japan like rich, gawping tourists. The rest of about 1.2 million foreigners resident in Japan are a motley crowd, including the lesser élite of western expatriates who occupy junior posts in financial and trading companies, youngsters who have paid their own way to Japan 'to experience the East', many of whom end up teaching English, and people from less wealthy Asian countries, especially Thailand, the Philippines, Iran and Bangladesh, who flooded in during the prosperous 1980s and early 1990s to try to pick up a few yen from the table of their rich neighbour. Most of them, apart from those on regular contracts by recognised foreign or Japanese companies, have an extremely difficult time. For a start, housing is expensive. In Tokyo, rent of $1,500 a month will bring only a modest three- or four-room apartment in the outer suburbs. Almost all teachers of English, apart from those with Ministry of Education backing, experience difficulties with their contracts, sometimes encountering failure to pay. If they try to protest, they are liable to be sacked. If the school goes bust, as many did after the economic bubble burst, they will be left with little redress.

Those in the worst plight of all are the casual labourers, who were welcomed with open arms by employers in the boom days to do the tough, dirty and dangerous jobs (called in Japanese the three Ks, *kitsui, kitanai, kiken*) that Japanese would not do at any price. Many of them came in without proper work permits or overstayed tourist visas, and when times were good the authorities turned a blind eye. Along with them came an underclass of women, mainly from the Philippines and Thailand, who were lulled to Japan by the promise of lucrative employment and then discovered they had to work as bar hostesses or prostitutes. Their passports were taken away from them and they were told they had incurred an impossible debt merely in getting to Japan. In one celebrated case, three Thai women had had enough, especially when they were told that their debts had multiplied several times from the 2 million yen ($20,000) that their 'protectoress' compatriot had 'paid' for them. So they murdered her to steal back their passports, and fled with her jewellery. They were caught, tried and sentenced to ten years in prison each, having made 'confessions' which they hardly understood.

The bar and prostitution trade involving Thais is not a small business. The 'protectoress' murdered by the three women, whom the prosecution presented as a loving mother to them, had bought 28 women in the nine months before her death for a total of 56 million yen. In 1993, according to government figures, 53,383 Thais overstayed their visits, half of them women sex workers. Some insiders estimate that the flesh trade between Thailand and Japan is worth $1 billion a year.

When the economy turned sour, Japan's authorities made a series of swoops to reveal illegal Iranians, Bangladeshis, Filipinos and other foreign labourers. It happens everywhere, but in Japan there was a nasty anti-foreign tinge to attitudes. Whenever crime rates went up, Japanese news-papers were quick to come out with headlines blaming foreigners for running rackets in doctored telephone cards and street robbery and bag snatching. Critics claim that Japan has made things worse for itself by laws that deny entry to manual workers and grant permission to work only in 28 specific skilled, mostly professional, capacities. According to Yasushi Higashizawa, a lawyer working to improve the rights of foreign labourers, by 1993 there were more than half a million unskilled foreign workers in Japan. That was more than double the Justice Ministry's esti-mate of illegal residents. Even in the good times, when Japanese employers were taking on unskilled foreigners and the authorities were happy to turn a blind eye, most such foreigners had little or no protection or insurance if they encountered an accident at work, such as losing a finger in unguarded machinery, let alone for being laid off. Japanese hospitals routinely refuse to treat foreigners even in the most dire emergencies, unless they can pay in advance or prove that they have the proper insurance cover for their treatment.*

The Japanese claim they are not racist in the conventional sense. Surveys have shown them to be blind to a person's skin and have indicated that they do not particularly discriminate against people who are black or brown. The problem is that Japanese discriminate against anybody who is not Japanese. This is seen every day in the attitudes towards the largest group of foreigners resident in Japan, about 700,000 Koreans whose fam-ilies have been resident for several generations, who speak fluent Japanese and often only Japanese, but who have not taken Japanese nationality

---

* It is not unknown for hospitals to check how much cash a patient has and then to set that as the limit of his or her treatment.

either because of pride or because of the onerous conditions attached, which include – perhaps the supreme indignity – changing their name to a Japanese one. In 1994, when there was increasing nervousness about North Korea's nuclear intentions, there was a spate of attacks on Korean schoolgirls, distinguished by their voluminous *chimachagori* uniform, some of whom had their dresses slashed in broad daylight at railway stations and elsewhere.* Respectable Japanese families will routinely use private detectives to check the backgrounds of candidates for marriage into their families, to weed out Koreans or burakumin or others of doubtful origin. It is made easier by the fact that, to be Japanese, a person must be included on a family register.

The reluctance with which Japan grants citizenship to foreigners was revealed when the giant Hawaiian sumo wrestler Salevaa Fuauli Atisanoe, who fought under the name Konishiki but was humorously known as 'the Dump Truck' because of his huge size and 256-kilogram weight, tried to become Japanese. At the age of 30, he had become the first foreigner to reach the second highest position of *ozeki*, champion, but was slipping rapidly down the ranks because of knee problems. He could only see a future in sumo and had married a Japanese woman. But the sumo association insists that only Japanese are allowed to receive the *toshiyori*, senior figure, status required for establishing sumo stables. So if Konishiki had left the ring before becoming a Japanese citizen, he would have had to depart permanently from sumo. Konishiki eventually got his Japanese citizenship and another new name, Yasokichi Shiota, using his wife's family name.

The Justice Ministry refused to say how many foreigners were applying to become Japanese, 'to protect the privacy of applicants' (just as it declines to say when a convicted murderer is hanged, to protect the murder's privacy and that of his or her family). But it disclosed some of the requirements and said that it normally takes about a year and a half to complete the review. Essential qualifications are that applicants must have lived in Japan for five years or more, must be twenty or older with a 'decent personality', must have the ability to make a living or have spouses or relatives who can, must not have participated in 'anti-government organisations' and must give up their previous citizenship upon naturalisation. Applicants must submit at least twenty different forms, including records of bank accounts, a list of all relatives with their occupation and addresses, certificates of tax payments, records of any debts and how

---

* John Loughran of Morgan told me that he had offered a job to an eminently qualified young man with a Japanese name who had degrees from Japanese and US universities, but who had not managed to find employment. 'I added that we did not mind if he wanted to call himself Park, and he burst into tears, saying that I was the first person who had said a kind word to him.' Park was his Korean name.

they have spent their income, including what kind of furniture they own. According to a lawyer who helps foreigners obtain Japanese citizenship, 'submitting the forms requires almost all the energy and time of applicants, so many foreigners give up even before applying. Officials investigate everything about applicants. Applying for citizenship is like losing your private life.'

Japan is by 1995 either the richest or the second richest country in the world. The government Economic Planning Agency declared in December 1994 that Japan had just pipped Switzerland the previous year for the title of world's richest country in income per person, thanks to a 14.5 per cent jump. Gross domestic product per person rose to $33,764, against $33,746 in Switzerland. Japan's rise was largely because of the strength of the yen: the figures used 111 yen to the dollar against 127 the previous year. Some international comparative tables still put Switzerland ahead. The World Bank, for example, gave Switzerland per capita income of $34,000 in 1992 and put Japan at $27,000. But with the rapidly appreciating yen and depreciating dollar, at mid-1994 exchange rates Japan was boosting its lead, and its income per person was about $41,000 compared to $40,800 in Switzerland.

Such statistics can be misleading, and in real terms the apparently high per capita income has to be set against the disadvantages of Japan's lifestyle, the cramped housing, the long commutes into work – an average of 90 minutes each way for Tokyo workers, equivalent to stealing three and a half years over a 40-year working life – the lack of parks and other amenities, and the high cost of living, especially expressed in dollar terms. Measuring these and other qualitative factors, such as social pressures, is difficult. Considerable numbers of young women, at least sufficient to be noticed by the Japanese media, began to be fed up with their lower status and keen to migrate to places like Hong Kong for work. One programme shown on NHK, Japan's public broadcasting service, even showed Japanese women in their twenties living in Hong Kong, earning barely enough to live on, sleeping three to a bed and yet still claiming to be happy about 'freedom we have here which we can never enjoy in Japan'.

What is certain is that Japan is increasingly vulnerable in the modern economic world. This became clear as the yen surged against the dollar in 1993 and 1994. The Organisation for Economic Co-operation and Development, the club of rich industrial nations, calculated that Japan's manufacturing labour costs had increased by 51 per cent between 1991 and 1994 against a weighted average of other leading international currencies. This was on top of the already rapid rise in the value of the yen after the September 1985 agreement made in the Plaza Hotel, New York, by leading industrial countries. Before the Plaza meeting, the yen was trading at between 245 and 255 against the US dollar. Afterwards it rapidly appreciated, passing through 190 and 150, and by 1990 it had strengthened further to 130. Leading Japanese industrial companies had calculated their profit forecasts in 1992 on the basis of a yen worth 120 to the dollar, in 1993 on a yen at 115 and in 1994 on a yen at 110, but each year it slipped away from their grasp.

In mid-1994 the currency suddenly rose from 110 through the critical 100 level against the dollar – critical because it meant that the yen was worth 1 US cent – and in mid-July it reached a record 96.60 during daily trading. The effect for major industrial companies was cataclysmic. Toyota Motor estimated that, for every one yen rise or fall in the dollar, there was a corresponding 10 billion yen rise or fall in its annual net income. If the dollar stayed at 95 to 100 yen, only one in 50 small to medium-sized exporters said they could make a profit. And yet in dollar terms, the value of Japan's trade surplus continued to rise and was on track for a second successive $140–50 billion surplus, thus triggering new demands from Washington that Japan should open its market and take more goods from America.

We have already seen some of the major differences between a defeated Germany and a defeated Japan. The other major differences are crucial political ones, which 50 years after the atomic bombing of Hiroshima and Nagasaki are coming back to haunt Japan and the relationship between it and the rest of the world. In Germany, Adolf Hitler committed suicide. His fellow Nazi lieutenants were also removed by suicide, death or the war crimes tribunal, and the whole Nazi apparatus was dismantled and held up as an evil thing that should never be allowed to be repeated. The Allied forces that drove into Berlin became an occupying power, or powers, given that the Soviet rulers of the East created a very different state, dismantled the old ruling apparatus and set up another dedicated to seeing that the old regime did not return. Konrad Adenauer, who took over as chancellor in the West when the Allies decided it was safe enough for the Germans to run their country again, was determined that Germany should not repeat its mistakes and should stay firmly wedded to a democratic West. Japan was different.

MacArthur, for all his idealistic intentions, did not take over the Japanese government lock, stock and barrel. He filtered his own requests through a bureaucracy whose civil apparatus largely remained intact and which, especially after the distraction of the Korean War, was able to distil what it wanted from what it did not like in instructions from SCAP. Once Japan had regained its independence in 1952, even some men found guilty as Class A war criminals came back into public life. Nobusuke Kishi, who had been held on war crimes charges and released in 1948, even became prime minister in 1957. Mamoru Shigemitsu received a seven-year sentence as a Class A war criminal, but was paroled in 1950 and four years later became foreign minister, a post he had held during the war. Okinori Kaya got a life sentence for his crimes, including being part of Tojo's government, but was paroled in the late 1950s and became justice minister in 1963. It was not just that a handful of war criminals came to cabinet office. More important, Japan has never faced up to its colonial and wartime activities as did Germany, or as did western colonial powers.

If you read the Japanese histories of the war, with their emphasis on the bombing of Hiroshima and Nagasaki, it is easy to come to the conclusion that Japan was the victim, not the aggressor, of the war. It was not until 1993 that Kiichi Miyazawa, on the verge of going out of office, accepted that a unknown number of 'comfort women' (usually estimated at 150,000 to 200,000) had been forced by the Japanese Imperial Army to serve as prostitutes within sound of the frontline guns. School textbooks dwell on the atomic bombs that the USA dropped on Japan. The bombs even intrude into unlikely places such as English lessons. But Japan's school texts play down the suggestion that the country was guilty of aggression. Authors who have tried to emphasise any of the murky aspects of Japan's role in the 1930s and 1940s have had their work rewritten by order. Unlike Germany, Japan never conducted a proper account of what caused the path to war. The fact that the emperor was allowed to remain, though he stripped himself of his godhood, also assured continuity and helped to dodge the awful question. Marquis Koichi Kido, the Lord Privy Seal and one of Emperor Hirohito's closest advisers, believed that after a decent interval he should have abdicated, but he never did, dying still as emperor in 1989, maligned in some western newspapers as evil incarnate, still revered as a god by some Japanese. Even today, leading Japanese politicians still come out and make statements declaring that Japan was not an aggressor, or was fighting a war against western colonialism.

The issue of wartime responsibilities is highly relevant today, half a century later. This issue involves not merely Japan's immediate neighbouring countries, which are sensitive about historical memories, but all the world powers because of Tokyo's aspiring role to be a big player in world political as well as economic matters. Constitutionally, article 9 still prevails, committing Japan never to use war as an instrument of policy, never to threaten force in settling international disputes, never to maintain war potential or land, sea or air forces. In return, Tokyo has been assured of the protection of the American defence umbrella, under which Washington promises to come to Japan's aid if it is ever threatened by a foreign country, and keeps a number of bases and 46,000 troops in Japan.

These arrangements are being assailed from two directions simultaneously. On the one hand, politicians have been prepared to undermine article 9 while pretending that it is still sacred and in place. The move was actually started by the Americans, who ordered Japan to create a national police reserve when they needed their own troops in the Korean

War. The police reserve later become the Self-Defence Forces. In numbers and more especially in fire power, the Self-Defence Forces by the 1990s had become one of the most powerful armies in the world, whatever pacific name they were masquerading under. Thanks in part to the rise in value of the yen, Japan's military spending had risen by 1995 to the second or third largest in the world, depending on definitions.

In all, in the fiscal year that began in April 1995, Japan's defence budget totalled more than 4,700 billion yen according to its own figures (and was still higher according to western defence economists – see Chapter 8). The Self-Defence Agency, the responsible ministry, claimed in a publication of March 1993 that 'If you compare Japan's defence capability to other countries, you will find Japan's defence capability is not very large. Particularly compared to other industrial countries like France and the United Kingdom – needless to say the United States and the former Soviet Union – Japan's defence capability is not large at all.' But the report was working on old international comparative figures, and even by then Japan's spending had surpassed France and the UK.

In terms of technology, there is no doubt that Japan's forces are among the best equipped in the world. Japan has Asia's largest bluewater fleet. Acquisition of AWACs (airborne warning and control) aircraft in the mid-1990s will give Japan a round-the-clock search capacity well beyond its shores. *Mainichi Shimbun* reported in August 1994 that the Defence Agency was considering how Japan could build its own spy satellite network; the agency's vice-minister said that the paper was 'at a study level' and 'no conclusions on the matter have been taken'. The nuclear potential of North Korea, and indeed of China, is another matter of concern. The defence agency firmly maintains the three 'non-nuclear principles as the fixed line of national policy. We will not possess nuclear weapons, we will not produce them, and we will not permit them to be introduced into Japan' (though what happens on the US air and naval bases is presumably a matter for US sovereignty, on which Tokyo would not want to intrude).

But in 1994 Kazuomi Uchida, head of the maritime Self-Defence Forces from 1969 to 1972, revealed that he did secret research on nuclear weapons. 'While I was serving, I believed that nuclear weapons were absolutely necessary for the defence of Japan, and my research was in line with this belief,' Uchida said in an interview with *Mainichi Shimbun* in August 1994. How many other military officers have similar views, and what they are doing to promote them, can only be a matter of worrying conjecture.

Japan is clearly anxious for its soldiers to play a bigger and more international role. In 1992 Japan passed a law allowing its troops to join United Nations peacekeeping operations, but not peacekeeping forces. The distinction is a vital one of whether the troops would be called on to use their weapons. Thus, under the 1992 law they were allowed to go to

Cambodia to assist the UN in holding elections, but would not be allowed to go to Bosnia where they might have to go into combat. Many Socialist opponents argued that even allowing Japanese soldiers to join UN non-combat operations was a breach of the constitution. By 1994 a report to the prime minister urged that the Japanese be allowed to join peacekeeping forces too. If it happened, it would be another, not so subtle undermining of the constitution. Some foreigners, like British foreign secretary Douglas Hurd, also hinted that, if Japan could not play a full role in UN peace-keeping, it might not be able to win a permanent seat on the Security Council, which had become a cherished ambition of Tokyo's Foreign Ministry by 1994.

The unique distinction of being anti-war was also coming under direct assault from some politicians who argued that this and their reliance on the US defence umbrella made Japan less than a full modern nation, and unable to make its own mature policies. The question of the constitution was still an emotive issue. Many of the older generation, especially those on the Left, believed that it was Japan's special saving grace to have made a commitment against war. But aggrieved Rightists still wanted to assert the old system in all its glory, with the emperor restored to his godhead. Coming up is a rising generation which feels a growing resentment that Japan continues to be pushed around by America and other countries. It is more worrying that this modern generation has little knowledge of what happened before and during the war.

In these contexts, the lack of information about Japan's role in the world, and the insistence on Japan being unique, are causes for concern. Of course, every country likes to appeal to its history, national independence, brave heroes, special flag and anthem. All nations have their myths and their historical heroes and heroines. But no other modern nation pretends, as Japan does, to have been created by the sun goddess, whose offspring became the first emperor, Jimmu, in 660 BC. No other country pretends to the mumbo jumbo with which Japan invests the installation of a new emperor, who is supposed to go to a small hut at night and commune with Amaterasu, as a result of which he is incarnated as emperor.

It is not clear how many Japanese believe this mythology, but the fact that it is taught and that the chamberlains of the Imperial Household Agency have resisted any attempts to allow proper research into the historical antecedents of the Imperial family is potentially dangerous. (Agnostic archaeologists suggest that there are similarities between seventh-century noble Korean tombs and burial grounds of the Imperial family, which, if true, would suggest Korean origins for the Japanese emperor, dynamite in itself, and that the imperial system is perhaps a millennium later than its defenders like to pretend.) All this, together with Japan's constant harping on its purity and uniqueness, sets up a dangerous course. It is too early and too alarmist to say that there is a danger of history repeating itself, but unless there are changes in Japan's attitudes, and a greater awareness of the outside world and how it sees Japan, there will be painful times ahead.

2

Giant among Pygmies:
Yoh Kurosawa and Industrial Bank of Japan

Yoh Kurosawa throws back his burly shoulders and laughs heartily: 'I had three career possibilities in front of me when I left university. I could have become an opera singer or a sumo wrestler, in which case I would have become rich and famous. Instead, I decided to become a banker.' He became not just any banker. In London in mid-1994, attending the celebrations for the 300th birthday of the Bank of England, he told Queen Elizabeth II that he was 'the tallest Japanese banker. She laughed, I am happy to say,' Kurosawa remembered, laughing again. By the mid-1990s it is fair to say that Kurosawa is Japan's most distinguished banker. As president of Industrial Bank of Japan (IBJ), he is chief executive of the very real powerhouse that helped to create Japan's modern industrial and economic miracle. As the exchange with the British monarch illustrated, Kurosawa could not possibly be considered a typical faceless Japanese banker. He is one of the few leading Japanese businessmen to be fluent in English, and in German too, and he is one of the even smaller number prepared to give his opinions and argue for them. 'Kurosawa is the opposite of bland or faceless, quite prepared to say what he thinks and argue to your face,' said an American banker.

Japan's tragedy is that it does not have more such independent-minded bankers, able to laugh and joke, and with a 'presence' on the international stage. Kurosawa's own tragedy is that, when it came to the crunch over a key business decision about lending money, he too proved very Japanese, following the pack of bankers into a misjudgement that cost his bank a lot of money and almost lost him his job. In retrospect, the particular incident would be highly amusing, but for the fact that hundreds of millions of dollars were involved. Tragically, it was an important example of the mess that Japanese banks – and the whole financial system as well – got into and from which they have not yet recovered. A few years ago Japanese banks were widely celebrated as 'bankers to the world', holding the huge assets of the Japanese people and feeding them to development projects all over the world. So today it is not just Japan, but the whole world financial system that should be worried about the problems in Japan's banks.

You might not realise this if you visited the big bankers in their stronghold. The towering modern bank headquarters buildings in central Tokyo look as safe and secure as any bank in the world – big, strong and not flashy, except for some of their modern gadgetry, including electronic women who appear on screens in the automatic teller machines, and bow and talk politely when you conduct a transaction. International league tables of banks show that Japanese occupy all the top eight places in terms of assets (Industrial Bank of Japan comes eighth). This is a big change from twenty years ago when there were just three Japanese in the lower half of the top ten (see Tables 2.1 and 2.2). These days few bankers aspire to bigness for its own sake.*

What counts today is strength and soundness, measured by capital and return on assets. In terms of capital, the Japanese banks are still strong, and occupy the six top slots in the world by tier 1 capital.† IBJ comes eleventh. In terms of return on assets, all the Japanese perform miserably, showing below 0.2 per cent and coming between 848th and 904th places in *The Banker*'s top 1,000 (apart from Bank of Tokyo in 18th place in the world ranking by capital with a return on assets of 0.39, coming 712th).

Such figures do not tell the whole story, which is of a Japanese banking system full of problems, crippled by bad loans, making poor returns and badly in need of new ideas, new talent and competition. Alicia Ogawa of Salomon Brothers, probably the most respected banking analyst in Tokyo, said gloomily after the banks published their results for the 1993/4 financial year, 'at best the system can survive for another five years'.

In some ways Yoh Kurosawa had a lucky start. 'I was just too young to be a soldier. I am the oldest non-soldier generation,' he said. 'If I had been born two days before, I would have been a soldier. I missed by a matter of two days. My memory of the war living in Tokyo is of lots of bombs. Fortunately, my parents' house was not hit, but lots of houses nearby were burnt down. When I was in high school, a big bomb hit the rugby field and made a large hole.' Getting into high school for the three final years of schooling before university was the difficult task, he recalled, since there were 30 students competing for each place. Like all the best students, Kurosawa was educated at the élite Tokyo University. 'When I went to university, the city was a full of burned down buildings and there were

* Barclays Bank chief executive Martin Taylor was surprised to hear that his bank had once been the biggest in the world, and said that it no longer aspired to such a title, 'though I would be happy to be the world's most profitable bank,' he laughed in a 1994 interview.

† Tier 1 capital, as defined by the Bank for International Settlements, is the core bank strength, available to cover actual or potential losses. It includes common stock, declared reserves, retained earnings and perpetual, irredeemable and non-cumulative preference shares.

Table 2.1 *Top banks in the world, June 1974 ($ million)*

		Assets	Deposits	Capital & Reserves
1	*BankAmerica Corp*	48,772	41,453	1,550
2	*Citicorp*	44,018	34,942	1,770
3	*Chase Manhattan Corp*	36,790	29,913	1,348
4	*Banque Nationale de Paris*	30,142	29,780	251
5	*Dai-Ichi Kangyo Bank*	28,467	21,298	845
6	*Barclays Bank*	28,304	24,748	1,586
7	*National Westminster Bank*	27,555	24,802	2,095
8	*Fuji Bank*	24,418	18,735	1,083
9	*Deutsche Bank*	24,389	22,847	836
10	*Sumitomo Bank*	23,905	18,233	879

Source: *The Banker.*

food shortages. My biggest problem was getting lunch. I was always hungry. Luckily there were lots of students who came from the countryside to Tokyo and they got food tickets from their local governments. I used to barter my examination papers for food tickets – civil law I for 50 tickets.' He read law, like many of Japan's future top officials. But, showing an independent streak, he opted not to go into the safety of the bureaucracy, where he would have been guaranteed a job for life and a place at the heart of Japan's decision making.

Kurosawa remembered: 'Throughout the war, we were fed up with controls imposed by the authorities, so I wanted to join the private sector. In addition, pay in the public sector was rather poor. The best pay was in a bank, but I feared that banking business might be boring. So for a time I considered becoming a newspaper reporter, thinking that that would be interesting, but my mother told me that if I became a reporter I would be working late at night and sleeping in the daytime, so it was not a healthy job. Then a friend told me that IBJ was somewhat different from an ordinary bank. "You can read a book, write a report and get a salary." I thought that is a wonderful job.' So Kurosawa joined Industrial Bank of Japan, commonly known in international banking circles as IBJ, or 'Kogin' in Japan from the initial letters of its Japanese name, Nippon Kogyo Ginko. If he and the bank are not household names in the West, that is part of the tragedy of the West, in that it regards economics as a dismal science and Japan as a far-flung exotic country not worth front-page newspaper coverage.

The IBJ that Kurosawa joined was going through a transitional phase. Founded in 1902, the bank had laid the foundations for Japan's modern

Table 2.2   *Top banks in the world, June 1994*

	Rank	Tier 1 capital ($m)	Assets $m	Assets Rank	Profits ($m)	Rtn on assets %	Rtn on assets Rank
1	Sumitomo Bank	22,120	497,781	3	900	0.18	855
2	Sanwa Bank	19,577	493,588	5	929	0.19	848
3	Fuji Bank	19,388	507,218	1	621	0.12	894
4	Dai-Ichi Kangyo Bank	19,360	506,563	2	676	0.13	889
5	Sakura Bank	18,549	495,975	4	578	0.12	902
6	Mitsubishi Bank	17,651	458,906	6	772	0.17	862
7	Indust. and Comm. Bank of China	16,782	337,769	10	1,417	0.42	695
8	Credit Agricole	14,718	282,911	15	1,522	0.54	642
9	HSBC Hldgs	14,611	305,214	13	3,828	1.25	356
10	Citicorp	13,625	216,574	27	2,888	1.33	325
11	IBJ	13,596	386,916	8	436	0.11	904
12	Union Bank of Switzerland	13,264	210,379	28	2,059	0.98	451
13	BankAmerica Corp	12,058	186,933	30	3,428	1.83	163
14	Deutsche Bank	11,723	322,445	11	2,664	0.83	510
15	Int Ned Gp	11,068	174,888	33	1,453	0.83	508
16	Tokai Bank	10,903	311,451	12	472	0.15	878
17	LTCB of Japan	10,850	302,185	14	599	0.20	841
18	Bank of Tokyo	10,570	242,445	21	956	0.39	712
19	Credit Lyonnais	10,386	338,848	9	−869	−0.26	935
20	Asahi Bank	10,311	261,963	16	452	0.17	861

Notes: Japanese bank results as at 31 March 1994; results of other banks listed as at 31 December 1993.

Ranking is of top 1,000 banks in the world. LTCB is Long-Term Credit Bank.

Int Ned Gp is Internationale Nederland Group.

When Bank of Tokyo and Mitsubishi Bank merge in spring 1996 they will create a mega-bank with assets of $875 billion and capital of $40 billion.

Source: *The Banker.*

development, especially its investment in heavy industries like steel, electric power, machinery and shipping. Besides raising domestic financial resources to support industry, IBJ had been active internationally in placing Japanese government bonds, issuing its own bonds in sterling on the London market, underwriting bonds and fostering Japan's capital markets. Unfortunately, among the industries that the bank had supported were those underpinning Japan's war machine.

The wartime IBJ was virtually semi-government owned. The victorious Allied powers deliberately clipped its wings. As Kurosawa recalled, 'When I joined the bank [in 1950], it was not so well established as a few years later. The US occupation authorities found IBJ as a funny animal. They took away its underwriting business. Doing lending was fine. Issuing debentures [long-term bonds, which was how IBJ raised its funds, since it did not have access to deposits from the public like the city or commercial banks] they regarded as funny for a bank. It seems that the US officers did not know about the European banking system. IBJ had managed to persuade general headquarters and [Supreme Commander Allied Powers] General [Douglas] MacArthur to maintain the basic character of IBJ. Only two years after I had joined, in 1952, were the existence and the operations of the bank rationalised by the long-term credit bank law, so that we were able to issue debentures and long-term loans.'

Kurosawa's first job was in the debenture department. 'The top management thought that the main problem of IBJ was how to get money, so they decided to put the new guys into the debenture department to learn about how to raise money ... It was an exciting business, with no time to read books, no time to write reports. I worked from 0900 in the morning to 2100 or 2200 at night,' recalled Kurosawa, always busy visiting clients or talking on the telephone to persuade people to buy IBJ debentures, and to keep all-important contacts with Ministry of Finance officials. In four years, he covered all aspects of the bank's funding. It was not just a question of hard work, but also involved very hard play, nights of entertaining important customers. 'I also had to learn how to play majong,' he said, this being just one of the things he had to do to keep essential contacts with IBJ's clients. Next, he was moved to Osaka into the bank's lending department, so that he could understand the other side of the ledger. His career was halted by illness, tuberculosis on a lung which put him in hospital for eight months, and saw his weight increase from 60 to 85 kilograms. His career did not suffer. 'I could have had up to three years off sick and IBJ would still have kept me on.'

These were the early post-war days when many aspects of Japanese life were carefully controlled, not least the banking and financial system. The rules of the game were rigidly laid down by the Ministry of Finance. Every bank had its allocated little box, its role and duties, so that none of Japan's precious resources, slowly growing from the dust and ashes of the war, would run to waste. Interest rates on savings and on loans were fixed. The big commercial banks (not, of course, IBJ and the long-term credit banks) built up huge networks of branches, so as to tap into the thrifty habits of Japanese and build up the store of savings that could be directed towards projects which the Ministry of Finance regarded as priority. To supplement the efforts of the banks there was also the postal savings system through the huge network of post offices, offering the incentive of tax-free interest, albeit at low rates, on savings of up to 3 million yen per account. People opened accounts in the names of themselves, their children and their pets to avoid paying tax. Just so that nobody escaped the network, the tightly run agricultural co-operatives also acted as banking organisations.

Banks, of course, were not allowed to indulge in stockbroking activities. That was for the securities companies. The US occupation authorities, following the 1933 Glass–Steagall Act in their own country, had made the basic distinction between banks and brokers. Within the banking framework there were distinctions between several types of bank, which were not expected to stray beyond their own compartments. IBJ, for example, was one of the three long-term credit banks, whose prime role was to provide finance for industry. They were wholesale banks dealing with companies, not with individual retail customers. A group of seven banks plus Daiwa Bank were designated as trust banks, which focused on pension fund management and fiduciary issues, from which other banks were barred.

The main retail banking operations were carried on by thirteen so-called city banks, the nearest equivalent to commercial banks in the UK or USA. But the writ of the city banks did not run all the way through the country. Once outside the big cities like Tokyo and Osaka, you may travel without being able to find a branch of Dai-Ichi Kangyo or Fuji or Sumitomo banks, the biggest city banks. There was a network of 63 regional banks, and under them came large numbers of saving banks and *shinkin*, or credit and co-operative financial institutions. One institution, the Bank of Tokyo, stood in a special category all of its own. The successor of the pre-war Yokohama Specie Bank, it served as a specialised foreign exchange bank, with few domestic branches, but with privileged access to foreign exchange and allowed to be Japan's leading bank operating in foreign cities.

Throughout the 1950s, when Japan's economic locomotive began to gather steam, and the 1960s and 1970s, when it picked up speed and saw Japan emerge as a major economic power, the system remained largely intact and unchallenged. Banks collected savings from the public and passed them on to industrial companies greedy for funds to keep the economy growing at close to double-digit rates. IBJ and the long-term credit banks fuelled the spurt in heavy industry. The city banks developed close relations with corporations. These were most obvious in the case of the *keiretsu* (conglomerates), such as Mitsui and Mitsubishi, where the links between business and banking were reinforced by strong cross-shareholders. But almost all companies had a 'main bank' from which they borrowed principally, with which there were special mutual responsibilities frequently underlined by shareholdings. Being a main bank involved bailing out a company that got into difficulties. The Ministry of Finance with its central bank agent, the Bank of Japan, policed the system carefully. About half of the governors of the central bank were ex-MoF bureaucrats. Companies got plenty of cheap finance, and obedient Japanese savers did not protest at the low rates they were getting. The finance mandarins kept a close, watchful eye on the banks, which was not limited to formal rules and regulations.

These were tough enough. The framework of Japanese laws is such that, unlike in the USA or Britain, where the law lays down exactly what can or cannot be done, Japanese laws provide a framework in which the bureaucrats actively fill in the details on a regular basis. A foreign banker expressed it this way in the early 1980s: 'In the West, if the law doesn't prohibit something expressly, then you can go ahead and do it. But in Japan the law expresses the general principles. If you want to do something you still have to ask the Ministry of Finance's permission, even when it seems in conformity with the law.'

So-called 'administrative guidance' is much more adamantine than the western translation suggests. No one would think of going against such guidance, not if they valued their future. On most occasions, the bureaucrats did not even have to consider giving anything as formal as 'guidance'. Close informal relations were maintained on a day-to-day basis between the banking bureau of the MoF and the banks. 'Even the bank president would be terrified of a formal summons to go to the head of the Banking Bureau's office,' recalled the foreign banker. The fact that the senior executives of the bank and the bureaucrats had studied together at Tokyo University, and that the bureaucrats were the top of the class who had taken the tough civil service exams, merely reinforced the aura of respect owed by the bankers to the bureaucrats.

There were some painful hiccups along the way. The oil price rises in the 1970s caused deep problems, immediately plunged Japan from growth to recession, damaged the cost structure of many companies and led to rapid structural changes. Even a 'miracle' economy was not immune from the ordinary hard facts of economic life. But Japan quickly swallowed the painful medicine of higher oil prices by introducing energy-saving measures, much faster than the West and especially the gas-guzzling USA. Even so, Japan was increasingly exposed to the winds and tides of the world economy, and caught a chill when the rest of the industrialised world suffered from influenza. At times of recession, bankruptcies rose, and there were some painful times when banks had to help bail out even big and famous companies. From the late 1970s until the mid-1980s, there were 15,000 to 20,000 bankruptcies a year, with debts topping 2,500 billion yen most years. Kohjin, a large diversified textile manufacturer, filed for bankruptcy in 1975 with debts of 150 billion yen, having speculated too heavily in real estate. Sankyo Steamship was the world's largest tanker owner when it declared bankruptcy in August 1985 with debts of 695.9 billion yen. Lesser names were quietly allowed to go under. But by and large the system held as Japan prospered. And Japan prospered.

Kurosawa had a good view of the rapid progress of the Japanese economic miracle. He noted that 'The bank today is very different from the one that I joined. When I joined, it was not long after the war and it did not have a clear picture of the future. We had to fight with General Headquarters [of SCAP], which said, "Which business do you want to do? A or B?" We said, "A and B", and we got permission to issue debentures and to lend money. The only restriction was that we couldn't take any deposit from private individuals. Nor could we do underwriting. After 1952, when the Long-Term Credit Bank Law was passed, justifying and legitimising IBJ's existence and establishing two other long-term credit banks, Nippon Credit Bank and Long-Term Credit Bank of Japan, we were very busy helping Japan to rebuild. We concentrated on financing the reconstruction of destroyed industries. We put the emphasis on four industrial areas: electric utilities, coal mining, steel and shipping, all of which were essential to reconstructing Japanese industry.

'Today, we don't finance coal mining. The shipping industry is still a client of our bank, but we don't put much emphasis on it. Electric utilities are still there, as is the steel industry. But the most significant thing is the range of new industries that we support, the motor industry, electrical and electronics, service industries, and in addition there has been globalisation on a massive scale.'

Kurosawa's own career reflected the changing times. After a time in the department for lending to small and medium-sized businesses, he said, 'At last, I was assigned to the research department, where I read books and wrote reports, etc. Then I was asked by the personnel department to go to Germany and study German banking with Deutsche Bank in Dusseldorf. This was 1961.' It marked the start of Kurosawa's international career and also gave him a chance to fulfil a boast that he might have made a career as a singer. 'In Dusseldorf, there was a good choir, the city choir which had a 200-year history and once [Felix] Mendelssohn was conductor and [Robert] Schumann was involved. With an introduction from some Deutsche Bank colleagues I went there and said that I wanted to join. The conductor was surprised that a Japanese should apply. There were around 200 German members of the choir and the conductor asked me, "We are now practising the Deutsches Requiem by Brahms: do you know the piece?" "From page 1 to 100, I know everything," I was able to reply,' said Kurosawa, chortling at the memory of Japan's small international success. 'I had sung the requiem in Japan with the NHK Symphony Orchestra. The choir conductor was most surprised and asked me to sing a piece, accompanying me on the piano. Immediately I started to sing, all 200 members of the choir began to applaud spontaneously. In Germany, I learned what was foreign business and lending business as well as colloquial German. I had the advantage of having studied German diligently in my high school for three years. During my thirteen months in Germany, my wife stayed in Japan with her family, something that does not happen now. Japanese going abroad for training are allowed to take their wives. IBJ has become rich and Japan has become rich.'

It was very much the start of IBJ's international experience too. 'These days,' continued Kurosawa, 'the bank is seconding about fifteen young graduate executives a year to business school in the US or Europe, some married, some not.' For him, it was a good move, since he returned to Tokyo as the youngest section chief in the funding department. At this time IBJ was largely a domestic bank. 'After four years in the funding department,' recalled Kurosawa, 'I was asked to go to head the Frankfurt representative office, which had been set up four years before. When I came back after five and a half years, I again was put into the domestic lending headquarters to learn about domestic operations,' he added pointedly, replying to critics who suggest that he is only an internationalist who somehow strayed on to the 11th floor powerhouse of IBJ and stayed by charm or force of personality.

'Then in 1974 I was made chief of the newly established international finance department. This was really the start of my international career. What I had learned in Frankfurt was about the export of German capital and the flourishing Deutschmark bond market. The highlight of my time was the first issue of IBJ Deutschmark-denominated bonds for DM60 million, the first by a Japanese issuer without government guarantee, and the first IBJ debenture issue outside Japan. At first, when I approached Deutsche Bank, they asked if we had a government guarantee. When I said no, they replied that it was very difficult. But we finally succeeded, though it took a year's work. This was my own idea: I persuaded head office to allow me to do it.

'When I started the international finance department, we had four staff, myself and three secretaries. Now there are more than a hundred people. In those days IBJ had just established branches in London and New York in 1973 and opened IBJ Germany, a joint venture with Deutsche Bank. We were learning how to compete with America in international banking. They were weak only in yen financing, but we were weak in dollar financing. Only after the Latin American crisis started in 1982 did the US banks become less competitive internationally.'

The big challenges to Japan's established financial order began in the 1980s when many disruptive factors came together simultaneously. Japan found that it was part of the rest of the world and influenced by winds blowing through the international financial markets. There were push and pull influences at work. Foreign banks wanted to set up in Japan and get a slice of the lucrative but carefully controlled business where margins (the difference between the cost of funds, expressed in low interest rates paid to savers, and the returns from lending the money) were high. Japanese banks began to set up offices abroad and found that they could do business abroad that they were not allowed to do at home, where they were more or less limited to 'plain vanilla' lending. Japanese companies, beginning to venture abroad for investment, found that they had access to money from a wider variety of sources than they ever dreamed of at home. Foreign companies could raise money by issuing commercial paper. The biggest and best of them could even issue their own bonds. Even before the coming of such financial derivatives as swaps, these were potential sources of money that was often cheaper and more flexible than that provided by banks.

With the dramatic growth in the Japanese economy, so the biggest and best Japanese corporations built up 'cash mountains', meaning that they did not have to depend so much on their traditional bankers for regular funds. Some of them, like Toyota Motor, still felt the pain of reconstruction forced on them years ago when they had faced the difficulties of industrial adolescence, and wanted to maintain financial independence. Others wanted access to cheaper and more flexible funds, but agreed to continue borrowing from the banks for old times' sake. In the period from 1970 to 1993, the percentage of corporate borrowing coming from bank loans fell from 85 to 70. As the Japanese banks grew, they also resented the restrictions on their traditional activities set by the Ministry of Finance. IBJ in particular wanted to get back to the underwriting business which it had dominated before the war, where its position had been taken over by Nomura Securities and the other members of the 'big four' brokers (Daiwa, Nikko and Yamaichi being the other three).

By the end of the 1980s Japan's economy had matured, so that its natural growth potential was much less than it had been in the youth or adolescent years of the 1960s and 1970s. Economists argue about exactly what the potential 'sustainable' growth rate had fallen to. Some optimists went as high as 4 per cent; others, including Kurosawa, suggested the figure was as low as 2.5 per cent. Any such arguments were obscured and forgotten about as Japan entered the era that subsequently was called the 'bubble economy'.

By the early 1990s, anyone simply reading newspaper headlines would have believed that Japan was the strongest economy the world had ever known, on its way to becoming the biggest economy in the world. Some bankers said that Japan would surpass the United States in overall size of gross domestic product by the year 2010; a respected Swiss banker, said that the banner year would come even sooner, possibly by the year 2006. Such arguments were enlivened by debate about what was the 'correct' international standard of comparison, a US dollar rate, which was liable to fluctuate depending on the strength or weakness of the US economy and the whims of foreign exchange dealers, or some artificial but fairer international standard like the special drawing rights or another basket of currencies. But by the start of the 1990s, some political commentators were talking of an impending era of *Pax Nipponica* on the basis of Japan's massive economic strength. Not only would Japan be bigger than the USA in terms of overall GDP, declared these futurologists, but it would be the biggest creditor in the world, with net foreign assets of $2,000 billion by the year 2010 (when net US foreign debts would be $3,000 billion).

But even for a country headed for the starry heights, the hubris was excessive. Bankers kidded themselves that there was nothing wrong with the Japanese economy, as economic growth rates soared and the Tokyo stock market rose towards the stratosphere, taking land prices with it, especially in the Japanese capital. The price of a single share of 50,000 yen par value in Nippon Telegraph and Telephone rose to 3.18 million yen (or $32,000 in 1994 values) as the company became worth more than all the shares on all the European stock markets put together. At its height, of 38,915 in December 1989, the Tokyo stock market was bigger than New York and was worth about 40 per cent of the total capitalisation of major world markets put together. The value of real estate in the centre of Tokyo rose and rose, so that the patch of land on which the Imperial Palace stood, altogether a mere 1,150,436 square metres or 284.27 acres, was worth more than the whole of the state of California.

Japanese companies and individuals poured money into investment and acquisitions, sometimes from the sublime to the ridiculous. Japanese even dared to buy slices of the Great American Dream when Sony bought CBS Records and then Columbia Pictures, and Matsushita took MCA and its Universal Studios, while Mitsubishi Estate bought the Rockefeller Center in the very heart of New York's Manhattan. Altogether in 1988 Japanese spent $16.5 billion in taking slices of corporate America, and another $13 billion in real estate. As part of the spending spree, Ryoei Saito, chairman of Daishowa Paper Manufacturing, paid a record $161 million in 1990 for a Van Gogh painting – and then caused a stir when he declared that he wanted the painting to be cremated with him when he died, a statement he later retracted as a joke. Banks competed to lend large sums of money, sometimes directly, sometimes to smaller banks and other non-bank financial institutions, which poured the money like petrol on to the overheating economy.

In the financial world, the buzzword was *zai-tech*, using the Japanese word for finance and the English for hi-tech, to mean financial engineering. The aim was to make more money from money, pouring funds into the ever-rising stock market and into schemes for land, the value of which rose month by month. Typically, the stock market became a merry-go-round, producing winnings that could be used to dream up ambitious development plans involving land that promised mega-yen profits as land prices reached for the sky. Given the ever-rising prices, the same collateral could be used to borrow larger and larger sums of money.

The banks should have known better. They had, after all, had an unpleasant experience in the 1980s when they had chased each other to lend money to Latin America and found themselves with huge losses. Kurosawa, who was then in charge of IBJ's international operations, ruefully admitted that his bank had got back 'about half' of what it had lent there. His only consolation was that 'I always watched our exposure [in Latin America] very carefully. When the crisis started we found that our position in Brazil and Mexico was number 5 to number 7 among the Japanese banks. And many Japanese bankers particularly were surprised. "How come?" they said. "We thought that Bank of Tokyo and IBJ were number 1." But I clearly watched the last stage of their borrowing. When I went to Latin America in the late 1970s, it was OK. But in the early eighties, they had started to borrow money rather short. At the start they were borrowing five years, seven years, ten years, but then in the early eighties, they changed to three years, two years, one year, ten months. Other Japanese banks thought that five year [loans] was a problem, but one year was OK, but my view was that five years was OK but one year was dangerous. Then I stopped lending and persuaded my colleagues that was the time to withdraw, so that was why IBJ was not number 1 but number 5 or 7.' The lessons of the Latin debt crisis, according to Kurosawa, were clear: 'too many banks, too many ambitious borrowers. We learned the lesson. We won't repeat it.' Perhaps the banks regarded Japanese as different from Latin Americans.

The Bank of Japan had been slow to react to the speculative frenzy, but under its new governor, Yasushi Mieno,* it put up interest rates. This was only one aspect of a multiple squeeze that brought home with a vengeance the folly of the competitive spiral of lending. Economic growth fell, helped by a worldwide recession. The stock market plunged. The value of a share in NTT eventually fell to 15 per cent of its one-time record. Though little publicised by the establishment Japanese press, the MoF received bomb threats from disgruntled investors who had lost heavily through the ministry's policies. It should be said that the Japanese are normally most peaceable, and that Tokyo is the safest city in the world, generally secure from terrorist or bomb threats.

By the end of 1994 the Nikkei was still hovering at about half of its 1989 record values. The stock market tumble not only reduced the value of companies, but meant that shares pledged as collateral for loans were no longer worth what they had been pledged for. Land prices fell, also lowering collateral values. The yen rose, pushed sometimes by the benign

---

* A career central banker, he took over in mid-December 1989 from the former Ministry of Finance official, Satoshi Sumita.

neglect and at other times by the malign intent of Washington, seeking to put pressure on Tokyo to curb its trade surpluses, which began to grow again in the early 1990s. Belatedly, even the banks began to repent of their lending frenzy and their failure to make even the most elementary checks of the credibility of the person or institution to which they were lending, the value of the project which attracted the loan, and the value of the collateral held against it.

IBJ was involved in one of the most celebrated of the scandals, a scheme so bizarre that it probably would not have got off the ground except in the mad circumstances of the bubble era. Nui Onoue was an Osaka restaurant owner with an interest in fortune telling. That was an unlikely beginning. She was no daughter of privilege, but was born to a poor family and divorced, aged 62 in 1992, when her name hit the headlines. She was obviously a woman of certain charm because of the distinguished list of banks which rushed to lend her money, and she clearly had devised a winning scheme.

She first became involved with IBJ in March 1987. She went into the Namba branch of the bank in Osaka and bought a billion yen worth of discount debentures issued by the bank. In any circumstances, it was such a large amount that it should have raised eyebrows. Onoue shrugged it off as if it were of no account, claiming that her restaurants were doing well. She was lucky in that the bank did not want to be left behind in expanding its lending, and was trying to expand by increasing lending to small and medium-sized businesses. Onoue kept in the bank's public eye by increasing her bond holdings in units of a hundred million yen. Her account was transferred from Namba to the main Osaka branch, where she got to know the deputy general manager. The sums of money were so massive that it is surprising that IBJ did not do a proper financial check on her background and sources of funds.

Not surprisingly, with this kind of investment Onoue was invited as one of the guests to the banquet hall in Osaka's Royal Hotel in 1990 to celebrate Kurosawa's taking over as the bank's president. Her motto was supposed to be 'With money all is possible'. So it might have seemed, as she joined the mightiest of rich businessmen and industrialists not only from Osaka, but also from the Kansai region. This was not just a trinket appearance, a passing reward to a valued customer. According to people close to the bank, the manager responsible for the account 'was really enthusiastic about doing business with her ... He felt like he was Kogin's pioneer in developing business with individuals.' He took other business clients to Onoue's restaurant, called the Egawa, and also spent his own money dining there. Other customers heard him say how much he liked the restaurant owner. The glittering reception at the Royal Hotel was not the only occasion when Kurosawa met Onoue. He went with his wife to Egawa at the request of IBJ's Osaka branch, and altogether met her twice when he was deputy president and once after he became president.

Not all IBJ executives appreciated Onoue's style. In summer 1990 she went on a tour of Buddhist pilgrimage places in India. Two IBJ executives were deputed to accompany her. Both grumbled that they had to wear rucksacks containing their own possessions so that their hands would be free to carry whatever Onoue wanted. She also further irritated them by urging them to hurry to carry out her errands. Onoue was impressed with the superior service and told one of the bankers, who was actually a departmental head, that she would like him to come again the next year. Colleagues said he fumed, stating 'If I am asked to do the same thing next year I am going to apply for a transfer. I didn't get a university degree to do this kind of thing.'

Someone who knew Onoue described her operating style: 'She would say something like "Even though we are Daiwa Bank's leading individual shareholder, the president hasn't dropped by to say hello." She would say she hoped someone would tell him to come by. Elite from IBJ were often in the restaurant at the time.' Apparently the name-dropping technique worked, and Onoue found a constant procession of leading bankers, section chiefs, departmental heads, directors and finally often bank presidents coming to pay court to her. Curiously, Sumio Abekawa, then the Daiwa Bank president, was one of those who refused to be lured into the spider's web. 'Abekawa felt that a visit to the *ryotei* [restaurant] of the leading individual shareholder might be misunderstood. He said he had an insight that it would be better not to pay a courtesy call.'

IBJ was clearly different, as a woman in the Osaka branch remembered. 'When Ms Onoue got in contact, the whole office would be on edge – you know – the big VIP treatment. Looking back, I can see she really stirred things up. The young male employees said that sometimes she would just suddenly call them on Sundays. They would rush to her place thinking something important was going on. But when they got there, they would find out that she had just made some curry or something and wanted them to try it. It got to be unbearable. She would keep calling them regardless of whether it was a Saturday or a Sunday.'

It is difficult to underestimate the leverage which Onoue got from the apparent blessing given to her by IBJ, and she used it to the full. Her trick was to show her discount bonds to get personal loans, not just from IBJ and its affiliates. An economic journalist, Seiichi Zaibe, explained the benefit: 'IBJ's investigation is considered to be authoritative. The government and other banks almost hold their breath waiting for the results of an IBJ inspection. But it is a novice in inspections of individuals, which is why it was soft on Onoue's credit.' At the peak she had more than 240 billion yen in loans from IBJ and associates, but she also used her discount bonds as collateral to get money from non-bank financial institutions.

With IBJ apparently behind her, Onoue almost always got her money. She used it to play the stock market. As she got more loans, she used part to buy more discount bonds and the remainder to buy stocks. When her gambling went well, she could even use her stockholdings as collateral, thus building a huge bubble of apparent wealth. At one stage it looked as if she had a fortune of 460 billion yen (to anybody who did not know about it being tied up in collateral). This was all achieved on the back of actual worth of an estimated two to three billion yen, the value of her restaurant in a valuable area of Osaka plus some land and some other smaller buildings. Her situation did not look so bad when the stock market was going up. When the stock market fell, so did the value of the collateral and of her wealth.

Eventually she was rumbled. Some bankers became suspicious when she made an application for a 500 million yen loan and then came back for a billion more. 'We found out that she was really not in a situation to get financing,' one banker said. He thought that she was being started off with 'black money' – proceeds of corruption or rackets by gangsters. What was finally revealed was that she had used the branch manager at a small credit institution, Toyo Shinkin Bank, to forge certificates of deposit which she used as loan collateral. By the end Toyo Shinkin was left with debts of 252 billion yen, equal to 83 per cent of its 304 billion yen in deposits. Altogether, when the fraud came to book, it involved 742 billion yen ($7.4 billion), and Onoue herself incurred truly massive individual debts of 400 billion yen. In total, she had borrowed from 62 financial institutions between 1986 and 1991 the colossal sum of 2,760 billion yen. To put it into perspective, that equalled more than twice Osaka's city budget.

Onoue, who was declared bankrupt, was arrested and charged with conspiring with Tomomi Maekawa, a branch manager of Toyo Shinkin seconded from Sanwa Bank to forge the certificates of deposit. They were charged for using the bogus paper as collateral for loans not only from IBJ, but also from Fuji Bank and ten non-bank financial institutions. Sanwa Bank resisted the Ministry of Finance pleas that it should absorb Toyo Shinkin and its debts. Because of this it took several months for a bail-out scheme to be put together, under which IBJ and Fuji wrote off 70 per cent and the non-banks 42 per cent of their claims backed by false Toyo Shinkin certificates of deposit; Toyo Shinkin itself sold 50 billion yen of assets to cover part of its remaining 130 billion yen in bad debts; Sanwa Bank assumed its remaining 80 billion yen debt, which was then offset via low-cost loans from IBJ, the Deposit Insurance Corporation and the Zenshinren Bank, the central shinkin bank body; and Toyo Shinkin's non-financial assets, including 25 of its 30 branches and most of its 650 employees, were taken on by other Osaka shinkin banks, with the remaining five branches going to Sanwa.

The episode caused such a stink that Kaneo Nakamura, chairman of IBJ, who was president at the time of most of the loans, resigned, in the immortal Japanese words 'to take responsibility'. Kurosawa kept his post and suffered a heavy pay-cut for six months. Kisaburo Ikeura, Nakamura's predecessor as chairman and before that president, resigned of his own initiative from his post as adviser. The general manager of the Osaka branch and a former Osaka branch head were asked to resign by advisers who were not on IBJ's board. Managers at Fuji, Tokai and Kyowa Saitama (now Asahi) banks also punished their executives.

In his resignation statement, Nakamura said: 'Our contacts with Onoue began when I was president, and Kurosawa was promoted to president just in June last year [1990]. As a result I [rather than Kurosawa] should take responsibility as the top executive.' That was not quite the end of the story. Kurosawa had to testify before parliament at the house of representatives special committee on problems in the securities and financial sectors. 'We were cheated . . . we were cheated repeatedly,' Kurosawa told the MPs. He refused to go into details about the losses, saying only, 'We will improve our management structure.' Onoue, meanwhile, in prison facing her charges, said she had taken to religion, was serving God and wanted to start a small restaurant when she was finally free.

In retrospect, Kurosawa denied claims that he cursed the evil influence of Onoue. One story said that he had called her a 'witch'. But Kurosawa denied this, saying, 'I try to be a good Christian. I don't have any warm feelings towards her, but I do not have any hostile feelings. My wife even wanted to visit her [Onoue] in prison and take her some sandwiches, but I said it was not good timing.' He points out earnestly, 'We were not involved in any wrongdoing. We were simply cheated. She was not involved in *yakuza* [gangster] activities. She was not being supported by any big shot or by politicians, though some small shots may have been there. It was rather simple fraud.' It was an expensive baptism for Kurosawa, who admitted that 'because of that fraud, we lost altogether $300–400 million, that's all.' In total, calculated Kurosawa, IBJ will probably have to write off 'more or less a billion dollars' because of its involvement in the bubble economy, 'but that will be over three to five years'. To claims that that is an immense sum to lose, he asserted, 'Our hidden reserves are 1,600 billion yen or $16 billion, so we can use less than 10 per cent of it.'*

IBJ may not have been involved with dubious underworld personalities, but another city bank, Sumitomo, the biggest, brashest and most profitable, was caught out. Its president, Sotoo Tatsumi, also appeared before parliament in March 1991 to apologise for being caught in scandals: 'It is true that our management put disproportionately high priority on

---

* IBJ's hidden reserves, he laughed, were more substantial than the Chagall painting on the wall behind him, part of the bank's splendid art collection.

increasing profits,' he conceded. 'It is regretful we could not break the reckless running of Itoman,' he added, referring to the medium-sized trading house that was teetering on the edge of bankruptcy. 'We feared unexpected developments for Itoman, with 750 billion yen in annual sales, would cause massive disturbance. We, as a leading bank, needed to maintain the order of the financial market.'

Itoman, which specialised in textiles, began to buy real estate to benefit from the bubble economy. Tatsumi said that Sumitomo repeatedly advised Itoman to get out of real estate, which was becoming increasingly risky, but the trading company had refused to listen. The Sumitomo president was only telling part of the story. He revealed a little bit more when he added, 'We made every effort to help Itoman since we knew about its irregularities in the spring of last year [1990], but we could not interfere with the management of a independent concern.' Again he was being economical with the truth. Pressed further, he denied speculation that Sumitomo was half-hearted because of close relations between its former chief executive, Ichiro Isoda, and Itoman's president, Yoshihiko Kawamura. Kawamura was himself formerly a senior executive of Sumitomo Bank and was subsequently arrested. Protests of the lack of bank responsibility were belied by the facts, which came out slowly over the two years after Tatsumi's appearance before parliament.

Isoda was one of the few colossus figures in Japanese banking. Known as 'the Emperor', he was president for six years and then chairman of Sumitomo for seven more, making the bank the most profitable in Japan and receiving the adulation of foreign journalists, respect from his banking peers and fear from his employees. He did this by aggressive lending policies, including in the real estate market, using the cheap credit that was freely available. It was ironic that Itoman was responsible for Isoda's downfall. Sumitomo, under Isoda's direction, had rescued the trading house in the 1970s and put its own executives in to bring stability and restore it to health. Itoman took its name from its founder, Mansuke Ito, who established it in 1883 as a fabric dealer, and then went into trading by importing cloth from Britain. The company specialised in textiles and later diversified into trading in foods and industrial machinery. One problem was that Itoman, dissatisfied with the slow pace of opportunities in its normal trading business, had turned to real estate, investing in a range of properties from apartments to golf courses. It had gone on to deal in the even more speculative art market, specialising in Modiglianis. This was bad enough, especially when Itoman had debts of 1,300 billion yen just before the economic bubble burst. Worse, there were constant stories about Itoman's involvement with underworld figures.

After the arrest of seven men on corruption charges, prosecutors said that Itoman's speculative ventures had cost it 300 billion yen. One director committed suicide before president Kawamura resigned. Isoda's own downfall and forced resignation from the post of chairman of Sumitomo Bank was triggered by the arrest of a former Sumitomo manager on charges of making illegal loans to a prominent stock market speculator. Sumitomo Bank's claims that it was no more than an ordinary small investor in Itoman, with a 3.2 per cent stake, did not fool anyone. It was Itoman's main bank, and a 3.2 shareholding is quite a strong one given that the legal limit for a bank holding is 5 per cent. At the time of its downfall, 13 of the 47 leading Itoman executives were from Sumitomo Bank. In the end, in April 1993, Sumikin Bussan, an unlisted subsidiary of Sumitomo Metal Industries, absorbed Itoman, the name of which disappeared.

By 1994, however, banks did not have to get involved with nefarious underworld or gangster figures, or even with fortune-telling restaurateurs, to be caught by bursting bubbles. The main problem was not criminal behaviour, but just stupid lending. The results of all of the major banks for the financial year ending in March 1994 were revealing, even though they had the benefit of the Japanese accounting system to hide as many of the problems as possible. None of the banks made losses, but all of them recorded plummeting pre-tax profits, the fifth fall in succession. More damaging, together the city banks wrote off 2,480 billion yen in bad debts, two and a half times as much as in the previous year. At the end of this, their declared problem loans were higher than at the end of the previous year, amounting to 8,948.1 billion yen, or five times the total pre-tax profit of all of the banks, or almost four times their total net business profits (the amount of money they made from ordinary banking business, taking no account of the bad debts).

The most damning commentary came from Alicia Ogawa of Salomon Brothers: 'We see little in the full-year results of the city banks which would encourage us to be more positive on the group. In spite of the banks having used nearly all of their operating profits, and a good deal of the hidden gains on their investment securities, to write off bad debts, the outstanding amount of problem loans increased over [the figures for the previous year to] March 1993. Loan spreads came under pressure and will continue to do so, limiting the pace of bad debt disposal further. Finally, we see little to suggest that the banks are doing anything to help themselves; costs remain virtually unchanged.'

Results of the three long-term credit banks, IBJ, Long-term Credit Bank and Nippon Credit Bank, were almost identical to those of the city banks. Only IBJ showed a steep drop of 7 per cent in its costs. The long-term credit banks, however, face a new difficulty not experienced by the city banks, with their access to customers' deposits as a source of funds. Since the long-term credit banks have to fund themselves by issuing debentures, they found that the interest rates they had to pay were essentially fixed, while interest rates on the loans they provided to make their money began to fall in line with interest rate reductions. The other group of Japan-wide banks, the trust banks, did better and actually reported increases in operating profits. However, this was mainly because of higher fee income from banking, rather than trust operations. Three trust banks reported negative net interest income – a dangerous sign. In addition, many of the major trust banks, unable to attract enough borrowers, have begun to lend money to themselves. This practice of shifting money from trust accounts to banking accounts, called *gingashi*, has weakened the profitability of the banks.

Equally worrying, many banks managed to keep up with their bad loans only through selling shares that they held in companies with which they had close relationships. Frequently, these shares were carried in the books at the historic cost, way below their current market prices, thus yielding a nice profit. Often, however, because of the close relationships through the *keiretsu* (conglomerates), the banks then immediately bought back the shares. Below the nationwide city, long-term credit and trust banks, regional banks reported heavy falls in their earnings, and a number of shinkin and smaller banks were in trouble.

The real difficulty for the banks is the level of non-performing loans. Generally, both the authorities and the banks themselves have tried to minimise the extent of the problem. Kurosawa of IBJ, for example, denied that there is a crisis. 'The crisis for the Japanese banking system is over,' he declared confidently in mid-1994. 'There are 14,000 banks in the US, and last year for the first time there was no bankruptcy. Usually they have 140 or 150 bankruptcies each year. We, in Japan, have had in the last 50 years no single bankruptcy. There might be bankruptcies, one or two, but this is different from a financial system crisis, which didn't exist. It has only been reported by foreign newspapers. The clouds over the financial system have gone, whatever difficulties some banks may be facing.'

Some banks said they should be congratulated for having disposed of more non-performing loans than ever before, and predicted that the bad loan problem would be over within two years, by 1996 or 1997. This attitude was upheld by Japan's leading financial newspaper *Nihon Keizai Shimbun*, which claimed to have got hold of figures for 'restructured' loans held by each bank and not publicly disclosed either by the banks or by the Ministry of Finance. It claimed that the total loans of the city banks had declined by 1.2 per cent between September 1993 and March 1994, suggesting that the levels of bad debt had peaked and would now decline. According to the newspaper's figures, total loans, including the value of restructured loans, of the eleven banks would be 15,765.7 billion yen. Restructured loans are those where the bank has lowered the interest rate below the contracted rate to help troubled clients. If total bad loans had dropped, this would have been reassuring news. But the article was misleading.

The newspaper admitted that the figures it published did not include loans to the Co-operative Credit Purchasing Corporation (CCPC), set up in 1993 to take over the worst of the banks' bad debts. Nikkei admitted that at the CCPC, 'recovery of the amount lent is very much in question'. Critics like Ogawa at Salomon Brothers saw the CCPC as an exercise in financial alchemy. The way the system worked was that the banks sold their non-performing loans to the body at a discount to full asset value, and booked the difference as a loss against their earnings. It sounded fine to have a real asset, though a diminished one, with the CCPC, which would then dispose of the loans and collect the collateral.

There were several problems with the scheme, however: the banks lent the money to the CCPC so that it could buy the loans; had to bear the risk of default; and would meet any difference if the CCPC was unable to sell the loans for what it paid for them. The expectation was that the new institution would at least help to create a market and begin to remove the problem of bad loans. Toyoo Gyohten, chairman of Bank of Tokyo, noted in 1993 that the real problem was to recreate liquidity in the property market. However, in 1994 the banks had been selling large numbers of loans to the CCPC. As of May 1994, a hardly vast total of 1.1 per cent of the loans on the corporation's books had actually been sold. According to Ogawa's figures, adjusting Nikkei's numbers to include the outstanding balance of loans to the CCPC, total problem loans increased by 4.9 per cent in the six months to March 1994.

On top of all this were questions over the definition of what actually constitute bad loans. The official Japanese definition is loans to companies that have gone bankrupt plus those where interest and principal payments have not been received for at least six months. In other countries, the standard is for non-payment for three months to put a loan into the non-performing category.

Reasons for concern were further prompted by disclosures in June 1994 by Mitsubishi Bank. This is regarded as one of the most conservative Japanese banks, likely to be the last with real problems. According to its declarations in Japan, its non-performing loans represented 1.8 per cent of its total, compared to the average for all city banks of 3.8 per cent. Ogawa, the pessimist, put the true figure of Mitsubishi's non-performing loans at 740 billion yen, higher than the 572 billion yen actually disclosed. But when Mitsubishi published its figures in the USA to conform with Securities and Exchange Commission criteria as a company listed on the New York stock exchange, it showed bad loans of 1,150 billion yen. If this is the state of one of the most conservative banks, then the Ministry of Finance might tremble at the prospects of smaller vulnerable banks which are disclosing non-performing loans at between 4 and 7 per cent of their total loans.

When she had had time to study the results more carefully, Ogawa took issue with statements from leading bank executives and the Japanese press who had declared 'the mountain [of bad loans] has been crossed'; 'our view', wrote Ogawa, 'is that the mountain is not even in full view yet'. Later the banks' half-year results in 1994 showed a slowing down of the increase in bad loans, but very little of the problem amount is being removed from the balance sheets. Early in 1995 Sumitomo Bank bravely decided to bite the bullet and announced that it would write off the huge sum of 800 billion yen (or $8 billion) in bad loans in one gulp, giving it a loss in its fiscal year to March 1995 of 280 billion yen. It still had 950 billion yen of non-performing assets on its balance sheet after the write-off.

Looking further ahead, Japanese banks have no room for complacency. Prospects for the property market in the mid-1990s are not regarded as very good, especially while economic growth is in the zero to 2 per cent range. If the market fell any further, then banks would be hit by a fresh wave of bad loans. Poor economic growth also means that demand for bank loans is low, giving them little opportunity of raising income. If interest rates rose, then there would be a new set of problems as some clients would not be able to pay the higher rates and would have to go into default. The problem is not limited to the banks alone, but is exacerbated by the tiers of non-bank financial institutions to which the banks in the heady bubble days lent money as they rushed headlong into the property market. They behaved just like lemmings.

It was not just a maverick few foreign analysts and journalists who questioned whether the crisis was really over. The big American debt-rating agencies clearly had their doubts too. Standard & Poors downgraded Japanese banks in a series of ratings in the early 1990s because of the overhang of bad debts, so that in its rating of March 1994, none of the banks enjoyed the top AAA rating. The best was Norinchukin Bank, the big agricultural bank, on AA +, followed by Mitsubishi with AA. IBJ was on A +, and Mitsui Trust and Yasuda Trust banks did not even get an A rating. In a report in May 1994, Standard & Poors also warned that asset quality problems would take years to resolve. It estimated that problem loans at 23 leading Japanese banks were in the region of 30,000 to 35,000 billion yen, or much higher than the banks or MoF were prepared to admit to. 'Japanese banks' biggest challenge now is how to extricate themselves from problem assets as quickly as possible without reporting red figures,' S & P said.

The other big rating agency, Moody's Investors Service, also had questions for IBJ, predicting that it would face increased competition in its traditional areas of business because of financial reforms and deregulation, and that it might not be able to find new business to offset these. Moody's also pointed to the very pertinent fact that the other troubling aspect is the poor profits of the Japanese banks. 'If Japanese banks had the same level of core earnings as US banks, the asset quality problem would be quite manageable, there would be no crisis, and Japanese banks as a whole would be much more creditworthy.' A very high 70 per cent of the banks' profits come from lending, much higher than in the USA or Europe, yet margins on loans are thin.

Apart from the immediate problems of bad debts are structural questions about the organisation of the whole Japanese financial system, with its tiers of compartments into which the banks are neatly packaged. Critical analysts ask whether there is a need for so many banks, all of them offering the same kind of services and hardly distinguished from each other more than Tweedledum was from Tweedledee, in name only. Two categories of banks, the long-term credit banks and the trust banks, are probably not needed as the late twentieth century moves towards the twenty-first. Under the city banks are regional banks, many of which are of variable quality. And beyond these banks are the highly vulnerable non-banks, still groaning from their excesses of the bubble years.

The attitude of the Japanese authorities, like IBJ's Kurosawa, is to boast that Japan – unlike the USA – has never had a bank bankruptcy. Rescue operations were carefully arranged before the crunch finally hit the wounded institution. The Ministry of Finance (MoF) has encouraged healthy banks to consolidate. Mitsui Bank and Taiyo Kobe combined to form Sakura Bank, and Kyowa and Saitama came together as Asahi Bank. Taiyo Kobe was itself the product of an earlier merger. The merger of Bank of Tokyo and Mitsubishi Bank, to be consummated in spring 1996, will be the biggest of all.

The MoF was also quietly trying to encourage regional banks to combine. In 1994 plans were devised to combine three regional banks in the Tohoku area in the north of the main Honshu island. In terms of capital, branches and deposits, the three were more or less the same size, but Kita-Nippon was slightly bigger and much stronger in profits and loan portfolio. Its pre-tax profits of 3.1 billion yen in the year to March 1994 were about 170 per cent of its total disclosed bad loans. But that was much better than its other proposed partners, one of which had bad loans of more than double its profits, while the other had bad loans of fourteen times its profits, illustrating just how poor and vulnerable are some of the smaller banks. The regional banks only disclose bad loans to borrowers in bankruptcy proceedings, and some Japanese financial sources said that, if the bad loans of the weakest bank had been assessed by the city bank standards, then its total would have been ten times higher or more than 100 billion yen, a horrendous sum for a bank with capital of 4 billion yen. In the end, the planned merger was killed by opposition from the Kita-Nippon Bank's union. The wider structural problems of the whole system remain.

This was again demonstrated in July 1994, when Nippon Mortgage, one of Japan's biggest property-backed lenders, decided to file for bankruptcy. It seemed to mock the MoF's protests that nothing was wrong. It was the third biggest corporate collapse in post-war history, with Nippon Mortgage's debts estimated at 500 billion yen, of which 120 billion yen were owed to Sumitomo Trust and Banking Corporation, 27 billion yen to IBJ and 25 billion yen to Long-term Credit Bank. It was set up by Sumitomo Trust and two property companies in 1982 specifically to be a property lender, an activity that the banks were excluded from. Other banks set up similar mortgage operations, so the fear was that, far from being an isolated bankruptcy, Nippon Mortgage was evidence of other horrors to come. Sumitomo Trust had written off 80 billion yen in bad loans in the year to March 1994, and the predictions were that the bankruptcy would cost it another 90 billion yen in write-offs. An MoF official played down the bankruptcy, saying that it would not precipitate a banking crisis, since there were no individuals among its creditors.

More problems followed in October 1994, when Mitsubishi Bank put up almost $2 billion to buy a majority 68.8 per cent stake in Nippon Trust Bank, the country's smallest trust bank, which was saddled with 200 billion yen in bad debts from property lending. The move gave Mitsubishi an opportunity to get involved in trust banking, though at a price. A director of the bank indicated that there had been resistance when he said, 'The best thing about this is that we won't be asked to rescue anyone else.' Bail-out by a big bank of a smaller institution may be seen as a way of restructuring the whole system. But it remains an open question whether healthier banks will pay the price or will want to pick up sickly institutions.

A few months later it became clear that there were limits to big brotherly rescues. In December, the Bank of Japan announced the setting up of a lifeline to two Tokyo-based troubled credit associations. It said it would set up a new bank to absorb the assets and liabilities of Tokyo Kyowa and Anzen (ironically, *anzen* means 'safe'), which were on the brink of bankruptcy, having each lent 50 billion yen to EIE International Corporation, a Tokyo-based real estate agency; they had more than 100 billion yen between them in bad debts. The Bank of Japan itself planned to provide half of the new bank's 20 million yen capital, with the rest coming from private banks, but it then became clear that 40 billion yen was an underestimate for the cost of rescue.

It was the first time since the war that public money had been used to bail out troubled financial institutions, and finance minister Masayoshi Takemura claimed that it was 'a temporary and unusual measure to protect depositors and the order of the financial system ... not intended to rescue independent financial institutions'. However, it could equally be used to pick up other banks facing difficulties, although some members of parliament asked whether it was a good use of public money. Equally, it was a sign of the central bank's failure to find banks prepared to rescue the two credit associations. The bail-out also cast doubt on governor Mieno's assertion that troubled banks could not count on being rescued by the government.

The mystery deepened and murky political clouds then developed when it was revealed that the two credit associations were the target of a criminal investigation and that Tokyo Kyowa had lent 35 times the legal limit to a single customer, the EIE International group led by Harunori Takahashi, who was also chairman of Tokyo Kyowa until late 1994 and adviser to Anzen. It was also alleged that secret payments were offered to people who would deposit money, in a desperate attempt to hide the gravity of the situation. More worrying were rumours of Takahashi's connections with underworld figures and leading politicians. The bad loans of the two credit unions, though large for them, hardly amounted to a threat to the financial system, leading to gossip that there was more to the rescue than the authorities were prepared to admit. Finance minister Masayoshi Takemura denied that there were any political pressures behind the bailout. The first politician to be smeared was the deputy secretary-general of the opposition Shinshinto, Toshio Yamaguchi, who resigned his party post to 'clear his name' after companies run by his family had been shown to be heavy borrowers from the troubled financial concerns.

The tight grip of the MoF has discouraged initiative. This has applied not only to large matters, such as forbidding banks to become involved in securities matters, or vice versa, even though they can compete abroad. Some of these bigger regulations are beginning to crumble – 'the fences get lower every year,' said Kurosawa – but the finance mandarins have been concerned to see that they do not disintegrate too rapidly, so that banks might gain an advantage over the securities companies, or vice versa, or that one institution might be able to make a sudden leap forward over its own competitors.

The restrictions also apply to small matters, not only banking hours – 0900 to 1500 Monday to Friday – but also the hours of automatic teller machines (ATMs). Uniformly, except for the US intruder Citibank, which has introduced 24-hour banking through its ATMs, the machines of the Japanese city banks work only until 1900 (to 1700 on weekends), take the day off completely on holidays, and charge 100 yen extra, plus the 3 per cent consumption tax, making 103 yen, for withdrawals made after 1800 on weekdays or at weekends. When Sakura Bank was formed, the MoF mandarins decreed that, although it could use the auspicious name Sakura – which means cherry blossom, a beloved symbol of the Japanese spring – it could not use the *kanji* Chinese characters in its signs and had to use the phonetic hiragana letters. The same applied when Kyowa and Saitama became Asahi Bank.

In other ways, too, the MoF policy is to see that there are no surprises. In international business, the failure of the ministry to give its approval to a European-based system called multilateral netting, designed to reduce foreign exchange risks, meant that no Japanese bank had joined it as of mid-1994. MoF approval is not needed, but the banks dared not go ahead without its blessing. A spokesman for Fuji Bank told Nikkei flatly, 'We don't want to talk about it.' The pervasive attitude in Japanese banking, as in many aspects of Japanese life, is not to stand out or to do anything fresh or different. The only excuse that the banks can have is that they have learned by painful experience. Any bank wanting to offer a new service or financial instrument was traditionally expected to obtain MoF permission first, which was usually delayed until other banks had been informed of the plan, so that all banks could introduce the new measure at the same time, with no bonus for original ideas. Competition has been devoted to small things, like reducing the wait for cash at ATMs from eleven to five seconds, rather than important things, like new services for customers or going into new businesses.

In the last few years, there have been some beneficial signs of a new competitiveness. Sanwa Bank has emerged as the most profitable bank by virtue of trying to attract medium-sized clients (who will pay more) rather than concentrating on blue-chip companies, but Sanwa had to because its keiretsu base was weakest. On the whole, it is still difficult to distinguish one city bank from the next. Kurosawa is even unusual in having a personality, holding sometimes controversial opinions and being prepared on occasion to utter them. Most leading Japanese bankers are bland, dark-suited and shiny-booted figures, dressed as smartly as a tailor's dummy, and having about as much wit. 'I will do my best to solve the problem,' is about the most forthright statement coming from any of them.

It is not that Japanese bankers are inherently stupid. Japan's big city banks annually attract the very best young graduates, and banks like Mitsubishi – and indeed IBJ – get the cream of the crop. IBJ is something of an exception. Its successive presidents, Ikeura, Nakamura and Kurosawa himself, have all been thoughtful and articulate. Conversations with junior executives, from manager to director and managing director, also normally yield interesting opinions and quotable quotes. But at the city banks it seems that the slow progress up the seniority ladder, the emphasis on consensus and the fear of offending lead to the crushing of thought and individuality. It would be unthinkable in Japan for a major bank to bring an outsider in to run the bank, let alone one as young as in his early forties, as was Martin Taylor, drafted in to run Barclays Bank in 1993. Moreover, Taylor was an ex-journalist, having started his career with Reuter and gone on to the *Financial Times*. The only executives catapulted into Japanese banks are ex-MoF mandarins, such as Yasuo Matsushita, former chief mandarin, who was chairman of Sakura Bank, and in December 1994 became governor of the Bank of Japan in spite of Sakura's bad debt problems.

One senior executive of Mitsubishi Bank was asked which foreign bank he saw as a role model for his bank. He suggested J.P. Morgan, the US house. This showed how far Japanese bankers can be from reality: Mitsubishi is far removed from Morgan, which gave up its commercial bank licence to concentrate on investment banking. It is hard to think of a city bank that would be disciplined – and discerning – enough to shed services to concentrate on its strengths. 'But we must provide everything our customers need,' is the plea of bankers when taxed. However, there is a very real question which Japan and its finance officials and bankers have refused to face squarely: how many universal banks can a country of 123 million people, double the population of the UK, afford?

The only defence of the MoF policies is that they plug short-term holes in the system. The CCPC may have prevented widespread panic about the impending collapse of the system under the weight of bad debts. Carefully controlling the turf of each narrow sectional interest may prevent chaos at a difficult time. However, sooner rather than later, the question of reform will have to be faced. In the area of banks against brokers, the MoF has loosened the rules to allow banks into securities business. Again, a plethora of rules and regulations hems in the freedom. The banks must set up separate securities offshoots, which cannot use the name 'bank', are not allowed to do stockbroking – which traditionally has been the most profitable core business of the securities houses – and must have a firewall keeping the banking and securities activities apart. And the MoF guardian looks after the smallest details – the staffs of the bank and its securities concern must wear different uniforms.

IBJ, which got a head start by being granted permission before the city banks, is showing its power. In 1994, its securities offshoot lead managed an underwriting for the first time, placement of domestic straight bonds worth 20 billion yen for Nissan Motors. Even though it was for Nissan, a company with which IBJ has long been linked, it showed the power of IBJ Securities, already making money after being in existence for only two years. Its securities arm also took nice chunks of new bond underwriting by Nippon Steel, Fujitsu, Orix and Sankyo Aluminium. By September 1994, it had underwritten 3.7 per cent of bonds issued by Japanese borrowers in the previous six months, had a staff of 130 and aimed to get up to 10 per cent underwriting with 200 staff in 1995. When the major city banks were allowed in late 1994 to start securities subsidiaries, they demonstrated their lemming-like behaviour as they all rushed to set up such offshoots, mostly staffed by bankers. It is tempting for banks with loan demand flat and with companies increasingly looking to bonds for funds. However, the experience of other countries where banking and securities have traditionally been split is that commercial bankers do not possess the skills to run securities operations successfully.

There is no sign that the MoF is thinking quickly enough to resolve the medium- and longer-term questions, such as whether Japan today really needs a special category of long-term credit banks or indeed of trust banks. Some of the trust banks should become specialists in fund management, but the longer they leave the decision to change role, the greater the risk they face of being challenged. Most important of all, the question is whether there is room for all the city banks, let alone the hosts of local banks. The precedent of mergers so far is not encouraging, since Sakura especially remains weak, even though it is the fifth biggest bank in the world according to *The Banker's* July 1994 ranking of banks according to tier 1 capital, and is the fourth biggest by assets. Yasushi Mieno, governor of the Bank of Japan, in March 1994 urged banks not to 'stay in the pack', but to become more competitive. There is little evidence so far that the city banks have heard or understood, though Kurosawa has clear ideas of where he is taking IBJ.

'We want to be a universal bank, but a wholesale, not retail, bank,' he said. This means doing securities operations, even trust banking, while continuing lending to companies. Kurosawa would not give up IBJ's ability to lend, as Morgan did. The IBJ president said, 'I think that the universal bank is the original form of banking, and the separation of banking and securities business was the very bad idea of Mr Glass and Mr Steagall in the United States in the 1930s, which was followed by Japan and Korea and Canada, that's all. We don't want to become bigger. If you look at Deutsche Bank, 2,000 branches and 60,000 employees; we don't have any such ambitions. We have 30 branches and 5,000 employees (plus another 30 branches and subsidiaries abroad), and don't have any idea to increase them. We will stay compact. We will still lend to industry. As long as they need, we will provide, and if they don't need, please go next door to IBJ Securities, which is doing very well. We are changing day by day. We will establish our own trust bank, hopefully in 1995, to do business with pension funds. The Japanese market is so huge that there is room for everyone.'

Kurosawa exudes optimism. Apart from the question of its badly inspired rush into personal and property lending in the bubble years, from which it is still suffering, IBJ has stamped out its strong, respected and feared presence. In Japan, it plays on the fact that it is not handicapped by being a member of any of the leading keiretsu, and therefore it boasts that it can give truly independent banking services and advice. It has been successful in this, in that its clients comprise 90 per cent of all companies listed on the first section of the Tokyo stock exchange. Regularly, IBJ wins top place in Japanese polls for the quality and depth of its advisory and consulting services, as well as for its burgeoning securities market expertise.

Abroad, it has more freedom to operate as a universal bank without being bound by domestic trammels. It is respected as an underwriter in the Euromarkets and for its strength in derivatives markets, not just in yen, where it is the leader, but in dollar, sterling and Deutschmark derivatives. It has also been active, but highly selectively since the experience of Latin America, in lending to foreign projects such as the Eurotunnel, linking England with France, and in the development of Shanghai and its new Pudong showpiece industrial zone. Every year Kurosawa goes to China, where he meets the very top leaders. He religiously attends the annual meetings of the International Monetary Fund and also the Asian Development Bank. US and European bank chief executives are conspicuous by their absence at the Asian meeting, but for Kurosawa it is a time for hard work. At the Nice meeting of the Asian Bank in May 1994, he pulled out a huge piece of paper with a grid of appointments – or more correctly a gridlock, since it was chock-a-block full and took him a full minute to count. 'By the end of the [three-day] meeting, I will have seen about twenty sets of people for formal appointments, another eleven for cocktails or over dinner and, if you count the formal receptions as well, I will have seen 1,000 people in all,' he said. And he got up at 6 a.m. for games of tennis at 6.30. 'We won,' said the ever-competitive IBJ chief, rejoicing in his latest victory.

He denies that IBJ executives can be divided any longer into 'domestic' and 'international', saying that in his career any bright rising IBJ executive will be expected to perform well in Nihombashi or New York, Hiroshima or Hong Kong, Shinjuku or Singapore. For all the claims against Kurosawa that he is too 'international', he keeps up with the domestic business and political scene and is able to offer penetrating insights into the major players, based on close personal ties (though he has become more reticent about going on the record about them as he has climbed the ladder). IBJ's most senior managing director, Yasushi Kajiwara, gave an interesting sidelight into Kurosawa's operating styles. 'When he asks me lots of detailed and complicated questions, I know that he is interested and the project is likely to get his backing. When he greets me with smiles, I get worried.'

But if IBJ and Kurosawa are to fulfil their dreams of being a universal (wholesale) bank, then they will have to do so at the expense of existing players. Securities companies were beginning to complain about bank intrusions on their turf, and it is likely that medium-sized brokers will suffer, especially if the stock market stays depressed. There will inevitably be losers as well as winners, but this means that the MoF will have to be prepared to tolerate failures.

When the stock market was falling towards 16,000 in 1993, the MoF called in executives of Japan's biggest life insurance companies, who are the biggest investors in the stock market. Nippon Life alone holds more than 2 per cent of the shares on the Tokyo Stock Exchange. The officials explained that if the market crossed below 16,000 there would be damaging consequences for the capital ratios of some of Japan's big banks, which count part of their stock market holdings towards their capital. This, the MoF said, could lead to a credit squeeze as the banks cut back lending to match their falling capital.

The message was understood: next day Nippon Life 'voluntarily' bought 10 billion yen worth of shares and the market picked up. Later, the banks themselves were prevailed upon not to issue preferred stock because the ministry urged that it could hit the stock market. The way to square the circle, at least in the MoF's view, and to tidy up the system while fulfilling the boast of never having had a bank fail is clear enough: it can be done by forcing the weaker players to merge with the stronger ones.

Unfortunately, the stronger ones can no longer be relied on to bail out the weak. Sanwa Bank resisted absorbing Toyo Shinkin, the unions at Kita-Nippon prevented it from merging with two banks in the same region, and clearly no taker could be found for the ailing Tokyo credit associations. The MoF has its hands full merely trying to plug the holes in the financial system, without having to orchestrate wholesale changes. The question is whether it has the time and energy, and someone else has the money, to keep on plugging the holes as fast as they appear.

Clearly, the mandarins are determined to try regulating the minutiae of the system. They may find opposition in unexpected places. In 1994 Jonan Shinkin Bank reacted to the deregulation of interest rates in October by announcing a lottery under which new depositors might win cash prizes of up to 50,000 yen. On cue, both the MoF and the National Association of Shinkin Banks criticised such a gimmick as a way of attracting customers. Jonan Shinkin stuck to its guns and was joined by other shinkin in announcing new schemes to win customers, some of them daring to raise interest paid on deposits, and the supervisors had to withdraw their opposition.

Eugene Dattel, an American who worked in senior positions in Tokyo for US investment banks in the 1980s, lambasted the MoF both for the failures of the financial system and for the inadequacies of the Japanese players. He claimed that the bureaucrats knew all about stockbrokers' links with criminal gangs and their common practice of compensating favoured clients, but did nothing about it unless it became public knowledge. In effect, the regulatory system was a cosy club for everyone. 'Unless there was negative publicity, the MoF was unconcerned about market manipulation, fraud, investor protection, poor performance and incompetence.'* In consequence, Japan's financial institutions, restricted by regulations but without the discipline of market accountability, frittered away billions of

---

* In *The Sun that Never Rose: The Inside Story of Japan's Failed Attempt at Global Financial Dominance*, Probus, 1994.

dollars, to the detriment of themselves and their shareholders, Japan and indeed the whole international financial system and economy.

What does it matter for Japan or for the rest of the world? One aspect is Tokyo's role in the international system; the other is the role of Japanese capital in the world. Increasingly, Tokyo's place as an international centre is being undermined by the failure of the MoF to think internationally or to understand the changing pace of internationalisation of markets. In the days when the Nikkei index was booming to absurd heights, it was widely assumed that Tokyo was one of the big world markets, sharing with London and New York the job of 24-hour trading, and likely to eclipse one of them.

In those heady days, when Tokyo accounted for almost 40 per cent of total world market capitalisation, its rapidly rising role seemed effortless. But after the bubble burst, and the market fell and fell and fell, and still has not recovered, either in the Nikkei index or in daily trading – a miserable 235 billion yen shares a day in 1994 – Tokyo's future seems less certain. A study for the Japan Center for International Finance, an affiliate of the MoF, found in 1993 that only 6 per cent of the foreign financial institutions questioned believed that Tokyo would come to be more important than New York and London as a financial market in the next five years. In 1989, just before the bubble burst, 32 per cent had expected Japan to lead the world. In addition, only 9 per cent said they were satisfied with financial liberalisation in Japan, and 49 per cent said liberalisation was inadequate. They cited a lack of disclosure by banks about their bad loans and obstructing accounting and tax rules. Some 67 per cent complained of obscure market practices and decision making.

County NatWest, the brokerage arm of the UK's National Westminster Bank, gave up its seat on the Tokyo stock exchange. So did Kidder Peabody, the investment bank subsidiary of the US industrial giant GE. Other brokers, including some of the biggest American houses, reorganised their Japanese operations and concentrated more resources on Hong Kong and other rapidly growing markets in developing Asia.

Another study in 1994 by the National Land Agency also joined in complaining about high rents and the low availability of lawyers and accountants who knew about overseas legal systems. It also mentioned the need to improve English language skills among Japanese bankers, to improve airport facilities and access, and to develop better tele-communications systems. Although Tokyo is the home of some of the world's biggest electronics giants, people in the communications business say the telephone and telecommunications facilities, besides being expensive, are not as good as would be expected in such a city. Although Tokyo retained its position ahead of London in terms of the market value of shares listed on the stock exchange – \$2,900 billion, compared with \$1,200 billion on the London Stock Exchange – in other respects Tokyo was much less international than London (and the New York Stock Exchange market value was $4,500 billion). Only 89 non-Japanese financial institutions had offices in Tokyo in 1993, said the National Land Agency, whereas 393 non-British financial institutions had offices in London, and 337 non-US ones had offices in New York.

In terms of international syndicated loans, Tokyo was a centre for only a fraction of New York's business, recording barely 1 per cent of New York's total in 1993. Hong Kong was almost six times bigger in terms of syndicated loans, and Singapore was almost one and a half times as big. Even Japanese grumbled about the MoF's interfering rules. 'Japan's capital and foreign exchange market is facing a severe case of hollowing out,' said Mikio Fujii of Nomura Securities' bond division, noting the shift of issuers and investors to places like Hong Kong, where they have more freedom.

Tokyo's shortcomings were further underlined in the mid-1990s. Several prominent international companies which had listed their shares on the Tokyo market in the exciting boom days decided to withdraw because there was not sufficient trading in their stocks, and because the procedures of staying on the exchange are tedious and expensive. They included British Gas, ICI, Chase Manhattan Corp, Eastman Kodak, General Motors, Goodyear Tire and Rubber Co., ITT, New York telephone company NYNEX Corp, Warner-Lambert (the drugs giant), Royal Bank of Canada and the Dutch investment concern Robeco. From 125 companies in December 1991, the number of foreign stocks quoted in Tokyo had fallen to 91 by early 1995. A General Motors executive put it brutally: 'There wasn't any bang for the buck.' The 20 million yen or so costs of keeping a listing, involving filing reports in Japanese, no longer match the benefits with trading volume in foreign shares down from 2 million in the boom of the late 1980s to 180,000 a day.

Raising money through a stock market listing was also becoming a problem for Japanese companies, thanks to the restrictions imposed by the Ministry of Finance. Because of the dull market, there was a lull in new issues, broken only by the public offering in 1993 of East Japan Railway Company, the biggest single part of the former nationalised Japan National Railways, which had been broken up into seven parts, and Japan Tobacco (JT) in 1994. Critics accuse the ministry of deliberately holding back other new listings so that it could safely sell off formerly nationalised concerns, such as the railway companies, the tobacco monopoly and, eventually, another tranche of Nippon Telegraph and Telephone. Mike Allen, stock market analyst with Barclays de Zoete Wedd, accused the ministry of bungling the initial public offering of NTT by helping to generate a 'frenzy of speculation', which saw the price of a single share set at 1.2 million yen, then soar to 3.18 million yen before dropping. 'It will be some years before the Ministry of Finance dare offer another tranche of NTT because a lot of small investors lost their shirts in the original offering,' said Allen.

The listing of Japan Tobacco (JT) was instructive of the MoF's determination to get a high price, and thus help to reduce bond issues. It had made 2,300 billion yen from the first tranche of NTT in 1987, and 5,000 billion yen from the second, and thus reduced bond issues from 12,300 billion yen in 1985 to 7,200 billion yen three years later. Initial bidding in the preliminary auction for the tobacco concern was mainly by individual investors, who pushed the price to 1.438 million yen a share, even though most institutional analysts valued the company as worth about 800,000 yen a share.

The MoF saw 666,666 shares (the first tranche of a third of the 2 million shares in the company) at 1.438 million yen each as netting it 958.7 billion yen, and set the listing price at that, even though, with a dividend at 5,000 yen, it was asking investors to accept an annual yield of a minuscule 0.35 per cent. But, seeing the high price, 60 per cent of winners in the lottery to buy tobacco shares decided not to exercise their right, and the MoF decided to withhold those shares. Nevertheless, the share price fell from the opening, and closed at 1.1 million yen on the first day, a massive loss of 300,000 yen in a day for anyone holding a JT share.

Analysts complain that not only was the Ministry of Finance intent on getting the best terms for selling off the former nationalised companies, but officials were actively discouraging other companies from listing on the market. These included smaller concerns that would have benefited from stock market money without absorbing the resources that a huge former national monopoly concern would. And of course, the vast sums of money raised from JT went straight into the Treasury rather than to fund an active business, as would money from a new private listing.

If the Tokyo market were to play an important regional and international role, it would be expected to be a magnet for companies from other Asian countries seeking to expand their international exposure. But when several Chinese companies looked for foreign listings in 1994, they chose to go to New York and apparently did not even consider Tokyo because of the rigmarole, restrictions and costs involved in getting a listing on the Tokyo market. The new president of the Tokyo Stock Exchange, Mitsuhide Yamaguchi, expressed his concern about up-and-coming foreign companies bypassing Tokyo, and introduced simplified rules and regulations from 1995, reducing the costs and making it possible for a company to appear in Tokyo even without a domestic listing in its home country.* 'These

---

* Vetting costs for a listing will be halved to one million yen; net assets of the foreign company will need to be only 10 billion yen (against 100 billion yen previously); and pre-tax profits over a three-year period must be a minimum of 2 billion yen (20 billion); the minimum trading unit will be 500,000 yen (3 million yen).

reforms can pave the way for at least 200 east Asian companies to join the exchange in the next few years,' Yamaguchi claimed. He may be disappointed, since decisions to list are determined equally by the actions of investors, and the Tokyo market still falls short by the standards of London and New York.

The stock market is only one of the financial markets, but it is note-worthy that, as foreigners have been fleeing from Tokyo, so trading in Japanese shares on foreign markets has increased. In 1993, turnover of Japanese stocks on the London SEAQ international market amounted to 20 per cent of the trading on the first section of the Tokyo market, and in some popular Japanese shares London was almost as popular as Tokyo. The US Treasury Department produced a long list of financial instruments that can be traded in New York, but not in Tokyo, including over-the-counter equity options, individual stock options, warrants on stock indices, junk bonds, index-linked bonds, strippable bonds and currency and commodity warrants. In addition, such internationally accepted instruments as zero coupon bonds, perpetual notes and asset-backed securities can only be issued with great difficulty in Japan. All of this helps to diminish Tokyo's and Japan's role on the international financial stage. Such restrictions and the MoF's nannying rules have caused Japanese to complain that their market is becoming a local affair.

The other important area where Japan is failing internationally is in the provision of funds to help development of the rest of the world. In the 1970s and 1980s, Japanese banks poured money into Latin American projects, many of which proved wasteful, so that they got their fingers badly burned and, noted Kurosawa, now have a much more selective and even leery attitude towards lending to developing countries. By the mid-1990s, they had resumed lending, but very carefully and selectively. China was an important target, especially as Japanese industrialists set up factories there. South-east Asia was popular, especially Malaysia, Singapore and Thailand, and some bankers were talking of Vietnam's market liberalisation as offering promising opportunities. But India was completely off most Japanese bankers' maps. Some of this was a function of Japanese ignorance. Even Kurosawa made disparaging comments about India, saying, 'India belongs to the Anglo-Saxons', though he admitted that he had not been there for 33 years.

Yet the surpluses are piling up, and Japan's net foreign assets are the biggest in the world. Some of the money s being recycled via Japanese corporate investment in south-east Asia and even some further afield as manufacturers seek production sources offering cheaper labour than expensive Japan, inflated further by the rising yen. But for a long time, large sums of money were being peddled back into the USA through Treasury bills and bonds, which was wasteful for everyone: for Japanese investors as the dollar fell and made the value of the instruments less with each fall in the US currency; for the ordinary Japanese, seeing the products of their work exported without any benefit being received in traded goods; and for other countries which would have benefited from real physical Japanese investment. When Japanese institutional investors became wary and held off putting funds into a weak dollar, that put more pressure on the yen. The worry now must be that some of the China loans may go sour, causing Japanese banks to pull in their international horns.

In all, international operations account for less than 15 per cent of the average city bank's net income, whereas for a European or US bank the figure is 45 to 50 per cent or more. In addition, most of the Japanese banks' foreign business consists of plain vanilla loans on which profit margins are thin. To some extent this is because the yen is not *the* international currency – a function still fulfilled by the US dollar – and to a large extent it is because of discouragement by the MoF. This is a contrast from the days when Britain and the USA were the financial leaders and bankers to the world, when their banks were everywhere and their currencies, first sterling, then the dollar, were the international currency. In summary, this performance is not a good advertisement for the international coming of age of the Japanese financial system.

3

International Flagship of Japan Inc.:
Mitsubishi

Of all the admirals of Japanese industry – no mere captains these men – Minoru Makihara, president of the giant trading house Mitsubishi Shoji, stands out from all the rest. It is not just the size or scale or octopus tentacles of the trading concern's operation – worth about $170 billion a year – but the career background of Makihara himself. He was not born in Japan at all, but in the London suburb of Hampstead early in 1930. He went to an exclusive prep school in New England. He obtained his university degree not from the élite Tokyo University, but from Harvard, and he acquired a western name, Ben. Makihara's career was largely spent not in Japan, but in the USA and Britain. These foreign assignments took 22 of his first 38 years with the corporation, against only 16 in Mitsubishi's Tokyo head office. Then in 1992 he was appointed president, truly an international executive of a company that has frequently been represented abroad as the flagship of Japan Inc. To friends, it offers the best of Japan, a worldwide reach and understanding, working in almost every country and dealing with up to 100,000 products; to opponents, it is the biggest, ugliest spider at the centre of a keiretsu web, preventing companies from other countries from getting access to Japan's markets.

In his first two years in office, Makihara raised some eyebrows, not only with his uncharacteristically unJapanese acceptance of bad debts, which he promptly wrote off, but also because of his embrace of the idea that, to flourish in the twenty-first century, Mitsubishi must become truly international. That he says will mean foreigners sitting on the main board of the company. The alternative to becoming international is to risk extinction. 'We either become extinct dinosaurs or homo sapiens of a new era,' he declared, putting the choice bluntly. It is heady, even revolutionary, stuff for a man who asserts that he is still quintessentially Japanese, in spite of his foreign education and work experience.

Mitsubishi has earned respect, fear and intense hatred at various times in its history as the epitome of Japan Inc. Before the Second World War, it rivalled Mitsui as the leading *zaibatsu* (meaning literally 'financial clique' but broadly plutocracy or conglomerate) and for the title of biggest company in the world. During the war, Mitsubishi's Zero fighter was one of the most dreaded aircraft, on a par with Messerschmitt in the western theatre, striking fear into the hearts of Allied pilots. After the war, the Supreme Commander Allied Powers, General Douglas MacArthur, and his team moved quickly not just to break, but to smash to smithereens the Mitsubishi empire. They broke the trading company into 170 different bits, and forbade the use of the Mitsubishi name for any of the activities done by any offshoot of the once mighty group.

But American hopes of killing Mitsubishi died soon after the Allied forces departed. By 1952 the parts of the Mitsubishi empire had begun to take the old name and to regroup. By 1954 the Mitsubishi group was formally reformed, not this time a single zaibatsu, but a grouping of 29 companies, many boasting the Mitsubishi name, meeting regularly and plotting together against the rest of the world, if you believe some hawkish American commentators, or loosely united for occasional friendly chats about good business opportunities, if you believe the Mitsubishi propaganda.

What causes foreign commentators to foam at the mouth and to see plots is that the companies involved are individually highly powerful, including Mitsubishi Bank, perhaps the most conservative of the city banks and therefore the one with the strongest balance sheet, Mitsubishi Trust Bank, Mitsubishi Estate Company, sitting on billions of dollars worth of prime land in Tokyo, – as well as owning the Rockefeller Center in the heart of Manhattan – Mitsubishi Heavy Industries, the biggest integrated industrial company in Japan with interests in shipbuilding and aerospace, Mitsubishi Motors, the third biggest car producer, Mitsubishi Electric, Tokio Marine and Fire Insurance, the biggest non-life insurance company with almost 18 per cent of the market, and even a couple of giants not bearing the Mitsubishi name, Kirin Brewery, accounting for about half of Japan's beer sales, and Nikon, the world-famous camera maker. Sitting at the centre of the web, turning this into the group that most closely resembles the old zaibatsu – or so the critics say – is the concern over which Makihara presides, Mitsubishi Shoji (Corporation).

The trading house's four-page monthly English newsletter, *MC Now*, offers a quick glimpse of the enormous range of its activities. A typical 1994 issue reported that a joint venture agreement had been signed between Mitsubishi, Shell, Exxon and the Venezuelan state oil company, Lagoven, to produce liquefied natural gas; that a UK-based financial services subsidiary was to help advise the European Bank for Reconstruction and Development on a project in Uzbekistan; that Mitsubishi had signed a deal to market software from Formtek, a subsidiary of Lockheed, in Japan; that Mitsubishi International in the USA was providing $30,000 to two Houston schools for Japanese teaching; that Mitsubishi had formed a joint venture to offer interior decorating in Shanghai; that South Korea had given permission to set up Korea MC to help boost Korean exports;

that MC Gold was celebrating ten years in the jewellery business (including running the Goldilocks shop in Tokyo's Ginza); and that the environmental affairs department had produced a video explaining how Mitsubishi was helping promote the revival of forests in its timber and pulp operations.

Altogether, Mitsubishi has partnerships with more than 40,000 companies in trading products from tea to telecommunications, and in research, exploration, production and marketing of goods from the everyday essentials to scientific and technological breakthroughs. It has the Kentucky Fried Chicken franchise in Japan, offers space in Tokyo for Harrods to sell its goods, is involved in research to produce calorie-free food and golf tees made from environmentally friendly soil.

One of the surprising things is that this vast corporation is not really that old. It dates back only 120 years or so to the infant years of the restored Meiji emperor. The young ambitious leaders of Japan who took over saw how far behind the West 300 years of feudal isolation had left their country, and determined to catch up quickly. They imported products and policies that led to the release of pent-up energies. The urgency of the quest to catch up was also fuelled by nationalistic fears. The Meiji rulers spotted and understood what was happening in nearby China, where the European powers were helping themselves to slices of the country. They were determined to build up their own forces so that the same fate did not happen to Japan.

The most important focus was the need to improve key resources with defence potential. The old wealthy interests were slow to respond to the challenge. Not so Yataro Iwasaki, son of a minor samurai family from a farming village on the island of Shikoku. Born in 1834, he went to Osaka to work at a trading house, became interested in international trade and in the early 1870s leased three obsolete steamships and used them to form a company called Tsukumo Shokai. This was the genesis of the future Mitsubishi Corporation. The name of the tiny company changed rapidly with its expansion, becoming Mitsukawa Shokai in 1872, then Mitsubishi Steamship Company two years later and finally in 1875 Mitsubishi Mail Steamship Company. The name and the familiar logo, still used by all Mitsubishi companies today and known as the 'three-diamond trademark', both come from the earliest days. Mitsubishi means three diamonds and originated from the three *hishi* or water chestnuts which were the emblems of Iwasaki's first ships.

Iwasaki's biggest step forward came early, when Japan needed ships to supply munitions to its forces involved on the island of Taiwan. The Japan National Mail Steamship Company (or YJK) line, which the government normally used, refused the opportunity for fear of suffering in the domestic market. Iwasaki leapt in, volunteering his vessels, 'moved less by the profit motive than by his fervent patriotism', says the company literature. 'His patriotism was so fervent, in fact, that he was unconcerned with whether he could make money on the commission or not. All that mattered to him was that he serve his country.' The government saw that he got his reward multifold. The following year he was given 30 ships disposed of by the government free of charge. This gave him the chance to take on the US Mail Steamship and P & O Steamship for shipping services in coastal Japan and between Yokohama, Shanghai and Hong Kong. The government, of course, was delighted at Japan's new ability to challenge the foreign intruders in its backyard, and Mitsubishi consolidated its position, transporting munitions for the government side during the Seinan revolt of 1877. Meanwhile, the old-established shipping company withered and died.

But in the swirling changes of the new era, Mitsubishi itself was soon to lose not only its domination of the shipping industry, but indeed its core business. In 1881 Shigenobu Ohkuma, the pro-Mitsubishi political leader, was unexpectedly defeated, and the new government launched a shipping federation to trim Mitsubishi's sails. It was as bad as any dogfight, with savage cuts in prices in order to secure passengers and cargo. It ended with a 50:50 merger creating a new shipping line called Nippon Yusen (NYK), which most Mitsubishi workers joined. The company had to find other lines of work. Iwasaki had already turned to coal mining and shipbuilding, renting from the government the Nakasaki Shipyard (later to be the core of Mitsubishi Heavy Industries and much later to be the target for the second atomic bomb in 1945).

Right until the Second World War, the Mitsubishi Company differed markedly from other growing groups, such as Mitsui and Sumitomo, which eventually became its rival powerful zaibatsu. It was controlled by the Iwasaki family and, more important, the founder laid down that the word of the president was to be law. Echoes of the dominance of a single man are to be found today in the modern Mitsubishi. Yataro Iwasaki laid down the rule. Even Mitsubishi's own potted history of the group concedes that 'Many biographies of Yataro Iwasaki portray him as a "bully", a "monster", or a "mettlesome adventurer".' Article 1 of the Mitsubishi corporate regulations of 1878 stated that 'Even though our company has adopted the name and structure of a corporation for the time being, the fact is that it is really a family run business entity and is quite different from companies organised with outside funds. Therefore, anything relevant to the company, every reward, punishment, or promotion, must be submitted to the president for his sole approval.'

The founder's younger brother, Yanosuke, who took over the helm on Yataro's early death at the age of 50 in 1885, started the process of diversifying the company. In 1890 he made a major acquisition, spending the equivalent of $1 million for 80 acres of wasteland on the then outskirts of Tokyo, a price that appalled his contemporaries, who wondered what sort of a mad spendthrift he was. That wasteland is now the centre of the Marunouchi banking and business district of Tokyo, prime land among the world's prime land and still in the hands of Mitsubishi Estate, worth billions of dollars.

The group continued to be built up by the Iwasaki family. Hisaya, Yataro's son, was the third president and set up divisions to deal with banking, general affairs, sales, coal mining, mining and real estate. Finally, in 1916, Koyata Iwasaki, the Cambridge-educated son of Yanosuke, took over and ran the group until the end of the Second World War, expanding it to more than 70 enterprises and giving it an increasingly international outlook. His focus on heavy chemical industries laid the foundations for Mitsubishi's prowess and technological development of a wide range of advanced products, which were soon to be typified by the Zero fighter and the Musashi battleship. Ownership of Mitsubishi and its growing family of companies was diversified through stock market offerings in Mitsubishi Sha (Mitsubishi Company) and in other affiliates, but Koyata Iwasaki remained the man at the helm.

Iwasaki's defenders – and not just those responsible for the company's good publicity – say that Mitsubishi was reluctant and indeed opposed to the militaristic policy that emerged in the 1930s. In 1925, prime minister Takaaki Kato, a former Mitsubishi employee who had married founder Iwasaki's eldest daughter and was funded by the group, cut the military budget by 25 per cent, resulting in a loss of four army divisions. For this, Mitsubishi itself was widely attacked as 'unpatriotic'. The Right accused Iwasaki of preventing Japan's imperial destiny, and the Left said that the wealthy capitalists cared only about themselves. Kato himself had studied in Britain, had served as Japan's minister there, and was a great admirer of the British parliamentary model. But the big trading groups also remembered how they had prospered during the First World War, when their rivals from Europe were preoccupied with war and fighting, and they were suspicious of what was achieved by military spending.

Popular criticism of the zaibatsu, and not just Mitsubishi, intensified in the early 1930s. Mitsui, the great rival of Mitsubishi, faced a series of newspaper attacks, and in 1932 a right-wing extremist killed Takuma Dan, its senior executive. Seeing the writing on the wall, the zaibatsu changed their tune to play along with the popular mood. But the military leaders never forgot and deliberately built up new groups that were given privileges particularly in China, the new frontier of military Japan. The Nippon Sangyo (Japan Industries) group was the biggest of these, including what later became (after its post-war dissolution by SCAP) Nissan Motors, Hitachi, Hitachi Shipbuilding and Nippon Mining.

With Japan's declaration of war through the attack on Pearl Harbor and the simultaneous invasion of Malaya, Koyata Iwasaki summoned all the leaders of the Mitsubishi companies to declare support for Japan at war. But he also included a plea to remember old friendships, as if his heart was not in the conflict: 'Mitsubishi has had many British and American friends who have co-operated with us in business. They have been working with us in the context of a friendly relationship up until this date, sharing the same interests in the same business, always co-operating. Now, unfortunately, we have been divided into nationalities, two sides to which we and they belong, and we are destined to fight each other. It is inevitable for our nation to take legitimate actions against their businesses and their assets. However, we should not impair our relationship with our old friends through such actions. Should peace some day be restored, they should again become good, faithful friends of ours, just as they have been in the past. There should be future opportunities for all of us to co-operate again to realise world peace and the welfare of mankind.'

In defeat in 1945, Iwasaki stubbornly tried to resist the suggestion by the victorious SCAP that the zaibatsu should voluntarily dissolve themselves. Mitsui, Sumitomo and Yasuda did. But Iwasaki protested: 'Mitsubishi has in no way performed in bad faith, nor has it done anything wrong to the nation or society. We have simply fulfilled the obligations that naturally had to be fulfilled by the citizens of this country. Should this "suggestion" be an imperative, then we have no options, but we have no reason to act on any suggestion of voluntary dissolution.' He even pleaded with Keizo Shibusawa, finance minister and chairman of the Postwar Government Liaison Office, to approve the payment of a final dividend to shareholders. But the new Allied rulers would not agree, and Mitsubishi too had to dissolve, pressured by the government, 'guided' by SCAP. Koyata Iwasaki died on 2 December 1945, aged 67, marking the end of the family rule and the end of the old Mitsubishi zaibatsu. He left behind a final poem:

> Autumn, a season of great variety,
> A diseased goose, motionless,
> Lies still on the frosty ground.

Mitsubishi lost not only its president and its headquarters. The presidents and executives of most member companies were purged, and their companies were forced to dissolve. Restrictions were placed on key people to prevent them from setting up new companies. Mitsubishi Shoji, the trading arm, found its 4,086 employees split among 139 different companies. At Mitsubishi Heavy, the hammer of SCAP was less thorough, and in 1950 three smaller companies were formed out of the old giant.

Some anti-zaibatsu measures taken in the early days of the occupation remain in place today. In 1947, parliament passed an American-inspired anti-monopoly law, article 9 of which made holding companies illegal.

The occupying powers saw the holding company as the vital force cementing the zaibatsu. Today it remains the law even though many corporate experts would like to see proper holding companies to make the accounts of Japanese companies clearer and easier to follow. The old zaibatsu names were changed: Mitsubishi Bank became Chiyoda Bank, Mitsui kept the Imperial Bank name it had used in wartime, Sumitomo became Osaka and Yasuda became Fuji. But the occupying powers misunderstood the driving force behind the old groups. The families were swept out of control, but the old corporate élite remained and waited until the Americans left, when they would be able to count on their old chums, the bureaucrats.

In other ways the reforming zeal was quickly diluted or bypassed. The occupiers had been highly selective in choosing the victims of their purges, which caused resentment. The military, of course, had been singled out, some of them tried and hanged, or imprisoned as war criminals. But apart from a few individuals, the bureaucracy, perhaps perforce since the Americans had neither the will nor the personnel to run the whole government, was largely left intact. Indeed, the two big ministries, Finance and what became International Trade and Industry (Miti) came away with enhanced powers. So there was a strong sense of grievance when the University of Tokyo business classmates of these rising bureaucrats found themselves forcibly removed from their jobs and livelihoods.

Bureaucrats aided by the political leaders quickly began to draw a distinction between the letter of the new regulations, which they kept, and their spirit, which they bypassed when convenient. Their freedom for manoeuvre was increased when SCAP was shaken in the period from 1947 by a series of strikes and labour unrest. This helped to undermine MacArthur's naive confidence in some kind of paternal kindly socialism, and gave a pivotal role to prime minister Shigeru Yoshida, who was almost the archetype of the smooth but tough nationalistic pillar of Japan Inc. Then the occupying force was distracted by its own problems, the Korean War and the dismissal of the stubborn MacArthur, which further played into the hands of the Japanese in running their own country their own way.

By 1951 the San Francisco peace treaty had been signed, effective from the following year, and the occupying forces had begun to pack their bags to leave. Japan was more or less master of its own house again. Restrictions on the big companies were dropped, 'to meet a rapidly changing world situation', as Mitsubishi puts it. By 1954 Mitsubishi Corporation had been reformed, and ten years later Mitsubishi Heavy Industries was put together again. The company asserts, contrary to sometimes vicious foreign claims, that the group today is far different from the pre-war zaibatsu. 'Today, Mitsubishi is an association of companies that share a common origin and management philosophy, but that are not subject to autocratic rule from headquarters. Though all companies are independent, all adhere to the three Mitsubishi principles.' These three principles were formulated by Koyata Iwasaki, the fourth president. They are: 'Corporate responsibility to Society; Integrity and Fairness; International Understanding through Trade.'

The idea of a variety of independent companies all proudly bearing the Mitsubishi name, but all operating completely autonomously of each other, is a neat one which Mitsubishi executives are keen to assert. It conveniently ducks several aspects which give the big Japanese groups common strong ties – apart from the family name and the fact that most Mitsubishi executives sport the same lapel pin with its three diamonds. One important link is the amount of business which Mitsubishi companies do with each other. Although president Makihara jokes that his years in America have left him with a taste for Budweiser beer – which his senior colleagues say is true – it is a common remark that it is possible to get any beer in a Mitsubishi canteen or dining room, provided that it is Kirin. Sure enough, when in 1994 the Mitsubishi president hosted a reception for foreign journalists in Tokyo, only Kirin beer was served.

These strong business ties are institutionalised by the cross-share-holdings that link and bind the Mitsubishi companies, and by the regular exclusive business sessions between the heads of all the group companies. In both aspects, Mitsubishi companies have statistically stronger links than any rival conglomerate group. In addition, the trading company Mitsubishi Shoji occupies a more central place in the overall structure of the Mitsubishi family than in other groups, where the lead is taken by a powerful bank. For all these reasons, American critics have been quick to complain that the keiretsu (or conglomerates) are latter-day zaibatsu with slightly friendlier disguise. Senior officials in the administration of President Bill Clinton have claimed that the keiretsu are themselves important barriers to trade, and are a major reason why the USA is unable to sell more and runs such a massive trade deficit with Japan.

The German Bundesbank also claimed that the keiretsu effectively blocked investment in Japan from its country. Affiliations between Japanese companies were so tight that it was difficult for foreigners to get in, the central bank claimed. Studies of particular areas of the Japanese economy, especially insurance and construction, have found that the keiretsu ties are strong there. A 1993 report by the American Chamber of Commerce in Japan claimed that member companies of the eleven major keiretsu account for more than 80 per cent of Japan's non-life insurance market – things like fire and car insurance – and a whopping 92 per cent if related and affiliated companies are included. 'We simply are producing the facts,' declared Evan Greenburg, head of the chamber's Financial Services Committee, who, coincidentally, is also the chief operating officer of the US giant American Insurance Group. 'And the facts seem to point very clearly that collateral relationships – namely shareholding, lending and other financial transactions – have a tremendous influence on where the insurance is placed.'

Greenburg's figures showed that, of the traditional big conglomerates, the Mitsubishi and Sumitomo groups were strongest in keeping their insurance business in-house. In both, 97.5 per cent of their non-life insurance was provided by their keiretsu insurers. If affiliates were included, the percentage climbed to 97.9 per cent for Mitsubishi and 98.1 per cent for Sumitomo. Other groups were less tightly bound: for example, 88.3 per cent for Mitsui and only 43.3 per cent in the case of the Dai-Ichi Kangyo Bank keiretsu, though in both cases the percentage leapt to 90 per cent if affiliates were taken into consideration.

Japanese insurers countered with a standard argument claiming that foreigners just did not try hard enough. 'Foreign companies often cite keiretsu ties as one reason that they are unable to crack the market, but from our point of view it's rather that the effort made to increase sales is just not enough,' said an agent from a big Japanese non-life insurer who did not want to be quoted by name. 'If you don't put in the effort and fail to visit clients, you can't very well expect to sign contracts,' he added, claiming that the Japanese did make such efforts and that foreigners did not. To this, Greenburg responded in a dialogue of the deaf: 'They say that keiretsu and cross-shareholdings are a figment of our imagination and there's nothing exclusionary about them. Let's quit saying that it's simply a myth, and that we don't understand, and we don't try hard enough. Obviously these collateral relationships have a tremendous effect on how the business is done, and that's hardly open and fair.'

Another area of business where the big groups dominate, not just because they are good and big but because of cosy binding relationships, is construction. The giant Kajima Construction in 1992 announced with a great fanfare that it was aiming to buy 5 billion yen ($50 million) worth of wooden furniture, tiles, stone, steel frames, glass and pre-stressed concrete from Asia, Europe and the USA. The purchases would be made – of course – through an affiliate trading company. (Even in giving orders to foreigners the keiretsu can do good business.) Given the fact that 5 billion yen in purchases would only be a drop in the bucket – about 0.265 per cent of Kajima's annual sales, for example – the announcement seemed no more than a publicity gesture of openness. But it threw light on the stranglehold of business ties preventing foreign construction sales to Japan.

A manager of a mid-sized general contractor said that his company was keen to use imported materials because they were generally cheaper than Japanese-produced materials. By buying abroad it could cut costs by up to 20 or 30 per cent, depending on how many of the inputs were purchased from abroad. However, he added, responsibilities to associates, reinforced by cross-shareholding ties, were more important than such matters as the price of the materials. Even if costs were reduced by importing cheaper materials, agreed the procurement manager for a larger construction company: 'You will still lose by offending your existing suppliers.' In Japanese business circles, trying to break away from existing obligations involves a round of visits and grovelling apologies, and would threaten to break several spiders' webs of carefully interwoven ties – which is also why there would be much resistance and why pressures are strong not to take such drastic steps as going outside the group, especially not to foreigners.

The generic word 'keiretsu' in fact embraces two broad kinds of organisation, the horizontal and the vertical keiretsu. Horizontal keiretsu are the traditional groups, the old zaibatsu in modern clothes, like Mitsubishi, Mitsui and Sumitomo, which consist of several companies, including a *sogo shosha* or trading company, a bank, life and non-life insurance concerns, and industrial houses, mostly linked by the same family name or once common ownership. The vertical keiretsu are divided into production and distribution types, but are basically the links in the chain to and from a giant industrial company, like Hitachi, Matsushita Electric Industrial and Nissan Motors. Kenichi Miyashita and David Russell, in their excellent account of the keiretsu,* compare the two kinds of vertical keiretsu to an hour-glass with the parent company in the middle, or to an inverted pyramid on top of a normal one. Products come in from a large number of components makers to a smaller number of subparts makers, then move on to a still smaller number of parts suppliers to the giant manufacturer, which then passes the finished products through a similar chain of wholesalers and retailers until they reach the marketplace and the consumer.

Development of the vertical keiretsu, its supporters say, has led to one of the peculiar strengths of the Japanese industrial machine; its detractors argue that it has also very effectively prevented foreign companies from selling into the Japanese market. Take the motor industry as a good modern example: use of a multitude of subsidiaries to supply components and parts is something that distinguishes a Japanese car maker from one in the USA where more of the manufacturing process is done in-house. The chain of subsidiary and affiliated companies helps take the strain off the industrial giant. If there is a squeeze because of recession or a rise in the value of the yen, the giant effectively forces the smaller companies feeding it with parts and components to bear most of the pain.

Japan's famous 'lifetime employment' system works very well at the big companies, but does not extend down the line to the suppliers. When the bad times occur and recession sets in, Hitachi or Nissan can simply tell its suppliers to reduce their orders. They have to accept the shorter working

* *Keiretsu: Inside the Hidden Japanese Conglomerates*, McGraw Hill, 1994.

hours, lay-offs or sackings that can result. Similarly, if the yen rises in value, the giant will tell its small offspring that they have to reduce the prices of the parts they are making for it. The fact that it is a pyramid structure with many layers should mean that the pain is dispersed widely. In fact, life is always tough for the smallest subsidiaries, which come under continuous pressure – in bad, normal and even good times almost alike – to reduce prices, refine their processes and reduce their manufacturing times.

The ties between the industrial giants and their suppliers are often strong enough to deter outsiders, as the American T. Boone Pickens found when he bought a 20 per cent stake in Koito Manufacturing Company, a supplier of car lighting equipment listed on the first section of the Tokyo Stock Exchange. The purchase made him the largest single shareholder in Koito, which should – he reckoned – have been worth at least a couple of seats on its board. His own American critics claimed that this was a clever attempt at 'greenmailing' the Japanese: that is, forcing them to pay a higher price to get him out of the company (with the classic greenmail threat of making a takeover for the company as the ultimate sanction). Unfortunately for the intruder, Koito was – and is – one of the major suppliers to Toyota Motor, which had a significant, though smaller stake, and which had seats on the Koito board. Indeed, insiders said that Toyota's was the effectively controlling hand over Koito; it was certainly strong enough to prevent T. Boone Pickens from gaining his ambitions. He protested, but eventually sold his holding.

Some Japanese supplier companies say that the disadvantages of being associated with one company are so strong that they prefer to avoid dependence. In good times, being a supplier and associate of a big quality-conscious company like Toyota may help, in that the giant will send its own engineers and control experts to help the small supplier refine and improve its own product. But the giant may want to examine the books and indeed all the manufacturing processes of the supplier to try to hone the prices finer. In many cases, suppliers complain, the bureaucracy of working for a giant can be time consuming. Each month the supplier may be asked to send in reports offering suggestions for improving operating efficiency; if there are not enough, the minnow will be told to go back and think of some more.

Some of the small suppliers laugh when organisations like Keidanren (Federation of Economic Organisations), the powerful club of big business, give their backing to shorter working hours and a five-day week to still foreign criticism of workaholic Japan. That is fine for the big boys, but small manufacturing industry may have to work round the clock to meet the demanding delivery targets of the giant and to allow it to work the five-day week. The executives and head office staff of the big companies have not had to worry about working Saturdays or Sundays for some time.

In the bad times, the small suppliers are the first to be hit. Until the recession that followed the bursting of the 'bubble economy', many Japanese industrial giants were able to 'rationalise' their production without too much trouble by simply squeezing their suppliers harder. Ota-ku, in the east of Tokyo, used to be full of thousands of tiny subcontractors, each with a speciality and a tiny workshop. By the mid-1990s they numbered several thousand fewer than at the start of the decade, as firms folded under the squeeze of the rising yen and recession. By 1994 the economic slump had got so bad that even the giants were beginning to be hurt, and had to curb new employment and make plans to slim down their white-collar office staffs. They were determined not to have to sack people – that would be bad for their image – but some of the best-known names were having to contemplate reductions of up to 40 per cent in their previously untouched office staffs.

Some of the vertical keiretsu are also members of a horizontal keiretsu, though this may be very loose depending on the muscle of the company. Toyota, for example, is sometimes listed as part of the Mitsui keiretsu, although it has more clout than most of the Mitsui companies, and its own unhappy experiences at the hands of its bankers taught it to be self-reliant. Toyota also built up its own distribution system and network of dealerships, development of which was one factor leading many Japanese analysts to predict that the giant trading companies could become the modern-day dinosaurs of the Japanese economy. They considered that the really powerful companies would fend for themselves in trading their products. The sheer size, professionalism and international reach of Toyota's distribution network has US rivals gasping with envy, and claiming that it is 'not fair' that the Japanese giant has a stranglehold on its own market and a strong presence in North America. Toyota certainly does not need Mitsui to show it how to sell cars.

Other motor car companies have links with the horizontal keiretsu. For example, Honda has banking links with Mitsubishi, and Mazda with Sumitomo Bank, though the fact that Ford Motors of the USA is the single biggest shareholder of Mazda, owning 24.5 per cent of the car maker, prevents it from being considered part of the Sumitomo family. Toshiba is also a loose member of the Mitsui family. Kajima, the construction giant, has ties with Sumitomo and even has a bank director on its board.

Working out just how big a slice of the Japanese economy is handled by the big horizontal keiretsu is difficult because not even one of the big spiders at the centre of the groupings can tell how big is the web that it has spun around it. Japan's Fair Trade Commission in 1989 counted 6,875 firms that were technically affiliates of the big six horizontal keiretsu: that is, with at least 10 per cent shareholdings. But this does not include large numbers of companies where the keiretsu have effective control without a substantial, sometimes without any, shareholding. And some of the bigger companies have their own vertical keiretsu below them. The Fair Trade Commission thought it was being generous in giving the keiretsu 12,000 companies, but Miyashita and Russell go as high as 100,000. Similarly, the figures for the total capital, assets and sales of the big six are impressive – respectively, 33, 25 and 25 per cent of all Japanese companies – but certainly understate their influence.

Of the big six, Mitsubishi stands out in two ways. First, the cross-shareholdings within the group are higher than those of any of its rivals: 35 per cent on average, against 27 per cent in the Sumitomo group, 19 per cent in Mitsui and smaller links in the other keiretsu. Second, the trading company is at the centre of the web in the real sense that its president is the person who chairs the regular meetings of all the group chief executives, whereas in other keiretsu the bank is the dominant player. The executive council of Mitsubishi, called Kin'yokai, has 29 member companies, but the group has 217 affiliates which are at least 10 per cent owned.

Mitsubishi, though it is often regarded as one of the old historic zaibatsu groups, is a youngster by comparison with Mitsui or Sumitomo. Outsiders saw it as the epitome of the zaibatsu because of the vigour and deter-mination first of Yataro Iwasaki, then of his family successors as president. But when he started the business, Iwasaki was regarded as an upstart from a minor samurai family, pushy distant cousins of the real aristocracy.

Mitsui undoubtedly had a longer pedigree. The group was founded in 1673 by Takatoshi Mitsui, who established dry-goods stores in Kyoto and Edo (the present-day Tokyo) and then became a moneylender and manager of the Shogun's tax revenues. In return he was allowed to issue currency and government bonds, a grand history which allows Mitsui to claim that it is Japan's oldest bank with more than 300 years of history (even though Mitsui Bank in the modern sense was only founded in 1876, lost its name when it combined with Taiyo Kobe Bank in 1990, and became Sakura Bank in 1992). Mitsui quickly recovered from being left at the modern starting line by Iwasaki. It was able to shrug off its handicap of being close to the Shogunate mainly because its general manager had established ties with anti-Shogun forces. By a combination of work and using its connections with government, it had become the world's biggest company before the outbreak of the Second World War.

Even today, Mitsui is the group that is regarded as having the best 'connections', though the disappearance of the bank's name symbolises the harder times that it is facing. Its executive council, with 26 members, is called Nimoku-kai or Second Thursday Club, though it actually meets on the first Thursday of the month. The chair is taken in rotation by the trading company, the bank (Sakura) and the real estate concern. In addition, there is another looser group called the Getsuyo-kai (Monday Club), meeting on the second Monday and open to 78 member firms.

Mitsui has a total of 171 affiliates that are 10 per cent owned, although only about a dozen companies now bear the Mitsui name.

Sumitomo is even older than Mitsui. It was founded by Masatomo Sumitomo, who lived from 1585 to 1652. It made its money and reputation as contractor to the Shogun and operator of a copper mine, which it took possession of when the Meiji emperor was restored. It used the income from this as the basis for branching into shipping, steelmaking and warehousing. Unusually for an Osaka-based company, Sumitomo proved too conservative to catch up with Mitsui and Mitsubishi in the pre-war period. In modern times, the Sumitomo Bank has been the spearhead of a more aggressive effort by the group to be a big player. Although only the third or fourth biggest bank in terms of assets, Sumitomo boasted that it was the most profitable. But its very aggression and some of its doubtful connections caused it some problems in the years after the bursting of the economic bubble of the late 1980s.

The trading company occupies a lesser position within the group because of its late start. In fact, pre-war Sumitomo was the only one of the zaibatsu not to have a general trading arm, since it relied on Itochu (C. Itoh in English until recently) and Marubeni, both of them from Osaka. Sumitomo Shoji was not founded until six years after the war. In spite of its rapid growth since then, the trading company is not a member of the core trio which dominates the regular get-together of Sumitomo group companies. Called the Hakusui-kai, meaning White Water Club, a name derived from the copper business that was the mainspring of the group's fortunes, the Sumitomo group is dominated by the bank with Sumitomo Metal Industries and Sumitomo Chemical. Membership of the executive club is held by twenty companies, and Sumitomo has 164 affiliates that are 10 per cent or more owned.

The biggest of the sogo shosha in terms of annual sales is not one of the biggest three, but Itochu, which does not have a keiretsu named after itself. It is half of the powerful duo controlling the DKB keiretsu with Dai-Ichi Kangyo Bank, consisting of 48 companies and 190 affiliates. Indeed, because of Itochu's past history, it may not be surprising that although DKB is the biggest single shareholder with 3.7 per cent, collectively the Sumitomo group companies are Itochu's biggest shareholder. Mitsubishi managers claim that Itochu is only biggest in total sales by virtue of including big gold trading operations, and what really counts is profits (where Itochu comes a poor fourth). By some counts, the DKB is the biggest of the keiretsu, but its links are also the loosest, with cross-shareholdings of the key companies averaging only 12 per cent.

There are also key rivalries among members in the insurance, steel and machinery sectors, and some members also belong to other keiretsu. Hitachi belongs to the DKB group and to two others. The role of the bank, until recently Japan's biggest, is an important factor in keeping old clients and bringing in new members. DKB's club is called the Sankin-kai, or Third Friday Club. It is symbolic of the looser arrangements of the group that this club meets only four times a year for lunch, though there are other more regular meetings of executives at general manager level.

The other two big six horizontal keiretsu consist of the Fuyo group, led by Fuji Bank, and the Sanwa group, built round the bank of the same name. Fuyo, with 29 members of the regular presidential meeting Fuyo-kai (*Fuyo* means 'hibiscus'), average cross-shareholdings of 15 per cent and 223 affiliates, includes the central companies of the pre-war Yasuda zaibatsu. Fuji Bank traces its origins to Yasuda, but chose not to take the Yasuda name (although trust banking and insurance members of the keiretsu keep it). Fuyo's trading house is Marubeni. Other members are well-known industrial companies, like the steelmaker NKK, camera maker Canon, the machinery concern Kubota and Sapporo Beer. Nissan Motors is a full member of the group, although it maintains historic ties to Industrial Bank of Japan, which is still its biggest shareholder. Hitachi, part of the same pre-war zaibatsu as Nissan Motors, is a member of the Fuyo keiretsu too. All this gives the present-day Fuyo industrial muscle which the pre-war Yasuda zaibatsu lacked. It lacks the old heavy industries of the big three.

Sanwa is a much newer keiretsu, though the bank itself dates back to 1933, when it was formed by a merger of three smaller banks, one of which was founded back in 1878. The group, with 44 members of its executive council (called Sansui-kai or Third Wednesday Club) and 247 affiliates, owes its strength to the zeal of Sanwa, which has taken over the title of Japan's most profitable bank, expanding lending to a large number of industrial companies, particularly to those that were not members of the big three groups. Sanwa does its best to straddle Osaka, where its head office is, and Tokyo, which has become its operational headquarters.

Of all the keiretsu, Mitsubishi is deservedly the best known, not least because so many of its companies are at the frontline of Japanese excellence. The trading company is at the heart of the group, at least *primus inter pares*, of all the Mitsubishi companies. This is quite an achievement considering the size and reputation of other keiretsu members: Mitsubishi Bank is regarded as one of the most solid; the heavy industrial company is Japan's largest; the real estate concern sits on the single most expensive plot of land in the world; and the motor car company has a growing reputation and has held its own against competition from the established bigger companies, particularly in recreational vehicles, where even Toyota acknowledges Mitsubishi's lead. The Mitsubishi Shoji of the mid-1990s is vast. It is divided into seven separate groups, any one of which would be regarded in most other countries as a giant company. It is worth looking at each of these groups individually.

(1) The newest of them is that for information systems and services, established in 1987 and still with its trading performance included in the machinery group. It is a response to critics who claim that in the modern age of higher-value, information-intensive industries there is no need for the soga shosha. It covers the fields of consumer and medical electronics, semiconductors and computer systems, and telecommunications and multimedia. As an example of how high Mitsubishi's ambitions fly, in December 1992 Space Communications Corporation, Mitsubishi's common-carrier satellite affiliate, successfully launched the Superbird A satellite to join Superbird B in establishing a dual communications system to assist growth in entertainment programming, satellite newsgathering and other communications.

The trading company's managers say that they aim to offer solutions-based business strategies taking advantage of developments right across the board of what is known as multimedia. It is linking with another affiliate, Memory-Tech Corporation, which manufactures compact discs and CD-ROMs (read-only memories). It has a joint venture with Battelle, one of the largest independent research and development organisations in the world, and Nippon Telegraph and Telephone (NTT) to manufacture and market novel planar lightwave circuit devices based on technology originally developed by NTT. In addition, Mitsubishi is offering its classical trading company skills to act as a systems integrator.

It made agreements with Apple Japan to market that company's personal computers to Japanese businesses, and then signed a deal with Apple Computers of the USA giving it exclusive rights to translate and distribute the Japanese version of the SNP-ps 3270 terminal emulator software, which links Apple's Macintosh computers with IBM's mainframe computers. It is also the sales representative in Japan for Sikorsky helicopters made by United Technologies Corporation of the USA, another area where it is doing a classical trading job. In 1994, the group was split into three divisions, computer systems, communications and aerospace.

(2) Mitsubishi's fuels group has gone beyond the role of a pure trader, although its trading activities are huge. Its total trading transactions are about 2,000 billion yen, or more than $20 billion. This represents about 11.4 per cent of Mitsubishi's total trading transactions, though a smaller portion, about 9 per cent, of profits. Given that Japan is energy hungry and short of its own resources, more than 90 per cent of the trading is importing. But Mitsubishi is increasingly becoming involved in a broad range of upstream and downstream activities, including production and development especially of major liquefied natural gas (LNG) projects.

The geographical spread of its ventures is impressive. In mid-1992 Mitsubishi formed a new joint venture company, Malaysia LNG Dua, with Petronas, Malaysia's national oil company, the Sarawak state government and Shell Gas. The new venture is building additional LNG facilities.

When these are completed, they will double the capacity of the Sarawak operation to 16 million tons annually, the largest production in the world for a single complex. Mitsubishi is also a major shareholder in Brunei Coldgas, which in 1993 signed a twenty-year contract to supply three Japanese power and gas companies with 5.5 million tons of LNG a year, higher than the previous contract and assuring Japan of long-term stable supplies of energy.

In other developments, Mitsubishi is participating in a joint feasibility study for developing oil and gas on the continental shelf off the Russian island of Sakhalin. It set up a joint venture company in Venezuela to supply the USA with 4.4 million tons of LNG by the year 2000. On top of this, it helped set up a downstream joint venture company to develop LNG in Oman, which is expected to produce 5 million tons a year from 1999. The fuels group was also responsible in 1992 for setting up a subsidiary called MC Asphalt to market asphalt, fuels and lubricating oils directly as well as through 25 distributors in Japan. It is Japan's leading supplier of asphalt and is planning to go into exporting in a big way to meet rising demand in road infrastructure, especially in Asia.

(3) The metals group is the biggest in terms of total trading transactions, coming to about 6,400 billion yen or $64 billion, thus contributing about 37 per cent to Mitsubishi's total operations, though only 16 per cent to profits in the early 1990s because of the depressed state of the industries served, such as steels and construction. In spite of the poor economic climate, the metals group has continued to expand, especially abroad. For example, in Brazil, Mitsubishi and Kawasaki Steel increased the capacity of their joint venture operation making high-quality ferrosilicon to more than 45,000 tons a year; in Thailand, the trading company and Mitsubishi Materials are involved in a feasibility study with a local company, Padaeng Industry, to build a copper smelter; Mitsubishi lent $25 million to Western Platinum for mining in South Africa, the first big sum by any Japanese business since the lifting of economic sanctions.

(4) Machinery business comes next to the metals group in total turn-over – almost 4,300 billion yen – and is bigger in terms of its contribution to profits, about 26 per cent. In spite of the economic downturn, the machinery group has benefited from a continuing demand abroad for new energy supplies, along with Japanese companies' determination to discover new business overseas. Mitsubishi's ability to take a worldwide view helped it to win an order from a Hong Kong-based developer for delivery of two 368,000-kilowatt coal-fired thermal power plants to the Philippines in 1992. It also won an order to supply Japanese-made electric railcars to Egypt, and gained an order for a flue gas desulphurisation plant in the Czech Republic as part of that country's efforts to control pollution.

Besides supplying power plants, Mitsubishi is involved in supplying power: its US subsidiary Diamond Energy began supplying electricity from its new 665,000-kilowatt gas turbine combined cycle power generation plant to a utility company in Virginia. The group has also begun importing Swiss-developed technology that turns urban refuse into solid fuel, a vital opportunity for Tokyo, where landfill schemes are full of refuse, and garbage is being produced faster than incinerators can consume it. More controversially because of the falling property prices in Japan, in mid-1992 the Sea Fort Square complex developed by Mitsubishi opened. It is designed to be the centrepiece of a new business development on the Tokyo Bay waterfront some miles from the present business and commercial centre of the capital. The adjoining Sphere Tower Tennoz, an integrated office complex, opened in April 1993.

(5) Mitsubishi is also active in the world's markets in chemicals. Executives of the chemicals group say that their aim is to work 'closely with local investors and use its skills to identify swiftly and take advantage of opportunities in areas with plentiful natural resources'. Recent developments have included setting up Nippon Jordan Fertiliser, producing 300,000 tons of compound fertilisers and ammonium phosphate in Jordan, which will be shipped to Japan and meet 10 per cent of the country's needs. In Thailand, Mitsubishi also set up a joint venture to make a variety of plasticisers, adhesives, formalin and other chemical products, including polymers. The group has eight subsidiaries in North America plus others in the UK and Belgium, mostly specialising in resins and moulded plastic products. Altogether the chemicals group turns in trading transactions of about 1,300 billion yen or 7.5 per cent of Mitsubishi's turnover, though its profit contribution is higher at 11 per cent.

(6) Besides its traditional connections with heavy industry through fuels, metals, machinery and chemicals, Mitsubishi is a busy trader of food and clothing, and other general merchandise. The foods group has trading transactions worth almost 2,200 billion yen ($22 billion) a year, or 13 per cent of the trading company's activities, and almost a quarter of its profits. Mitsubishi is trying to take advantage of the opening up of Japan's markets and increasing imports of fresh foods, and has already gained the number one slot among general trading companies in the food industry. It has established subsidiaries in Australia to supply premium grade meat to Japan through its food wholesaler subsidiary, has set up a joint venture apple juice processing plant in China. It also owns the Princess food concern in the UK. But the group has also tried to keep its eyes on smaller opportunities too. In one of these, to tap what might be called the niche *kawaii* (cute) market, an important one in Japan, it set up Chocolate House, a retailer in the Nagasaki Holland Village, an amusement park.

(7) Textiles was long an important group, which 30 years ago Mitsubishi's high-flying young graduates were anxious to join. The glamorous aura of the group was hit by international restrictions on trade in textiles and clothing. Nevertheless today the group provides about 7 per cent of

Mitsubishi's total trading transactions, or 1,200 billion yen, and more than 12 per cent of its profits. In recent years the company has tried to use fashionable brand name imports to Japan as a profit earner or, as its managers put it, 'to offer consumers a wide array of affordably priced apparel of outstanding quality and design'. It is distributing Roberta di Camerino, Old England (a French concern), Reporter clothes and Ferragamo clothes and shoes. The general merchandise side of the group is also involved in trying to develop environmentally sound pulp operations, with a joint venture tree-planting scheme in Chile and involvement in the world's largest single-line bleached kraft pulp mill in Alberta, Canada. Other wide-ranging operations done just by subsidiaries under the textiles and general merchandise group (and leaving out associates or affiliates) include production of wood chips in Chile, mining of solica sand in Australia, manufacture and distribution of clothing in Hong Kong, and spinning of cotton yarn in Japan.

Altogether, this adds up to a formidable company. Total trading transactions fell in yen terms in the year to March 1994 to 17,277 billion yen from almost 20,000 billion yen three years before. But thanks to the rising yen, this amounted to $170 billion, a size that puts Mitsubishi into the really big world league. It operates like a vast worldwide intelligence operation. It is not just the number of employees, just under 10,000 in Japan and another 4,000 abroad, which would put Mitsubishi only in the medium-sized bracket. What is impressive is the trading house's network of offices, 55 throughout Japan from Hokkaido in the north to Okinawa in the far south, and another 113 all over the world. Mitsubishi's map extends as wide as the world, with branch offices in most of the important trading cities and also some in lesser places like Cochin in India, Kitwe in Zambia and Santos in Brazil, and subsidiaries in major capitals like London, Paris, Hong Kong, Sydney and Lagos. Mitsubishi has 22 subsidiaries in North and Central America, including New York, Palo Alta, Pittsburgh and Portland, and 15 subsidiaries in Europe.

But of course a big trading company such as Mitsubishi is not like a manufacturing concern, which has more freedom to set its own profit margins, subject to competition in the marketplace. The sogo shosha traditionally makes its profits on high volumes but wafer-thin margins, and is always highly vulnerable. Manufacturing companies which it serves may easily decide to bypass it and set up their own specialised trading networks. Toyota is a prime example of a company that is big, specialised and has its own sophisticated system of shipping and transporting its vehicles to a vast network of loyal dealers worldwide. Indeed, the very special sophistication of the industrial companies and their detailed knowledge of their own industries makes the general trading company, which has to know many things about a welter of operations everywhere, look amateur.

Critics have long claimed that the big trading houses are doomed in sophisticated modern economies, and whole books have been written about their impending demise. Other countries, from the giants to the fast-growing 'dragon' economies, get by without such general trading companies. Even in Hong Kong the old British hongs have been eclipsed by newer Chinese entrepreneurs. Those that remain are better known for their offshoots with specific assets, like the Hongkong Land Company, Jardine Matheson's property company, Jardine Fleming, the investment house, and Cathay Pacific Airlines and Swire Properties, the subsidiaries of Swire Pacific.

Mitsubishi's new president, Makihara, recognised the dangers to large trading companies in his new year address to all staff in 1994, when he warned that Japan was going through a period of profound structural change that went beyond the mere problems of the bursting of the 'bubble' economy. 'If we do not change and adapt,' Makihara warned, 'we risk succumbing to the crises before us, going the way of the hapless denizens of the Jurassic Age.' The new president quickly set up a committee to look at reforms, whose leader, director Mikio Kawamura, noted the danger signs. 'If operating expenditures keep growing at the current rate, they might exceed operating profits sooner than expected,' he warned in 1994.

Makihara's own answer is that Mitsubishi must become more and more international, which is perhaps the kind of answer you might expect from a man who has spent so much time abroad and indeed appears more 'international' than Japanese. He is quick and forthright in denying that he lost his Japanese character through his foreign birth, or foreign education. 'My thinking patterns or tastes are not radically American. They are basically Japanese,' he claimed. He contrasted himself with other Japanese who had gone abroad for education and gone native. 'I am a very traditional person, fairly Japanese in my thinking. Some people go abroad a short time and come back very different. Others go abroad a long time and come back unchanged. I think that I am one of the latter.' Nevertheless, he acknowledged that his years of education and work in the West have given him an appreciation of their strengths. 'I feel comfortable in both worlds,' he said.

Makihara's daughter, Kumiko, who works as a journalist, told a reporter that for relaxation her father liked to curl up with an English-language spy novel. But people who know him well say that Makihara has a very Japanese side and is steeped in Mitsubishi culture. A long-time friend says, 'Beneath his business suit is a Japanese gown.' He was born in London because his father was general manager of Mitsubishi Corporation's branch there. His father died in 1942 when the ship he was on, the *Taiyo Maru*, was sunk by US submarines in the East China Sea as it went to help develop Japanese-occupied south-east Asia. The young Makihara and his mother lived in an annexe of the house built by the Mitsubishi founder, Yataro Iwasaki, in Tokyo. After the war, Iwasaki's residence was taken over by the occupation forces and used by the Episcopal church, whose bishop encouraged Makihara to go to his alma mater, Harvard. Makihara's wife, Kikuko, whom he met when he was asked to give her English tuition and married a year after he joined Mitsubishi, is from the Iwasaki family, the third daughter of Takaya and a great-granddaughter of founding father Yataro.

The slender Makihara spent most of his time on the sales and marketing side of the corporation. After his initial training he was posted to London for a long stint. His two spells in Tokyo, with Seattle and Washington, DC, in between, were in the marine products department, dealing with imports of shrimps and tuna, to which he again returned as general manager in 1980 for three years. He was then made general manager of the marketing co-ordination department, before being sent back to the USA, first in charge of Washington and then to run Mitsubishi International Corporation from New York. He was boss in New York when he was called back to be the president in 1992.

He laughs and denies that his marriage into the Iwasaki family had any influence on his promotion, a judgement with which other senior Mitsubishi executives concur. 'The only way in which you could say he was lucky is that his predecessor was from the "hard" side of the corporation – meaning metals and minerals – so it was the turn of the soft side to be president,' says a colleague. No doubt the clinching factor in the mind of predecessor Shinroku Morohashi, who appointed him, was his overwhelming international experience.

And Makihara has dedicated himself to turning Mitsubishi into a truly international company. Speaking almost flawless English, with a British rather than an American intonation, Makihara declared, 'The circumstances surrounding ourselves and other trading companies are changing very dramatically. Until now, say the past 20 or 30 years, Japan was more or less protected by the ministries, not so much in tariffs and quotas, but in their guidance system. I would say that the situation was that we were like a flower in a hothouse. There were certain rules of the game. But now with deregulation all those rules are changing: with deregulation the relationship between ourselves and our clients, which up to now were mainly producers, were bound to change. Consumer tastes are changing, methods of distribution are changing, and we have to keep up with that. There is a dramatic change in advancing communications and travel, which undermines our traditional role as translator and communicator. We really have to improve and even change our approach to overseas markets. For that I really think that Japanese trading companies will have to become – though I don't quite like the word – global enterprises. This means that in terms of personnel, now we are 99 per cent Japanese, but that should change to maybe 70 per cent or 80 per cent Japanese and 30 or 20 per cent non-Japanese to begin with.'

Makihara said that Mitsubishi will begin its international drive in Asia and then will look at the USA, 'perhaps because I am prejudiced because I have spent so much time in the US'. Of Europe he is less sure, uncertain which way the European Union is going to turn, or what it will become. He has confidence that 'businessman to businessman, we can settle our differences' and that trade frictions will disappear if businessmen like him are left to discuss and settle things with their counterparts. 'It is the bureaucrats who get in the way,' he says of trade squabbles. Bureaucratic and political interference is one danger. The failure of the politicians to settle currency controversy, thus prolonging economic recession, could be another that will prevent Makihara and Mitsubishi from fulfilling their bold international dreams.

Asked what time frame he was thinking of for transforming Mitsubishi into an international corporation, Makihara suggests ten years, but then has to admit it will probably be longer because of the slow growth of the Japanese economy and the fact that Mitsubishi follows a lifetime employment policy, and finds it difficult to lay workers off even when the economy is in a downturn; it would certainly be unthinkable to do this so that foreigners could be taken on. 'A reduction in our staff would take a long time,' he admitted. The way forward is obvious enough. Mitsubishi will have to be more active abroad, 'and by abroad, I don't mean export–import business, but investment projects abroad, business between third countries, etc.' Makihara says that so far Mitsubishi 'has taken some small steps. We have established within our personnel department an international staff development team headed by one of our Canadian executives.' Mohan Patel achieved the elevated rank of general manager, the immediate stepping stone to director, for the job. 'I called him in and asked him what he was going to do, and he said, "Write a manual." I replied, "That's fine, but I want you to change the culture of our company."'

Becoming a global rather than just a Japanese corporation means putting non-Japanese directors on its board. Ironically, in 1994 Mitsubishi's only non-Japanese director, Korean Choi Moon Ho, general manager in charge of its Seoul office, retired, so the company once more became exclusively Japanese. The only outsiders on the board are the chairmen of two Mitsubishi sister companies, Yotaro Iida of Mitsubishi Heavy and Moriya Shiki of Mitsubishi Electric. Makihara continued, '[The expansion of Mitsubishi Corporation's board to include foreigners] will start off with people from within our organisation and then the next step is not necessarily restricted to Japanese or non-Japanese but more outside board members.'

Makihara admits that becoming international means travelling along a difficult road. Other Japanese companies, notabaly banks, set out flush with funds, believing that they could take on the world, and paid the price. 'I think we have to change our culture,' repeated the Mitsubishi president. 'I feel that Japan and the United States have quite a few things in common. We are both basically pragmatic, commonsense-oriented countries; both countries, if not classless, lack an aristocracy. The United States in the area of soft, information networks finance is probably taking a lead globally right now. Probably that lead will continue for ten years or so. It makes sense for us to work together with the US. I have come across some of our young US staff who could function quite well in our Tokyo office, possibly because the US is a hybrid country with such a variety of peoples. The first step we have to do is to take those people into head-quarters. Ideally they should speak Japanese, but if we put that as a condition it will limit our choice. We find that those who are here pick up Japanese in a couple of years.'

President Makihara admitted that so far he is ahead of his own board members in his vision of an international company. 'I have discussed it quite a bit with board members, though not at board meetings, so most people know my thoughts. I would say some of them think that [my idea] is impossible and if it happens, the whole culture will change, will have to be changed so much that we will disintegrate. About an equal number of people think very positively that this has to be done even if there is unhappiness in some parts. I think a large majority says, "We quite understand what you are saying, let's think about it." The more people realise the importance of change and the difficulties in the situation we are confronting now, they will come to my side.' Makihara is hoping to lay a sufficiently firm foundation during his tenure of the presidency that his successor will be able to fulfil his international hopes for the company. Traditionally, most post-war Mitsubishi presidents have served for six years, comprising three two-year terms, though one president did eight years. The importance of the job, says Makihara, is that the president 'may not have absolute choice but has a very strong say' in deciding who will take over from him.

The Mitsubishi president predicts that in the years ahead 'trading activity will still constitute the bulk of our business, but I think the pattern will change. There will be much more business outside of Japan, say from Brazil to the US or from China to Russia. In terms of manufactured products from Japan, the products will be much more sophisticated equip-ment. Labour-intensive things will be shifted abroad. If we are still involved with televisions, I am sure it will be from overseas plants. Auto-mobiles will be shifting quite a bit too. Much more of our trading [activity] will originate or be with companies in which we have an investment abroad or subsidiaries.' Makihara sees Mitsubishi making investments in companies abroad and forming 'strategic alliances'. 'For example, we have had a strong relationship with [Royal Dutch/]Shell. I hope that will expand. It started in Brunei with oil and gas, and I hope it will extend to chemicals and other areas. There are quite a few other possibilities.'

Makihara also caused a stir by his bold policy of massive write-offs in the company's accounts for the first two years of his presidency, amounting to 80 billion yen ($800 million) each time. The company had to sell shares to realise the money to pay for the write-off. Some of the losses stemmed from the activities of Mitsubishi's financial team, which was very active in the years of the bubble economy in what was known as *zai-tech* – financial engineering or 'financial fiddling' as critics derided it.

The department, under deputy president Shinichiro Ohta, was regarded as the most active of financial teams among Japanese trading companies, and was earning more than 30 billion yen annually in its best years, or the equivalent of a third of the company's profits at the time, propelling the finance department into the top tier of business earnings. Mitsubishi was active in *tokkin* and fund trust accounts. There was much sense in the financial activities, which set up a '*shosha* bank' within Mitsubishi, using the massive cash flows of the trading company to make more money. But with the bursting of the bubble, a senior Mitsubishi executive lamented, 'We don't know who our friends are and who our enemies are. The whole trust system is paralysed and nothing works like it used to.' Ohta and senior members of his team were the first to retire under Makihara.

The president was criticised both inside and outside the company for writing off such large sums of money when there was no obligation to take the hits. Indeed, accountants studying the tax burden warned that Mitsubishi would lose money by taking the losses early. But Makihara insisted that he wanted to preserve a clean balance sheet: 'I don't have the answer to how much money we might have saved [by delaying the write-offs]. If you have to take [a hit], it's best to take it. These are bad times. The best thing to hold the company together, as long as we have the capacity to write off bad debts, is to write them off, let people know what happened in the past three, four, five years and get on with the new business. I think that we have been fortunate to be able to do it ... I did not face any opposition from the board from my decision. When I wrote off the first chunk [in 1993], I did go to a few elders [in Mitsubishi] to tell them, "Look, I am doing this and I don't know what the reaction of the stock market is going to be and we may get an adverse reaction." I was very surprised. One person said, "You don't know, the stock price might go up because you are taking a courageous step." [After the 1994 write-off] we still have bad debts, but these are normal.'

Makihara's appointment as president was the culmination of more than three decades of managerial skills and good luck. One director of Mitsubishi said that 'Only one executive in a hundred makes it to a director's post. Getting there involves a mixture of intelligence, good business abilities and luck.' This is because at the start of their Mitsubishi career, young graduates are allotted to one of the main business groups. Under normal circumstances they will stay with the same group for the whole of their career. Anyone joining the financial group would know that none of its executives had ever been president. Luck comes in because the strong and powerful groups at the start of a young graduate's career may no longer be so significant in the middle years. 'People who excitedly joined the textile group in the 1950s and early 1960s because that was the glamour area are now regretting it,' said the director ruefully. Textiles today no longer have either glamour as a growth area or power in the company.

To an outsider, the career structure is unusually rigid and does not make the best of rising talents. Usually the only way of moving to a new area is to get involved in a totally fresh area of activity, as with the recent formation of an environment group, tapping both an international vogue and an area of increasing importance for Mitsubishi. When such new business development is started, it generally offers opportunities to applicants from a wide range of existing business groups. The ambitious executive then has to judge whether the new activity is merely the flavour of the month or something that is going to be of lasting importance in the power structure. Mitsubishi can also be accused of not making use of its female employees. Until now the successful Mitsubishi executives have all been men. Women graduates were first hired at executive level a few years ago, and the number of women hired each year can still be counted safely on the fingers of two hands, while 150 male graduates are recruited in a normal year.

'There was some nervousness about us and how we would fit in,' said one of the women. There's also still an attitude at Mitsubishi, especially among the older managers, that women are meant to work for a short while, then get married and leave, or at least leave when they become pregnant. 'In these recession times we are having problems because even the women secretaries are reluctant to leave when they get married,' grumbled an elderly senior manager. 'It is creating a barrier to our recruitment because normally we hire newcomers to replace women on marriage or pregnancy, but now they are not moving on.'

Turnover of staff is, however, being increased by the fact that Mitsubishi men often meet their wives when at work in the company. One junior manager estimated that 50 per cent of Mitsubishi men married Mitsubishi women. 'Where else would we meet our wives, since we spend so much time working for the company?' laughed one young man. Since two members of the same family are not supposed to work for the corporation, this normally encourages the wife to leave and devote herself to being a good wife. From the comments of Mitsubishi men, women's lib has not yet reached the big trading house.

Often young graduates apply to several trading houses. Mitsubishi believes it gets the cream. 'Well,' said one bright manager, 'we reckon Mitsubishi is the best in that it treats its managers really well.' Less committed people say that Mitsui is still attractive to people who feel they are already well connected, or from old families. Sumitomo is the most aggressive.

A Mitsubishi manager who makes it to director knows that he will be looked after on full pay until the age of 70, and a managing director will receive full pay until he is 73. As with other big companies, when managers at Mitsubishu reach their mid to late fifties, they are likely to be retired from the main company and given another job with a subsidiary or associated company. 'When you become a director, you sign your letter of resignation so that the president can activate it whenever he chooses,' said a Mitsubishi director. A director who retires to a subsidiary will give his salary from that company to Mitsubishi, but in return will receive the full director's pay. 'It doesn't encourage you to stray from the comfort of Mitsubishi,' said the director. Some presidents are more active than others with regard to their close associates. Makihara seems to be determined to put his own appointees into key slots, so there were a spate of retirements in his first years in charge.

Makihara himself praised the 'support given to the president. The job of president is much more demanding that I had imagined. There were occasions in the past when I accompanied the president and wondered why I had to do it. Now I understand and I also realise that the support system is almost too good. I only have to mutter something and suddenly before too long a whole report on the subject appears before me,' he added laughing.

Perhaps the most vexed question of all concerning the keiretsu, especially the 'big six' horizontal ones, is the extent to which they co-operate or collude in business. The big groups do themselves little good when they protest that the regular meetings of the heads of big companies in a keiretsu are merely social gatherings, and then refuse to disclose any details, or to release minutes of the meetings. Such attitudes damage the interests of the keiretsu. The veil of secrecy over the meetings – of all the keiretsu groups and not just those of Mitsubishi – has fed mischievous if not malicious speculation in the Japanese press that the presidents must be up to no good, perhaps breaking the anti-monopoly law, fixing prices or, worse still, plotting to keep foreigners out of Japan's markets. Professor Yoshinari Maruyama, an expert on the big six horizontal keiretsu, pointedly commented, 'Why would you gather together the only men in a company who have the legal right to make decisions for their companies if not to make some decisions? The *shacho-kai* [presidents' assembly] members are the men who control the *daihyo-in* [the corporate legal seal necessary for making any contract or document legal]. Why bring such men together to talk about golf?'*

This is precisely why Washington officials complain. Official Japanese reports have tried to play down the impact of the keiretsu and to suggest also that the links are diminishing. The normally toothless Fair Trade Commission (FTC) claimed in 1992 that links between companies in the big six horizontal keiretsu are not very strong and are declining. The report claimed that each company within the groups held an average of 1.42 per cent of the total shares of another company in the same group in March 1990. This was a reduction from 1.52 per cent three years earlier. This seems minuscule, but is not the relevant figure. Much more important is the combined shareholdings of keiretsu members. The FTC found that other members of the same group held an average of 21.64 per cent of the shares of the keiretsu member company, also reduced from 22.65 per cent in 1987. In the recession of the early 1990s, many well-known companies sold some of their shareholdings in order to boost profits. Keiretsu shares carried in the books at low historic values were particularly attractive, and it is estimated that in 1993 about $20 billion worth of keiretsu crossholding shares were sold on the Tokyo market.

Such reports do not satisfy foreign critics, who point out that keiretsu ties have not weakened to the extent that any outside company – let alone any foreign business – could contemplate a merger or acquisition approach to any keiretsu family company being considered on its commercial merits.† There remains the sinister stumbling block of the secretive nature of the group meetings, and especially the regular get-togethers of presidents of the family companies.

Another Japanese line of defence is to claim that the keiretsu are not unique to Japan. Especially in Europe, but even in the USA, close groupings of enterprises are common. Deutsche Bank, for example, owns big chunks of German industry, including 28 per cent of car maker Daimler Benz, 25 per cent of Karstadt, the biggest department store, and 23 per cent of Linde, the machinery maker. In the USA, Morgan Guaranty Trust Company has shareholdings in IBM, Mobil and Digital Equipment. Exxon is the biggest shareholder in 14 of the top 252 American companies, and IBM and Eastman Kodak are the biggest shareholders in 13 of them. But it may be foolish of the Japanese government to draw attention to its own keiretsu in this way. The American crossholdings, for example, are much smaller and weaker. Links in Germany, especially with Deutsche Bank, are well known, but they are the individual octopus-like tentacles of selected

---

* Quoted in Miyashita and Russell, *Keiretsu*, op. cit.

† Such a complaint would be considered a particularly foreign one, since mergers and, less still, takeovers are an uncommon practice in Japan.

strong companies, not the systematic Japanese spiders' webs of linked shareholdings.

Makihara denied grumbles from Washington that the links between Mitsubishi group companies turn the notorious keiretsu system into a major constraint on trade. He gave a few details of the famous or infamous Friday meetings between all the Mitsubishi family chief executives, and said there were no deep dark plots. 'The strength [of the Mitsubishi family] is that it certainly makes communication between the companies easier. What does the Friday Club meeting do? Normally we have a very quick lunch, a discussion or report on companies that want to use the Mitsubishi trademark, proposals to give donations to a foundation jointly, and then we have an outside speaker. That's the normal procedure.'

The whole session lasts up to two hours, and Makihara denied that there was ever any heavy business discussion done. The outside speakers, he said, tend to be unrelated to any pending business matters – for example, bureaucrats, doctors and even journalists have addressed the Friday Club presidents. Makihara added that the regular lunches offered opportunities for getting to know other Mitsubishi heads. 'Before I became president, of the 30 or so presidents, I only knew 10 of them; but now I know all of them, so that if I want to do something or get their advice, I can just get on the telephone to them. That is very useful when you have to have a quick meeting of minds.'

He cited one important time when quick consultation was of the essence, the Pennzoil takeover of Getty Oil, as a result of which Mitsubishi Oil could have been sold on the open market. 'Very quickly the interested Mitsubishi companies could get together to buy out those shares.' Trying to dispel the claim of keiretsu collusion, he quickly added, 'based, of course, on their individual interests. It would have been very difficult to structure that without their common background.' Mitsubishi executives claimed that when the Estate company decided to buy the Rockefeller Center in New York, there was no prior discussion with the trading company, 'or we might have tried to dissuade them from throwing their money away at the top of the market'. Mitsubishi Estate also got its timing wrong in planning Japan's tallest building, the 70-storey Landmark Tower on Yokohama's waterfront, right at the top of the property boom, for completion in mid-1993 during the middle of the recession. Group companies declined to help out by taking space in the building, but Mitsubishi Estate is strong enough, with help from its friends at Mitsubishi Bank, to hold on to the investment in expectation that better days will come and its asset will be realised. Mitsubishi co-operation is also in evidence in Vietnam, where the trading company stands ready to benefit from the major discovery made by Japan Vietnam Petroleum Company, a subsidiary of its sister oil company.

Occasionally, Makihara suggests, there have been arguments between some of the Mitsubishi companies on environmental issues. Mitsubishi Kasei Corporation came under fire in the early 1990s for a joint venture plant in Malaysia producing the rare earth metal yttrium and other radio-active by-products for use in electronics. The high court in Ipoh ruled that the plant's operations were endangering the health and safety of nearby residents. Some press reports, both in Asia and the USA, just blamed 'Mitsubishi' or 'the giant Mitsubishi conglomerate'. Mitsubishi Corporation itself has come under fire and been accused of destroying the world's forests through its involvement in south-east Asian logging operations. It claims that these are the assertions of 'Japan bashers', and protests that care of the earth's environment is of primary concern. Makihara asserted that Mitsubishi during his reign has had a keen eye not only on the environment, but on social consequences of economic policies: 'Which should come first, the economy or the environment? That is a question I often meet. But the question is misconceived; it assumes that the two are distinct and incompatible. The truth is that rational environmental stewardship integrates environmental, economic and a vast range of social considerations.'

Another Mitsubishi executive added that Friday Club relationships also helped greatly in the budding relationship between the Mitsubishi group and Daimler Benz of Germany. In 1990, to great interest in Japan and accusations in the rest of the world that the old wartime 'Axis' was being restored, Mitsubishi Corporation and three sister companies, Heavy Industries, Electric and Motors, announced that they would seek a comprehensive tie-up with the German giant. 'If it hadn't been for the Friday meetings,' said the Mitsubishi executive, 'it would have been more difficult for the three group companies to come together with the Daimler Benz group.' Fears of the united axis were slow to be realised. It took more than three years before the promises bore fruit in actual business deals between Mitsubishi and Daimler. In December 1993 the two groups agreed to co-operate in six business areas, including semi-conductor manufacturing technologies, assembly and sales of Mitsubishi lorries in South Africa, and recycling of used motor vehicles with the use of Daimler Benz technology. The agreement requires an investment of only 6.5 billion yen ($65 million), so it is minuscule in terms of the total business of either conglomerate.

There are also signs that big Japanese companies are becoming increasingly price conscious, and will not just stick with an associate company if it cannot deliver at the most competitive terms. Mitsubishi Heavy opted to use Nissho Iwai to sell its heavy machinery in Indonesia, even though Mitsubishi Corporation has two offices in that country. Mitsubishi Heavy was disappointed when Nippon Yusen, the shipping line member of the family, decided to buy South Korean ships because they are 30 per cent cheaper than those built in Japan. Mitsubishi Motors also set a precedent by going to South Korea for steel for its car bodies.

The Fair Trade Commission had already found that by 1992 sales generated by intragroup business, apart from financial transactions, were only 7.28 per cent of aggregate sales of member companies. Moreover, the commission reported, keiretsu members in 1990 accounted for only 0.12 per cent of each group's trading companies sales and for 0.38 per cent of procurement. The lesson is that these are big companies, dealing in big businesses, and cannot afford to deal exclusively within the same family if they want to stay in business.

That still leaves open the question of the future of the big trading houses like Mitsubishi. The experience of other countries suggests that Makihara is right to be worried. A conglomerate trading house that does not continue to adapt risks dying. In a report published in November 1994, Leon Rapp, an analyst with Baring Securities in Tokyo, suggested that trading companies are in the vanguard of deregulation of the domestic economy and are an important vehicle for lowering the differential between Japanese prices and those in the rest of the world. He noted that the big sogo shosha were shifting their emphasis to profits rather than mere revenue growth, and in the longer term were trying to capitalise on their strengths, which will mean becoming less general. In Mitsubishi's case, he pointed to telecommunications, food and energy as its three main thrusts.*

The arguments between Japan and the rest of the world about the unfairness of business practices will no doubt continue. Japanese companies, not just the big trading houses, get angry when foreigners, especially Americans, make loose allegations about unfair collusion in Japanese business. 'Foreigners sometimes come to Japan and make great efforts to show that they know how to handle chopsticks or to take off their shoes when entering a room or to drink their tea properly using both hands to lift the cup,' said a trading house executive, 'but they are surprised because they haven't done their proper homework on how we do business and don't understand the importance and power of long-standing business relationships. That is more annoying to us, and proof to us of the failure of the West. We don't mind if a few mangle some of the key points of Japanese etiquette, but it suggests you aren't really competitive if you don't know what potential partners or potential rivals are up to.

'The very first thing that a Japanese company does is make sure that it has got a complete dossier on anyone it is doing business with. We trading companies do this extraordinarily well because of our vast networks. But it is typical of the competitive edge that the Japanese have. Is it wrong to have close friends in business and to depend on each other?'

---

* *Trading Houses: Here Today, Here Tomorrow*, Barings Japanese Research.

4

The World's Biggest Steelmaker Suffers Corrosion:
Nippon Steel

Maybe it is the fury of the flames in the blast furnace; or maybe it is the silken smooth yet deadly edge of the final product; or maybe it is the use for centuries of iron and steel to make weapons of war from swords and axes to pistols, heavy artillery and missiles; or maybe it is their immortalisation in such expressions as 'a taste of cold steel'. Whatever the reason, production of iron and steel has down the centuries been seen almost as a touchstone of a country's masculine strength. Jacob Bronowski, in his magnificent television series *The Ascent of Man*, took the example of the making of a traditional Japanese sword to demonstrate the special properties of steel and the almost magical regard in which it is held. He told the story through the swordmaker, Getsu, proud possessor of the title of a 'living cultural monument'. Bronowski watched fascinated as he saw the swordmaker controlling the carbon and heat, doubling the billet fifteen times and making 30,000 layers of steel. Each layer was bound with the others to create an immense sandwich combining, as Bronowski said, 'the flexibility of rubber with the hardness of glass', after which the sword was 'heated until it glows to the colour of the morning sun'.

The ancient ritual of sword making still goes on in today's Japan, part religion, part culture, all weapon. But in its modern industrial version, in its steel plants, Japan is losing the battle to younger upstart countries. Nippon Steel is still the world's largest steelmaker, but it is facing falling demand, rising costs and increasing international competition, so the title is a costly one. It lost money in the year to March 1994 and will continue to do so until at least 1996 – proof that, if steel is Japan's 'industrial rice', then it is suffering blight.

Yet Takashi Imai, president of Nippon Steel, aficionado of the game of *go*, where the object is to win by outflanking your opponent, is thinking ahead to the twenty-first century, when he sees Nippon Steel as not only the world's largest but also its best steel company. As of mid-1994 this seemed a virtually impossible dream. The company's annual report for the year to March 1994 reported a loss of 18 billion yen and a net loss of 30.9 billion yen after taxation. (Tax still had to be paid even after losses because of deferred obligations.) The total after-tax loss rose to 54 billion yen on a consolidated basis, including the parent and its subsidiaries, and would have been higher still had Nippon Steel not made 65.7 billion yen from the sale of shares it held in other companies. The situation was so grim that the company was losing 3,000 yen or $30 on each and every ton of the 25 million tons of steel it produced.

Imai and his chairman, Hiroshi Saito, recorded laconically in their message to shareholders: 'Due to intensified stagnation of Japan's economy resulting from the yen's unprecedented appreciation against other currencies, demand for steel in fiscal 1993 [ending in March 1994] declined. In addition to a broad drop in demand for steel by the construction industry, demand in every other major area of manufacturing also fell. Both production and shipment of steel products by the Japanese steel industry in fiscal 1993 were below the previous year's levels. As a result, crude steel production stood at 97.1 million tons, a drop of 1.83 million tons from the year before and the second consecutive year of production under 100 million tons. Nippon Steel's production of crude steel also fell 190,000 tons below the previous year to 25.12 million tons in fiscal 1993, the lowest level since the company's inauguration in 1970.'

As the yen continued to rise to new post-war records in 1994, there were plenty of prophets of doom predicting that this could be the end of the line for the Japanese steel industry. After all, said analysts in foreign stockbrokerage houses, labour costs in neighbouring Korea are about a quarter of Japan's and the Koreans are busy building up capacity. Pohang Iron and Steel (Posco) is not far behind Nippon Steel in terms of total production, is profitable, produces more cheaply and with lower labour costs, and with its more modern facilities seems to be the rising giant. After Korea may come rapidly rising China, an even bigger country with potentially greater thirst for its own iron and steel facilities, and with a larger pool of cheap labour. So the prospects seem bleak for high-wage Japan and Nippon Steel.

In December 1994 three of Japan's big motorcar makers, Mitsubishi Motors, Nissan Motor Company and Honda Motor Company, delivered a body blow when they signed deals with Posco for the Korean steelmaker to supply cold-rolled steel sheet, the key material in making car bodies, at a price of $620 per metric ton, or 15–20 per cent lower than Japanese steelmakers' prices. It is hard to overestimate the strength of this bombshell. Not only is the auto industry the second largest customer for steel after the construction business, but the steel companies thought their ties with the motorcar makers were watertight. Until this time, the Japanese considered themselves protected by the superior quality of their steel, and also by the cosy club of Japan Inc. No longer: a Mitsubishi official said bluntly, 'With the strong yen, we will buy from anybody who can give us reliable quality for less money.' And Nissan added, equally uncompromisingly, 'The results of our study showed that Posco's steel was as reliable as the domestic product.' Truly a test of Takashi Imai's business acumen and diplomatic skills, as well as his four decades of experience in the steel industry.

Although President Imai had been with the company for more than 40 years before becoming president in 1993, Nippon Steel Corporation itself has only been in existence for a quarter of a century, since 1970. The inconsistency is easily explained: after the Second World War the victorious Allied powers determined to smash Japan's war machine for ever, and so broke up the industrial giants which they believed were the key creators of its military might. Nevertheless, Nippon Steel executives have a longer view and like to trace their corporate history back long before Imai was born, to 1857 when Takato Oshima became the first Japanese to smelt iron in a western-style blast furnace. His achievement was an incongruous mixture of modern science and industry and old-fashioned manual labour: he did it at Kamaishi, 300 kilometres north of Tokyo, by using oxen to bring ore from the nearby mountain, carried in bags made from the bark of grape vines, and turning the ore into pig iron. His success led to the birth in 1886 of Kamaishi Mines Tanaka Iron Works, which is still one of the factories of the Nippon Steel group.

The next step was the foundation of the government-operated Yawata Steel Works in 1901. Nippon Steel executives say that 'Japanese industrialisation took its first step at Yawata, where the vision of creating modern factories in Japan began with iron and steel making – the mother of industry.' Yawata Works are also part of Nippon Steel's group. In 1934 the two founding plants were put together to form Japan Iron and Steel Company. This was the organisation which the victorious Allied powers broke up after Japan's defeat in the war. The giant was split into Yawata Iron and Steel Company and Fuji Iron and Steel Company. Imai joined Fuji after graduating in law from Tokyo University in 1952, and started his steel life at the Kamaishi works. In 1970 the refoundation of Japan Iron and Steel as Nippon Steel was accomplished, though the two separate executive streams have continued with the appointment of the Nippon Steel president alternately from Fuji and Yawata executives.

Today Nippon Steel operates ten different works sited strategically all over Japan, from Hokkaido in the north to Oita in Kyushu in the south. To maximise operating efficiency and productivity, iron making is concentrated at Yawata, Nagoya, Kimitsu and Oita. Besides supplying its own region, each plant has its own line of specialist products. Thus, Kamaishi, the oldest plant, is the production base for high-grade radial tyre steel cords. Kimitsu, founded in 1965 and located just east of Tokyo, is the supply base for the Kanto region around the capital, and also produces a showcase of steel products, such as plates, sheets, sections, wire rods, colour coated sheets, and pipes and tubes. Oita, the most modern of

Nippon Steel's ten plants, founded in 1971, supplies in all-continuous casting system for slab production as well as making high-grade heavy plates and hot coils; it is the principal supplier of slabs and hot coils to the company's other steel works.

To Imai and other senior executives of Nippon Steel, it is unthinkable that the company would be thrown off its historical course by the rise in the value of the yen or the challenge from steel plants in other developing countries, built with the advantage of later technology and of cheaper labour supplies. One of the more poetic executives claimed that steel production was a historic mission: 'You should see iron as a gift from the sea, since more than three billion years ago iron dispersed in the earth was slowly dissolved by rainfall and washed into the sea, where it was oxidised by blue-green algae and accumulated on the sea floor. After time the sea floor rose, depositing the iron ore on to dry land.' Continuing his water metaphor, he saw the foundation of the Kamaishi works as the first drop in what became a stream and then a river with the founding of Japan Iron and Steel. 'Nippon Steel has had its strength tested by many difficulties, the oil crises, trade friction, environmental problems. At times the river of its history has been turbulent, at times running strong and deep.' By now Nippon Steel, he asserted, has become a great delta with many tributaries, some of which are important rivers in their own right. 'It is tradition and transition together.'

As far as the steel itself is concerned, the product has been continually developing and changing along with society. Back in the nineteenth century, the steam locomotive created a need for rails made of steel. Wars created demand for food that could be moved easily in cans, triggering a need for tinplate lining on the cans. The advent of the motor age prompted demand for steel sheets for the car bodies. Creation of bigger container ships promoted the development of bigger steel plates. The coming of high-rise buildings stimulated the production of a whole range of new steel products from coated sheets to wide-flange beams and pipes, rods and wires.

'In this, Nippon Steel always aims to stay a step ahead of what society needs,' stated the company. To think of steel just in terms of massive slabs or even rods or sheets is misleading. Production has been diversified into new products, some of them very hi-tech. According to Nippon Steel: 'Our intensive research and development efforts in steel have generated a great variety of products, some of which are in general industrial use and others which are high-grade and specialised. Among the specialised steels are those capable of withstanding ultra-high or ultra-low temperature, ultra-high pressure, strong corrosive attack and other adverse conditions.'

Some steel executives even talk of the 'ultimate products', the very best achievable in purity, freedom from segregation, dimensional accuracy, thinness and fineness, with enhanced strength, toughness and resistance to corrosion, and with their magnetic or non-magnetic properties enhanced depending on the customer's requirements. In the Minato Mirai 21 waterfront project at Yokohama, there is an example of modern Nippon Steel advanced technology. Its Landmark Tower has risen rapidly to be Japan's tallest building at 70 storeys above ground and 296 metres high. Extra-heavy large-diameter pipes of high-grade steel developed by Nippon Steel are used in the four corner columns of the building. These welded pipes have a large outer diameter of 800–900 millimetres and a heavy wall thickness of 70–90 millimetres, and, more important, have a strength level of 570 newtons per square millimetre. Such strong steel pipe columns boost the efficiency of constructing buildings with a complicated design.

Since the Landmark Tower was started, Nippon Steel has increased the strength of its special steel to produce tensile strength of more than 780 newtons per square millimetre. This, the company boasted, will allow economical construction of high-rise buildings up to 1,000 metres high, three times the height of the Yokohama tower or more than 200 storeys high, almost twice as tall as any building in the world today. The new steel contains less carbon, but more copper and nickel, and no boron because steel containing boron requires a high pre-heating temperature for welding. Nippon Steel claimed that this strong steel will significantly reduce the amount of steel needed for building frames. Slabs are hot-rolled into place under temperature and rolling reduction control, and the plates then undergo critical heat treatment so that their ferrite and austenite crystalline structures mix well and are tempered. The new steel is good for welding, since it requires no high temperature pre-heating. 'The steel will allow buildings of the future to employ slender columns that have strong earthquake resistance,' said Nippon Steel. 'It is an economical material for the 21st-century era of super skyscraper construction.'

Other prominent and internationally acclaimed buildings that display Nippon Steel's technology include the Bank of China building in Hong Kong, which is even bigger than the Yokohama tower, reaching 310 metres high or 370 metres to the top of its giant chopsticks. It is a monument in steel and glass, with glistening knife-sharp edges, controversial because in Chinese folklore the sharp edges of a building can be compared to daggers; they point at the nearby Legislative Council building and the Hongkong Bank's local headquarters, the Bank of China's rival for banking predominance in the colony.

The building, for which Nippon Steel was general contractor, posed technical difficulties, and not only because the uppermost portion has a floor area a quarter of the ground-level base. In addition, the wind load in Hong Kong is twice that of New York because of frequent exposure to typhoons, and the seismic load is four times the greatest seismic load in Los Angeles. The solution was to counter the enormous lateral forces by eight mega-structures incorporating X-braces and earthquake-resisting steel plate walls. The Bank of China initially refused to accept the X – considering the shape unlucky – until architect I.M. Pei told its directors that it was a diamond. It means that the Bank of China building is steel-rich and contains as much of the material as buildings half its height.

More delicate use of steel is seen in two of modern Japan's bridges, the double-deck Rainbow Bridge across Tokyo Bay, which opened in 1993, and the Akashi Kaikyo suspension bridge, which will take over the title of longest single-span suspension bridge in the world from Britain's Humber Bridge when it opens in 1997 or 1998. The bridges show that steel is not just a muscular heavy-duty product, but can have grace as well as strength. The Akashi bridge, with a massive 1,990 metres span between the two towers, will link Japan's main island of Honshu with the smaller island of Shikoku across the Inland Sea. The cabling for the bridge requires extreme strength, development of which was a triumphant advance for Nippon Steel's technology.*

Before work started on Akashi, wires had been developed with the strength of 1,600 Megapascal. To use these on the bridge would have required four cables, two on each side, which would have caused safety as well as construction problems. The strength of the wire is governed by the distance between the iron and iron carbide plates of high carbon steel. 'Narrowing the distance between the iron and iron carbide plates in the wire manufacturing process – in heat treatment, drawing and galvanising – is the key to increasing its strength,' explained Toshihiko Takahashi, general manager in charge of the bar, shape and wire rod research laboratories at Nippon Steel's technical development bureau at Futtsu. 'The problem was galvanising because the wires must be immersed in a hot zinc bath to 450 degrees Celsius. During heat treatment, the iron carbide plates break into small particles, and this decreases the strength of the wires.'

Using an atomic probe field ion microscope, Takahashi and his team discovered that, by increasing the amount of silicon in the steel, a protective layer formed around the iron carbide plates, preventing them from changing shape. 'Our discovery in 1989 was a world first,' Takahashi boasted. As a result of this work, Nippon Steel offered 1,800 Megapascal wires with 1 per cent silicon bearing steel for the Akashi Kaikyo bridge, permitting the use of just one cable on each side. Each cable will be 1.1 metres in diameter and will contain 37,000 strands of wire. The advances continue. 'Ultra high-strength wire of 2,000 Megapascal has been developed using silicon and chromium steel, and our aim is to lift the threshold to 2,200 Megapascal,' added Takahashi. Nippon Steel now has its eye on playing a major part in helping to develop the planned Messina

* The Great Hanshin earthquake of 1995 caused slippage of the land, so that the bridge will have to be slightly more than a metre longer than planned.

Strait bridge linking the Italian mainland with Sicily. This bridge will set another new world record, since it will have a centre span of 3,300 metres.

Besides steel products going into highly visible, massive buildings, Nippon Steel has been developing specialised steel for oil and natural gas development, especially in severe environments. This includes low-temperature service steel for natural gas pipelines. It is also getting good business from making tailored steel products for nuclear as well as geo-thermal and solar power plants. Its high-strength steels are used in power transmission towers, while laser-irradiated electrical steel helps to reduce core loss and improve power transformer efficiency.

As noted above, the automobile industry has always been a good cus-tomer of the steel industry, and Nippon Steel has been developing products to give value added in its supplies to the industry. Recent innovations include the introduction of steel cords for radial tyres, and of high-quality spring materials for suspension devices, the development of high-performance shaft materials for drive systems, and the supply of stainless steels which should help improve the performance of car exhaust systems.

Nippon Steel is also involved at the cutting edge of new technology, and claims that another new product coming from the research lab-oratories into production of viable advanced materials may soon allow trains to fly propelled by magnets. This will be through the development of a high-temperature yttrium oxide superconducting bulk magnet. Nippon Steel said in the early 1990s that it had developed one with the world's strongest magnetic field (1.35 tesla) when cooled with liquid nitrogen. Even neodymium magnets, which have the strongest magnetic fields among permanent magnets, show a magnetic field strength of 0.45 tesla. Nippon Steel claims to have maintained an yttrium oxide magnet with a field of 1.0 tesla even after three years at a temperature of 77K (Kelvin or absolute scale).

Researchers are hoping that Japan's new Maglev (magnetic levitation) train will be able to fly just above the ground at 550 kilometres an hour, propelled by such a superconducting magnet. Unfortunately, although the idea is more advanced than science fiction, there is still a big leap to be made before the advances in superconducting magnets can be trans-lated into hard commercial success. Awkward problems of economics and prices have also hit Nippon Steel in its more down-to-earth businesses.

In the mid-1980s, partly because of the 1985 Plaza agreement, which led to the rise of the yen from 250 to 150 against the US dollar, partly because of sluggish demand at home and partly because of growing US barriers against imports and rising demand from transplanted Japanese car factories in the USA, Japanese steel makers began to invest in America. They did this primarily through joint ventures rather than by outright purchase of American companies.

Nippon Steel in 1987 set up operations in the United States through a joint venture with Inland Steel Industries, called I/N Tek. I/N Tek began cold-rolling operations in 1990 and has since produced cold-rolled products at a rate of 1 million short tons a year in order to supply the US market with high-quality cold-rolled materials. Nippon Steel provided I/N Tek with a highly advanced, fully integrated processing line. In 1989 co-operation between the two companies was expanded with the foundation of I/N Kote, another joint venture with a 500,000 short ton a year continuous hot dip galvanising line and a 400,000 short ton a year electro-galvanising line, which became operational in 1991. I/N Kote's operation has provided Nippon Steel with an American base for supplying high-grade coated steel products, mainly to automobile manufacturers, including Japanese operations in North America.

The venture was established in a highly unlikely place for a steel mill, in the middle of the American corn belt in Indiana and 60 miles from Inland's integrated steel complex near Lake Michigan in the US 'Rust Belt'. Most of the workers are local people who had no previous experience of steelmaking. However, the supporters of the two plants say that, like the Japanese car companies, Nippon Steel wanted to make a 'green field' start away from the old culture of traditional steelmaking America. It has paid off in generally trouble-free labour relations. The Japanese giant has been criticised for spending far too heavily on getting set up, and start-up difficulties were also experienced. But on the other hand, said executives on secondment from Nippon Steel, customers claimed to be satisfied with the products. By 1994 the company said it was within sight of the equally important goal of making a profit. President Imai said without a flicker of hesitation, 'This has been a successful venture.'

In the early 1990s, the American protectionist cries began again, and the Commerce Department filed dumping charges against foreign steelmakers from Europe as well as from Japan. The Japanese particularly were infuriated because they had helped modernise the American industry and many of them had spent – and some lost – large sums of money in the process. Nippon Steel chose its investment rather well compared with its main domestic rival NKK,* which took 50 per cent of National Steel Corporation and spent $2 billion to modernise National's decrepit facilities, but by 1994 was still losing money and finding its American managers resistant to more efficient Japanese methods. In mid-1994 Nippon Steel announced plans to buy a 10 per cent stake in New CF&I, the holding company of Colorado-based CF&I Steel Corporation, for about 1 billion yen. Under the deal, Nippon Steel will provide the American electric furnace steelmaker with the technology for manufacturing quality rails, and will supply heat treatment facilities to it.

*   *   *

* The other members of Japan's big five steelmakers are Kawasaki Steel Corporation, Sumitomo Metal Industries and Kobe Steel.

Today Nippon Steel is more than just the world's biggest steel producer. It has diversified into a large number of associated, ancillary and sometimes apparently barely connected activities. The first obvious move was to get involved as purchaser of the raw materials it depends on – the iron ore and coal essential for steel production, which comes from as far afield as Australia (which supplies 46 per cent of its iron ore and 46 per cent of its coking coal), Brazil (30 per cent of iron ore), Canada (23 per cent of coal), India (16 per cent of iron ore) and the United States (15 per cent of coal). Nippon Steel managers boasted that 'we are competitive, but not in the sense of "the world's toughest negotiator". We are bringing materials in on energy-efficient, specially built cargo ships that help to keep operating costs low.' The company also explained with pride that it has succeeded in making quality steel with lower-grade fuels by the development of pulverised coal injection techniques and technology for using large quantities of semi-soft coking coal in coke making. 'We've made this effort not because it was advantageous for us, but because the efficient use of natural resources is our responsibility.'

Moves into two other specialist metals, titanium and aluminium, also seemed to be part of a logical progression. A few years ago titanium products were in great demand as uses of the metal expanded rapidly, especially in building materials and consumer products markets. Nippon Steel established close relations with Titanium Metals Corporation of the USA, which has plenty of experience in the use of titanium in aircraft manufacturing. The particularly attractive properties of titanium are its durability and superior corrosion resistance.

Unfortunately, the good times and high promises did not last long. Demand for titanium in aircraft production fell, and Nippon Steel had to face the challenge of the rising yen just as competition in the market started increasing. Nippon Steel Chemical Company, another close associate of the steelmaking business, also faced a harsher environment, leading the company to reformulate and concentrate its management resources in areas that could take best advantage of Nippon Steel's corporate strength. Imai said that the development of chemicals was natural, involving the gases that the steelmaking process produced; the activity was worth about 15 per cent of the sales of the main steelmaking business in 1994.

Nippon Steel has also developed considerable expertise in engineering and construction, making use of its strengths as the most advanced steel company. Japan's recession of the early 1990s had an impact, but by the year ending in March 1994, engineering and construction activities accounted for 17 per cent of total company sales, the highest ever. These engineering and construction activities grew out of Nippon Steel's long-standing role as a supplier of technical co-operation to steelmakers worldwide. This is something that it has been doing for more than 30 years, providing services including construction engineering of plants and machinery, technical and operating guidance, diagnosis of equipment and operations, and transfers of technology.

Nippon Steel received an order for an electric arc furnace from South Korea's Posco. This demand from its main international rival was something of a tribute to the Japanese company's new technology – basically, the system uses one power source for two vessels that operate alternately, saving energy in a highly efficient and clean operation. In 1994 British Steel received blast furnace throat armour cover plates from Nippon Steel for its Teesside works. The plates prevent damage to the throat of the blast furnace during charging of raw materials. With more than a century of experience, Nippon Steel offers its expertise in construction and operation of integrated plants throughout the world, not only in steel plants and equipment, but in innovative plants and industrial machinery of various kinds. In the 1993 fiscal year, for example, Nippon Steel received an order from Ibaraki for two waste-melting plants able to cope with 150 tons a day.

It is something of a jump from offering advice on steelmaking and other plants, but the company's engineering and construction activities also include an expanding role as a comprehensive urban developer. The rationale for this is that Nippon Steel has plenty of building experience, including with environmental concerns. In Japan, it has been heavily involved in the construction of the Makuhari Techno Garden, a twin-tower intelligent building complex, and the development of residential and commercial areas for 40,000 people in the Makuhari business district of Chiba city, bordering Tokyo. Another landmark project was the construction of the Kawasaki man-made island as part of the Trans-Tokyo Bay highway scheme. Abroad, Nippon Steel has also served as a general contractor in large-scale building projects, especially those, like Bank of China's Hong Kong headquarters, which have high-rise steel frames.

Perhaps the most surprising development – adventure, it is tempting to call it – of the engineering and construction business is a project in Kita-Kyushu, in the northern part of the southern island of Kyushu. As the publicity handout tells it: 'a leisure boat, travelling peacefully down a stream in a forest, encounters the hull of a UFO which fell from outer space. Suddenly, the boat is drawn inside the wrecked UFO through a crack in the spacecraft, and a dazzling adventure begins …'. With an introduction like that, it can only be a gameshow or an adventure park. It is the latter. Nippon Steel established Space World in April 1990, under a licence from the Space Camp Foundation in Alabama.

The UFO experience is part of 'the Planet AQA' water ride and is supposed to remind visitors 'of childhood games with water pistols and water balloons and days filled with play'. A corner called Space Camp allows a slice of the experience of an astronaut, including part of the training schedule and a moonwalk. The uncomfortable mixture of educational and rather childish fun is maintained with the Earth Garden, a green area with 2,000 trees and rocks and waterfalls supposed to represent the beauty of Planet Earth viewed from outer space. But there is also Free Fall G.0, a 'screaming machine' which offers an instant plunge of 40 metres, testing whether visitors will scream or faint first.

In March 1994, the Space World venture introduced the ultimate in roller coasters, called Titan after the giants of Greek mythology. It is 60 metres high* and has a drop of 54 metres, 'the world's longest straight drop'. The car drops at 60 degrees, the steepest slope in the world, at 115 km an hour, then goes up a 45-metre hill and down a 45-degree slope, offering riders (to quote Nippon Steel's publicity department) 'the sensation of gravity (maximum centrifugal force 3.7G) that astronauts feel when they are launched into outer space and return to Earth, and the fear and thrill they feel when being in a spacecraft as it moves at superhigh speed between the planets'. Japanese apparently like it, because Space World is getting almost a million visitors a year.

Steel was often regarded as the 'industrial rice' of Japan, so it may not be totally surprising that, in the age of computers and information superhighways, Nippon Steel has been tempted to plant and grow the modern variety of 'industrial rice' and get into the electronics and information/communications business. The 1993 annual report justifies the move, saying it was to make 'the most of expertise as a world class major computer user'. If that sounds a bit thin, then even Nippon Steel's president at the time (and now chairman), Hiroshi Saito, admitted that the pursuit of some diversification projects had been 'amateurish' and 'haphazard'.

Many of Japan's steelmakers took the big step into computers and semiconductors in the savage recession of the mid-1980s; none of them has proved profitable, and few are likely ever to make big profits. Nippon Steel admitted its own mistakes by pulling out of notebook computers in 1992, a victim of the savage international price war in the personal computer business, which has seen even specialist computer makers reeling. It had plunged in, hoping that this was the fastest-growing area of the computer world. But in spite of having its fingers burned, Nippon Steel retains its optimism about making inroads in computers and semiconductors. In 1993 it bought a controlling share in NMB Semiconductor, previously owned by Minebea, the bearing maker. NMB was a promising semiconductor maker, but at the time of the purchase it was 'bleeding red ink', according to the Japanese press. The steelmaker paid 30 billion yen and used the acquisition to establish Nippon Steel Semiconductor

* Later, in 1994, Blackpool in England opened a roller coaster that was even bigger, 71 metres high.

The 1995 Great Hanshin earthquake not only killed 5,400 people, it devastated the once elegant city of Kobe and more than 300,000 people were made homeless as fires swept through the city. This family had to dig with a tablespoon in an effort to retrieve ashes of treasured possessions.

A small part of the Kobe earthquake damage. Many buildings in Kobe were destroyed or rearranged.

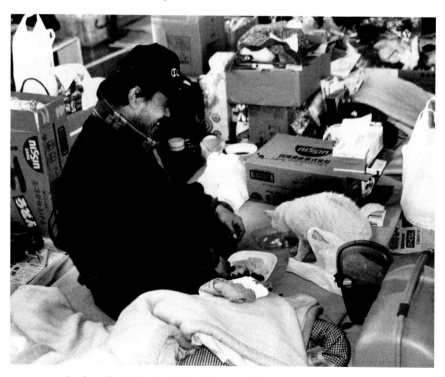

Earthquake victim in Kobe shelter, with his cat.

Yoh Kurosawa, president of Industrial Bank of Japan, denies that Japan has a financial crisis.

Minoru Makihara, president of trading giant Mitsubishi Corp.

The most powerful brothers in Japanese industry, Shoichiro (left) and Tatsuro Toyoda, chairman and president of Toyota Motor. Shoichiro is also chairman of the powerful Keidanren.

Production line at Toyota's Kyushu plant can be adjusted to suit the worker.

Yoichi Morishita, president of Matsushita Electric Industrial Co., has the difficult job of steering family-oriented Matsushita safely into the multi-media age.

Japan still leads the world in consumer electronics.

Admirer of the Iron Lady Margaret Thatcher, Takashi Imai, president of Nippon Steel.

Fumio Sato, president of Toshiba and lover of shogi, now has to plot business battles with rival Sony.

Entry to Toshiba's 'clean room' at Ome, just outside Tokyo, is strictly controlled and requires special clothes and an air bath.

Toyoo Gyohten, chairman of Bank of Tokyo, and former 'Mr International' and chief 'Barbarian tamer' at the Ministry of Finance.

Isao Kubota returns to his old desk in the MoF 'schoolroom'.

Even young schoolgirls flock to Kyoto to learn their fortune in exams and love.

Going home from the 'hothouse', two serious schoolboys carry heavy bags but one of them also carries a comic.

Corporation, got assistance from Hitachi on technology, and was trying to make a big push in 1 and 4 megabit dynamic random access memory chips.

In 1994 Nippon Steel made another move into computer software development by agreeing to co-operate with Electronic Data Systems Corporation of the USA, subsidiary of General Motors Corporation and a world leader in the business of helping companies to use computers more effectively. The link had two potential advantages: it could give Nippon Steel an edge in the crowded area of integrated data-processing services; and it could also help the steelmaker's efforts to rationalise its hi-tech operations. Makoto Hiranuma, chief steel analyst at Nomura Research Institute, said that 'EDS is a company that everyone wants to co-operate with', noting that 'the computer industry is shifting from mainframe-based systems to client-server systems, requiring vendors to offer solutions on systems construction and data transactions, not just computer hardware'.

But if Nippon Steel is to make credible advances in computers, it must get more than the EDS name. Previous joint ventures, including a 1989 deal with Hitachi, IBM Japan and Itochu to provide computer systems integration services, and others with Sun Microsystems and Oracle of the USA, have proved disappointing. The steelmaker is well behind its 1987 plan that electronics, information and telecommunications would be a business worth 800 billion yen by 1995. In the three years from 1991 to 1993, revenues from the businesses were about 150 billion yen and were not profitable.

The recession of the 1980s helped to push Nippon Steel into stranger ventures than adventure playgrounds and computers. Kamaishi, the original company town of Nippon Steel, suffered badly. Its two blast furnaces were closed in 1984 and 1989, leaving the wire-making plant for radial tyres. But because of its obligations to provide continuing work for its long-time employees, Nippon Steel went into other businesses, including producing meat substitutes from soya beans, selling bottled fresh water that seeps into the old mineshaft, making office furniture and turning out bodies for lorries. A mushroom-growing operation was started and then abandoned as a failure.

The toughest economic facts remain – lingering recession and a continuing strong yen have hit Nippon Steel hard. Critics claim that last time round, in the 1980s, the company experienced a shock, but the recession ended before it got to grip, with its costs properly. Over the Japanese steel industry as a whole, the index of fixed to overall costs rose by 3.6 per cent between 1987 and 1993, instead of falling by 30 per cent as promised. The industry's failure then to grasp the nettle continues to haunt it today, and provides the fiercest challenge to Imai since he took over as president in the middle of the slump.

Nippon Steel executives said that, in Imai, they had just the right man for the troubled job. He spent 30 years in the raw materials division, where he oversaw the development of mines throughout the world and learned to be rigorous and clear in his negotiations. 'My thought processes originate from the days when I was in charge of raw materials,' said Imai, who was 64 in 1994. To help drive home the gravity of the 1990s recession, which he said is worse than that of the 1980s, he met the company's 300 general managers individually before launching an ambitious plan to slash costs and restructure the company.

Imai acknowledged the situation: 'The auto and home appliance industries had been leading the Japanese economy for the past twenty years, but their markets matured and they are now experiencing a period of inactivity. That caused a decline in the demand for steel materials and pushed the steel industry into trouble. Up until now, half of Japan's steel production, including processed products, was exported, while half was used at home. Now, exports are down and domestic demand is depressed. Our options for action are either to raise prices or to reduce costs across a wide spectrum.'

The option of raising prices is not one that it has been necessary for Nippon Steel to choose – the rising value of the yen has already done enough damage. It has directly hit exports. At home, prices expressed in yen are not affected, and steel companies even benefit from the falling yen price of raw materials, all of which, from the basic iron ore to the energy used in making the iron and steel, have to be imported. But the rising yen also makes imports cheaper. That is why the three car makers' decisions to import Posco steel has made the Japanese industry extremely nervous. It is not just that the knife-edge arithmetic of how to get back into the black has been blown away. Now other major steel-using industries, such as construction and shipbuilding, will be encouraged to press the steel companies to lower their prices, and threaten to import foreign steel.

Nippon Steel itself reacted quickly to the likelihood of South Korean imports challenging it inside its stronghold. It promised 10 per cent discounts from April 1995 to any car maker signing a long-term contract for its cold-rolled steel sheet. That would bring Nippon Steel's prices to within 5 per cent of Posco's. Disingenuously, Yoshiro Sasaki, the company's executive vice-president, insisted that 'The timing of our price cut has nothing to do with the contract between Mitsubishi Motors and Posco. There is no possibility that the prices of domestic steel products will be brought down to those of Posco's.' Pointedly, the same discounts were not on offer to other industrial users, though they may have to be if the pressures intensify.

To some extent the early announcements from the car makers represented a 'phoney war' of bluff and bargaining. The initial amount that

Mitsubishi planned to import from Posco was only 500 tons a month – as if it were a challenge to the Japanese steelmakers to do better. But the threat to the Japanese industry is real enough. Imai had previously forecast that Japanese domestic steel demand would remain steady at 75 million tons a year, on top of which they could count on exports of 20 million tons a year, including demand from Japanese manufacturers going abroad who 'will continue to use Japanese steel products to ensure quality and stable supply'. But if the Japanese steelmakers are being deserted by their most faithful customers, all bets are off that demand will stay high.

Imai is by no means complacent, but claimed proudly that for all the Koreans' progress, the Japanese still have an edge in quality steelmaking: 'the Japanese car industry uses Japanese steel, but the Korean car industry also uses Japanese steel'. With a touch of sad pride he added that '25 years ago Nippon Steel educated the Koreans in making steel from the very first steps and also set up their first factory.' Posco, Imai pointed out, owes its international edge to the fluctuations in the foreign exchange markets. With the currency rates at his fingertips, he reeled off the figures that showed the damage: '25 years ago, at the time of fixed exchange rates, the yen and the South Korean won were both at 360 to the US dollar; by the time of the Plaza agreement in 1985, the yen was 250 and the won about 950 to the dollar; after that both currencies appreciated, the yen to 150 and the won to 680; since then the yen has strengthened to 100, whereas the won has weakened to about 810.' One of the hopes of the Japanese industry is that South Korea will soon join the club of rich industrial nations, the Organisation for Economic Co-operation and Development, and this will lead to strengthening of the won.

Like leaders of the car, electronics, home appliance and most other Japanese industries, Imai was quick to complain about the strength of the Japanese currency: 'A hundred yen is too high,' he said. 'If you look at purchasing power, the yen should be at something like 180.' To suggestions that this was like King Canute shouting to the waves to go back, and that the prospect is that the currency will increase in value rather than diminish, Imai commented, 'If the yen continues to strengthen, it will mean that our rationalisation policy is no good. That's why the government's macroeconomic policy is very important.'

Unlike makers of cars or electrical goods, it is not easy for Japanese steel works to move abroad or even to enter foreign joint ventures. Apart from in the USA and Britain, many steel companies are nationalised, and then there is the nationalistic industrial pride which argues that steel must belong to the nation. Even where countries have allowed a foreign company in to set up a steel plant, there has been a temptation for the government to intervene and change the terms against the foreign partner once it has got going. However, Nippon Steel has established ventures to produce some downstream products abroad, notably tinplate in Thailand and China.

Imai sees Nippon Steel as caught in Japan's general economic malaise, and has urged the government to cut through the plethora of regulations, which he describes as 'a cancer' killing the country. He pleaded that 'Japan's economy stands at an important juncture today. Two pressing issues the government faces to break out from the present economic impasse are raising the quality of life at home and achieving a high level of harmony internationally. Therefore, in order for Japan to respond to the current economic situation and perform on the global stage in ways that befit its status as an economic power, it must take two principal steps: first, it must move away from its traditional dependence on exports; and second, it must promote expansion of the domestic market.' This means giving a helping hand to imports: 'Measures have to be introduced to make it easier for imported products to come into Japan. Along these lines, there is a strong move now under way towards wide-ranging deregulation.' Imai is chairman of a high-powered committee making recommendations regarding deregulation. But he went further than most other big business leaders in urging that deregulation and opening of markets should not be limited to the obvious areas of goods manufactured abroad.

The Nippon Steel president suggested that steps would have to be taken that might prove painful to some of his industrial colleagues. 'Steps are needed to ensure that the benefits of the strong yen reach the marketplace. For example, about 40 per cent of total Japanese industries such as electricity, finance, transportation, communications and retail sales are protected by the government. That's why such industries can't raise their productivity and decrease their costs in a less competitive, less international market. Legal restrictions also preclude the entry of foreign companies into those industries. Deregulation and the strong yen will introduce formidable competition that should lead to lower prices. That's precisely what happened, for example, after Japan's telephone monopoly was broken several years ago. Telephone services quickly became more competitive and charges came down, eventually reaching approximately 50 per cent of what they were before. So regulations need to be eased or removed in industries where there is little or no competition at present. Such action will make it easier for foreign companies to enter Japanese markets to compete.'

Laughing, Imai asserted, 'I think that Japan's civil servants are excellent, but since they retire around the age of 55, they need to secure their second jobs and their rights to give approval to industries they supervise.' He added that he spoke with personal knowledge because his older brother worked for the Ministry of International Trade and Industry, retiring as vice minister (permanent secretary).

To do its best to keep its costs down, so that it can keep up with the competition, Nippon Steel introduced a new business plan not only to cut costs, but to shake up the company from top to bottom. As far as improving the profitability of its basic steelmaking is concerned, the aim is to reduce costs by 300 billion yen ($3 billion), 'in order to rebuild its international competitiveness to a level better than or even equal to the strongest competitors both at home and abroad'. Imai hoped for a 15 per cent reduction in product cost over three years. This will mean a radical reduction in the company's steel workforce from 27,000 to 20,000. Of the jobs eliminated, 4,000 will belong to white-collar workers and 3,000 to technical employees. Nippon Steel described it as a 'drastic cost-trimming plan'.

As an indication of the new slimmed-down look, at the height of its growth in 1962, Nippon Steel took on 5,000 people. By 1994 the executive-level intake was 749 new graduates, including 201 engineers, and in 1995 only 325 new graduate recruits will join, including 105 engineers. Imai said that a third of the reduction would come from cutting management costs, another third from reducing procurement costs and a final third from curbing the costs of raw materials. 'We want to be the world's most competitive company,' he said with grim determination. Imai did not exempt either himself or his fellow senior managers from financial stringencies. In 1993 he did not receive his annual bonus, which, amounting to several months' salary, is normally considered an essential part of a person's pay in Japan. Senior executives' salaries were cut by 10 per cent in 1992, and by a further 5 per cent in 1994.

But more than attention to the pennies is involved. Nippon Steel will try to get a better projection of steel demand in the future and will improve marketing and co-operation between itself and its affiliates so as to achieve the best combined strength. Besides this, the management will be shaken up. Many jobs will go at corporate head office by slimming down corporate planning in administrative departments and halving their personnel. Administration, including at steel works and research laboratories, will be greatly simplified. When the plan is completed by March 1997, there will have been a 30 per cent reduction in the corporate steel business departments from 156 to 111. In addition, in the company's steel operations, marketing, engineering and manufacturing capabilities will be combined, including the resources of the steel works and research and development divisions, into a single unified force, running product-by-product business divisions. This, said the company, 'will help realise a quicker response to customer needs, and complete total profit and loss control by product and steel works'.

The rationalisation very much bears the hallmarks of Imai's rational thinking. 'We have so many management levels that we must go through to make one decision,' he grumbled not long after taking over. 'When you look at the production side, the superintendent of the steel works does not have concrete targets; and when you look at the sales side, they should have concrete targets, but they do not. I want to minimise the size of head office, and I want to abolish the tedious vertical system of decision making. Under the president, we have an executive vice president, managing director, general manager, deputy general manager and so on, but authority is not clearly delegated.' It will be henceforth.

The plan also embraces Nippon Steel's affiliates. The company's executives explained that the aim was to expand the profitability base, both domestically and abroad, of already established engineering businesses dealing with plant and machinery, civil engineering, and marine and building construction. The group will also be on the hunt for new business areas, including electronics and information, and new materials. It will also look for business opportunities abroad, both in steelmaking and outside.

As part of the medium-term plan, Nippon Steel will slim down its total assets and try to reconstitute the financial structure. This will be done by looking at each business segment and strengthening the profit bases. In addition, plant and equipment investments will be reduced by 40 per cent over the previous three-year period to 340 billion yen. Finally, working assets will be reduced by 60 billion yen, or a 15 per cent slimming-down of the steel business inventory.

Imai said that diversification into non-steel products would continue and grow. He predicted that in ten years' time, 'The steel business will probably stay about the same, at 2,000 billion yen, but I would expect the non-steel operations to grow from the present 1,000 billion yen to 2,000 billion yen, so that about half of Nippon Steel's activities will be in non-steel business.' Profits may be a different matter, and Imai said that the bulk of the profits would continue to come from steel. 'Non-steel businesses will become more profitable, but we cannot expect them to be as profitable as steel because we are the world leader in that. I would like to develop a niche product where we can build up our reputation and profits.'

The president questioned whether some of Japan's cherished business practices could continue in a changing age of recession: 'Until now, the accepted thinking was that the real owners of a corporation are its employees. This fact was reflected in the way companies took care of their employees, providing lifetime employment, health and welfare facilities, and guaranteed pay increases and bonuses. However, in the context of the present difficult economic situation, some Japanese companies are beginning to reconsider certain employee-related policies. Part of the reason is that change is being forced on Japanese managers because of a situation where it is no longer possible to borrow heavily from banks. Instead, corporations have to depend more and more on raising capital through new stock issues. In other words, there is a heavier reliance now on borrowing from the public, and corporate managers are having to listen more to the wishes of shareholders.'

To a westerner, Imai's wide-ranging comments may not seem too surprising. But for a Japanese, they are eloquent and indeed radical. More impressively to the point, they come from knowledge and from the heart.

When it comes to personal matters and ambitions, Imai retreats into typical self-effacing Japanese executive mode. After more than 40 years in the steel business, the Nippon Steel president said that his greatest achievement had not been accomplished in Japan, but in the steamy Amazon jungles of Brazil, where he had been instrumental in opening up the world's biggest iron ore mine at a cost of $5 billion. It was an adventure in itself, requiring him to commute frequently between Tokyo head office, the mine site in Brazil and Europe 'to arrange the finance without which it would never have been opened. But I have the satisfaction of knowing too that without me there would have been no mine.'

The president's comfortably appointed office did offer a few clues as to his opinions. A golf club and ball rested beside the wall, and he grumbled that his golf game had suffered since he had become president because he had so little time to play. 'Well, my private life, to tell you the truth, has just about evaporated. I still try to play golf on Saturdays, but since becoming president I have become much busier than before with public duties.' Sunday is for catching up on reading, though most of it is business or committee reports. Close to the golf club there was also a photograph of Imai with former British prime minister, Margaret Thatcher. He is very casually dressed in a sports jacket, and on further inspection the British leader looks rather drawn. He confessed that the shot was taken on an admiring visit to Thatcher's wax image in Madame Tussaud's and laughed at the idea of himself with a wax heroine.

Imai is direct enough in conversation, but modestly matter-of-fact. He understands English, though he was more comfortable answering in Japanese. Asked how he wanted to be remembered as chief executive of Nippon Steel, he responded with typical Japanese cliché: 'I want to enhance and strengthen the company and make it profitable again.' That was more eloquent than the typical 'I want to do my best', beloved of everyone from sports stars and sumo wrestlers to business leaders; but considering Nippon Steel and the whole industry's plight, it would be a shining epitaph worthy of a man of steel.

5

Kings of the Road:
Toyota and the Toyodas

Eiji Toyoda's childhood in small-time, small-town, hand-to-mouth rural Japan is far, far removed from life in the fast lane of the late twentieth century. Yet Toyoda can claim an important place as one of the movers and shakers of the industrial twentieth century, and as one of the shapers of the twenty-first century. He joined the Toyota Motor Corporation almost at the same time as its foundation by his older cousin, and rose to become president, later chairman and today honorary chairman of the company. He was at the helm when the car maker rose from obscurity in provincial Japan to become the internationally known name for motor car manufacturing, respected and feared in Detroit as well as at home. Toyota became not just the equal of the American giants, but their beater and the standard-setter for the world's motor car industry.

The motor car is often seen as the symbol of the twentieth century, offering people mobility and independence as never before. In the same way, of all the powerhouses of Japan Inc., Toyota is the flagbearer. It proved that Japan was one of the world's industrial giants. Today it and Japan are facing their fiercest tests, with questions being asked whether the motor maker can maintain its lead in the face of a comeback from Detroit; the handicap of a high yen and economic mismanagement at home; and the growth of ambitious challengers in Japan's backyard, including South Korea and, potentially, China.

Out in Kyushu, the most southerly of Japan's four large islands, Toyota's latest plant hardly looks like a factory, it is so pleasant. It is set in countryside at Miyata, about an hour's drive away from the spaghetti junctions and traffic jams of Hakata and Fukuoka. It has been carefully landscaped and surrounded by a small forest, including 1,500 cherry trees. The outside has been painted grey-white, mixed with blue and green pastel colours, so that when the trees are in full bloom, the factory will be almost camouflaged in an apparently natural landscape.

Inside, the most remarkable thing is how clean and tidy it is. Some Toyota executives claim that it is so quiet that you would not know you were in a factory at all. That is obviously an exaggeration: when you stand close to the well-muffled thump and crunch of the 4,000 ton stamping machine, it drowns normal conversation. But the final assembly line runs as smoothly and cleanly as Swiss clockwork; this is the very model of modern motorcar manufacturing.

Few people could have imagined this when Eiji Toyoda was born near Nagoya in 1913, or in 1937 when Toyota Motor Company Ltd was formally established, or in 1945 when the company restarted after the war, or even in 1957 when Toyota proudly exported its first cars to the USA and saw them laughed at as ugly and underpowered. No longer: Toyota's story very much mirrors that of Japan's own industrial rise, and indeed offers an object lesson to Europe and America in how to take, modify, use, polish and perfect advancing technology and make it more advanced.

In Toyoda's schooldays, Japan was still emerging into the steam age. He had the advantage of being born into a family interested in mechanical things and in developing industry. His grandfather, Ikichi, lived as his forebears had done for years, simply and according to the changing rhythm of the seasons, planting the staple grain crop of rice at the right time before the onset of the annual rains, seeing that it got enough of the precious irrigation water during the long hot summers, harvesting it before the destructive arrival of autumn typhoons, going hungry when for some reason the weather patterns misbehaved. Daily life revolved round the sun. There were strict obligations to the extended family and to the village, so that a person's life was hardly his or her own. Social mobility was extremely limited.

Then came the shock visitation in 1853 of Commodore Matthew Perry and his 'Black Ships' from across the ocean, and the forced ending of three centuries of Japan's near isolation. In their wake a whirlwind of changes occurred: the Restoration of the Meiji Emperor in 1868, the abolition of the domains of the *daimyo* (regional barons) and their standing armies, the establishment of a national army and conscription to man it, the creation of a strong central bureaucracy, the replacement of the lunar calendar with the western solar version, and compulsory elementary education as part of a determination to turn Japan into a rich, technologically advanced nation – like those of the West which had rudely interrupted the centuries of isolation. Such changes shook up the established lifestyles and were resented in traditional Japanese villages; but they also offered opportunities to restless youngsters like Sakichi Toyoda, son of Ikichi and uncle of Eiji.

Sakichi Toyoda, born in 1868, the year of the Meiji Restoration, read Samuel Smiles' book *Self-Help*, a best-seller when translated into Japanese. He listened to teachers from Tokyo telling young men that the samurai and force could not defeat the West, but that Japanese had to imbibe and understand the new technology and then do better. Toyoda courageously rejected his father's expectations that he would become a carpenter, and turned his interest towards improving the traditional hand loom, which had been a mainstay of village cloth production but was now under threat from the intrusion of better-quality imported cloth from the West.

He struggled for five years with all the problems of his isolation in Yamaguchi near Nagoya, visited Tokyo to look at an exhibition of foreign machines, and then went to see new factories in the capital and in Yokohama, where western looms were installed. He finally produced an improved loom, still wooden and hand-powered, and used it to improve the quality of the cloth and worker productivity, which rose by 50 per cent. Sakichi spent the next two decades in a constant struggle to find capital to continue the research to build a better and better loom, a fully automatic power machine made of steel and capable of producing 36 inch broadcloth that could compete with the materials made on western machines. By the early years of the twentieth century he had made his steel loom, but tests showed that machines made by Platt Brothers and Company of Manchester were superior.

His struggle continued, through the founding of several Toyoda companies and factories in Japan and China, through the often vicious vicissitudes of a fluctuating economy that was striving to modernise and compete with imperial British might and with the raw adolescent power of America, through the devastating great Tokyo earthquake of 1923, and through stormy family relationships which saw a manager and administration expert, Risaburo Kodama, marry Sakichi Toyoda's daughter, be adopted into the family as Risaburo Toyoda and become first-born son by proxy.*

In 1924 Ford of Japan was established with a capital of four million yen and set up a factory in Yokohama to assemble cars from parts shipped from the USA. General Motors followed a year later, set up in Osaka with capital of eight million yen upon promises that it would be exempted from city taxes for four years. Ford promptly doubled its own capital as Japan's first car battle raged. The first Japanese competitor was still several painful years away from its efforts to build a car.

A big advance was made in 1929 when Sakichi Toyoda's hard work paid off and his youthful dreams became reality. Platt Brothers, the world's biggest makers of textile machinery, asked to conduct a performance appraisal of the new Toyoda automatic loom. Having seen the result, they offered to buy the patent rights exclusive of Japan, China and the USA for the fabulous sum of one million yen. This money was to be the seed capital for the start of the Toyota motor enterprise.

Sakichi Toyoda offered the money to his son Kiichiro to build Japan's first motor car. In part, this was an attempt to make up for the fact that he had allowed his adopted son to displace his natural son as the effective

* This was not unusual in Japan – and indeed happens today when a family without a son and heir adopts the son-in-law.

manager and heir of the Toyoda loom company. In part, too, it was a recognition of his own engineering and inventive talents in his son, and a desire that the quest for new and better machines should go on.

Kiichiro Toyoda had many educational advantages over his virtually self-taught father. Sakichi had initially been sceptical of the values of education, but Asako, his second wife, encouraged Kiichiro to become a boarder at the famous Number Two High School in Nagoya, and then to go on to study mechanical engineering at Tokyo University. In spite of his educational qualifications, the son was at first appalled at the ambitions of his father, and pointed out that Japan's big *zaibatsu* (conglomerates) had so far refused to take up the American challenge, recognising that the motor car was a much more complicated and expensive machine than the loom. Nevertheless, slowly, his father instilled his own new dreams into his son, so that when Sakichi Toyoda died in 1930 at the age of 63, Kiichiro was studying with all his might and imagination how to make Japan's first motor car.

It was a long and tough struggle which took years. Few Japanese companies were brave enough to challenge Ford and GM, which assembled 29,338 cars in Japan in 1929. Another 5,018 vehicles were imported, while domestic production was just 437, all of them assembled by hand. Yukiyasu Togo and William Wartman recount in their book about the origins of Toyota* that one of the supporters of domestic car production arrived for a meeting in a Chevrolet taxi; when this was pointed out, he resolved never to use a foreign vehicle – and subsequently had to travel by rickshaw, the only domestic transport he could find.

Kiichiro Toyoda had to fight not only the head start of the American giants and the economies of scale, but also the sceptical attitude of his adoptive brother, Risaburo Toyoda, who had taken over as head of the family after Sakichi's death and was jealously determined to preserve the financial stability of the family company. He had reason to be worried, since the paid-up capital of Toyoda Automatic Loom Works was only one million yen in 1933 and its profits were 182,000 yen. Poor Risaburo had to agonise and cough up extra cash several times before the car-making company even got on the road.

In fact, it took a stirring speech by Kiichiro Toyoda at a directors' meeting on 30 December 1933 to get the articles of association changed to permit automobile making as part of Toyoda's activities. He urged that theirs was a living and changing company. 'Sakichi's courage and spirit have something to say to all of us about the development of automobiles. At present, the United States and Europe are going great guns making cars. Whenever you look at the industrialised western world, cars are being

* *Against All Odds: The Story of the Toyota Motor Corporation and the Family that Created It*, St Martin's Press, 1993.

made by human hands. Mitsui and Mitsubishi say we can't do it in Japan, but that's only because they're conservative aristocrats whose power lies in their money. And that's their shortcoming: they won't do anything risky. If someone does take the risk and succeeds, people will say anyone could have done it, just as I say anyone could have invented what Sakichi invented. What I'm saying is this: It's not a matter of whether or not it can be done, but of who will do it. You understand that, don't you? It is in the national interest to start an auto industry in Japan. That is why my father instructed me to enter this business.'

The struggle to understand what was involved in making a car and then to make it proved exhausting as well as expensive. At one stage Kiichiro Toyoda and his team disassembled a Chevrolet and noted down its parts and their shapes, sizes and how they fitted together so that they could understand the complex jigsaw puzzle of a car. Each piece revealed a new part in which Toyoda – and often Japan – lacked manufacturing expertise or even experience. Toyoda himself realised that time was limited, since unless he could get car production into gear and be registered as a producer, he would lose the benefits of protection that the government planned to introduce. His contacts in government also told him about the importance of lorry production for the military as a potential revenue earner – since production of a lorry was both simpler and offered a large number of potential orders. So he decided that Toyoda would go for *both* cars and lorries.

The strains on the company were enormous, both on its cash and on personal relationships. New recruit Eiji Toyoda quickly noticed that Kiichiro Toyoda took himself off to Tokyo to get away from Risaburo, who was fuming about the continuing soaring costs, which he could do nothing about. A partial solution came from the contribution of three million yen from Toyoda's highly profitable China operations (notwithstanding the legal difficulties of transferring money).

It was September 1934 before the first engine was produced and May 1935 before the prototype car, the A1, was ready, copied shamelessly from three foreign models, the Chevrolet for engine and frame, Ford for the drive train and DeSoto Airflow for the body. Kiichiro Toyoda drove the car out to the cemetery where Sakichi's ashes were buried, to tell his father that he had fulfilled his final wishes.

Then relief came from the government, which was stung into action by Ford. The US manufacturer stubbornly decided to expand in Yokohama in spite of clear obstacles being placed in its way by the Japanese military, which saw the action as foreigners threatening to strangle Japan's motor industry at birth. The soldiers persuaded the Ministry of Commerce and Industry to draw up laws requiring any car manufacturer wishing to make more than 3,000 vehicles a year to be licensed and to be majority-owned by Japanese. The laws offered considerable reliefs for licensed manufacturers, including five years' exemption from both national and local taxes and similar exemptions from duties on imported parts, and imposed additional burdens on foreign car makers. The existing makers, Ford and GM, were allowed to continue at their existing capacities, but not to expand.

Toyoda meanwhile set about building his lorry before the deadline for licensing. The prototype of a 1.5 ton lorry – G1 – was finished in August 1935, then five vehicles were rushed to be ready for a special exhibition. Their showing had to be postponed by three days, and they took 23 hours to cover the 200 miles from Nagoya to Tokyo. The sale price of the lorries was put at 2,900 yen, or 200 yen less than the rival GM product, but also much less than it had cost to build them. Once the lorries were ready for their first public appearance, Kiichiro Toyoda delivered a ringing speech about his determination to lead the Japanese domestic motor industry. Whether it could really be called 'domestic' is a moot point, since Eiji Toyoda admits that almost all the parts making up the first vehicles were imported from the USA.

The final stages of the setting up of Toyota came in September 1936 when Kiichiro Toyoda's automotive department of the Toyoda Automatic Loom Works gained its coveted licence, one of only two to be awarded. Then came the new name, Toyo*ta*, rather than the family name, Toyo*da*. It happened after a competition to design a logo for the new car maker. Risaburo Toyoda intervened to insist that the name in Japanese characters should be changed from Toyoda to Toyota. Eiji Toyoda remembers today that one of the reasons was to avoid confusion in legal documents. The name-change had an additional superstitious advantage. In Chinese characters, 'Toyoda' and 'Toyota' are the same, but in the Japanese hir-agana, 'Toyota' required only eight brush strokes, not the ten of the family name, and eight is regarded as a lucky number, synonymous with growth. However, Toyota's road ahead was still highly troubled. Its products acquired a reputation for breaking down, such that one Nagoya newspaper ran a cartoon showing a vehicle stuck with a broken axle under the caption, 'Toyota lorry in Zen meditation'.

Eiji Toyoda had also inherited the mechanical bent of the family. He was the second-born but eldest surviving son of Sakichi's middle brother, Heikichi. His own father had parted company with his older brother to set up his own cloth-weaving mill. Japan in those days was miles behind the West. Eiji was brought up, he recalls, literally into the steam age: 'Electrical power still was not available when the mill was built, so steam engines were installed and the plant ran by burning coal. At night, those engines were used to run generators that supplied electricity for lighting. In other words, we generated our own power. Most houses back then, like my grandfather's in Kosai, had one light at most. Naturally, few homes near the factory had any lights at all ... The boilers were cleaned once a year. A worker would strip down to his loincloth, get inside the boiler while it was still warm, and scrape the walls free of deposits. I must have made a real pest of myself, but I managed to get inside on a few occasions myself. This gave me a good idea of what the inside of a boiler is like. Later, one of the courses I took in college was boiler design. I'll bet that of the 70 students in that class, I was the only one who had seen the inside of a real boiler.'*

In those days of Eiji Toyoda's youth, radio broadcasts had just started and people built their own sets to listen in. Cotton quotations came in by telephone and young Eiji quickly became expert at complicated mental arithmetic and market pricing. This was because the company had to know what price was profitable for spinning cotton and making it into cloth for sale in China. Sums had to be calculated against the prices of silver bullion (since China was on a silver standard), sterling (since London was the centre of the international silver market), dollars (because New York dominated world cotton dealings) and yen.

Eija was close to Sakichi Toyoda, who regarded him with grandfatherly affection given the eighteen-year age difference between Eiji and his older cousin, Kiichiro. Just before Eiji graduated from the engineering department of Tokyo Imperial University, Kiichiro claimed him to work for the infant car company. His first instruction from Kiichiro was 'Go set up a lab at the car hotel [fireproof structures built because of the shortages of parking places and the fears of the explosive element in petrol, equivalent to a modern garage] in Shibaura [district of Tokyo].' The younger Toyoda recalls, 'I was to do this entirely by myself.'

The job, at 1.7 yen a day against the five yen that Ford paid its starting workers, was varied. It included checking defective cars – frequently – taking apart and examining foreign cars, looking for parts makers near Tokyo, studying machine tools for making cars, doing research on helicopters – of which Toyota later test-built a few – and studying rockets, all suggesting the keen, inquiring and determined mind of the cousins. It led to some amusing incidents, which revealed the plight of the fledgling Japanese industry. Among the would-be parts makers that Eiji Toyoda visited was a manufacturer of meters located under a railway line, so that each time a train passed, 'the whole place shook like crazy. Any meters made here must have been totally worthless.'

The formal establishment of Toyota Motor Company Ltd came in summer 1937 with a capital of 12 million yen and backed by a line of credit of 25 million yen. Risaburo Toyoda was president and Kiichiro became executive vice president. Togo comments, 'Toyota Motor Company came into the world, its ledgers awash with red ink and its

---

* *Toyota: Fifty Years in Motion*, an autobiography by the chairman, Eiji Toyoda, Kodansha, 1987.

parking lot filled with unsold cars and trucks.' The method Toyota chose for pricing its vehicles was to take the price of Ford or GM products and undercut them, since Japanese consumers would not buy anything more costly than the marker price established by the US giants.

For lorries, the production price was set at 2,400 yen, based, so Eiji Toyoda recalled, on a Chevrolet sticker price of 3,000 yen, meaning that dealers would be invoiced at 2,800 yen. Kiichiro Toyoda calculated that at production of 500 vehicles a month, the costs would drop to 2,140 yen, a good enough profit margin. When the new plant at Koromo (now Toyota City) was opened, it would have a capacity of 1,500 vehicles a month, and costs would drop to 1,850 yen, giving a handsome profit. The trouble was that actual production fell well short of the target and the costs rose way above the target.

Salvation was at hand. To quote Eiji Toyoda: 'War in China broke out and the army bought up all our trucks, cleaning out our entire stock. Military procurements for the war were what saved the company.' Japanese forces had been involved in Manchuria since 1931, annexed it in 1933, and then marched into China in undeclared war in 1937. With the attacks on Pearl Harbor and British and Dutch Asia-Pacific colonies in December 1941, Japan's total war machine went into full swing.

During the war, Toyota was an essential part of Japan's military struggle, churning out lorries as fast as shortage of supplies and conscription of manpower would permit. Eiji Toyoda expressed his relief that the war had not been prolonged beyond the 15 August 1945 surrender by Emperor Hirohito (posthumously referred to as Emperor Showa) because, according to the American bombing schedule, 'Toyota City was to have been bombed and burned to the ground on 21 August.'

After the war, the Toyoda family had to worry whether their company would be taken away from them or broken up by the Allied occupying forces. Executives began to cast around for what they could do to keep their employees employed: making textiles, investing in a sewing machine concern, running a chinaware franchise, producing concrete for houses, opening dry-cleaning ventures and making fish paste were just a few of the ideas. Shoichiro Toyoda, Kiichiro's eldest son, who is today the chairman of the company, went to Wakkanai in Hokkaido and began to make fish paste there. Luckily for the company, the occupation forces fairly quickly allowed Toyota to resume making lorries and buses, though not cars, and the first post-war lorries began rolling out from the plant eighteen months after the end of the war.

Toyota's struggle was still in its infancy. Japan's recovery from war and defeat was slow and beset with difficulties. Toyota was targeted for possible punitive action by the occupation authorities on two counts, as a member of the Mitsui zaibatsu, since Mitsui companies owned 14 per cent of its shares, and for its involvement in the war effort. Luckily for Toyota, it fell into the second rank in each case and got away without seizure of equipment or being forced to pay reparations. It had to detach Toyoda Spinning and Weaving and Nippondenso, its parts supplier, and make them independent companies.

Having escaped the worst fates, Toyota had to face the ordinary harsh economic facts – raging inflation, difficulties in getting supplies like steel, and burgeoning labour unrest. The Dodge Line of 1948 put the brakes on inflation, but promptly threw Japan into recession, and meant that many lorry purchasers were not able to keep up their instalment payments to Toyota. This pushed the company into a perilous financial condition and sowed the seeds for a new crisis, with the company fighting desperately to survive bankruptcy.

For Kiichiro Toyoda it was heartbreaking. He literally had to go out and beg the banks for money as debts mounted and surpassed a billion yen, or ten times Toyota's capital. The company founder went to his workers to plead with them to accept huge pay cuts to avoid the job losses that had savaged Nissan and other motor companies. They agreed, but it was still not enough. Toyota was saved only through the intervention of the Nagoya branch manager of the Bank of Japan, Takeo Takanashi, who realised the devastating chain effect that the bankruptcy of the motor company would have on the area by forcing large numbers of supplier companies to follow suit and fold.

Takanashi had to fight hard to convince the governor of the central bank, who was quite prepared to see Toyota go under, but he eventually got permission to put together a consortium of banks with a rescue package of loans. Poor Kiichiro Toyoda had to return on what he saw as a betrayal mission to his men, telling them that as a condition for pumping new money into Toyota and keeping it afloat the bankers insisted on 1,600 workers being sacked, those remaining taking an additional 10 per cent pay cut, and the manufacturing and sales arms being split into two companies, so that the manufacturing unit would make only vehicles that had been ordered. (The two companies were remerged as Toyota Motor Corporation in 1982.)

Eiji Toyoda, head of the engineering unit, told 2,000 angry workers that 'Toyota is like a boat that is foundering. Unless someone jumps off into the water, the boat will sink. That's why I want you to recognise the need for personnel cuts.' Workers felt betrayed and made the plight of the company worse by a series of strikes. In June 1950 Kiichiro Toyoda bit the bullet and tearfully told his workers, 'Much as I'm against it, unless we make these cuts, the company doesn't stand a chance. I'm personally taking responsibility for this by quitting.' And he resigned.

Taizo Ishida came in from Toyoda Automatic Loom Works to be the new president of the manufacturing operation. He had no experience of cars, but ran a profitable company, which made him acceptable to the bankers.

In addition, a Mitsui Bank executive took a senior position to oversee the financial reorganisation. This crisis caused a deep scar in the minds of the Toyota family and left them determined never again to leave themselves vulnerable to their bankers. The need for financial strength and independence has become one of the abiding folk memories of the company.

At this stage, Toyota was not only in a financial mess, but it had not been able to put together the technology of its own to make a car, which had long been Kiichiro's founding dream. In his mind, lorry production, which Toyota had achieved, was fine, but the real test was to build a car. Nissan was already using licensed western technology, and the idea was put forward that Toyota might co-operate with Ford in a joint venture to make the Consul car, thus leapfrogging some of the painful learning experiences. Advanced negotiations were thwarted when on 25 June 1950 North Korea invaded the South, triggering the start of the Korean War.

Washington decided that skilled technical personnel could not leave the country. Eiji Toyoda nevertheless went to look at Ford plants in America. He returned with two reactions. One was that the US giants were far ahead in size. 'Their daily output was 8,000 units; ours was a piddling 40. You might as well compare a pebble with a boulder,' he reported. But on the other hand, he was not so impressed by US technology. 'I remember thinking: "Detroit isn't doing anything Toyota doesn't already know".'

The Korean War and the US military saved Toyota. There was no time to get vehicles for the war from America, and their price would have been too high, so the US forces ordered from Japan. From teetering on the edge of bankruptcy, Toyota received what Eiji Toyoda called 'a gift from heaven' in the form of the military orders. It made money, was able to pay a dividend and had enough spare to put muscle into its domestic sales. The situation became so good by early 1952 that the new boss, Ishida, asked Kiichiro Toyoda to come back to the helm. The founder replied, 'An automaker that doesn't make cars is no automaker at all. I don't have any intention of running such a company.' He was coaxed back with the promise that he could begin car production. But he never made it. On 27 March 1952 he died suddenly of a stroke at the age of 57. 'I strongly suspect that what killed him may have been the intense excitement he felt at the thought of returning to the company,' said Eiji.

With the founder gone, strangely, his ailing adoptive brother Risaburo took up the cause of car making, to which he had originally been vehemently opposed. Risaburo himself was terminally ill, too sick to attend Kiichiro's funeral, about which Eiji went to inform him. 'He moaned from his bed, "Whatever you do, have Toyota make cars." The one person who had been the most opposed to Toyota making passenger cars was spurring us on from his deathbed. "Toyota should no longer be making just trucks," Risaburo was saying. "Whatever you do, go out and make passenger cars!"' Risaburo died two months later, aged 68. Car making gained its new inspiration from the death of the founding father, Kiichiro.

Back then, in 1950, Eiji Toyoda's comments about Ford must have seemed a rather arrogant view for a young man from a small and sickly company. But Toyota began making cars and grew in confidence. By the mid-1950s, it had developed the Crown model, the first 'real' passenger car of its own. On New Year's Day 1955, Eiji Toyoda drove the first Crown off the line to applause and showers of confetti, watched by executives in morning coats. Rival Nissan had just introduced a new model, but it was based on the British Austin technology, and was both smaller and 150,000 yen more expensive than the Crown. The Crown quickly captured the popular Japanese imagination, with a deluxe whitewall-tyred version plus radio, heater, electric clock, tinted glass and fog lights for the small private-owner market.

Proudly, Toyota became carried away with the prospect of exporting to the USA, to show the old master that the young apprentice had learned its lessons well. This was high ambition given that Toyota was selling fewer than 2,000 cars a week in Japan and Eiji Toyoda's new small car, the Corona, had been almost a bomb. The common joke was that goldfish could live in the Corona when it rained. Nevertheless, Toyota executives said it was not just a matter of pride in building smart cars. They saw European cars making inroads in the American market and feared that, if they did not get a foothold soon, the USA might start to close the door on newcomers.

At first all went superbly well. There was great expectancy when the first two Crowns, one painted dark and the other light, left Yokohama on 25 August 1957 for Los Angeles. Miss Japan and Toyota executives in dinner jackets were on hand, along with many reporters and photographers, flashing away at cars that, so its instant fans said, looked like a baby Cadillac. Overjoyed Toyota Motor Sales president Shotaro Kamiya basked in calls from potential dealers and would-be owners, did quick calculations and sent a telegram off to headquarters in Japan asking for production to be increased to supply 100,000 cars a year to the American market. This was before Toyota had actually hit the road.

Sadly, instant fame quickly turned to instant notoriety as local officials examined the vehicles and declared that they would have to be modified considerably to meet California's safety standards before they could get certificates to go on the roads. When they did start the journey from Los Angeles to San Francisco, it was quickly apparent that the Japanese had not done their homework about US market conditions. The car's biggest handicap was its 1,500cc engine, which did not have the endurance or the high speeds essential on American freeways. Cars in Japan hardly had an opportunity to travel at 50 miles an hour because of the narrow, twisting and bumpy roads. Consequently, the engine began to knock and overheat.

Worst of all, Toyota discovered that the car was not at all efficient, and both oil and petrol consumption were high. Eiji Toyoda confessed that 'In retrospect, that first initiative of ours was very poorly thought out indeed.' But, he added, that was not a reason for giving up. The contrary: 'In fact, having this bitter experience behind us helped us work that much harder afterwards to build cars that were right for the US market.'

Now roll fast forward 35 years. Toyota is *the* standard for the world's motor car industry. It still commands a huge 33 per cent of its domestic market, so there is no question that it is the dominant player. The initial plant at Koromo has become part of Toyota City, a company town with ten of the factories located inside it and another two just outside. It has a major factory in the USA, which in March 1994 doubled its capacity to 400,000 cars a year. In addition, it has a joint venture with General Motors, through which Toyota turned round a hopelessly unprofitable GM plant to make it a success. It has a new plant in the UK at Burnaston in Derbyshire, which in 1995 will produce 90,000 cars, successfully completing the first stage of £400 million investment that is part of Japan's tutorial to the UK on the importance of manufacturing industry. Worldwide, Toyota employs 73,000 people. Japanese domestic production in 1995 will be about 3.4 million vehicles, of which 1.25 million will be exported. Overseas production will be almost the same as exports – the first year in which foreign production will match exports from Japanese factories. The conservative Toyota is the last of the major Japanese manufacturers with exports greater than overseas production.

On the world car-making map, Toyota is not the biggest, but it is the leader in terms of quality. Some sceptical Europeans question such a bold assertion, presenting BMW, Mercedes, Saab, Volvo or even Rolls-Royce as their paragons, but this is a measure of the blinkered view from 'Fortress Europe' and perhaps of Toyota's late manufacturing arrival in Europe, with the British plant opening only in 1992. In the USA, Toyota cars regularly win the coveted J.D. Powers awards for quality. When Eiji Toyoda's pet project, the Lexus luxury car, rolled off the production line in the late 1980s, the US auto analyst Maryann Keller sang its praises, saying that it showed that Toyota could not only produce quality mass production vehicles. Lexus, she commented, 'proved that a luxury performance car could be produced at mass-production costs. It turned the industry upside down.'*

In spite of the success story, plenty of questions now loom. US motor

---

* See her *Collision: GM, Toyota, Volkswagen and the Race to Own the 21st Century,* Doubleday, 1993.

car analysts claim – controversially – that Toyota's days as the world beater are numbered, thanks to the high yen and the revival of Detroit. In Europe, the company delayed its plans to double capacity at Burnaston. And in the third world, it may be handicapped by its conservatism and reluctance to set up new plants.

The Miyata plant on Kyushu is different from other factories in the Toyota empire, but such is the heavy investment that all plants are creatures of their time and place. Total investment at Miyata, including the 20 billion yen for the purchase of the 160 hectares of land, was 150 billion yen ($1.5 billion in early 1995 dollars). It was Toyota's first domestic plant to be built away from Aichi prefecture, where Toyota City headquarters is.

The investment decision was made in the heady days of the 'bubble economy' when the stock market and land values were going up and up, through the ceiling, beyond the sky and challenging the stratosphere, when economic growth was good and job-seekers were able to pick and choose what they would do and began to regard motor industry work as one of the 'three Ks' – *kitanai* (dirty), *kiken* (dangerous) and *kitsui* (demanding). Some people added two other Ks. *kurushii* (painful) and *kusai* (stinking). Whatever the reasons, Toyota perceived that workers were a scarce commodity. The Miyata plant was meant to be attractive to a local pool of workers and to be open to women too.

Eija Toyoda, chairman of the Kyushu company, boasts in the glossy brochure that 'Toyota Motor Kyushu was started with the aim of achieving harmony between people, society and nature ... born in the midst of the natural beauty of Miyata. We wanted to make it a place where people could enjoy working and relaxing; a beautiful facility that anyone could love, immersed in the area's natural beauty.' This, an outsider has to say, is pure hype. Public relations people are so easily carried away by the purple mists of their own prose.

The countryside around the plant is tolerably pretty, and on the journey there you can see egrets wandering through the paddy fields, or perhaps a kingfisher swooping across a river and triumphantly disappearing with its wriggling silver prey into a bamboo grove. But the Japanese have been too quick to plunder natural resources as they have tamed them, and even in Kyushu there are no free-running streams, since they have all been dammed, and electricity pylons and wires festoon the landscape as if a giant spider has been on the rampage. This is not the wild or natural beauty of the American Rockies or the Scottish Highlands.

Having made that warning, the Miyata plant is lean and mean and clean. Away from the thuds and trembling of the body-stamping shop, there are places where work goes on with such a quiet hum that you would not imagine you were in a factory. The streets of any Japanese town are a cacophony, a din, after this. And the factory floor is as clean as a whistle. The assembly line conveyor system is a new roller-friction type, much quieter than the standard chain version of most motor plants. On top of this, says Mikio Kitano, the engineer and Toyota director who helped set up the plant, 'We have tried to establish a new assembly concept, a people-centred factory that offers challenges and satisfaction to workers, in which the equipment is the partner of the members of the team.'* Instead of a single assembly line, there are eleven mini-lines, with work divided among teams of 20 to 25 employees under a group leader. Workers rotate between jobs to improve their skills and boost their motivation. Unlike most Japanese car plants, there are a number of women on the production line.

At any time, says Toyoto parent senior managing director Kenichi Kato, a worker may stop the production line by pulling a cord – like those on the old London Transport Routemaster doubledecker buses. This is now standard equipment in all Toyota plants. It is a device that other manufacturers have adopted with variations. For example, at Nissan in the UK, pulling the cord does not directly stop the line, but it alerts a supervisor to help make the decision; at Toyota the individual worker has the initiative to stop the assembly line. Buffer areas at the end of each mini-line mean that there is time for one to stop working for a few minutes without the whole assembly coming to a halt or cars stacking up. Another innovation at Miyata is a device allowing each individual worker to adjust the height of the platform by up to 60 centimetres to give a more comfortable working position.

Robots are increasingly being used in car making, albeit that they are disappointingly impersonal by the standards of children's comics – faceless and with no human features unless you count stick-like arms. But the whole object of the robots, say the Toyota executives, is to be the servants of the employees, to do the heavy and back-breaking work and take the strain off the humans. In Miyata's paint room, the sheet metal is immersed in anti-rust treatment, then the actual painting is done in a room completely free from dust, with three coats of paint applied by robots and automatic equipment. Welding is also done by 250 robots, which help to ensure smooth and swift assembly of the car body. The heavy tasks of stacking and transporting the bodies no longer need human help.

At Miyata, new robots are employed that are more and more intelligent: they not only lift the several ton load of engine plus axles, but fit it into the vehicle; they are able to distinguish between three types of vehicle body and can even tell whether the vehicle is front or rear wheel-driven. In other factories of other companies, the lifting is done by machine, but the assembly and the final screwing of nuts and bolts is done by the workers. The robotic assembly is so modern that Toyota forbade visitors from taking photographs of it.

This is an advance on the plant at Tahara in Aichi, three hours from

* In late 1994, Kitano went to the USA to take charge of Toyota's Kentucky plant.

Tokyo and surrounded on three sides by sea. It was specifically set up in 1979 as a highly automated plant, to the consternation of the accountants as the economic ice-age began to hit home. The abiding impression at Tahara, besides a cleanliness common to Toyota, is its spaciousness – an impression increased by the sight, from time to time, of a man on a bicycle riding to check a red warning light. An overhead central control panel shows a string of green lights that will turn to red if someone stops the assembly line because a problem has occurred. 'Any worker can stop the line at any time, and it is no disgrace to do so,' said Takeshi Sakakibara, Tahara's project general manager, explaining that Toyota's abiding commitment is to eradicate faults before they happen.

At Tahara it sometimes seems as if the robots rule the roost. They can carry their loads along pre-programmed routes from the stacking areas to the line. The loudest noise on the factory floor comes from tinkly versions of 'Für Elise' and 'Campdown Races' played by the robots warning humans to get out of their way. The robots at Tahara's number 4 assembly line, with the help of 197 humans, produce a car every 150 seconds. Tadaaki Jagawa, general manager and main board managing director, offered a variation on a familiar tune: 'The basic concept of the plant is to try to eliminate those jobs that are uncomfortable for the workers. A summary of my philosophy is that there should be more fun, more comfort and more sense of value brought to the process of assembly.' Jagawa admitted that the extra space, the additional electricity used and the heavier construction costs raised the cost of a vehicle by 3 to 4 per cent – worth it in bubble years so that Tahara could keep workers with itchy feet. But in 1993 Tahara shut down the entire number 2 assembly line – 'the first time for an entire Toyota plant to be shut down,' said Jagawa sadly.

The twin problems of the rising yen, making the export of Japanese cars more expensive, and threats of direct controls on those exports by foreign countries led to Toyota setting up plants abroad. It was slower to make the move than some of its rivals, reflecting the conservative management of Eiji Toyoda and his nephew Shoichiro, Kiichiro Toyoda's son, who was to succeed him in 1982 as president, then in 1992 as chairman. – It also reflected Toyota's dominance of the Japanese industry. Honda, founded by a maverick motorcycle maker, was the first to set up in the USA, but it was forced to be adventurous because of its domestic weakness (with about 10 per cent of Japan's auto market in 1994). Nissan followed suit and Toyota only began car-making operations in the USA in 1988 and in the UK in 1992.

For the Japanese giants, there was an immense problem to be overcome before they could operate comfortably abroad. Car production in Japan is based on close, almost family, relationships between the manufacturer and hundreds of parts suppliers. Yoh Kurosawa, president of Industrial

Bank of Japan, described Toyota and Nissan themselves as 'like the snow on the top of Mount Fuji, the visible part of Japan's car making, but they are supported by hundreds of suppliers and parts makers who are just as much part of the mountain, though not always so visible to the outsider'. Another important consideration is that in Japan the suppliers are physically close to the mother plant, a factor which helps to achieve the concept of 'just-in-time' deliveries, so that the plant itself can keep a matter of a few hours of inventories. This cuts the clutter of the car plant and reduces the costs.

These close ties, both geographically and in shareholdings, of course were impossible to replicate abroad. Toyota Motor Manufacturing (TMM) USA Inc.'s factory at Georgetown, near Lexington in Kentucky, was deliberately set up far away from America's traditional auto heartland, employs about 5,000 workers and turns out 400,000 cars a year. Fujio Cho, the Japanese president and one of only 60 expatriates at the plant, was proud that the company has recruited workers from all but a handful of Kentucky's 120 counties. A quarter of its workers are women and 13 per cent come from minorities, a higher percentage than the 7 per cent minority population of the state. He called his team 'my so excellent workforce' and noted that Toyota had more than 100,000 applications for the 3,000 jobs originally offered.*

Overall, Toyota has invested more than $2 billion in Kentucky as well as providing jobs for almost 200 parts suppliers from 32 states of America. A diagram of a Toyota Camry saloon made in Kentucky shows that the car wheels come from Kentucky, the tyres are made in seven different states, the steel for the body is supplied from four states, the drive shafts come from North Carolina, the cylinder heads from Missouri, the bearings from South Carolina and Iowa, the horns from Illinois, the airbags from Mississippi, the exhaust systems from Indiana, the radiators from Michigan, the catalytic converters from California, the glass and shock absorbers from Ohio and the windscreen wipers from New York.

It is, said Cho, an American car in any commonsense meaning of the word. By the end of 1994, 90 per cent of the steel used by TMM would come from the USA. Of the 174 US parts suppliers in 1993, 114 were 'traditional' US-owned companies, only 18 were owned by Japanese concerns, 7 were US companies bought by Japanese, 6 belonged to the Toyota group and a further 29 were joint ventures. The 'domestic content' of the cars coming off the Kentucky line is 75 per cent according to Cho, or as the company says, 'We use American workers, American manufacturing plants, American suppliers ... and $1.2 billion of American parts.' That was the 1992 figure and will double to more than $2.4 billion by 1995 when the expanded plant is fully operational.

* In late 1994 Cho went back to Japan as managing director in charge of public affairs.

When TMM started making the Avalon, a new large sedan for the American market, its initial local content was 75 per cent, and the vehicle was the product of much advice and expertise from the Kentucky plant's American suppliers and US technical experts. Exports from the USA of more than 30,000 vehicles a year have begun to be important, especially with the rise in the value of the yen. In addition, Toyota takes great pride in being a caring corporate member of the local community, contributing with cash and time to Kentucky events and causes.

The Kentucky plant is quite unlike any of Toyota's Japanese factories, for the simple reason that the workers are American. One of the managers laughed and commented, 'Yes, in Japan you can give a two- or three-hour lecture to Toyota workers, but here we fall asleep sooner.' The Americans come from a wider social spread and have a wider variety of education and experience than is found in the Japanese factories. 'They are not a quiet bunch,' said Sam Heltman, vice president of human resources and information systems. But he added with a great deal of pride, 'We have the best workforce that I have seen assembled anywhere because of the effort in working, the dedication to improve things.' American temperament means that managing involves more of a team effort, whereas Toyota Japan can get away with more of a top-down approach. It is quite clear that the 'John Wayne style of management', the troubleshooter who rides into town with all the answers, is not welcome at Georgetown. One of the proofs of the success of Toyota is that headhunters spend a great deal of time and are prepared to throw a great deal of money to tempt its experienced managers away from Kentucky.

President Cho contrasted the working styles of Japan and the USA. Japanese workers are more flexible, but those in the USA are excellent at standardisation. In America, decisions are taken more quickly, and 'sometimes many related departments don't know what has been decided'; whereas in Japan they are the product of slow consideration and consensus, which generally ensure that all the snags have been considered and dealt with first. 'Here, I need quick decision making, but I also need consensus,' said Cho, explaining the challenge that faced him.

Cho expressed his admiration for American workers. 'The US is still very strong in manufacturing because of the excellent workforce. In Japan the focus of responsibility gets blurred, but in America it is very clear. The great difference is that Japanese don't know how to make female workers work, whereas the US does. I wish I could take that aspect back to Japan. Before I came here, we had this stereotyped feeling that female workers were only good for filing work or making tea and other such tasks. Japanese are very strong at using tools, but cannot invent new tools, which is something that Americans are good at. Japanese use chopsticks, and with these two sticks can do everything; but in America they have a great variety of implements, like knives and forks and spoons, which offer new opportunities.'

Michael DaPrile, general manager manufacturing for TMM, was a 25-year veteran with General Motors, ending up as a general manager before he joined Toyota. He commented that 'At GM it depended on who you worked for: if you were not in line with the philosophy of that person, you were out.' He is clearly proud of what TMM has achieved, and indeed used the word 'elated' to describe the accomplishments. 'I think that the American workforce is the best in the world given the right environment and empowerment of the people.' The lesson that Toyota has taught is the importance of making the workers feel part of a family with common interests. 'If you lose people, you lose everything,' added DaPrile, a lesson which Toyota taught its first American partner GM in their Nummi (New United Motor Manufacturing Inc.) 50:50 joint venture, which in 1984 began making Toyota Corolla cars for GM's Chevrolet division.

The operation used an old GM factory at Fremont, California. Under the old system, employees were treated like 'human robots', expected to obey every order of their managers. The animosity between the two sides seems almost impossible to believe: it was not just a them-versus-us attitude which split the two sides; the plant was a battleground. The workers specified in their contract that they wanted telephone booths with extractor fans in them, but the management refused to supply electricity for the fans, claiming that the contract did not say that the fans had to work. To stop workers sitting on rubbish bins during their breaks, the management soldered nails on top of the bins. Workers stuck to the very letter of their highly detailed job descriptions, and there was a huge repair area set aside for defective cars.

The new deal that Eiji Toyoda hammered out for the Nummi factory had several revolutionary clauses for a GM workforce, including a no-strike clause, penalties for absenteeism and a reduction in the number of job classifications from a hundred to four; in return, the workers were given long-term job security and a voice in the way the factory operated, both unprecedented for a US auto factory. The initial deal was for twelve years, but in 1993 it was agreed that the joint venture, producing pick-up trucks as well as cars under GM and Toyota brands, and turning out more than 300,000 vehicles a year, would continue indefinitely.

The Georgetown factory builds on the Toyota lessons in car making and human relations, with a large open-plan office where even vice presidents sit, and general meeting rooms off the corridors rather than exclusive offices for managers. President Cho was dressed like many of the line workers in an open-necked dark blue Toyota shirt with a Toyota hat, which he took off as we spoke. He and the other managers are not remote, but familiar figures on the assembly line, checking and chatting about the progress of work and any problems. Equally important is the flow of ideas from the workers to the team and group leaders and managers about how the production process can be improved.

Two of the most attractive innovations pioneered in Kentucky and as of 1993 not yet featured in Japan, not even in Kyushu, were seats to help remove the backstrain of bending when installing wiring inside the car and when fitting and checking items on the wheels. The seat swinging the worker inside the car was a real hit, allowing the fitter to whiz in and out without strain. Altogether the number of suggestions received from workers at Georgetown has increased to more than 40,000 a year, or about nine per worker, ranging from simple things, like reducing the walk time to get a small part from three seconds to one, and rigging up a small light so that the worker can see what he or she is doing better.

But the most important factor is the quality of the cars. Toyota's in-house magazine boasted that, according to the J.D. Power quality survey of the best North American auto plants in 1993, Toyota Georgetown came out top with just 65 defects per 100 cars. Toyota in Cambridge, Ontario, was second with 71 defects, followed by a Ford plant, also in Ontario. There was only one small fact that spoiled the triumph – that the car with the fewest defects of all was not the Camry from Kentucky, but the Lexus LS 400 (only 54 defects per 100 cars), Toyota's luxury car made in Japan. Altogether, Toyota and Lexus had seven models in Power's 1993 top ten.

DaPrile said that it took 18.3 hours to build a car in Kentucky in 1993, though the target was to get it to 18. But he admitted sadly that, in Japan, the same car took only 16 hours. Kentucky still has a road to travel to match Japan. Cho said that the assembly line is good, but the real problems occur in the body-welding shops. 'We are using so many machines and maintenance is a problem,' he complained. 'If a machine breaks down, something that in Japan would be fixed in ten or fifteen minutes, here can take two hours.'

Toyota's British operations, Toyota Motor Manufacturing UK (TMUK), did not start producing cars until 1992, with the first car coming off the line in December of that year. By early 1994 the first phase of the £400 million plant was in full swing, with capacity of 100,000 vehicles a year, producing the Carina E model. As in the USA, Toyota chose to go far away from the traditional heart of car production in the country, and set up its factory in rural Derbyshire, 7 miles into the countryside south of Derby. Toyota president Tatsuro Toyoda in February 1994 declared himself satisfied with progress and said that the company wanted to move on to the second phase, another £300 million of investment to double capacity to 200,000 vehicles a year.

'The UK plant started up exactly according to our schedule and it has attained very high local content, producing 100,000 cars,' Toyoda said. 'We would like to double the capacity and we have already acquired a large piece of land to accommodate the factory expansion.' He added that what stood in the way was poor demand in Europe. Toyoda 'ardently desired' an end to the slump. He brushed aside any fears that Toyota might have difficulty selling its British-made cars as fully European vehicles. Restrictions on sales of Japanese cars in Europe did not apply to the British Toyotas. 'We are in a transition period during which levels of imported cars [to Europe from Japan] are being monitored. But those Toyota cars produced in our UK plant are cars made in Europe. The UK government has already made a strong assertion of that, and that has already been determined. We do not know that in some quarters, some people are saying that, although they are made in the United Kingdom, they are a Japanese brand and Japanese cars. But given the current local content level, I am confident that consensus will be reached that these cars are considered fully European.'

Generally, he was all smiles about the British factory. Other Toyota executives also expressed satisfaction with the quality of the Carina E models coming off the Burnaston line, but commented that productivity was still far below levels in Japan. When pressed to give an estimate of the shortfall, they replied that the British factory was 'about 80 per cent' of the mother plant. The 'local content' – defined in good European terms as coming from European suppliers – of the UK Toyotas reached 80 per cent six months ahead of schedule in 1994, as the company built up its list of 200 suppliers stretching from Wales and Scotland to Germany, to make the vehicle a truly European car. The engine for the Carina is also British-made at Toyota's £140 million engine plant at Deeside in Clwyd. The 300 employees there are turning out 200,000 units of the 1.6 litre engines a year, enough for the British Toyota and others for export, thus helping Britain's trade as well as contributing to the development of its industry. About 75 per cent of the Burnaston cars are exported, and with exports of engines and components, they contribute up to £500 million a year to Britain's exports.

In some circles in the UK, Toyota is seen as an important and possibly vital part of the rejuvenation of British industry. The brochure for would-be employees illustrates the demands that Toyota makes on its workers. 'Toyota is not just hiring "workers",' it states. 'We are hiring Team Members who will work together to accomplish tasks or a series of tasks. Every Member needs to be open to new ideas and challenges every day. You will be encouraged to listen, learn and understand not only your own but other members' jobs as well; to show patience; to express ideas. At Toyota we all need to adapt rapidly to changing conditions, and to work with or, on occasion, substitute for our colleagues. Toyota believes that teamwork is an essential part of the workplace. We have created a positive team spirit in the Company, as everyone knows that everything they do affects many other people in the Company. Company success is necessary for security and long-term prosperity for all Members. Quality is another key factor at

Toyota and góes hand in hand with teamwork. High quality standards start with every Member. All Members are expected to take part in quality discussions, to meet together and discuss ideas about quality. It is every Members' [sic] responsibility to correctly complete their job and only to pass on 100 per cent quality to the following process.'

Applicants for jobs with TMUK have to face a searching test and interview procedure that lasts more than 11 hours, including 4.5 hours each for tests and assessments, a 45-minute interview and a full 1.5-hour medical check. Surprisingly, in view of Japanese companies' supposed reluctance to deal with stroppy British trades unions, the British company states, 'We have developed a very good understanding and relationship with the AEEU and as a result we believe that it is in all Members' interests to join. However, it is not obligatory and there will be no difference in treatment of Members whether they are in the Union or not.'

Toyota's contributions to the international car-making industry are considerable. Had it not been for the Japanese invasion of what the American 'big three' automakers considered their backyard, it is unlikely that the Americans would have improved their efficiency, discipline and quality to be able to return to healthy profits in 1993. Honda, of course, was the first to take the American market by storm, but this was the maverick Soichiro Honda's typically cheeky response to being the weakest of the Japanese car makers at home. Toyota was the last because it was the strongest, but by 1995 it will be the biggest of the Japanese producers in the US market (counting its Nummi vehicles). Apart from the tribute of the J.D. Powers awards for quality, Eiji Toyoda's production system was dubbed in a 1990 book published by Massachusetts Institute of Technology as 'the machine that changed the world'.

The key factors contributing to Toyota's mastery can be summed up in four Japanese words – *jidoka, heijunka, kanban* and *kaizen*. 'Jidoka', as translated in common Japanese–English dictionaries, means 'automation', but that is the literal word-for-character translation of the three Chinese kanji that make up the common word. At Toyota, managers boast, they have added two small strokes to the central Chinese character to change its meaning slightly but importantly. The change is to add the abbreviated character for human being to the middle kanji normally meaning motion or movement: the character is thus changed to mean 'work'. Jidoka, according to the Toyota production system, then means 'investing machines with human-like intelligence'. 'Management and employees at Toyota share a very strong opinion about the role of machines and people in their production system,' said one director. 'They believe in using machines in ways that make life easier for employees. For that to happen, the machines must have a built-in capacity for detecting abnormal events and responding accordingly.'

The principle goes back to Sakichi Toyoda's looms that would stop automatically whenever a thread broke. The idea is that it is better to catch and remedy any defect before it passes through and is potentially magnified by the production process. It also reduces the danger of a complete batch of parts being defective. Toyota's workers co-operate with the machines in also identifying troubles or defects before they can pass along the line.

'Heijunka' means distributing work intelligently and efficiently, so that it can be done evenly and without bunching over the production schedule. 'The output of our plants thus corresponds hourly and even by the minute to the diverse mix of model variations that our dealers market every day,' said the company. Each motor car has about 2,500 parts. With multiple choices frequently available for colours, types of seat, steering wheels, covers and carpets, this means that Toyota has many thousands of different parts and components that may be fitted to its vehicles. By one estimate there are 75,000 different variations of parts that might be fitted to any single car model. Toyota even provided 32 different types of sound system on cars exported to America.

Heijunka is itself an important component of the 'just-in-time' production process for which Toyota is rightly famous. Car plants in Japan keep spare parts for only a few hours, knowing that they can rely on the suppliers to deliver just-in-time, neither too soon, which would mean parts piling up and costing warehouse space, nor too late, which would mean that production would have to come to a halt. One of the features of any Toyota factory anywhere is its uncluttered look: it does not have boxes of supplies littering the passageways. This means that the factories are more attractive places to work, but it also helps limit accidents and mistakes.

But this system would not work without the contribution of kanban. The Japanese word means 'signboard', and Toyota's kanban are nondescript printed pieces of cardboard sandwiched between clear plastic covers. They supply the essential information about which parts have been used in the production and should therefore be replaced. The system operates on the basis of a 'pull' method and is similar to those that supermarkets use to keep their shelves supplied with goods in the right type and quantity. This similarity is not surprising because the originator of the kanban method, Taiichi Ohno, got the idea in 1956 when he visited the United States and admired the way that supermarkets, then virtually unknown in Japan, were able to supply the merchandise required in a simple, efficient and timely manner. Toyota uses two categories of kanban: withdrawal kanban to secure additional parts to replace those that have been used; and production instruction kanban attached to parts sent out for the next stage of the production process.

All this helps the production line work smoothly, while accommodating the variety of choice that modern consumers insist on. Toyota developed some of the techniques because the production line that was Henry Ford's brainchild was too long and required too many cars to make it economical for more modest Japanese requirements; other stemmed from increasing consumer refusal to accept Ford's demand that a customer could have any Model-T that he or she wanted provided that it was black. But Toyota has gone further in developing the modern production line.

An equally important contributor to Toyota's superiority is kaizen. The company at least has a sense of humour in conceding that foreigners may be bored with all the talk of kaizen, which literally means 'improvement'. 'Three businessmen, an American, a Frenchman and a Japanese, get caught up in a revolution,' said a Toyota manager. 'The revolutionaries sentence them to a firing squad and grant each of them a last wish. The Frenchman asks to be allowed to sing a final chorus of "La Marseillaise". The Japanese asks to give a final lecture on kaizen. This proves too much for the American, who breaks down and pleads, "Then please shoot me first! I couldn't stand another lecture on kaizen." ' The Toyota executive added: 'But no company can have too much kaizen, for kaizen is the real dynamic of quality and productivity.'

At Toyota, kaizen involves everyone, but especially the shopfloor workers. At every Toyota plant everyone is always studying new ways to improve the workflow, measures great and small which will enhance the quality or reduce the waste. Sometimes these involve tiny precautions, like fitting a small strip of rubber on to door panels to prevent the danger of scratching; sometimes they are large improvements, such as the swing seat in the Kentucky plant, allowing the worker fixing the electrical wiring to swing in and out easily without straining his or her back.

The US and UK plants of Toyota are not the only foreign manufacturing operations, though the Kentucky plant is obviously the biggest and that at Burnaston offers the great hope of penetrating the vital European market from the inside. Altogether Toyota makes cars and car parts at 38 places in 24 countries outside Japan, including Canada, Brazil and Venezuela, Portugal and Germany, Indonesia, Pakistan and Thailand, Kenya and South Africa. Both president Toyoda and his brother chairman Shoichiro in separate interviews rejected the idea that Toyota was too conservative and slow in establishing foreign factories. Both take a rosy view of the future both for the international motor industry and for Toyota.

Chairman Shoichiro Toyoda bases his optimism on his essential claim that the motor car is a fact of daily life everywhere round the globe, and there is nothing that can successfully replace it, whether for going to work or to do the shopping or to play golf. 'Being optimistic might not the right word, but we think that the market for motor cars will continue to grow. There is no device to replace the automobile as a means to move around in a very convenient manner,' he said. 'Our philosophy is to contribute to the building of a more affluent society through making cars, and we want all the people in the world to benefit, so the future of the industry is bright and promising.' He admitted that in the early 1990s the economies of Japan, the USA and Europe were all depressed, but his faith in their future burns brightly. 'There is a business cycle, so there is a recession, but there will be a boom as well.' He pointed to the growing markets in south-east Asia as new booming markets of the future.

Nevertheless, in spite of this optimism, Toyota has a number of points of vulnerability. US motor car analysts in particular are already saying that the mid-1990s and early twenty-first century are witnessing the comeback of the American 'big three', especially the biggest of them all, GM. Even the Japanese press began to think this way when they saw Chrysler's dashing new Neon car and predicted that it would run away from the boring Japanese opposition. Critical American automobile magazine writers have begun to complain that design of new Japanese cars like Toyota's Avalon, launched on the American market in 1994, offer nothing new and are boringly the same as in the past.

Maryann Keller, one of the most respected of New York motor industry experts, declared that 'Japan's auto industry has certainly reached middle age ... and it has to prepare itself for much more volatile swings in production, as well as more formidable competition.' In her 1993 book, *Collision*, about the three major international players, GM, Toyota and Volkswagen, she questioned the appointment of Tatsuro Toyoda to succeed his elder brother Shoichiro as president and chief executive, on the grounds that he lacked his elder sibling's steely drive. But the American optimism that the 'big three' are latter-day phoenixes may be premature – and a warning note against premature US pride was sounded when the Neon was twice recalled for defects.

Time will tell, but Toyota executives say it is unfair to damn the younger Toyoda – 'a nice man' – before he's had a chance. The Toyoda family question is a sensitive one. More than one Japanese newspaper claimed that Tatsuro moved into the chief executive's job because he was the son of the founder. Toyota PR people asked me not to raise the family question with Tatsuro since it was 'too sensitive', but he himself had faced the criticisms head on at his first press conference. 'I don't think my being a Toyoda is the reason for my becoming president. I have no doubt that I was chosen because I have the right kind of experience. Allusion to nepotism is simply ludicrous.'

In the end, the question of the Toyodas and Toyota is an amusing red herring because the founding family holds fewer than 1 per cent of the shares. The next president will not be a Toyoda. Toyota is a big company, with many competent managers, including some members of the Toyoda family. (Two sons of Shoichiro are rapidly climbing the corporate ladder.)

The relevant questions are whether those managers are good enough to cope with rapidly changing times.

Toyota's weak points are its conservatism and its vulnerability to international trade and political pressures. Tatsuro Toyoda said he looked forward to the company producing six million cars a year by the turn of the century, of which 4.5 million would be made in Japan, a slight increase on the 1994 levels, and 1.5 million would be made abroad, a 50 per cent jump on the 1993 overseas production of just about one million. In its domestic backyard, Toyota is doubly vulnerable as the events of 1993 and early 1994 showed. Profits tumbled at the start of the 1990s as recession began to bite. In its financial year to the end of June 1994, Toyota's profits from its car-making operations plummeted by 25 per cent to 136 billion yen. Without a savage cost-cutting operation, Toyota might have gone into the red in its car-making operations. And the company was still waiting for an upturn after an unprecedented four successive years of falling profits. Its highest operating profits were in the year to June 1990, when it made 643 billion yen, more than 4.7 times the 1994 figure.

The reasons for the decline were obvious enough: recession in Japan cut into sales at home, while the rising yen made exports less profitable. In 1993 Tatsuro Toyoda admitted that car making was not profitable when the yen rose to 110 against the dollar. In 1994 trade frictions with the USA sent the yen to new heights against the dollar. In its overall operations Toyota was still healthily in the black, thanks to earnings from its massive cash mountain of billions of dollars. In the year to June 1994, profits before tax were 235.5 billion yen, with money from non-operating sources bringing in 199 billion yen. But even the total pre-tax profits showed a huge fall from the 837.8 billion yen profits in the bumper 1990 year. In strict financial terms, it may soon pay the company to stop making motor cars and do something else.

The 1994 results would have been worse and would probably have pushed the company's car-making activities into the red if Toyota had not reduced costs by a massive $1.5 billion. Indeed, underlining how serious the situation was, the (English) annual report that followed the results was entitled, 'How we saved $1.5 billion'. Among the changes were reductions in the number of models and the varieties of parts offered, along with examination of the strict testing standards and a new thrust to kaizen improvements on the assembly lines.* Equally important, much effort went into improving the productivity of white-collar workers in the offices, through reducing personnel by 20 per cent, getting rid of reams of paperwork by using computers, and reducing work hours by 10 per cent. In all, Toyota improved white-collar productivity by almost 30 per cent.

---

* In the financial year 1993/4, Toyota employees came up with 929,257 ideas for improvements, of which 99 per cent were implemented on the factory or office floor.

In its exhaustive re-examination of all its operations, Toyota discovered that its quality testing rules demanded that sunroofs must be opened and closed 1,500 times in a room where temperatures were 30 degrees below zero Centigrade. 'When we thought this through, we realised that in such low temperatures, few people would open their sunroof,' admitted a senior executive, 'so we saved money by reducing the test so that the sunroof is opened 500 times at minus 20 degrees.' Akihiro Wada, executive vice president, said that 'With excessive standards, we overengineered cars. We had a philosophy that as long as we made good quality vehicles, no matter how expensive they were, people would be satisfied.'

Toyota also found that one model of its cars had 21 different varieties of turn-signal switches; they were reduced to seven. A main model of car had 97 variations at the end of the 1980s, of which fewer than half accounted for 95 per cent of total sales. Japanese car makers have much room for manoeuvre in the efficient re-engineering of their vehicles to reduce the numbers of components and parts. Yoshifumi Tsuji, president of Nissan, admitted that the Chrysler Neon had advantages over Japanese cars: 'Where we would use five parts to make a component, the Neon has three; where we would use five bolts, the Neon body side was designed so cleverly, it needs only three.' One European design specialist working in Japan said it would be possible to reduce component costs by 40 per cent or more through better design and reduction of parts such as the Neon had achieved. Indeed, Toyota launched its RAV4 recreational vehicle in 1994, making it almost entirely from off-the-shelf parts used in other vehicles.

Executives also announced that they were taking up the challenge of making a simpler car. The target was a model made in Japan that would be competitive even if the yen rose to 80 against the dollar – or 30 per cent cheaper than the currently cheapest Toyota small car available. Japanese newspaper reports said the new car would be on the roads by 1998; Toyota itself said the start-up date was incorrect, but refused to say more. Some critical motor industry analysts sniffed that the reports were just headline-grabbing attempts and that such price reductions would not be possible.

Domestically, auto analysts believe, Toyota could improve its position by behaving more aggressively, seeking to capitalise on its strengths and fight hard against the competition – as any western company probably would. 'In any other country, Toyota would be using its strength and muscle as the biggest producer to dominate and bruise its competitors in a falling market,' said one experienced European analyst. 'The Japanese automobile market is surely too small to accommodate eleven vehicle manufacturers. But it's not the Japanese way to be brutal and force rivals out of business.' A briefing paper from the stockbroker Barclays de Zoete Wedd was confident that 'A higher level of capacity utilisation, a seemingly unassailable scale advantage, and a leaner and more efficient production system will allow Toyota to retain cost advantages which it can apply to reducing its debt, or, through more aggressive pricing, to crippling the opposition.'

But Tatsuro Toyoda deprecated the idea that Toyota would force any rivals out of the industry. In an interview early in 1994, he expressed his confidence that Japan could continue to support the present structure of vehicle companies. He pointed out that for all practical purposes Hino and Daihatsu were part of the Toyota group and Nissan Diesel and Subaru were linked with Nissan. On top of this Mazda has strong – and growing – links with Ford, so the eleven named vehicle makers in fact become six or seven. His optimism may be misplaced, however, especially if the car market in the late 1990s recovers only modestly, as many economists think it might. Japan's overall economic boom times are over, and demand for cars will no longer be as buoyant as in the 1970s or 1980s even when the county can shrug off its recession.

One problem is that Shoichiro Toyoda is chairman of Keidanren (the Federation of Economic Organisations), Japan's most powerful business body, and his brother, Tatsuro, is chairman of the Japan Automobile Manufacturers Association, so in consensus Japan they would feel inhibited from doing anything competitive enough to drive a rival out of business. One small indication of how Toyota felt impelled to toe the general line came shortly after Shoichiro took the Keidanren job: effective from 1995 it would change its financial year from a July to June period to the April to March wed by the rest of Japanese industry.

Toyota's second vulnerability is making so many of its cars in Japan, where labour costs are high and the company has to suffer the fluctuations of the yen. With the yen at 112 to the dollar, president Toyoda said that the company was 'comfortable'. He protested that on a purchasing power parity basis the yen should be at about 190 to the dollar, but added that 'stability in the exchange rate is the most important factor'. His comfort did not last long. The trade spat with the United States and rumours that President Bill Clinton and his hawkish economic advisers saw a rising yen as one way of choking off Japan's exports were sufficient to send the yen rising to the 102–5 range, and then through the 100 barrier. At various times in 1994, most foreign economists in Japan were predicting the imminent weakening of the yen to the 110–15 range, but it did not happen. At rates of 100 against the US dollar, Japanese car makers will find it expensive to export cars against the competition of German and American companies with more stable currencies.

Political pressures are likely to continue to squeeze the Japanese. Clinton is showing himself to be a US nationalist in his anxiety to reduce his country's trade deficit, and cars and car parts are among his top targets. It is easy to sympathise with the Japanese: the Americans, for all their protests about 'closed Japanese markets', did not take the pains to study the Japanese market that Toyota, Nissan and Honda had to suffer in the USA. Toyota has been there since 1957, built up its own dealer network and opened its own plant as a price for challenging Chrysler as the third biggest car seller in the USA.

When Eiji Toyoda ordered studies to be done for his dream product of the Lexus luxury car, Toyota executives staked out upscale Los Angeles restaurants, talked to hotel and restaurant doormen, and quizzed Cadillac dealers, all to examine the demands of customers of luxury cars. By this test the US 'big three' were models of arrogance in their expectations of Japan – it was the early 1990s before a US company decided to bring out a right-hand-drive car for Japan, where driving is done on the left. Nevertheless, American pressures were paying off: Toyota agreed in 1993 to sell 20,000 GM US-made Chevrolet Cavalier cars from 1996 under the Toyota brand name. This was a major gesture, since the Cavalier will compete with Toyota's own Corolla. But it may not satisfy the American political pressure for targeted inroads into Japan.

One way of showing how much the big Japanese car-makers were hurting, and how much ground the 'big three' had recovered, is to look at the acid test of the financial results. By late 1994, the Americans were twice to three times as profitable as Toyota, while Nissan was heavily in the red and – sign of the turning tide – Mazda was pleading for Ford's help to rescue it. Expectations in Mazda's hometown of Hiroshima were that Ford, with a 24.5 per cent stake in Japan's fifth biggest car maker, would soon take over its management. Mazda had taught Ford all about small cars and still supplies the technology for popular Ford models like the Escort, but by 1994 Mazda's $294 million losses in the six months to September were the best sign that the Japanese are no longer invincible but on the rocks. Another acid test is the price of cars, where the high yen by 1994 gave the big Americans a huge $2,000–$3,000 price advantage over cars made in Japan. Table 5.1 (overleaf) shows results converted to dollars at the time of the announcement.

In Europe, the slump in the car market hit Toyota badly. Quota restrictions negotiated with the European Union put strict limits on exports from Japan to key markets. The British Burnaston plant went into production just as the European market entered recession, and progress was clearly slower than Toyota hoped. In December 1994, managing director Yukihisa Hirano set a target of 90,000 for production in 1995, below the original 100,000, but rejected speculation that the second phase of the plant's expansion to 200,000 cars would be delayed.* Expansion to produce 130,000 to 140,000 vehicles a year is necessary to put the UK plant into profit. Concentration on the USA had also hurt the luxury Lexus in Europe, especially against competition from Mercedes and BMW.

---

* In March 1995 Toyota finally announced it would spend an extra 7200 million to bring production to 200,000 cars a year by adding the Corolla series from autumn 1998.

Table 5.1   *Pre-tax profits, 1990–4 ($ million)*

	1990	1991	1992	1993	1994
Chrysler	147	−810	934	3,838	4,199
Ford	1,495	−2,587	−127	4,003	6,570
GM	−2,217	−5,862	−3,333	2,575	5,991
Honda	1,054	934	981	796	435
Nissan	1,576	907	1,248	−509	−1,877
Toyota	5,695	5,178	3,257	2,691	2,228
Fiat	2,604	1,276	666	−879	442
Peugeot	2,585	1,502	805	457	n.a.
Renault	253	728	1,193	193	297
Volkswagen	1,480	1,076	386	−990	32

Note: With US car companies, 1994 results are first nine months; for Japanese, except Toyota, all figures are years to March; Toyota is year to June; for European makers, 1994 results are first six months.

In Japan in 1993 more than 20,000 Lexus were sold, and in the USA almost 24,000, but in the UK a mere 1,100 Lexus took to the road.*

The Toyota way forward is to step up its production abroad. In late 1994 it announced that production in Canada will be more than doubled to 200,000 cars a year by the late 1990s. By 1996 more than half of Toyota's cars sold in North America will be made there. In addition, by the end of the century about 100,000 Toyotas a year will be exported *from* North America *to* Japan. But the awkward flip side of this is that exports from Japan will fall, and Toyota will have to struggle to keep Japanese factories employed.

Toyota's conservatism also showed in the president's comments about the two potentially biggest markets in the world: China, where an economic boom is already steaming ahead; and India, where the government in the early 1990s began dismantling the controls which had held back the economy for decades. Toyota has a tie-up with a company in Shenyang, and its associate Daihatsu is assembling cars, but both of these are small ventures, nothing like full-scale Toyota production. President Toyoda said in early 1994 that 'At this point there are too numerous uncertainties in China and its infrastructure, especially the road network, remains

---

* The 1995 US price of the Lexus was $51,200 plus another $2,120 luxury tax, while in the UK it was £42,900. When Lexus hit the road in 1989, rival European luxury car manufacturers had a grumble – that when driving at speed, you had to look at the tachometer to see if the engine was running, but drivers wanted to feel and hear the engine.

underdeveloped. Issues such as intellectual property rights need to be clearly defined. We have been asking the Chinese government about them.' He was also negative about India, saying 'It is a very difficult country in which to work, and unfortunately there is no indication that the Indian market is going to grow rapidly in the near future.' Toyota has an assembly plant in neighbouring Pakistan which has a population only a sixth the size of India's and is at roughly the same stage of economic development.

Later in 1994 Toyota was singing a slightly different tune. As president Toyoda visited China, a company spokesperson spoke of 'our ambitions for the Chinese market', and Toyoda himself said, 'our chances of being selected as a joint-venture partner [in China] are good'. By late 1994 the hopes had grown and Toyota had devised plans to build a car in China with an engine of 1,500–2,000cc to complement the Daihatsu 1,000–1,300cc cars already being built.

For all the undoubted weak points, Toyota still has great strengths lacking in other car makers. By common consent, even among the most patriotic US auto analysts, it was the Japanese, and particularly Toyota, which taught Detroit the way to revive their depressed factories. In spite of the gloom, Toyota still demonstrates a dedication to be the best, which was lacking in the dog days of American and British car making when unions and management were at each other's throats. The 1993 Toyota report that asked for cutting of costs went on: 'But never compromise on quality. And keep making it better, and better still.'

The emphasis on superior Japanese quality was driven home in a 1994 study of car parts makers which found that the Japanese retained 'only' a 30 per cent advantage over US makers, but had a four to one advantage over those in France and Germany, and at least eight to one over parts makers in the UK and Italy. Japanese components makers outperformed those in the UK by two to one in productivity and 100 to one in quality.*

When it announced its profits for the six months to December 1994, Toyota showed how formidable it was. Although the continued appreciation of the yen bit another 40 billion yen from its earnings, and sales had risen by a paltry 2.1 per cent, the parent company announced a massive 834 per cent rise in its operating profits to 87 billion yen, the first turn-round for five years. Pre-tax profits were up more modestly by 79 per cent to 149 billion yen.

Henry Ford is supposed to have said that if you build a better mousetrap, the world will beat a path to your door. Without the damage done by the

* Worldwide Manufacturing Competiveness Study, done by Professor Dan Jones, co-author of *The Machine that Changed the World*, Cardiff Business School, Cambridge University and Andersen Consulting. Altogether 71 components plants in nine countries were studied, though none was identified by name.

soaring yen, it is doubtful whether anyone would be talking of the demise of Japan as a motor car maker. Toyota executives still like to quota Kiichiro Toyoda in expressing their continuing dedication to quality: 'An engineer who does not oil his hand every day cannot rebuild our industry.'

6

From Brobdingnag to Lilliput:
Toshiba

Just after he took over as president of Toshiba Corporation in 1992, Fumio Sato played *shogi*, a kind of Japanese chess, against a legendary master, Yasuharu Oyama, and almost beat him. Asked where he went wrong, Sato replied, 'I was thinking too many moves ahead.' In business, Sato has the almost impossible tasks of having to think and plan and commit investment for several years ahead, while juggling with immediate plans battered by financial stringency, recession, the high yen and falling profits. Additionally, the world he faces is changing so fast technologically that – rather like the Red Queen in *Alice Through the Looking Glass* – Toshiba has to run as fast as it can to stay in the same place. But economic growth is so slow that it is not generating the profits to allow an athletic pace. Sato himself admitted that there will have to be big changes in the way Toshiba and Japan do business.

Toshiba has a special place in Japan's industrial structure. In the archives of what is now called Toshiba Corporation is a document which the company executives handle with a special pride – it is a letter from American inventor Thomas Edison expressing his thanks and happiness that Toshiba was using technology that Edison pioneered in making electric light bulbs. Toshiba is Japan's oldest industrial company and in most ways one that is archetypically Japanese. In spite of this, it has a long history of forming strategic alliances with leading foreign companies. Its roll call of partners includes General Electric, IBM, United Technologies, Motorola, Siemens, Ericsson, Olivetti and Time Warner. Until now it has also been lucky enough to have its specially protected and preserved Japanese fields of interest. In the future, Toshiba may need all its skills to fight off competition coming from home, from abroad and from the challenges of a shrinking economy. In 1995 Toshiba began to take on Sony in a battle for world dominance in digital video discs.

Like other distinguished Japanese giants, Toshiba is almost a mini-conglomerate, involved in a wide variety of businesses, from making common household items sold through Japan's corner 'Mom 'n' Pop' stores to producing the very latest technology, including computer chips, personal computers and highly specialised equipment for offices and hospitals. It means having to keep up with the latest changes in fad and fashion as well as the cutting edge of technology, understanding what the 'with it' teenager and modern housewife want, as well as designing the latest generations of computer chips and flash memories that will shape the world of the twenty-first century, and making devices that can pack millions of pieces of information into an area no bigger than a pin-head. On top of all this, Toshiba is also one of Japan's three giant producers of heavy-duty equipment that is the backbone of power stations. Straddling these several very different worlds will take all the imagination, energy and financial resources that the company can muster.

What is now Toshiba extends its roots back to the nineteenth century, when Japan had restored the Meiji emperor to the throne and was just starting the battle to catch up with the West and develop a modern economy. The single individual whom Toshiba regards as its founder was Hisashige Tanaka, an enterprising inventor who set up a telegraphic equipment manufacturing plant in 1875, later to be called Shibaura Engineering Works. Fifteen years later, Ichisuke Fujioka and Shoichi Miyoshi established a company to make electric lamps, which in 1899 was renamed Tokyo Electric Company. In 1939 the two companies, Tokyo Electric and Shibaura Engineering Works, merged to form Tokyo Shibaura Electric Company, even then popularly known as Toshiba from the first syllables of the names of the two companies, though it was not until 1978 that Toshiba was formally registered as the company name.

Toshiba's science institute in Kawasaki, only twenty minutes by fast train from the centre of Tokyo, provides a fascinating glimpse of the company's past and present production. There are models of an Edison lamp; the first Japanese refrigerator, a huge battered box with a bulky electrical plant on the top; an early washing machine, just a rusting tub on legs with wheels, with a hand-driven wringer on top; and a television set, a tiny pale monochrome screen set in a vast box with speakers on either side. Tokyo Electric in 1921 developed the coiled-coil incandescent bulb, one of six major electric light inventions. Three years later, it produced Japan's first radio receiver, and in 1928 it began research into television. It was the first company to begin marketing Japanese-made washing machines and refrigerators in 1930, and a year later it put on sale Japan's first vacuum cleaner. Shibaura Engineering meanwhile had its own firsts, including, in 1913, Japan's largest generator, a 6,250-kVA, three-phase hydroelectric generator, and in 1915 it began Japan's manufacture of X-ray tubes.

After the companies had combined to form Toshiba, the latter's progress was interrupted by war. But in 1949 it began manufacturing black and white television sets, and three years later it completed Japan's first television transmitting equipment to ensure the successful telecasts inaugurated by NHK (Nippon Hoso Kyokai, Japan Broadcasting Corporation, a public broadcasting service similar to the British Broadcasting Corporation) the following year. It was Toshiba that delivered the first Japanese-designed digital computer – the TAC – to the University of Tokyo, a huge monster of a thing with much less power than today's tiny laptop personal computers made by the millions by the company. Later, in 1957, Toshiba produced Japan's first domestic transistor radio, and two years after that the first colour television set. The start of the 1960s saw microwave ovens, transistorised television sets, Japan's first 12,500-kilowatt nuclear turbine generator and transmitting equipment for space communications.

Away from its historical section, the science institute shows modern products, some of them frivolous, others almost offering a glimpse into the future. There is an electronic parrot. From a distance it looks like a real multicoloured bird in a cage, but close up you can see that it is a robot with a beak and beady eye true to life, and its feathers are made from various types of electronic component. It is not totally useless. If you go over and say something to the 'bird', it will mimic your voice and make corresponding gestures. There is an electrostatic generator, which if you put your hand on it, literally makes your hair stand on end. Toshiba also displays a popular electronic height and weight measuring indicator, which can provide a person's gross height and weight at the same time without anything touching his or her body.

Another amusing feature which combines elements of the toy and useful modern electronic devices is a full-colour computer simulation machine. This allows a picture to be taken, displayed immediately on a computer screen, then played with almost as will – for example, recolouring the hair to any colour of the rainbow, adding moustache or beard, altering eye shape or colour, and changing features. The result can then be printed out within minutes. The machine can be used for police photofit simulation, or in publishing work, or just to create a new-look person with the distinguishing features of his or her dreams. Changing a balding, middle-aged Japanese into a blue-eyed person with a mop of bright red hair took just four minutes.

Other products on display at the institute include various kinds of robot. As in motor car factories, they look nothing like the humanoid robots of science fiction. Instead, they are just like spindly detached limbs. But some of them can work as freely as any human arm or as nimbly as any finger, using six axes. Normally they are used for assembling products at factories, but at the institute the arm robots show off traditional Japanese skills like fighting with swords, while the finger robots conduct dancing trigonal glass tips on a stage showing off a light and colour display of the four seasons. Besides displays of scale models of Toshiba plants, including a boiling water nuclear reactor power plant, a 4-megabit memory integrated

circuit including 8.7 million elements on one chip, and a magnetic res-
onance imaging system used for hospital diagnosis, there are also doll's
house models of the homes of the future, in which controls are worked
by computers that can react to the human voice. There is also an instamatic
camera that takes your picture and tells your fortune at the same time.

Toshiba's new president Sato in 1992 and 1993 conducted a major reorganisation of the company's activities to create four main business groups:
information and communications systems; electronic devices; heavy electrical apparatus; and consumer products and others. By share of sales,
information systems and electronic devices together accounted for 49 per
cent of Toshiba's total sales of 4,631 billion yen ($46.3 billion) in the year
ending in March 1994. Heavy electrical apparatus comprised 25 per cent,
and consumer products contributed 26 per cent to sales.

There is a world of difference between the plants where the nuclear,
thermal and hydroelectric energy equipment is produced, and those
responsible for making personal computers and the integrated circuits
that drive the office and factory machines now and into the future. Going
across Tokyo from the Keihin Heavy Engineering Factory to the Ome
'intelligent' works where computers are made is like Gulliver travelling
from Brobdingnag to Lilliput. At Keihin there are massive generators and
turbine blades which literally dwarf any human worker standing alongside
them. Some of the equipment weighs up to 3,000 tons; the assembly lines
are high and vast and governed by massive overhead cranes required to
shift the various pieces of equipment from one point to another.

Toshiba is the biggest of the giant Japanese power-station makers, just
ahead of Hitachi and Mitsubishi Heavy Industries. The Keihin plant, which
extends over half a million square metres by the waterfront, with splendid
views across Tokyo Bay and the new bridges linking it and Yokohama
port, is reached by some of Japan's old-fashioned trains. Altogether 4,300
workers produce turbines of up to 1,000 megawatts, generators, trans-
formers and condensers for conventional power stations. The works also
is responsible for total assembly of nuclear power plants, and executives
proudly boast that Toshiba nuclear plants 'have never been involved in
any accident or incident' – even in the Kobe earthquake.

In the 30 years from 1960, Toshiba produced an accumulated output of
80,000 megawatts of turbines for all kinds of power stations comprising
1,500 sets. It can make 1,100-megawatt nuclear steam turbines and 700-
megawatt tandem-compound and 1,000-megawatt cross-compound
machines for fossil power plants, which are the largest steam turbines in
Japan. Toshiba is producing a 40-inch titanium blade for the turbines,
bigger than the 33.5-inch previous maximum. The workers pride themselves on the fact that, although the machinery is big and heavy, the

blades are delicate and precision engineered for smooth fitting and most efficient work.

Altogether 95 per cent of the workers are men and only 5 per cent women. Surprisingly, 58 per cent of the total workforce is employed in offices. Most of the shopfloor workers are high school graduates who joined Toshiba at the age of eighteen and are given a year's on-the-job training, consisting of lessons, lectures and training in key technical skills, such as welding, working on machinery, operating lathes, fastening bolts and, surprising to relate for such massive power projects, important hand finishing operations. After a few years on the job, there are provisions for workers to upgrade their skills with a further one year schooling involving lectures and practical tests. Almost all the workers had a badge on the left sleeve marking the 'three ups' campaign. 'Not give up,' said one of the managers, trying a joke, 'but they mean image up, morale up and clean up, since we must have a clean factory.' 'We do not apply mass production techniques here,' said another of the managers. 'We are making 100 per cent order-made products.' There was a lot of proud love involved as the workers showed off their final gleaming products.

The output figures for Toshiba's heavy energy production show considerable year-to-year fluctuations, depending obviously on demand for power plants. The Japanese government had originally expected to build more and more nuclear power plants by now, but pressure from environmentalists had slowed the programme down and contributed to slower order books. In some years, up to 30 per cent of output was exported to countries as far away as Brazil and Bangladesh, but in the early 1990s export output dropped to 10 per cent, obviously hurt by the strength of the yen.

Some managers are worried about modern trends. 'Japanese industry has maintained its lead by keeping the highest levels of quality,' said one of the executives. 'This has been done mainly by having the highest levels of labour.' But he noted with alarm that modern Japanese high school graduates wished to avoid jobs they considered dirty or hard work or painful, and migrated instead for white-collar office jobs that are considered cleaner and more attractive to future brides. 'Hereafter I am not sure whether we can maintain these high standards,' the manager added.

The difference in scale between Keihin and Ome is marvellous to see. At the heavy engineering plant, the machines overpower the men; at the electronics factory, the workers are many times bigger than the tiny computer chips they are nimbly assembling to turn into the latest personal computers. Most of the factory workers on the assembly line at Ome are women, in contrast to the men who dominate at Keihin. The emphasis is on cleanliness throughout the factory, and all the workers wear Toshiba caps to keep their hair back. At various stages of the assembly line, the products go through a blower device to keep any minute specks of dust from interfering with the smooth process.

At one section, however, even these high standards of cleanliness are not sufficient. The clean room at Ome looks as if it is staffed by creatures from another planet, but they are ordinary humans clad from head to toe in protective clothing. Before entering the room, the worker has to put on a protective suit, long boots, tight rubber gloves (with tags showing they were made in England by the London Rubber Company) that extend over the arms of the suit, a cloth helmet covering the head and neck, and a gauze face mask. Kitted up like this, the only parts of the flesh left exposed are the eyes and part of the forehead. But before actually being permitted to enter the clean room, the worker has to go into a small ante-chamber where, once the doors are tightly closed, he or she will be sprayed with air to remove any intruding dust particles from the suit or tiny bits of exposed flesh. It is like having a shower, but the nozzle sprays fierce air rather than water. I was permitted to go through the experience, the first foreign journalist, Toshiba said, it had ever permitted into the clean room. Being blasted with air was not unpleasant, and gives a refreshing feeling of being thoroughly cleansed. Inside the clean room, the air is constantly purified to less than five microns per unit of air, against more than a million microns in the ordinary atmosphere. A micron is a tiny particle of dust, much smaller than the eye can see.

Some parts of the processes require even purer air than the clean room in general, so they are done under even more special dust-free conditions with strictly filtered air. The air quality in the clean room and the processes are all controlled by computer. Partly for this reason, although I was allowed in the room, photographs were strictly prohibited, both from inside with a properly dusted camera and even from outside, lest pictures betray the secrets of Toshiba's holy of holies.

The company boasts that it uses a computer-integrated management system at the Ome works. This means that computers integrate and control all stages of the operations, from design through manufacture to production control resource management, testing, shipping and marketing of the goods. The actual flow of the production lines is controlled by computer and responds to orders from customers. The company says that 'the system keeps alert to the market scene, never allowing the works to be caught unprepared when an order comes in. No one can predict if a certain product will sell well, so the computer-integrated management system waits for confirmed orders before it sets the system to "go". This intelligent production-controlled system responds quickly to market demand, which means that you can always rely on Toshiba's promptness.'

Akira Saito, the manager of international production planning for personal computers at the Ome works, said that Toshiba is a 'totally integrated company', something which helps to shorten the lead time from design to product, as well as creating more value added and ensuring that the hi-tech components have flexibility in design. In the final assembly of computers, the human touch allows flexibility, which can be important, whereas in the trickier printed circuit boards, assembly is done entirely by machine because automation adds strength. Other procedures such as hard disk assembly are semi-automatic.

The Ome managers say that their research and development staff work in close harmony with Toshiba's leading research and development institutes throughout the world. These include one at Cambridge in England headed by Professor Michael Pepper, who also holds a Physics chair at the university's world-famous Cavendish Laboratory. The company has other R & D facilities at Irvine in California and at Princeton. 'Toshiba is a very warm company in which the human network is very important. We try to bridge each science discipline,' said Akinobu Kasami, director of the R & D centre, altogether embracing eight laboratories. He contrasted this approach with that at rival Hitachi, where, he claimed, the priority was the personal work of the individual scientist and what he or she put first.

The decision to fund the research lab at Cambridge looked as if it was beginning to pay dividends – in kudos if not in cash – in October 1994 when Michael Pepper announced an important breakthrough on the road to the next but two or three generation of computer chips. Pepper and his Toshiba team declared that they had actually been able to develop a process for producing chips that will be somewhere between 500 and 1,000 times faster and 1,000 times smaller than existing silicon ones. One excited scientist claimed that commercial development of the breakthrough chip would vastly shrink the size of computers and enable the processing power of a present-day personal computer to be packed into a device 'the size of a small mobile telephone or even a wristwatch, given that big battery power would not be needed'.

What Pepper has achieved at Toshiba Cambridge is a workable process for building quantum effect integrated circuits exploiting the wave-like properties of electrons at an atomic level. Instead of modifying a layer of silicon or gallium arsenide by implanting or diffusing impurities (as happens with conventional silicon chips), Pepper used molecular beam and vapour phase epitaxy to grow semiconductor materials, one atomic layer at a time, and introduce impurities in the process. Apart from allowing the creation of tinier devices, this technology will permit the use of new concepts of operation that come at near-atomic dimensions.

The development comes at a time when the conventional silicon chips are reaching their practical limits. The latest 64-megabit dynamic random access memory (DRAM) chips about to go into widespread production in 1995 are less than a centimetre across and contain 140 million devices. Researchers at big computer companies all over the world are already working competitively to be the first to produce the much more powerful next generation 256-megabit chip – and may spend up to $1 billion each in development costs – and this will be followed by the 1-gigabit chip.* Already, however, there are problems. Pepper commented, 'The optical systems used to define integrated circuit features are reaching the limits of resolution, set by the wavelength of light. Although the diffusion control can be very shallow, it lacks dimensional control and smoothness of potential.' The absolute barrier may come somewhere between 4 and 10 gigabits.

The new quantum chip which Pepper has made in the laboratory uses components no more than 10 atoms across – or 100,000 times thinner than a human hair – and such a chip could contain 1,000 billion memory cells, switching at 1,000 billion times a second, with the additional advantage of using virtually no power, whereas today's computer chips drain batteries. Pepper is not yet boasting that the quantum chip will be available next year or even early in the twenty-first century. The snag is that, although he and his researchers have shown the potential to make quantum chips, they have only done it at very low temperatures, close to absolute zero. He estimates that it may take fifteen years or more before the processes can be developed to make the chips at close to room temperature, to enable commercial production.

What is interesting is that Toshiba has been prepared to take the plunge and back fundamental research at leading foreign universities, in the hope that it will pay off in the distant future. Pepper and his team of fourteen, which will probably grow to thirty scientists by the end of the decade, are involved in research which will not result in practical applications for years to come. The research centre works closely with the semiconductor physics group of the Cavendish, and, judging by Toshiba's publicity materials, the Japanese company is proud to be associated with a famous university laboratory that saw the discovery of the electron, splitting the atom and pioneer work in discovering DNA. It is ironic that the Japanese have been quickest to join hands with university labs, leaving British companies behind.†

Toshiba spends just over 6.7 per cent of its consolidated net sales on research and development, amounting to 312 billion yen or more than $3 billion in a year. Kasami explained that the time span depends on the nature of the research. Corporate laboratories at the R & D centre carry

---

* In early 1995, Toshiba's Japanese rival NEC announced it had made a prototype 1 gigabit chip, though commercial production is still years away.

† Pepper added that his work might stimulate improvements in conventional technology, and indeed Toshiba claimed a breakthrough in making the world's first experimental transistor with a gate length of just 0.04 microns; technically this should make it feasible to produce 100-gigabit memory devices.

out basic research with a five- to ten-year time horizon; development laboratories operate on product-oriented technologies with a three- to five-year framework and are attached to an individual business group; the results from these laboratories become new products and models at the divisional engineering departments found at all Toshiba manufacturing plants.

The laboratories are divided into four main business groups: information and business systems; information equipment and consumer electronics; power systems and industrial equipment; and electronic components and materials. In addition to the R & D centre itself, there is one other corporate laboratory, the manufacturing engineering research centre, which develops manufacturing technologies widely used throughout the company. There are three points that Toshiba tries to achieve, said Kasami: 'how to deepen the technology; how to integrate the technology; and how to educate the scientists'.

President Fumio Sato quoted a former Toshiba president, Kisaburo Yamaguchi, who 'once said that a manufacturer without R & D facilities is like an insect without antennae. Strong technological capabilities provide the basis, the driving force, for corporate growth. This means that the ability to create innovative products is a key factor determining corporate strength in this severe business climate.' Sato also tied R & D into Toshiba's slogans of 'the three Gs' and 'E & E': 'R & D also plays an important part in our "three G" policy, covering Growth, Group and Global. To achieve growth, we have to direct our resources to facilitate expansion in promising areas. Our group policy is geared to enhancing group R & D and so strengthening the overall capabilities of Toshiba group. Our global target is continued promotion of globalisation, including expansion of overseas R & D and production. Here, we are also pursuing greater localisation in the management of our overseas subsidiaries and realising our policies for competition, co-operation and complementarity through global alliances with major international companies.

'Our business interests are very diverse, ranging from information and communication systems and electronics devices to heavy electrical apparatus and consumer products. We see our field as "Electronics and Energy" from which we have derived the Toshiba slogan "E & E". We carry out research in the wide variety of technologies required to support E & E.'

Toshiba has been prepared from time to time ruthlessly to discard some of its old products, or to commit large-scale resources in a desperate search for a new breakthrough. As one small example of the junking of old products, the Toshiba museum proudly boasts Japan's first tape-recorder and old-fashioned steam radios, but you will not find any tape-recorders or radios in Toshiba's present range. It bowed to the superiority of Sony and no longer makes them. Indeed, quietly in 1992 the company pulled out entirely from making radio-cassettes, compact disc players and all kinds of audio equipment. It was done without fanfare or closing of factories or sacking of people. Instead the workers involved were brought into Toshiba's television and video business as its name disappeared from hi-fi stores all over the world.

Conversely, the greatest recent gamble was to go for broke to produce 1-megabit DRAM semiconductor chips. At the time that the decision was taken, in the early 1980s, Tsuyoshi Kawanishi, who retired as senior executive vice president in 1994, recalled that 'Toshiba was struggling to produce the 64-kilobit DRAMs that were then the mainstay of the computer memory market.' Struggling was the correct word. Toshiba executives admit that their company was widely whispered by competitors to be backward, and there was newspaper gossip about how long it could remain in the semiconductor game at all.

The sums of money needed were huge. But Kawanishi, who had just been appointed to lead Toshiba's semiconductor business, asked then president Shoichi Saba and got a 32 billion yen promise in the president's 1982 address, with the pledge that 'the industrial revolution in eighteenth-century Europe was a revolution in mechanical power replacing human force. From now on, I believe, semiconductors will become the driving force replacing mechanical power of the first industrial revolution. Semiconductors are vital for further development of Toshiba as a whole; for our industrial electronics business as well as for consumer electronics, and for heavy electrical apparatus business.' With typical Japanese ingenuity, Saba and Kawanishi initiated 'project W'. Let Toshiba explain in its tortuous English: 'The W symbol was made up of 2 Vs: one for victory in making semiconductors a mainstay of Toshiba, the other for value added to Toshiba products by the incorporation of company-developed semiconductors. Their combination in a W pointed the way to the company's goal: worldwide success.'

In 1983 Toshiba invested even more money in the new semiconductor, 97 billion yen, about 35 per cent of its total capital investment for the year. It was February 1985 before the company revealed that it had developed a prototype 1-megabit DRAM. But two crucial decisions had to be made. The first concerned whether the structure should be N-Mos (negative channel metal oxide semiconductor) or C-Mos (complementary). Unusually, Toshiba set two research teams against each other to test the structures. After evaluating the results, the company decided to go against the industry trend and adopt a C-Mos structure.

The second choice was whether to adopt a 'planar' or 'trench' structure. Research engineers preferred the trench structure, but the production people pressed for the planar version, arguing that these were made for better mass productivity and earlier commercial production. Again, Toshiba gambled and went for the planar. Again it had made the right choice. The benefit was seen during the worldwide DRAM shortage of

1987 and 1988, when Toshiba was the biggest producer of 1-megabit DRAMs which were in increasing demand.

Similarly, the company decided bravely to get out of mainframe computers in the late 1970s, and to put its resources into personal computers and especially into developing a new smaller model, a so-called laptop. It was a decision widely queried at the time, but it paid off handsomely, especially in the early 1990s when rival Fujitsu was struggling and losing money in the mainframe business, while Toshiba was powering ahead and setting international standards with its laptops. With hindsight, it seems to have been easy, but it involved correctly guessing new social trends, or perhaps just being lucky. Kazuo Ishiguro, general manager of international operations for information and communications systems, noted the changing times: 'In the 1960s, executives I saw boarding planes in the US looked as if they enjoyed their food and got stuck into the gin and tonics. In the 1970s they had tennis rackets under their arms for a game after their business meetings, and in the 1980s they carried laptops, most of which were Toshiba models.'

Progress was not as effortless as it might seem, however, and involved difficult choices. Even though Toshiba adopted the IBM-compatible standard, its engineers had to work out new, almost miniature, technology. This included designing the world's first flat liquid crystal display; remodelling the industry standard 5.25-inch floppy disk with a 3.5-inch disk (because the larger floppy was too big for a laptop model); battling to get the software for a 3.5-inch format; and replacing all the components on to a single printed circuit board, rather than the three or more boards used in the traditional desktop computer. The last task was by no means simple, since it involved reducing the size of the chips and changing the methods for mounting them on the boards, because they were too small to be assembled by hand and had to be mounted by robots. But it succeeded and Toshiba set the standards for the rest of the world, for a few years at least, until it was challenged again by a resurgent America benefiting from a high yen.

Then at home in Japan, Toshiba had to do its work all over again, convincing its compatriots that a computer did not have to be an immense, bulky thing. 'When we took laptops around Japan, people did not think that they could be real computers as they were not like the large machines they were used to,' recalled a Toshiba manager. Getting software for a Japanese version was the next struggle. Eventually the Dynabook released in 1989 proved a best-seller in Japan. Masaichi Koga, senior vice president and director in charge of information equipment, attributed Toshiba's success as a pioneer of laptops to the company's 'capabilities as a comprehensive electronics maker', involving skills in making large-scale integrated circuits, thin plasma and liquid crystal displays, and miniature large-capacity hard disk drives. Even so, Toshiba lags behind its rival NEC in the Japanese PC market, such is the intense competition at home.

Toshiba claims to be a technology leader in a number of areas, including work on superconductive magnets that are the key for the next generation of supertrains. The Maglev (short for magnetic levitation) trains are expected to travel at speeds of between 500 and 600 kilometres an hour (up to 400 miles an hour). The idea is simple. The train will have a bed of magnets along its track to provide lift, and will be propelled by rows of magnets alongside which are continuously switched on and off to give a 'kick' to similar magnets on the train. 'The result will be smooth, virtually friction-free transport, capable of reaching very high speeds,' according to Toshiba engineers. Because the trains skim over the rails, they do not generate friction and can offer a ride that is both faster and smoother than existing trains. The principle, however, is simpler than the practice. International competition is tough, and Germany, Russia and the USA are planning similar vehicles. Germany has an experimental train, the Transrapid, but Toshiba says that the Transrapid uses conventional electromagnets and 'flies' at only 1 centimetre. The most ambitious scheme is that of Japan, whose train will use superconductors and fly at a height of 10 centimetres (3.9 inches).

The contribution of Toshiba is to produce about half of the magnets for the three railway organisations co-operating in the work. It has been a long struggle. In 1971 Japan's tests confirmed that the magnets do float, but a magnet of 2,000 kilograms could only generate enough propulsion to lift one-tenth of its weight. The following year, Toshiba superconducting magnets achieved enough power to lift their own weight, and later a lighter version encased in aluminium rather than steel was developed and achieved speeds of 60 kilometres an hour. By the end of the decade, a train with 32 passenger seats managed 400.8 kilometres an hour.

There are still years to go before the new supertrain will be in service. A 42.8-kilometre (26.7-mile) test track will open in 1995 west of Tokyo, but Toshiba and the other companies making the magnets are still working to perfect a propulsion device that can not only propel a whole train at 500 kilometres an hour, but which can handle trains that have to go into and out of tunnels, pass on opposite tracks and run for 10,000 hours without servicing. As an example of how complicated and expensive the work is, the superconducting magnets consist of a coil made from wires of niobium and titanium (Nb and Ti) and a cryostat to cool the coil to working temperatures of minus 269 Centigrade, which is the temperature of liquid helium. The wire that makes up the model coil of the test vehicle consists of 2,689 separate filaments of Nb–Ti, measuring 20 microns, or thinner than a human hair. This has to be wound by hand 1,167 times, so that it takes a week to prepare a coil with a piece of wire 5,000 metres or three miles long.

Toshiba has developed ceramic superconductor wires using yttrium-based oxide, but this requires the basic quality to be improved because ceramics are hard to process into wires. If the ceramics technology can be improved, it will be possible to use cheaper liquid nitrogen rather than helium for the cooling. Anything that can be done to keep the costs down will be welcome because the estimated price of building the expressway between Tokyo and Osaka, Japan's second largest city, has been put at 5,000 billion yen ($50 billion). Sceptics abound, saying that even if the Maglev can fly, it will never be a commercial proposition.

Another new technology where Toshiba's electronics experience is helping is in developing ultrasound diagnostic systems for medicine. Such a machine emits inaudible sounds of 2–10 megahertz which penetrate into the human body, with the sick organs giving off a distinctive sound. It is similar to sonar devices used deep in the ocean. It has advantages over X-ray and X-ray computed tomography in that it is painless and harmless because there is no exposure to radiation, and allows real-time display of the dynamic state of the body. Ultrasound diagnostic systems today have automatic focusing and can probe into both shallow and deep organs, using coloured display screens with different colours for the blood from blue to red as the probe gets near the blood flow. Higher frequencies, up to 7.5 and even 10 megahertz, are used for eye-tests. By attaching the ultrasound probe to an endoscope, ultrasound can also be used for checking prostate glands and the womb. Ultrascan can detect cancer cells hidden deep inside the body in places like the pancreas, liver and gall bladder, and can discover cancers as small as 1 centimetre. By the start of the 1990s, Toshiba claimed a 40 per cent market share of ultrasound scanning devices, and as high as 60 per cent for diagnosis of the heart and circulatory systems.

High-definition television is another area where Toshiba has invested lots of money, but the results are less certain because of doubts about whether Japan is using the right system. It has stubbornly stuck to analogue rather than digital technology. By 1994 even the conservative-minded Ministry of Posts and Telecommunications (MPT) seemed about to change its mind and go with the rest of the world to digital, but it met howls of protest from manufacturers and makers of programmes. In terms of colour quality, high-definition television (or HDTV) is certainly impressive, but at a cost of 4 to 4.5 million yen ($40,000–45,000) for a set, it is a long way from economic success, as Toshiba admits. It estimates that the cost will have to come down to a million yen and possibly even to 500,000 yen for a set before every family will be clamouring to put HDTV in its home.*

---

* Toshiba is continuing work on digital HDTV, and recently developed the world's first $\frac{3}{4}$-inch digital, high-definition video cassette recorder based on a universal digital high-definition recording format jointly developed with Broadcast Television Systems of Germany.

In nuclear power, Toshiba was very much the student of General Electric of the USA. When Japan went nuclear on 26 October 1963 at 16.59, the Japan Atomic Energy Research Institute generated its first electricity from a 2.4-megawatt plant supplied by GE. When Toshiba came into the act in 1966, it licensed technology from GE, as did Hitachi, the other Japanese student of the American company. From 1981 the former teacher and student began a technology co-operation contract, which was renewed in 1991 for another ten years.

One of the most serious problems in building boiling water reactors was stress corrosion cracking of pipes, which occurred because water exposed to radiation decomposed into hydrogen and oxygen, which tended to corrode pipes, while pressurised water led to stress difficulties. Five international companies, Toshiba and Hitachi from Japan, GE, ASEA Atom from Sweden and Ansaldo Meccanico Nuclears from Italy, formed the Advanced Engineering Team to solve the twin hazards of corrosion and stress. The team's work led to development of plans for advanced boiling water reactors (ABWR) by Toshiba, GE and Hitachi. The consortium is building two ABWR units, the world's first, for Tokyo Electric Power Company, the world's largest electric utility. Toshiba was chosen to lead the joint venture for what will become in 1996 Japan's fiftieth commercial nuclear power plant when it takes its place as the number 6 unit at Kashiwazaki-Kariwa, supplying Tokyo Electric Power.

In its production and development of power generation equipment, Toshiba takes full advantage of its electronics capacity, especially using large information and automation display screens and advanced robotics technology for automatic plant maintenance. The company in fact boasts that, with greater construction experience of nuclear plants in recent times, it may be able to teach GE things. Jiro Kani, general manager of Toshiba's nuclear energy division, described links between GE and Toshiba as 'a close co-operative relationship in a broader area on the basis of equal partnership instead of the old teacher–pupil relationship'. Yasumasa Yahagi, executive vice president, expressed it diplomatically: 'There are many things that we, the former student, can learn from GE, even though we will have equal standing. But I think that Japan is probably more advanced in some aspects of plant construction, while the US lacked the construction experience in the past decade. I believe we will maintain a relationship with GE in which the two sides can complement each other.'

Co-operation with other international companies in just one aspect in which Toshiba stands out from other Japanese companies which are noted for their competitive attitudes towards foreigners. President Sato said simply, 'It is no longer an era in which a single company can dominate any technology or business by itself. The technology has become so advanced, and the markets so complex, that you simply cannot expect to be the best at the whole process any longer.' His colleague, Kawanishi, who has played a major role in developing semiconductor appliances, including the ambitious tripartite venture with IBM and Siemens to develop the next generation semiconductor, stresses that the important thing is to devise a proper contract outlining the roles and rights of each company as well as the terms if it fails. 'During honeymoon time, everything is great,' said Kawanishi. 'But as you know, divorce is always a possibility, and that's when things can get bitter.'

Kawanishi said jokingly, 'They call me Mr Semiconductor' because of his career in the industry. 'Toshiba should be an international company,' he asserted, explaining his argument thus: 'Technology-wise, marketing-wise, manufacturing-wise, semiconductors especially are a borderless business. There are several ways of being international. Globalisation is one method, to have factories in many countries, with regional offices. This is very common but is not perfect because occasionally some political issues or emotional issues will occur. Toshiba will continue to do this kind of internationalisation. But there is another route – that is, making strategic alliances. If you can find a good partner and collaborate together, you can have a synergy effect on each other. This is a new way to internationalisation, especially to reach the leading edge of technology.' Increasingly, he suggested, such strategic alliances would become more and more important, especially with more complicated technology in semiconductors, liquid crystal display and the buzzword of the twenty-first century, multimedia.

'These are huge and complicated areas. One company cannot do everything on its own. This is true in terms of the technology and in terms of the money. [The next but one generation of semiconductors], the 256-megabit DRAM, needs an investment of $1 billion, too huge for one company, especially when the process is very complicated. We have to sum up the highest level of technology for a number of processes. That's why we have combined with IBM and Siemens for the 256-mega-DRAM, developing one memory correlating three chips. By coming together it is possible to reduce the investment money to get higher excellence and shorten the development time.

'When we collaborate together, the relationship between Toshiba and its partner should not be like a married couple, but that of friends. There are some differences. With friends, it's possible to have several partners, whereas married couples should be just one. In addition, it is important to keep some tension in the relationship. In the case of a married couple, the husband relies on the wife and the wife on the husband too much, so that they can forget to go forward. This way, we can have one friend to play tennis with, and another friend to play golf. For example, Toshiba is collaborating with Motorola regarding memory and microprocessors; in the semiconductor field, we are collaborating with Samsung of Korea regarding non-flash memory. We can find good friends in each area, though not so many. It's important that each has strong core skills, and there should be respect and trust for each other.'

Sometimes, the friendships grow, then wane, as happened with links between Toshiba and LSI Logic, which were once strong but are now less so. Kawanishi said that 'We had a close relationship with LSI Logic for many years. We exchanged our computer technology with their design expertise. Now Dataquest says that LSI Logic is number one and Toshiba is number two in the area, so there will be some conflict, good conflict, but essentially LSI Logic does not need aid from Toshiba, nor Toshiba from LSI Logic. At a personal level, I am still friendly with Mr [Wilfred J.] Corrigan, chairman of LSI Logic, but we are competitors.'

The partnership with Samsung surprised analysts, who see the Koreans as the ultra-competitors of the Japanese. Kawanishi offered an explanation: 'We did not want to shake hands as a friend two or three years ago with Samsung, but the company is now becoming very, very strong. It has had to change its attitude and become more international. We too had to change. If we had to co-operate together, it is much better than competing only, so we are collaborating, but only in the memory field. Samsung is not just a semiconductor company, but also uses our products, so things are working out well.'

In fact, Toshiba has not been afraid to make collaboration arrangements with companies that might be considered its rivals, as well as with concerns that are competing with one another. In 1992 it made an agreement with Apple Computers to develop multimedia computer products for business, education and entertainment. The two cited 'Apple's software technology and Toshiba's manufacturing knowhow in making smaller and powerful consumer electronic products'. The next year Toshiba struck a deal with Microsoft Corp, Apple's great rival, for hand-held computer systems. 'Hardware is important, but software is critical,' said a Toshiba spokesman. The device will be sold in the USA but not in Japan, although many computer specialists doubt the size of the market for such hand-held devices, which are supposed to replace pens and paper for personal records, and telephones, faxes and pagers for personal communications.

At least Toshiba was right at the cutting edge when it made a tie-up with not just one but two intercontinental giants, IBM and Siemens, in the key semiconductor area. Kawanishi's colleague, senior executive vice president Hideharu Egawa, expanded on the rationale for the link and the advantages which each partner brought to the party. You have to realise, he said, 'The development cost for the 1-megabit DRAM was about $20 million, whereas for the 256-mega-DRAM, it will be $1 billion or more. It's very difficult to invest this kind of money on our own.' Each of the companies in the partnership has a special skill: IBM in lithography, Toshiba in etching and Siemens in engineering. 'This way we can not only share the cost, but combine the best technology of the three companies,' Egawa added. Production of the 256-megabit DRAM means putting 256 million memory cells on to a slice of silicon the size of a fingernail. It means being able to etch lines that are a quarter of a micron wide – or about 400 times finer than a human hair – on to the device.

Development work is being done in New York state at an IBM facility. Egawa is optimistic about the progress. 'We sent 52 engineers over there, IBM assigned approximately the same number of people, and Siemens sent a slightly smaller number. They all live and work in the same community, making one team, divided into different groups of specialists. It was a very difficult decision for me to send engineers over there. I had some concern that many engineers would complain and say that they would prefer to develop everything in Toshiba or in Japan and insist that our technology is superior. That is the usual tendency of engineers. But actually because they have had good experience of working with other companies, almost all of them have expressed a good desire to work together.' He says that the development is 'ahead of schedule, progress is very good and with lower expenses than predicted, surprisingly. Usually, we have some delay on the schedule and more expense [than budgeted]. This is very rare. IBM has been so supportive for us and helped to get over any cultural problems.' Egawa laughingly noted that there are attractions to working in the USA: 'They enjoy a very good life. They can stay in a house that may be ten times bigger than what they have in Japan.'

The planned commercial production date for the 256-megabit chip is 'very confidential. If I disclose our plans, it will give a very good target for our competitors.' Even so, Egawa predicts that it may be produced six months to a year ahead of schedule – very important in this game, where the whole point is to steal a march on your rivals. By being brave and getting ahead of the rest of the world with the mega-DRAM, Toshiba made a record $5 billion on the chip, a sum not seen before or since as competition has again intensified. Egawa remembers it well, since he was the chief engineer when the mega-DRAM was being designed, and then became the general manager who saw it into commercial production and sale.

Rapid progress with the 256-megabit chip could mean that it will be available from early 1997. Although they are working together on the research for the chip, when it comes to commercial production and marketing, Toshiba, IBM and Siemens will be on their own, and Toshiba will be able to sell round the world in competition with its co-researchers. Egawa does not expect the competition to be intense. 'Fortunately, IBM is our very good customer rather than a competitor. IBM's consumption is huge. Siemens is not very aggressive in producing DRAMs. They want to use the technology for telecommunications,' added Egawa, 'so I believe we will not compete and Toshiba will get the main benefit of selling on the open market.' Then the battle will be on for the 1-gigabit chip, containing one billion bits of information stored on a tiny silicon chip. Egawa can see ahead to the 4-gigabit chip, and after that 'I don't know.'

Another exciting venture is flash memory devices. These are semi-conductors which retain information when the power is switched off, as hard disk drives do today. The hope is that they will replace the bulky hard disks and even floppy disks in today's computers, and also take over from magnetic recording devices in a wide range of electronic equipment – especially in portable equipment, since flash memories will reduce both the weight and the power used by the machines. Their products of the future could also include items like tape-recorders and toys that are a long way from being considered computers, but which need disk drives. Flash memories use about a tenth of the power. The problem is that the memory content of flash memories is currently small – 20 and 40 megabytes against 200 to 300 megabytes on hard disks.

Toshiba is generally credited with inventing flash memory, but has lagged in developing it into usable products. The American company Intel has dominated the marketplace, and in February 1992 announced that it was teaming up with Japan's Sharp Corporation to develop flash memories. To hit back, Toshiba later the same year formed alliances with IBM and National Semiconductor of the USA to develop such devices. With IBM it agreed to share its technology in return for IBM technology for a controller device allowing high-speed read and write functions. The deal with National Semiconductor licensed Toshiba technology to the US company in return for Toshiba acquiring rights to derivative technology developed by National Semiconductor. The market for flash memories is expected to grow from about $200 million in 1993 to about $10 billion by the turn of the century. Toshiba is again taking a gamble by concentrating on NAND-model flash memory chips, which program and erase information faster than the NOR model which Intel has made dominant.

Asked how Toshiba had gone about the question of finding partners, Kawanishi responded, 'It is the same question to me as how I found my wife. In the case of Time Warner, our chairman, Joichi Aoi, had a close relationship with Time Warner's president. Regarding Motorola, Mr [Robert] Galvin [chairman] of Motorola [for 26 years and son of its founder] was close friends with our former chairman and president, Mr Saba. Top executives knew each other. In the case of IBM we were collaborating with each other in some areas before we made a formal alliance, and that experience was good, before we came on to LCD, then flash memory, then to 256-mega-DRAM. In the first stage it was not so big, but if we at Toshiba keep trust and respect and some patience, the relationship will grow, grow, grow. As far as transnational strategic alliances are concerned,

Toshiba is the top, but other companies are following, so they recognise the importance of such relationships.'

In spite of the importance of alliances, Kawanishi added that 'Competition is first, co-operation is second, because if we have no competitive power we cannot find friends. Competition is our potentiality. If we haven't got it, perhaps no one will respect us.' Though he refused to contemplate the demise of any of Toshiba's competitors – and asserts that the troubled 'IBM is on the way back with the help of our liquid crystal display technology' – Kawanishi added, 'our team should always be winning. If we lose the fighting spirit then we will be beaten.'

Curiously, Toshiba has few major alliances with Japanese companies and has chosen instead to make friends with Americans. Kawanishi pointed out that Toshiba has a partnership with Asahi Chemicals to try to improve technology in perhaps the weakest area of the business – batteries. 'Whereas the power of semiconductors has gone up by a thousand times, that of batteries has advanced by only ten times,' he noted. Batteries are very much the weak link because of their weight, but Asahi Chemicals (part of the Dai-Ichi Kangyo Bank keiretsu) reputedly has very good technology in lithium ion batteries. Through their joint work Toshiba is hoping to increase power per unit of weight by three to four times by around the turn of the century.

Kawanishi admitted both a personal and a Japanese debt to the USA in the development of the semiconductor industry. Laughing again, Kawanishi said 'When I joined Toshiba it was the first chapter, the very very beginning time of the semiconductor industry. As you know, Dr [William] Shockley and others invented the semiconductor in the US about 45 years ago. We at Toshiba started the business approximately ten years after. At that time I was an engineer, and for the engineers the semiconductor field was paradise because there were many things to do. But for managers it is hell. So I am now a manager and have gone from paradise and am now in hell.

'After doing semiconductor business for five years, I had a chance to learn the technology from General Electric. Now GE has no semiconductor capacity, but 30 or 40 years ago they were a very strong company. At that time and until now, Americans were very kind to foreigners. They taught us many things, perhaps more than were laid down in the contract. I learned everything from America. I cannot forget the kindness of Americans. So nowadays I can understand their irritation: because America invented the semiconductor; America taught us everything; now the student is bigger than the teacher, so it's very difficult for the teacher to bear. Basically, our technology came from the US and also our biggest market is still the United States. So we should be very patient.'

Asked whether he sees any prospect that Japan may go the way of America and lose its predominance to the Koreans, or even in some years' time to rapidly growing China, there was a hint of disappointment in Kawanishi's voice. He recounted that 'Last year I met Mr [Jack] Welch [chief executive] of GE and told him that I had been a student of his company, but Welch answered, "I don't like the semiconductor industry", so it's up to Welch's philosophy because Welch decides everything in GE. But I expected some answer from Mr Welch on why GE changed its attitude because 40 years ago it was the strongest company in semiconductors. Unfortunately, he had no time to discuss the details. If Toshiba got out of semiconductors, I'd be retired, but I don't believe such a thing would occur.'

Kawanishi conceded that there were many businesses within the electrical and electronics field, and that a company had to decide which to specialise in. 'In the past we [Toshiba] gave up big computers and we concentrated on small ones. After we gave up the large computers, they got money, huge money, so some people said Toshiba made a mistake. But now everyone thinks this is a good decision because Toshiba was the fastest company to enter into the personal computer era and our competitors Hitachi delayed and Fujitsu is losing big money on big computers.'

He is not so gloomy about the future of America, or trade and business relationships between Japan and the USA. 'There are three key components for the twenty-first century, LCD [liquid crystal display], rechargeable batteries and semiconductors, so any big excellent modern company should have these three. Of course, software and systems are also important, but these three components are essential for the multimedia era. In that sense, GE, RCA and Fairchild disappeared from the semiconductor field, but other companies such as Intel, Motorola, National Semiconductor and Micron and other new private-sector ventures are now very strong in the semiconductor field. It's a very good thing for America as a whole.'

Japan, he added, is still 'weak in the logic and software areas. We are very strong in the technological process of mass production, and show high excellence in manufacturing; perhaps here we are better than the United States. But in software and how to systemise one component to apply it to the system, America is much better. In some sense it depends on the culture, though very recently in other fields such as games, Nintendo and Sega are much bigger than American makers [and have seen off the competition from] Atari and Mattel. So it's partly history. Japan is trying to build up its software and systems, while other developing countries, such as Korea and mainland China, are trying to emulate Japanese production. This is the process of history.'

He expressed concern about 'a hollowing out from manufacturing in Japan because of the high appreciation of the yen and the lack of young engineers who are willing to engage in manufacturing industry. But

America had the same history many years ago. It's a megatrend from an industrial society to an information society. Now there is something of a comeback in America. For ten years America has been relying on Japan or south-east Asia for hardware, while it concentrated on software and systems. As a result of that, it has had some problems, so they now want to come back to manufacturing hardware again.

'Japan has no natural resources, only human resources. We are a very small country and we cannot survive without technology potential. Technology consists of hardware and software, I don't know if it should be 50/50 or 60/40, but we have to have a balance. If we lose everything regarding hardware, it is a time when Japan's economy will drop. So even though the high appreciation of the yen will cost us, we have to have both. Until now we have been very strong in hardware. We are trying to rev up our software, but we should retain our strength in both. If we are following the trend of history, then fifteen years from now, perhaps Japan will lose.'

Of one thing Kawanishi is confident – that there is no reason for Japan and the USA to quarrel over semiconductors. He echoes the remarks of other business leaders in believing that 'left to themselves [shorthand for being free from interference by politicians], the businessmen will be able to solve all the problems. As far as America is concerned, with our system of alliances, we are so close we cannot divorce.' GE and Toshiba's other partners certainly speak well of the company. GE's relationships in fact go back to before the war, when Toshiba learned from the Americans all sorts of things from making simple light bulbs to building heavy power generation equipment. Before the war GE owned almost half of the Japanese stock, which it was forced to divest during the war. But afterwards the relationship was resumed, especially in the heavy energy-producing area. Jack Welch of GE paid his tribute, telling *Fortune* magazine in 1993: 'I've dealt with Toshiba for fifteen years, and it's always been a very easy relationship. When things go awry, a call to [Toshiba president Fumio] Sato-san will take care of the problem in 24 hours.'

Egawa's assessment of Toshiba's competitors also plays down the battle, often seen in the media, between Japan and the USA. He commented, 'We are not competing very much, since Japanese are going one way and US companies are going another. They are more capable in systems-oriented products, such as microprocessors or processors for special operations. US semiconductors and Japanese semiconductors are necessary for our customers, and there is only a small competitive overlap between us. Micron Technology, though, is a company forecasting its dedication to the DRAM business. The size of the company is not so big, but they have very talented people, and they are a company coming into the market.' He said that South Korea's Samsung had made giant strides, agreeing with analysts who said that Samsung had released the 16-megabit DRAM at the same time as Japanese and US makers. The Korean company started by selling low-cost chips through computer shops, but by the mid-1990s it was making big sales to almost all major US personal computer makers. It benefited from the boom in the early 1990s which saw capacity for chips growing by 50 per cent, but demand rising by 80 per cent.

'Samsung started as a latecomer to the industry,' said Egawa. 'It was two years delayed in 256K DRAM, about one year delayed in one megabit, maybe six months in the 4-mega, and zero – well, no they were leading – in the 16-mega. They have very good technology and work very hard, and they have the advantage that the yen has risen against the dollar whereas the won [Korea's currency] has declined.' He predicted that the coming of the 1-gigabit chip would see 'three Japanese companies and one, maybe two Koreans. NEC is very aggressive, so they will stay in the market. I am not sure whether Oki or Fujitsu will stay, and there are questions about Hitachi. Hitachi has very good technology, but it seems to me that they like to provide their technology to other companies, for instance Goldstar and Nittetsu Semiconductor, and get oem [original equipment manufacture] supply from their own company. That is a clever approach for a short period of time, but I am not quite sure whether it is basically good or not.'

If nothing else, Egawa is fiercely loyal to Toshiba. 'Sometimes I am asked by new graduates why I work for Toshiba. My answer will be like this: Toshiba is a company which provides us with various opportunities, but generally allows us *jiyu-na funiki* – how shall I translate it? – a free atmosphere to do what we want to do. That is the general feeling of Toshiba. Hitachi and NEC are different, more straightforward, ordered from the top to the workers. "You have to do this, in this way." Even in the top management decisions we see some difference. I am not saying that Toshiba is a bottom-up decision-making company, but we discuss, always we discuss, and finally we reach a decision, so that it adds up to a bilateral management style.'

A successful electronics company cannot live on a diet of chips alone. Forecasts of the future value of semiconductors or consumer products pale beside some of those quoted for what is called 'multimedia'. John Sculley, the then chairman of Apple Computers, guessed that it would be worth $3,500 billion a year. Other estimates have ranged up to $5,000 billion and even higher.

In the early 1990s, Toshiba and the trading company Itochu paid $500 million each to join forces with the US media group Time Warner and later with US West telephone company to create Time Warner Entertainment Company. The arrangement gives Toshiba and Itochu 5.61 per cent each, US West 25.51 per cent and Time Warner the remaining 63.27 per cent of the new company, which holds the filmed entertainment, cable and programming activities of the Time Warner group. This includes Warner Brothers, its Hollywood studio, Home Box Office, its cable television production unit and Time Warner Cable. The publishing and music activities of Time Warner were not put into the new company.

In addition, Toshiba and Itochu took 25 per cent each, US West 12.75 per cent and Time Warner the balance of a new company called Time Warner Entertainment Japan, to offer filmed entertainment, home videos, consumer products and a slot entitled 'new business'. Analysts said that the deal gave the Japanese companies a small foothold in the great adventure of multimedia, with assets potentially worth a lot more than their upfront stake, and helped to reduce Time Warner's debt and strengthen its balance sheet. How the partnership will work out depends on a lot of complex factors, including how the partners get on and how multimedia develops.

According to Toshiba executives, this gives the company stakes in all aspects of what it sees as the telecom–cable–studio alliance, with Time Warner supplying the movie capacity and cable television programming, US West being the telephone operator, Toshiba providing the electronics, and Itochu offering other back-up support. Toshiba believes that none of its rivals is as far advanced. Sony and Matsushita both have movie assets through Columbia Pictures and MCA respectively, but they have no television capacity or telephone links. Other US telephone networks, such as Bell Atlantic, Southwestern Bell and NYNEX (the New York telephone provider), have links with television stations and even plans for movie tie-ups, but they do not have a deal with a major electronics producer for a complete multimedia system from entertainment provider to the home and office of the next century.

'Regarding Time Warner, they are like Hollywood and we are like Silicon Valley, so the combination is pretty good,' said Kawanishi. To add another dimension, Toshiba agreed to link with General Magic of the USA to develop jointly a personal digital assistant tool using General Magic's Telescript and Magic Cap technologies. General Magic hopes that its Telescript will be the world standard computer language for fibre-optic and wireless communications networks.

Toshiba, however, has come under fire for its failure in software. When it unveiled its widescreen television in June 1994, it used a laser disc of *Terminator 2*, the film made by Carolco Pictures of the USA, an associate of its rival Pioneer, to demonstrate the model. This set competitors chuckling, ridiculing Toshiba for having to rely on a rival's software, and claiming that the company was too focused on hardware. (Toshiba and Pioneer joined hands to develop the digital video disc.) Although the company has set up a software creation team at head office and a Software Liaison Council with its group companies, it also sold 5 per cent of its 50 per cent stake in Toshiba-EMI to Thorn-EMI of the UK, and thus lost its position as the largest shareholder. 'It is the perennial Japanese problem,' said a European analyst. 'They don't have the software to appreciate the importance of software and how it fits in.'

Toshiba allied itself with as many friends as it could when it geared up in 1995 for the big battle of digital computer discs, which promises to be as bruising as the videotape wars of the 1980s when Sony fought Matsushita and lost. This time Sony and Toshiba declared war on each other in late February. Sony has Dutch maker Philips on its side, but Toshiba has put together a powerful international alliance of seven companies including Matsushita, Pioneer and Hollywood movie studios Time Warner and MCA. Digital video discs are the next generation of compact discs that are expected to take over today's video cassette market. The rival contenders are a single-side disc developed by Sony and Philips and a double-sided format developed by Toshiba, which has a larger memory capacity. Both discs are expected to make their commercial debut at about the same time, in autumn 1996.

Hopes that the two sides would get together, pool resources and develop a common standard were dashed when both companies issued uncompromising statements that they would not co-operate with each other. Sony announced that it had doubled the storage capacity of its digital video disc to 7.4 gigabytes (billion bytes) and would go ahead with its commercial production. Toshiba hit back immediately with its own promise to support its system as the international standard, retorting that its own disc, a double-sided one with 10 gigabytes of memory – or 15 times as much as a music CD – was both superior in storage capacity and offered better picture and sound quality. 'We cannot let the movie industry down,' a senior manager added, noting that the Sony disc had not yet met film industry needs.

Toshiba's disc is being developed with Pioneer Electronic and is backed by Matsushita. It has also lined up Matsushita's film subsidiary MCA and Time Warner on its side, both attracted by the greater storage and potential for the film industry. Sony executives claim that the single-side format of their disc allows greater synergies with existing CD technology and is easier to operate since it does not have to be turned over. The company says that with a blue semiconductor laser diode it will try to raise capacity to 11 gigabytes, which would provide better pictures and accommodate next-generation digital television signals.

There is still a long way to go to multimedia, as the flow charts that Toshiba offered amply demonstrated – and sketching the charts is the easy part. Today's technology will need considerable upgrading to produce the information superhighways that are the stuff of multimedia dreams. Cable television connections today, for example, are mostly coaxial, of limited band width and one-way; telephone connections are two-way, but the traffic on them varies. The information superhighways of tomorrow will have to combine the best of the two systems and of advances beyond them.

According to Toshiba, the superhighways will have a fibre-optic back-bone with coaxial tails; will be of unlimited band width; will be two-way; will have constant traffic; will be unswitched; will be subscription based; will offer simple billing; will be hi-tech and reliable; will have high customer interaction; and will have high channel capacity. The company imagines a control box at home, which will be connected by telephone to a control centre, which in turn links the subscriber via telephone and cable to his or her bank, shop, security company and hospital. The subscriber will also probably have a portable multimedia product, offering connections and transactions with the control box at home, plus television, telephone, fax and computer links as well as access to share information and dealings on the move. It is an exciting vision.

As president Sato noted, under the old analogue system, different kinds of information could not be handled together; but under the modern digital framework, 'all information sources will be fused in digitalised data and we will be able to process it in one unified framework'. In other words, the use of fibre-optic channels will open the libraries of the world to everyone just as easily as telephone conversations occur now. Television advances will give everyone a camera's eye view of the world. And improved software will allow anyone anywhere to browse through this material to find what satisfies them.

It is not a far-fetched dream, but it is an optimistic one. You have only to look around: billions of the world's people living in poor countries have limited access to computers, or even a hospital. The big groups involved in multimedia admit that they are not sure where the biggest money will be made. 'People know what the skeleton looks like, but they don't know what the muscles look like,' admitted Frank Biondi, chief executive of cable operator Viacom in 1993. Andrew Grove, chief executive of Intel, was still more honest, telling the *Wall Street Journal*, 'I don't know what the hell I am talking about really ... We will know the truth when we get there.'

It is ironic that Japanese companies should be pushing to the forefront of the multimedia business when at home the government has not laid the foundations for any kind of information highway; instead, it has set up roadblocks. A critical American analyst commented that 'There are three letters which protect the Japanese electronics companies and handi-cap consumers – they are MPT, meaning the Ministry of Posts and Tele-communications.' He and other critics claim that, by keeping a tight grip on the industry and refusing to admit new processes, ventures or licences, the ministry provides a feather bed for Toshiba and other electronics and telecommunications companies, keeps prices high, but ultimately damages Japan because it does not get the benefit of either competition or new ideas.

The critic singled out Toshiba because of its close relationship with Nippon Telegraph and Telephone (NTT), with which it used to share headquarters in Tokyo and whose main office building still has space occupied by Toshiba's executives responsible for heavy electrical equipment. NTT benefited, and Japan suffered, from its monopoly control of the domestic telephone market. The company is still 65 per cent owned by the minister of finance.* Its comfortable monopoly and the negative attitude of the MPT to innovation has prevented Japan from enjoying the range of telephone and electronic options that are available in the USA and which have helped to fuel the communications revolution going on in that country.

In Japan, bureaucratic control through the MPT is still very much the order of the day. To quote the critical analyst: 'They are unimaginative and plodding, small-town postmen rather than telecommunicators or technocrats who appreciate the advantages of the information revolution.' Even the *Nikkei Weekly*, the English offshoot of the leading financial daily paper *Nihon Keizai Shimbun*, weighed in with its bitches against the MPT: 'Permission from the posts minister is required either to install telecommunications lines and offer services or to withdraw from the business. Even when enthusiastic engineers want to start new services at their own risk, the government takes away the business demand. Even supposing permission to start a new telecommunications service is granted, the newcomer then faces a sea of red tape in actually carrying out the project ... Should a CATV [cable television] firm decide to start broadcasting in Tokyo, it faces a six-month wait before it can even apply for permission to build, then another year before permission may be granted. Then construction can finally start. Companies must not only offer detailed explanations of their planned services, including future projections, but also obtain a veritable mountain of approval forms and certificates before they can actually start installing lines. They must prepare a plan and obtain a permit for each and every working site, for everything from the use of roads and utility poles to the crossing of rail lines to the laying of lines underground.'† Toshiba and other Japanese companies have much more freedom abroad than at home.

Only in mid-1994 did recognition begin to sink into the official mind that Japan was lagging behind the USA and throwing away perhaps millions of jobs as well as potential for economic growth. The MPT, ignoring the fact that it was to blame for the laggardly start, estimated

* One of the burning questions for the mid-1990s is whether NTT should be broken up, as AT & T was in the USA, to increase efficiency and competition.
† *Nikkei Weekly*, 23 May 1994.

that multimedia could account for 5 to 6 per cent of gross domestic product by 2010, and 2.4 million jobs. The Ministry of Construction proposed an underground cable box network that would be able to house fibre-optic cable for the information superhighway. The scheme would cost 40,000 billion yen ($400 billion), but it would be 2020 before the bulk of the work would be finished.

One major issue is whether the fibre-optic network should be monopolised by NTT – which aims to link every household to a fibre-optic system by 2015 – or whether it should be open to competition, as the Construction Ministry's scheme would allow. NTT is anxious to provide new services beyond its conventional telephone operations, and has set its sights on video communications, shopping and interactive games, but at the moment it is inhibited by the law, which states that it cannot set up other businesses outside the telecommunications field. As a result of MPT restrictions, cable television hardly exists in Japan; with only 5 per cent of households hooked up for it in late 1994 (against 60 per cent in the USA), the computer networks are set to be ten years behind the USA. Use of mobile telephones was 1.8 per cent at the end of 1993, against 4.4 per cent in the USA and 7.9 per cent in Sweden.

Even when in 1994 the MPT relaxed its regulations to permit easier entry to cable television, including with foreign investors, potential operators found that their path was through a maze of paperwork. TCI of the USA formed a partnership with Sumitomo Corporation, the major trading house, to bring its superior technology to the lucky people of Suginami ward in Tokyo, in all 220,000 households. In the USA, the cable companies simply send lorries laden with cable to run it from one telegraph pole to the next. Not so in Japan, where poles are already festooned with wire. The cable company was prepared to go underground. But it found it had to get permission from the Ministry of Construction each time its cable crossed a national highway, and permission from local authorities for local roads. A single or multiple permit was not possible, so the company had to make its pilgrimage for permission for each individual road. On top of that, it had to pay a fee for taking up space underground and a separate usage charge for transmitting signals. It discovered that construction costs were 70 per cent of total investment in equipment.

Toshiba is still vulnerable even in its strongest areas. It has been protected through the periods of economic uncertainty by its heavy energy-producing sector. Here it seems comfortably ensconced and regularly wins the biggest share of orders in Japan for setting up power stations. It is especially comfortable in the Tokyo area, thanks to its links with Tokyo Electric Power Company. But some foreign analysts say that its days of clover may be threatened as Washington puts political pressure on Japan to open its market to foreign contractors in power generation. 'American companies could certainly give the Japanese a run for their money. Especially if the yen remains high, I am confident that the US could come in and really shake up the Japanese,' commented a US power specialist. A mixture of political and other pressures have meant that foreigners have found it hard going in the general contracting and construction area, and even if the barriers were removed, outsiders would still find it more difficult than they imagined.

The strength of the yen is certainly challenging, especially to a company like Toshiba. It has set up overseas offices and facilities in North and South America, Europe and Asia, where it makes electronics products. Many of its personal computers, for example, are made in Germany or the USA for its non-Japanese markets. Toshiba's Asian diversification has recently reached China. Altogether it has fourteen Chinese factories, including one in Dalian which makes printed circuit boards and small industrial motors. The Chinese ventures started as satellites for assembling Japanese-made components for export back home and to Europe and North America, but now Toshiba is looking more at China as an important market in its own right.

However, in the key area of semiconductor production, Toshiba has opted to make the bulk of its chips at home in Japan. In this it is unlike its rival NEC, which is concentrating more and more of its chip making abroad. By 1994 NEC was already making 15 per cent of its chips outside Japan, and was planning more and more investments, developing major new production centres in Livingston, Scotland, and in Roseville, California, close to the major markets of North America and Europe, and building up its manufacturing with hundreds of millions of dollars of investment. These plants are doing front-end processes such as wafer processing. NEC's senior vice president Yuichi Haneta claimed in late 1994 that productivity in Scotland and California was 'already at the same level as our plants here in Japan'. In addition, NEC has set up labour-dependent back-end processes, meaning assembly and inspection, in Ireland and Singapore. But when it came to the $1 billion investment for mass production of 256-megabit DRAMs beginning in 1999, NEC decided to build at home in Japan.

Other Japanese chip makers, including Fujitsu (in Durham, England), Hitachi and Mitsubishi Electric (in the USA and Germany), have also been building capacity abroad. 'Simply due to the rising yen, we can no longer continue manufacturing in Japan for foreign markets,' said a senior executive of one of the chip makers. Toshiba, by contrast, is the only major manufacturer without any front-end processing abroad. It was slow to go abroad because of the energies it put into the 1-megabit DRAM production, and now it rationalises its decision by saying that it would take too long to set up new plants abroad, that it had expected the yen to climb through the 100 mark against the US dollar, and that there is no reason to panic. Luckily the world is hungry for chips, but if the yen starts rising again, its decision will be called increasingly into question.

Fumio Sato, in his spacious office at the top of the Toshiba building, commanding a splendid view (on a clear day) of Mount Fuji and (on any day) of the imaginative skyscraper housing his rival NEC, has plenty of worries on his mind. Years of economic recession and almost imperceptible growth, accompanied by the high yen, have taken big bites out of Toshiba's income and seen its profits tumble. In the year to March 1994, pre-tax profits perked up a bit to 90 billion yen, but this was just a third of those in the year to March 1990. In 1993 Toshiba announced that it would cut 5,000 workers from its Japanese payroll of 75,000 over the next three to five years. This would mainly be done by cutting back on new hiring to about 1,800 a year, rather than the 3,000 new recruits it was accustomed to take on each year.

Worldwide, almost a quarter of a million people work for the 800 companies and affiliates that form the Toshiba group. Sato sadly admitted that the role of a president has changed with the changing economic circumstances: 'I assumed the job when Japan entered this recession, something more serious than a mere cyclical recession. Today the Japanese economy has matured and we need restructuring. I have reviewed the overall business content of the company to produce concentration and selection of our activities to prepare for the informational era. I have also restructured the management to make it able to cope with the rapid changes of the era.'

He explained more fully: 'We are in a period where technical changes are very rapid and demand from the market also changes very swiftly, so we have to take management decisions equally quickly to meet these changes. This means that even in Japanese management there will be more tendency for top-down decisions, otherwise companies will not be able to cope ... I believe that we will be gradually approaching a more western style of management,' Sato added, breaking out of the Japanese and into English for the words 'western-style management'. 'But we have to preserve the best of the Japanese practices.'

Asked what were the main virtues of the Japanese system that he wished to preserve, he immediately replied, 'Harmony and the strength that Japanese companies can demonstrate as a group.' He was more doubtful about lifetime employment, under which – at least as far as Japan's big companies are concerned – workers stay with the same company from school or university until retirement. This creates two-way obligations: workers do not quit to go job-hopping; and companies do not lay off workers when the economy turns sour. 'Lifetime employment is prob-lematical if the economy is in recession,' Sato claimed.

Pressed about the level of growth needed to allow lifetime employment to continue, he doubted whether 2.5 per cent, now estimated to be the medium-term trend rate for Japan, would allow the system to flourish. 'If the growth rate is low, lifetime employment creates a tremendous burden on any company.' He was not prepared to be dogmatic about Toshiba and added, 'We can be flexible because we have areas of activity which are growing at 4 to 5 per cent.' He claimed that 'Our younger generation has little resistance about changing jobs', so 'what we have tried to maintain will crumble over the years because of the ease with which people now change jobs'. However, the Toshiba chief, who was 63 when he was appointed president in 1992, was less sure about any switch away from the seniority system. He actually pulled a face at the suggestion that Japanese companies might adopt western practices and appoint bright young whiz-kids to top jobs. There would not be a chief executive of Toshibo in his late forties or early fifties for the foreseeable future, Sato predicted.

Like many Japanese chief executives, Sato would be considered colourless by western standards. He is a graduate of Tokyo University. He came up – as his predecessors have done – from the ranks of the heavy energy machinery-producing business. Constant choice of presidents from Brobdingnag, rather than Lilliput, which is where all the exciting new developments are occurring, has brought the criticism that Toshiba's future lies with hi-tech electronics and that it should give them a turn at managing its future. Other critics attack the élitism of choosing Tokyo University graduates, who are sucked into the pernicious cosy club of Japan Inc. through their personal connections with high-ranking bureaucrats and other industrial leaders. Throughout the interview, Sato was the epitome of a grey man, wearing a grey suit to match his greying hair. He made no grand or grandiloquent gestures or statements. The nearest he came to dynamism was when he brought out a chart to show how Toshiba was preparing 'a project to study family life in the twenty-first century, an advanced life project', but he quickly withdrew it, claiming that it was a top company secret.

Toshiba colleagues stress Sato's qualities of being firm yet having a clear view of the complications of the company and of its future. Being a good manager who can also think ahead and choose the best allies for the twenty-first century is vital, they assert, since Toshiba has plenty of scientists and researchers who will see that it continues consistently to be in the top three in the world when it comes to registering new patents or inventions.* Sato himself sees an important connection between his favourite game and business: 'Success in shogi,' he said, 'presupposes careful attention to detail and the ability to devise a systematic plan to see you through to a strong finish. I believe that similar qualities of mind

---

* In 1993 Toshiba was disappointed only to be second, to IBM, in the number of patents registered with the US government; it had 1,064 patients, 24 fewer than IBM.

are helpful in implementing a successful plan to manage a company' – provided that he is not thinking and planning so far ahead that he misses the opportunities immediately in front of him.

7

Mom 'n' Pop are not Enough for Matsushita

Yoichi Morishita is different from most senior Japanese corporate executives. He has a distinctly aggressive outlook. He is also the outsider who has been given the difficult job of turning round a large but traditional enterprise, lumbered with a strong sense of its own importance and with the brooding presence of the founding family. His unequivocal message to the 252,000 group employees immediately after he took over in early 1993 was that the old methods and especially the reliance on 25,000 corner stores – typically called 'Mom 'n' Pop stores' because that is how they are owned and run – will no longer suffice. The company, he declared, would have to move with the times, modernise and accept new management methods. 'We became lax and extravagant,' Morishita proclaimed, refusing to mince his words in the time-honoured fashion of typical Japanese executives.

He took over as president and chief executive of Matsushita Electric Industrial Company after his predecessor, Akio Tanii, resigned to 'take responsibility' for a 50 billion yen ($500 million) fraud scandal involving a subsidiary, a defective line of company products and plummeting profits. This trio of difficulties was only the start of Morishita's difficult baptism. The change of leadership was not made easier by reports – duly denied in chorus by the company – that the outgoing president was a victim of pressures from the founding family, and particularly from chairman Masaharu Matsushita, the son-in-law of Konosuke Matsushita, who set up the concern in Osaka in March 1918. The hot question is whether Morishita will have the time to be his own man, or whether the family just expects him to keep the top seat warm for the founder's grandson and chairman's son, Masayuki Matsushita, who is in his late forties and moved into the fourth-ranking job in the company at the same time as Morishita took over.

The questions are important not just because Matsushita is a big company, the world's biggest producer of consumer electrical products. It was until 1995 also the owner of MCA, the Hollywood film giant and its Universal Studios. Most important, Matsushita epitomises the traditional Japanese corporate management style now coming under pressure.

Outside Japan, Matsushita is probably less well known than Sony, one of its main rivals. Sony has become an international household name, synonymous throughout the world with the highest quality audio-visual products, thanks to its maverick co-founder Akio Morita. But inside Japan, Sony is the Johnny-Come-Lately and is a much smaller, younger relation to Matsushita. Matsushita is almost twice as big as Sony in terms of sales and employees. In the year to March 1994, Sony's sales were 3,734 billion yen or $37.3 billion, whereas Matsushita's were 6,624 billion yen. Sony employed 126,000 people worldwide; but Matsushita workers numbered more than a quarter of a million for it and its more than a hundred subsidiaries round the world.

One reason for the disproportionate international fame is that Sony's Morita had an international outlook and deliberately courted good opinions round the world; Matsushita's founder, apart from being older and the product of a different time, was more introverted and quintessentially Japanese.

Another reason is that the Sony parent company exports 65 per cent of its products, whereas Matsushita relies on exports for only 35 per cent of its sales. Yet another is that Matsushita does not appear on the company's brand names, which are sold under the labels 'National', 'Panasonic', 'Quasar' and 'Technics'.

Matsushita's whole sphere of operations is just much bigger than Sony's, although it is widely spread. One senior executive said dismissively of the smaller, younger company, 'Yes, Sony is one of our main rivals, but just for one of our product lines, audio-visual products. But we are much, much bigger than that.' Indeed, production of audio-visual equipment is big at Matsushita. It makes televisions of all kinds, video cassette recorders and camcorders, video disc players, satellite broadcast receivers and satellite communications equipment, radios, tape-recorders, compact disc players, stereo hi-fis, car audio products and even electronic musical instruments.

One of Matsushita's claims to fame is that it took the video cassette recorder system pioneered by Sony, developed a different format, and by virtue of its production, sales and marketing muscle not only overturned Sony's lead, but made the Matsushita VHS format *the* international standard and Sony's Beta the also-ran, undermining the upstart young company in the VCR market and raising doubts about Sony's staying power. All its audio-visual products together account for less than a third of Matsushita's total sales.

The company is a major producer of home appliances – items like refrigerators, washing machines, dishwashers, irons, vacuum cleaners, microwave ovens, electric fans and heaters, and electric blankets and heated rugs, as well as rice cookers, a vital ingredient in every Japanese kitchen. Together these account for about 13 per cent of its sales, and its major competitors in these appliances are companies like Toshiba and Hitachi.

According to Matsushita's classifications, under which video and audio equipment are counted separately, making up 21 and 8 per cent of sales respectively, the largest single component of its sales consists of communications and industrial equipment, which together make up 24 per cent. This subgroup includes a welter of products, some of which are familiar parts of late twentieth-century offices, such as fax machines, copying machines, word processors, personal computers, telephones and PBX systems and vending machines. Another subgroup embraces other items, which are more likely to be found in factories, including industrial robots, welding machines, measuring instruments, compressors and electronics-parts-mounting machines. In this huge area of activities, the competition is different again and comes from NEC, Fujitsu and other Japanese companies.

Even this is not the end of the Matsushita production story. Another 12 per cent of its activities come from making electronics components, including integrated circuits, discrete devices, image pick-up tubes, tuners, capacitors, resistors, magnetic recording heads, motors and electric lamps. Matsushita and the US Symetrix Corporation recently developed the world's first gallium arsenide integrated circuit with a built-in capacitor. About 5 per cent of Matsushita's sales come from making batteries and kitchen-related products: another wide group of products from batteries of all kinds to gas cookers, baths and sanitary equipment, even including kitchen sinks. A further 8 per cent of Matsushita's products are classified as 'other', including some of the original products the founder was involved with, such as bicycles, along with a complete assortment of cameras and flash units, electric pencil sharpeners, water purifiers, lumber, paper and medical equipment and imported goods.

Since late 1990 Matsushita has had to squeeze in yet another category to its already lengthy list of items. Entertainment by 1994 accounted for about 9 per cent of the conglomerate's consolidated sales. This is thanks to the purchase of MCA, the American film business, for a whopping $6.6 billion, just before the end of the carefree 'bubble economy' years when Japanese companies had money pouring in and went on a huge spending spree. Critics claimed that Matsushita bought the film maker in copycat response to Sony's purchase of Columbia Pictures (for a mere $3.4 billion), a charge which Matsushita denies. Nevertheless, its top executives admit that there is virtually no one in the parent company who knows much about films and how they are made, let alone about the whims and fancies and fantasies of the US entertainment business. This ignorance became a major problem in late 1994 and early 1995, leading to dangerous flaring of tempers between Tokyo and Hollywood.

Matsushita was so preoccupied with the repercussions of domestic recession that it had little time to attend to the demands of the temperamental Hollywood moguls. In Japan's golden days of high and steady economic growth, being big was almost a virtue in itself for Matsushita. Very size attracted the best choice of employees. The range of products meant that, although one of them might be in recession or temporarily out of favour, there was a varied line of goods, many of which would be selling well. If the real crunch came, such as a challenge from Sony with its video cassette recorder, then Matsushita's size was part of its strength. Through its large number of corner stores, it had a lock on traditional outlets for electrical goods, which it used to good effect to kill off the opposition, which had fewer exclusive sales points.

But by the early 1990s, times had changed. Recession in the West was bad enough, but it was accompanied by deep and lingering recession in Japan that hit corporate profits hard, not for one year, but for four in succession, unprecedented in the post-war economy. The rapid rise in the value of the yen merely made it harder for big industrial companies to export their way out of economic difficulties, as they had sometimes done in the past; it also trimmed profit margins savagely and raised questions about long-term business practices in Japan. As Matsushita's annual report for 1993 summed up, 'The harsh operating conditions that characterised fiscal 1993 made the year a trying one for Matsushita. More than a temporary adjustment phase, this downturn seems to foreshadow a fundamental change in the economic and social orders ...' This was just as Morishita took over as president, and was one aspect of the problems that he had to face. The other was taking over the helm of what was still very much a family company. The strength of Konosuke Matsushita's presence years after his death was seen not only in the continuing family name, and the presence of his descendants on the board and among the managers of the company, but also in a very powerful industry devoted and dedicated to the memory of Konosuke Matsushita, frequently called 'the god of management'.

The original Matsushita personified a number of important aspects of the modern Japanese industrial miracle. The company he started began relatively recently, in 1918, had to fight its way up without privileges of wealth or connections, and displayed an individualist and entrepreneurial spirit that seems ancient history and totally alien to modern, wealthy, conformist and bureaucratic Japan – and which indeed sits awkwardly with the big, late twentieth-century Matsushita Electrical Industrial.

Konosuke Matsushita was born in 1894 in Wasamura, a small village south of Osaka, the youngest child in a family of three boys and five girls. His early childhood was pleasant, even idyllic. But when he was four years old, his father's speculation on the rice market cost the family its comfortable farm property and even its house, enforcing a move to the nearby city of Wakayama into a cramped tenement house. The three oldest children, including both brothers, died young mainly because of simple infections that could not be cured by the primitive medical facilities and which developed into deadly illnesses.

At the age of nine, Konosuke Matsushita was put on the train to Osaka and apprenticed to a maker of *hibachi*, portable charcoal stoves widely used to heat the home in those days before central heating or electric or gas fires (and still in use even now in some Tokyo homes). When the owner moved out of town, Matsushita shifted his apprenticeship to a bicycle shop. Part of his duties there consisted of turning the mechanism to operate a lathe used in repair work, since the shop did not have electric power. It was a tiring and painful job. 'If the machine slowed before it ought, the craftsman would hit me on the head – with a mallet. This may sound a bit rough, but craftsmen in those days expected apprentices to work hard and they disciplined us with a heavy hand. The rough treatment, in fact, was part and parcel of becoming a good craftsman. To complain or to show indignation about such treatment, moreover, was bound to bring on greater wrath than the original transgression. In retrospect, it seems to me that the simple thumpings and thrashings we received at the hands of masters and senior craftsmen responsible for our training had a human warmth that is hard to find in this post-industrial age.'*

At the age of fifteen, Matsushita, 'fascinated by the potential of electricity', left the bicycle shop to get a job with the Osaka Electric Light Company doing interior wiring. Promotion to the coveted position of inspector at the age of 21, and his delicate health, prompted Matsushita to re-examine his career and decide to go into business on his own, making electric sockets. With words of warning from his boss, who had seen his prototype – 'that socket's not as good as you think' – ringing in his ears, Matsushita set off on his own.

The giant known today as Matsushita Electric Industrial Company, with hosts of subsidiaries employing people in almost 40 countries, started with less than 100 yen in capital. Even with the help of his 33.20 yen severance pay, compulsory savings of 40 yen and personal savings of 20 yen, the young entrepreneur could only put together 93.20 yen, 'even in those days a paltry sum when it came to setting up a business'. Two other former colleagues joined him, and his wife's younger brother, Toshio Iue (later to found Sanyo Electric Company), offered help. They borrowed 100 yen as additional capital and set up in Matsushita's two-room tenement house in Osaka.

'We had plenty of manpower, but that was all,' he confessed. 'None of us knew where to purchase materials, how to make a socket or what price a socket could be sold for ... My wife had to make frequent trips to the

---

* Account in Matsushita's autobiography, *Quest for Prosperity*, published in 1988.

pawn shop to exchange what good clothes we had for small amounts of cash.' Formal establishment of the Matsushita Electric Appliance Factory was done the following year with the family's move to a larger two-storey house/workshop in Osaka. Matsushita attributed his rapid success to a mixture of hard work and good luck. The foundation was laid on an improved version of the two-way socket that Matsushita himself had first designed.

Matsushita quickly diversified his activities by developing a new battery-powered bicycle lamp to replace the old candle lamp which would blow out in a gentle wind. This was ready from 1923, but he found that bicycle dealers were reluctant to take a new-fangled product. His revolutionary method of convincing them was to persuade dealers to take the lamp, but not to pay until their customers were happy with the new technology. It may seem a simple idea, but it meant that Matsushita had to risk making and distributing up to 10,000 lamps worth 15,000 yen, an enormous sum for those times, before seeing its return and reward. It paid off handsomely. A later improved square version of the lamp was given the newly invented 'National' trademark, which became synonymous with battery-powered lamps. This logo was later used for all household electrical appliances. Matsushita himself confessed that he had no idea what the English word 'national' meant; he initially thought that it must have something to do with the Russian Revolution before he looked it up in a dictionary and decided that 'the meaning was perfect for a product I hoped would become indispensable in every household in the country'.

In these early days, Matsushita showed that he was a true Osakan. The dialect spoken in this city differs crucially from that spoken in Tokyo and other parts of Japan, especially in showing life that is trade and money driven. In general greetings, rather than say, *'O genki desuka?'* ('Are you well?'), which is the normal Japanese expression, Osakans are down to earth in greeting acquaintances with *'Mokari makka?'* ('How much money are you making?') Matsushita upbraided his young brother-in-law, Toshio Iue, for daring to spend three yen on 'a good linen mosquito net that will last a long time'. 'For whatever reason,' Matsushita wrote sternly, 'you are in no position to buy an expensive linen mosquito net that costs three yen. If you thought more carefully about the financial state of Matsushita Electric today, you would realise that you could do just as well with a simple one-yen cotton net.'

During the Great Depression that began in 1929, Matsushita, again sick in bed, began to develop his home-spun philosophy. He refused requests to lay off employees, deciding to pay normal rates for half-days of work without holidays, while urging staff to sell the backlog of stocks. It worked, boasted Matsushita, who could not understand the lack of dynamism and failure to act on the part of Japan's leaders. 'Quite unlike the period just before and during World War II, when there were dire shortages of goods, it was a time of considerable material abundance. If this abundance were actively consumed, I believed, it would encourage new production. Business would improve and the depression would come to an end. People would recover their vigour and energy, and national strength would increase, making the goal of a prosperous society and nation a reality. Retrenchment would only result in the opposite outcome . . .'.* Matsushita Electric prospered and began to diversify the range of its products. From making electric irons and heaters, it moved into producing radios. 'I had a radio set that seemed to break down whenever there was a programme I really wanted to hear,' complained Matsushita. The company expanded production of dry batteries for lamps and other purposes.

With the strengthening grip of the Japanese military in the late 1930s, some items in Matsushita's production line, such as fans and heaters, were banned as luxuries, and other goods were curtailed. When full-blown war was declared, Matsushita became an integral and important part of the war effort, making bayonets, parts for guns, wooden propellers, wireless receivers and transmitters, and finally wooden ships and aircraft. It did this so wholeheartedly that the occupation forces put Matsushita on its blacklists, and an order was issued stopping production.

The Supreme Commander for the Allied Powers (SCAP), however, took action against Matsushita not merely for being part of Japan's war machine. It placed the company on the same list as some of Japan's oldest and most distinguished families, along with Mitsui, Mitsubishi, Sumitomo and Yasuda, as a *zaibatsu* (an industrial and financial conglomerate). Such conglomerates were the prime targets for breaking up during the regime of the victorious powers. This itself placed restrictions on the company's plans for getting back to full production, since it meant that its smallest activities were 'bound hand and foot by the zaibatsu dissolution directives'. Much bigger rivals like Hitachi and Mitsubishi Electric were split off from their parents and allowed to get on with business, while Matsushita had to sit and fume.

The reason was that Matsushita had spawned 60 subsidiaries for its varied activities, and to the Allied officials now running the defeated country, it looked just as much of an ugly spider at the centre of a vast web as did Mitsui or Mitsubishi. For Konosuke Matsushita himself this had the worst consequences, since he was not allowed to be involved in management or to set foot on Matsushita's premises. His assets were frozen and his living expenses were set by SCAP, to whom he had to report on his budget and expenses, and from whom he had to get monthly permission to pay his housekeeper. Indeed, like other zaibatsu presidents, he should have resigned.

Stubbornly, he did not and fought to save and resurrect his company

* *Quest for Prosperity.*

from what he saw as blind, stupid, foreign officialdom. 'At the time we received notice of our designation as a zaibatsu, I realised that the authorities did not have their facts straight,' he complained in his autobiography. 'For one thing, Matsushita Electric was not among those enterprises that had been in business for generations; for another, it had not had a hand in controlling Japanese industry as had the big combines. I had started from nothing and built up the company little by little; it was a mere twenty-odd years since it had been founded in the Obiraki-cho tenement house. We were little more than a small electric shop grown rather large, and yet we were being treated like the great Mitsui, Mitsubishi and Sumitomo concerns. In a way, I suppose, it was an honour to be put in such illustrious company, but I was sure it was all an absurd mistake.'

Correcting that mistake took more than 5,000 pages of documents, all transcribed from Japanese into English, more than 100 trips from Osaka to Tokyo, more than 50 personal appearances by Matsushita himself at SCAP headquarters, 'riding into Tokyo in trains that were invariably overflowing with passengers', and waiting for more than four years while the 'investigating' went on. He was supported by otherwise obstreperous trade union members, 15,000 of whom signed a petition, and whose leaders tried in vain to meet SCAP himself, General Douglas MacArthur, to argue with him that Matsushita Electric was Matsushita himself, not some vast empire. The battle was slowly won. First, in May 1947 Matsushita was redesignated from Class A to Class B for purposes of the purge of management, the only 'zaibatsu' to be downgraded. Then, slowly, other various corporate and personal restrictions were lifted. Finally, in July 1950 Matsushita Electric and Matsushita himself were released from their 'bondage' (as he put it), and were free to work and produce again.

He restarted with visits to the USA and to Europe. In New York he was amazed at the material prosperity and to find that an American worker could buy a General Electric radio for the equivalent of two days' pay, whereas a Matsushita radio in Japan would cost a worker a month and a half's total wages. In Europe he made the contacts for a deal with the Dutch electrical company Philips Gloeilampenfabrieken to form a new electronics company. This was to be a joint-venture operation under which Matsushita would receive vital European know-how. The bargaining session was long and hard, and Matsushita showed his own fighting spirit in the negotiations. He accepted Philips' demands of a payment of $550,000 plus 30 per cent of the company stock, but objected to its claims for a 6 per cent technical fee. Instead, Matsushita agreed to pay a 4.5 per cent technical guidance fee, but demanded that Philips agree to pay a 3 per cent management expertise fee, which it did.

The technical deal – not a tie-up, said one Philips executive, but a marriage – resulted in the creation of Matsushita Electronics Corporation, established in December 1952, which began to make light bulbs, fluorescent lights, vacuum tubes, transistors, semiconductors, television picture tubes and other modern electronics parts, thus giving Matsushita a part of the hi-tech electronics world that was just beginning to boom. The joint venture, with its terms gradually revised towards equality (although the Japanese company preserved its majority stake), lasted until 1993 when Matsushita bought out Philips' stake.

Konosuke Matsushita stayed at the helm of the company he had founded until 1973, when he retired as chairman to become special adviser. But there is no doubt that his was very much the guiding hand at Matsushita at least until his death in April 1989, when he left an estate worth 244.9 billion yen, the highest figure in Japan's history. In a very real sense, he is still the most influential figure overseeing the company. This is not merely a trivial question of reverence for the founding father who is not long dead, although that influence is stronger in Japan than in typical western countries. Matsushita himself believed strongly in the correct order and place of things. He said once that he was 'a creature of the Meiji era', referring to the emperor under whose rule from 1867 to 1912 Japan was opened to the rest of the world.

His views about emperors being august beings encountered a culture shock when he went to the Netherlands to be invested as commander in the Order of Orange Nassau, an honour for Matsushita's business co-operation with Philips. He and his wife expected pomp and circumstance and instead were shown 'into a chamber that was obviously not a throne room. As we hesitantly stepped inside, a woman in her fifties with an easy air came forward to greet us. We took her at first to be a lady-in-waiting. Imagine our surprise when she turned out to be the queen!' So surprised was he by Queen Juliana's informal manner that when she offered a cigarette, he accepted, even though he was a non-smoker.

Matsushita the founder was full of homespun philosophy. The key to success, he said, lies in persistence. 'Failure comes only when one stops making an effort.' He also declared that 'Any organisation, no matter how big it may be, is destined to decline when it loses its philosophy or goal.' He pioneered the idea that corporate loyalty is not only the most important thing in life, but goes beyond life itself and into the grave. Matsushita was the leader in what by the 1990s had become something of a trend of establishing corporate tombs. He established the Matsushita cenotaph as far back as 1938 at Koyasan near Wakayama, in an area surrounded, appropriately, by tombs of samurai warriors. By the 1990s more than 300 companies had established corporate graves in the area.

Jyosho Kirimura, a local priest, commented that 'The rise and fall of corporations is the same phenomenon as the rise and fall of feudal lords. In this context, the practice of corporate tombs is not new, but comes from the age of battles.' The company asks for the consent of the families of the bereaved person before adding them to the roll of those commemorated in the corporate cenotaph, but only a handful of the 100 or so Matsushita people dying each year decline, so that now several thousand employees are united to the company in death as they were in life. Matsushita is thinking of offering the facility to its foreign employees.

There is a favourite trick question which is sometimes asked of newcomers to Japan. It is – which is the most popular song in Japan? The answer is not something by Sting, or some golden oldie by the Beatles, or a soulful Japanese pop tune, or a historic song. The correct answer is '*Ai to Hikari to Yume de*' 'With Love and Light and Dream'. Most Japanese probably have not heard of it, but the almost 100,000 employees of Matsushita and its associates sing it promptly every workday morning. It is the company song, the first version of which was sung in 1933. This was another pioneering invention of Konosuke Matsushita, and started a wave of such songs by other companies. The management says it creates an 'emotional medium' tying employees to the company. To westerners this practice smacks of groupism, if not totalitarianism, but Japanese respond that the corporate singers gain joy from singing as part of a big happy family.

The company refuses to provide the words of Japan's most popular song 'because of the copyright issue', but some employees were happy to oblige. Clearly the corporate spirit infuses the song with something that is missing in the words. The opening verse goes something like this: 'Love and light and dream, cheerful heart full of life, Matsushita Electric connects them abundantly. Time passes and youthful days come again. Let's surround the blooming world and green country with love, light and dream.'

But Matsushita left more behind than the idea of the corporate samurai fighting spirit and the obligatory busts in the company headquarters as a reminder of his continuing presence. His 'Basic Management Objective', written in 1929, appears frequently in the company's brochures and in its offices: 'Recognising our responsibilities as industrialists, we will devote ourselves to the progress and development of society and the well-being of people through our business activities, thereby enhancing the quality of life throughout the world.'

He also left behind an institute to continue his work, called PHP, which has published many of the founder's writings, including several books of essays published in English. Indeed, the industry of turning out his thoughts continues after his death. In 1993 PHP (standing for the English words 'Peace, Happiness and Prosperity') published *A Piece of the Action*, effectively a series of short sermons on life originally written in Japanese by Matsushita in 1981 and 1984. In these he comes across as a kindly, but elderly clergyman of the conservative school.

For example, he advises junior executives to show consideration for their superiors. He offers the record of a dialogue between himself and a young colleague. ' "Young man, can you do a shoulder massage?" "No, sir, I can't." "What, you never massaged your mother's or father's shoulders?" said I, surprised. "No," the young man answered in embarrassment. "At least, not very often." "Well," I warned him, "that means you won't get very far in business." ' To the tired Matsushita, the offer of a massage for a weary superior was a way of showing thoughtfulness, which would be rewarded with respect, growing partnership and potential promotion. 'I am not talking about apple-polishing or seeking brownie points,' added the businessman-author-philosopher, 'but the kind of genuine concern that endears people to each other.'

Matsushita subscribed to the 'equal but different' view of women, ascribing to women the prime role of bearing and rearing children and to men the position of main bread – or rice – winner. He regretted the modern idea that 'men and women are increasingly assigning themselves identical roles'. He lamented male chauvinism and welcomed the entry of women 'into more visible positions in society and their efforts to pursue lifelong careers, but ... [the] advance of women into the work force will only succeed if it is premised on a full understanding of the role they have played in the household, whether their role was moulded by history or biology'.

The influence of Matsushita is reflected not only in this reverence for him, but also in the continuing and important presence of members of his family in key positions in the company. His son-in-law, Masaharu, has the pivotal position of chairman. Normally, in a Japanese company, the chairman's job is more decorative than powerful. Though he chairs the board of directors and represents the company nationally and internationally, the day-to-day power of running the company is held by the president, who is the chief executive.

In most Japanese companies, the rule is that the president – unless he has disgraced himself or unless there is a tradition that a government ministry placeman will take an *amakudari* (literally 'descent from heaven', meaning retirement) post – will step up to be chairman, where he may take an active part in industry-wide activities. But in Matsushita, the family has kept the chairman's job, first through the brother-in-law of the founder, then through his son-in-law. Given the family name and continuing influence of the founder, this gives the chairman more leverage than in any ordinary company. Japanese newspapers have also been full of speculation for several years about whether the founder's grandson, Masayuki, aged 48 in 1994, would be the next or perhaps the next-but-one president.

In spite of the reverence for the founder, life has evidently not always been smooth between the president and the family chairman of the company. Akio Tanii, who resigned abruptly in the middle of his term of office in 1993, was generally supposed to have upset the family by trying to dismantle the management structure that Konosuke Matsushita had set in place. Tanii had set up a so-called 'Living Department' and two other supra-divisional departments dealing with construction electronics and information and communications.

This was done in April 1990 as part of Tanii's 'Human 21' programme, aiming eventually to split Matsushita's operations into separate subsidiaries. It was an attempt to keep Matsushita vigorous and prevent its corporate arteries from hardening. But company insiders also saw it as an attempt to assert Tanii's independence from the founder by dismantling his system, under which each division functions as an independent profit centre. The direct impetus for the creation of the new departments came from the purchase of MCA Inc. in November 1990. Matsushita clearly wanted and needed to exploit MCA's film and music software on a company-wide basis.

But Tanii's experiment was flawed. In spite of their responsibilities, the departments had no authority over their own personnel or budget affairs, which were left in the hands of the separate divisions. Chairman Masaharu Matsushita himself was one of the strongest critics of the scheme, arguing that the company's organisation should consist of divisions and division headquarters reporting to the president. In another move which upset the family president, Tanii tried drastically to reorganise the 'family' of retail shops, the very 'Mom 'n' Pop' stores which Matsushita himself had nurtured as the centre of the company's marketing strength, and as key players in his management ethos of 'co-existence and co-prosperity'. Retailers were quick to complain to the chairman about the cutting off of rebates, another factor which helped to undermine Tanii as president.

When he actually stepped down in February 1993, with fifteen months to go in his two-year term, Tanii said he was resigning 'to take responsibility' – a favourite Japanese term – for several mishaps. One was the discovery of defects in 700,000 refrigerators. More important was the involvement of Matsushita's National Lease subsidiary in a massive fraud, in which several institutions, including the internationally respected Industrial Bank of Japan (IBJ), had lent huge sums of money to an Osaka restaurant owner and spiritualist (see Chapter 2). National Lease had lent her 50 billion yen ($416 million in 1993 when Tanii resigned) and had suffered a loss of 20.9 billion yen from the episode.

The real surprise in Japanese corporate and financial circles was why Tanii had not resigned earlier, if it was just a question of the financial scandal. The chairman of IBJ had stepped down in 1992 to accept responsibility for his bank's involvement in supplying money to the conwoman. Tanii had evidently fought for his position – though he denied that he had been pressured into giving up the post – but the declining financial fortunes of Matsushita may have been the clinching factor. On the same day as he resigned, the company announced that its quarterly profit had plunged by 76 per cent. 'In addition to the worsening business environment, Tanii could not exert his leadership as freely as his predecessor, Toshiro Yamashita, who enjoyed the strong backing of the late founder,' said one leading Japanese analyst. Chairman Matsushita gave what might be seen as a 'good riddance' comment to the departing chief executive. He said that he would be remaining at his post and added, 'Matsushita should go back to the time of the Konosuke era, when diligent and honest corporate culture was valued.'

In spite of this assertion, the problems of Matsushita will not be so easily solved, and one of them, though secondary to restoring the company to good financial health, is the role of the family. New president Morishita did quickly scrap his predecessor's 'reorganisation dream'. But he made it clear, in interviews, in internal comments to members of the Matsushita army of employees and in his actions, that the company is going through a difficult time and needs to take special business measures to meet the changing environment. 'What we're dealing with is not simply another cyclical downturn, but a structural problem stemming from how Japanese industry developed,' he warned bluntly. 'We have to recognise that to make progress, we must do things differently.'

The weaknesses of Matsushita's position are clear enough. The network of 25,000 Mom 'n' Pop stores which served so brilliantly in the past have become something of a liability when consumers are seeking both better service and cheaper prices than the local corner stores can provide. In the days of light bulbs, radios and refrigerators, when prices were fixed, the corner store was fine, especially if it stayed open until late at night and the shop owner also tinkered as a repair man carrying a stock of replacement parts. But in the closing years of the twentieth century, the corner shop was under fierce pressure from rebellious consumers increasingly resentful of the high prices charged in Japan.

The small stores enjoyed protection from supermarkets and other giants because of strict land-zoning laws. This hindered but did not prevent the burgeoning of speciality discount stores offering both more variety and cheaper prices. In places like Akihabara in downtown Tokyo, shop after shop was piled high with immense varieties of electrical and electronics goods made not just by Matsushita, but by Sony, Hitachi, Toshiba, NEC and even some foreign makers. Shoppers could instantly compare the variations in the latest technology and prices in one place. When the recession of the early 1990s began to hit, even the Akihabara stores suffered undercutting by discount stores located away from the high rents of downtown Tokyo. In all this, the corner store owner could cope neither with the price cutting nor with the advances of technology. He was quite able to replace a light bulb or a small faulty part in an electric iron, but he had little idea what was wrong with the motherboard of a personal computer and might not be able to tell a warper from a woofer on a stereo system.

Signs of the growing clout of Japan's discount retailers became clear in early 1994 when Matsushita and the supermarket leader, Daiei, announced that the electronics giant would continue to supply Chujitsuya when that supermarket chain was absorbed by the bigger Daiei. For 30 years the supermarket and electronics giants had been at virtual war by personal order of Konosuke Matsushita, incensed by Daiei president Isao Nakauchi's discounting of suggested retail prices. The Matsushita founder believed that price competition harmed both manufacturers and consumers, and refused to supply any goods to Daiei. Officially, Matsushita spokesmen said that it was still the case that their company would not sell to Daiei, and there was a 'gentlemen's agreement' that Chujitsuya would not ship Matsushita products to other Daiei stores. But this was an attempt to put a brave face on a defeat. Chujitsuya stores, which benefit from direct purchase from the electronics company, were making discounts of 10 to 50 per cent on Matsushita products, as was being done regularly at other discount stores.

An intermediary for the deal said that there were threats of a reference to the Fair Trade Commission (FTC) should Matsushita discontinue supplies to the supermarket, and president Morishita was specifically told that his company could find itself in the same position as the cosmetics maker Shiseido, which was humiliatingly raided by FTC officials in September 1993 after refusing to supply a mass-merchandiser. For Matsushita, the question of whether or not to supply Daiei may be a minor allergy only, but it is symptomatic of a disease that will not be so easily curable, that price cutting is part of the world of the late twentieth century, and that the dedicated retailers who were part of Matsushita's strength are now part of its vulnerability.

The second weakness stems from the rise and rise of the Japanese yen. Until the early 1970s, the yen had stayed at 360 to the dollar, affording a certainty that was reassuring at a rate that allowed Japanese goods to take on and conquer the world. By the mid-1980s it floated happily for Japanese manufacturers and exporters in the range of 240 to 260 against the dollar. At that point Washington exerted pressure through the Plaza Accord (named after the Plaza Hotel in New York where the key international meetings were held) to force the yen higher. It soared to the 150 level against the dollar, such a rapid increase that it set Japanese exporters squealing. But as the Japanese economy recovered, so the big companies forgot their worries, buoyed by rising economic growth, profits and stock market.

Matsushita was so optimistic that it spent a huge slice of its cash mountain in buying MCA just before the economic bubble burst and growth stopped. But it did not stop the yen from rising, propelled partly by the trade surplus that continued to increase and partly by American anger and determination to force open Japan's markets. The grim bottom line for Matsushita and for other leading manufacturers, which occasioned Morishita's warning, is that at 120 yen to the dollar, if the domestic market is growing, it is possible to make money; but at 100 with slow domestic growth, most Japanese factories are not profitable.

Like other companies, Matsushita has already shifted considerable parts of its production offshore, either to places where labour is cheaper or to be closer to the market. By 1995 or 1996 it is likely that sales from its 150 overseas outposts will contribute more than 50 per cent of the total. In the USA it has twenty subsidiaries, together responsible for sales worth $6 billion a year and putting Matsushita US in the top 100 companies in the country. It has regional headquarters in the USA, London and Singapore, and has been rapidly increasing production in fast-growing but lower-cost Asian developing countries like Malaysia, Thailand and most recently China.

Malaysia is already an important regional manufacturing base, producing a quarter of Matsushita's air-conditioners and televisions, altogether 1.8 million air-conditioners and 1.3 million TVs a year, on computerised production lines more modern than those in Japan and able to work, for example, on 60 different models of television simultaneously. Its investments there mean that Matsushita alone contributes 3 per cent of Malaysia's exports and a huge 4.8 per cent of its gross domestic product. Some items, like medium-sized air-conditioners, which were originally developed in Japan for the Japanese market, and even colour television sets, are now exported from Malaysia to Japan.

China is already developing into a similarly powerful Matsushita base. The company has 16 joint ventures and officials say the company may build up to 30 factories. The Chinese operations are limited to specific items, such as washing machines and televisions for the rapidly growing consumer market, but the volumes coming off the production lines are potentially massive. Matsushita has been a pioneer in teaching the Chinese the new kinds of operation and the standards necessary for an aspiring industrial country.

In its plant making a million tubes for colour televisions in Peking, the strictest standards of cleanliness are maintained, and visitors have to wrap their shoes in plastic at the door to help keep the factory dust-free. The assembly line came from Japan; it was dismantled by the Chinese workers and put together again in Peking. The plant was all set for its trial run in early June 1989 – and then the Chinese People's Army began the bloody crackdown on pro-democracy protesters in Tienanmen Square. The city ground to a halt and public transport stopped – but Matsushita's dedicated workers triumphed, and 90 per cent of them turned up for work, arriving by bicycle or on foot. The company booked a whole hotel to save workers long journeys home during the week of the crisis.

In late 1993 Matsushita took a giant 10 billion yen step forward in China with a joint venture to make 1.5 million video cassette recorders a year for the Chinese market, the biggest single such Japanese investment. It has not been a completely smooth ride, and the Japanese executives often complain about Chinese standards of timekeeping and teamwork. 'They don't want to share their knowledge with their colleagues,' grumbled one, 'but we are working on it and seeing progress.'

Matsushita's Japanese managers have also had to cope with tricky cultural practices in the American factories. In Japan, workers will stay on to finish the tasks of the day, whatever the clock says about the time; but in the USA, as one Japanese commented, 'Five o'clock is five o'clock and that's the time to go home.' Some Americans also resented the tight cost controls imposed from Osaka, including high standards of cleanliness and insisting on things like turning off the lights when leaving a room.

President Morishita presented many plus points of the foreign expansion. 'Our success in manufacturing abroad helps us more than it hurts us because that is where the fastest-growing markets are and because it gives us even more incentive to develop new products and technologies back here in Japan. Besides, it is our responsibility to help other countries to develop.'

Nevertheless, in spite of this offshore diversification to cut costs, president Morishita admitted in an interview in 1994 that the rising yen was such a problem that a single yen rise or fall would affect annual profits by between 5 and 6 billion yen. Even savage cost-cutting measures are hard to achieve, to make up for blows that land in $50 million lumps at a time. His best hope was that 1993 'will prove to be the bottom' and that the government's various packages to promote economic recovery would actually promote new growth and take some of the pressures off. Hopeful signs appeared with Matsushita's pre-tax profits for the six months to September 1994, which jumped by 46 per cent to 84.6 billion yen, after a hot summer drove up air-conditioner sales in Japan and a computer boom started abroad. Inspired by this, Matsushita forecast that it would make 210 billion pre-tax in the full year to March 1995. But this was still about 35 per cent of its profits in the year to March 1991, so no one was getting carried away.

The other critical question mark over Matsushita is whether it can show the leaps in creativity needed to conquer the brave new world of the twenty-first century, expected to be dominated by multimedia. US commentators, who had been filled with gloom during the 1980s, were beginning to crow again by the 1990s. At the creative end of the hardware, semiconductor chip makers like Intel kept their ground and were beginning to be challenged by new American, not Japanese, products such as the Apple–IBM chip, which will challenge Intel's Pentium in providing the brains for newer, faster, more creative computers. Software is still the prize preserve of American companies, with their looser, smaller, more individualistic structures than the regimented Japanese corporate armies can dream of. One jubilant New Yorker went so far as to boast, 'Let the Japanese keep their lead in the hardware – the boxes that house the new electronic gadgetry. In those areas competition is fierce and the profit margins are tiny. The Americans will retain their lead in brainwork – the software where the prizes are rich and the profits are high.'

Rival Sony's massive $2.7 billion write-down in late 1994 on Columbia/Tristar, which it bought in 1989, raised questions about the Japanese ability to cope with their purchases of American film studios. It seemed to confirm the American claims that the Japanese had plunged into a new world where forces of imagination were at play, and where their regimented minds could not cope with the restlessness and freedom that was needed to win. Sony certainly wrote its own starring role in a great horror movie. Soon afterwards questions were raised about Matsushita too.

Its venture into motion pictures had been a bigger surprise than Sony's, since Sony already knew about the entertainments and records business. By mid-1994 Matsushita was basking in the money and the glory of its MCA offshoot, including Universal Studios. This was thanks largely to Steven Spielberg, whose film *Jurassic Park* had swept aside all previous records, surpassed (his own) *ET, the Extra-Terrestrial*, and become the most profitable movie of all time, grossing more than $900 million worldwide. For honour and glory, MCA and Matsushita could also rejoice in Spielberg's *Schindler's List*, which swept the 1994 Oscar awards and will keep profits churning in. *The Flintstones* was also a useful winner.

However, the consensus of American film industry critics is that, apart from Spielberg's megahits, MCA's performance has been 'ho-hum', as one of them puts it. There were a handful of classy films, such as *In the Name of the Father*, some modest successes in *Dragon: the Bruce Lee Story, Carlito's Way* and the *Beethoven* films about a dog, and a lot of flops. *Junior*, the Christmas 1994 film starring a pregnant Arnold Schwarzenegger, proved only a modest success, and in 1995 MCA were risking a lot with a problem-plagued *Waterworld*, a science fiction adventure with Kevin Costner. Costing almost $150 million to make, this was the most expensive film ever, more expensive than Sony's flop, *Last Action Hero* (also starring Schwarzenegger). One cynical critic, Jessica Reif, entertainment analyst at Oppenheimer & Co., summed up the feeling that the Japanese did not know what they were doing in Hollywood: 'At Columbia, the Japanese let the lunatics take over the store. And at Universal, they [Matsushita] have one man representing them there, but he's in an office across the hall. I don't know what he does. This would be a good time for the Japanese to get out.'

Stock market perceptions in 1994 were somewhat different, rating the film companies at all-time highs. Sony paid about twelve times Columbia's cash flow (net income plus depreciation expenses) when it bought the movie maker, and Matsushita paid about fourteen times MCA's cash flow. But by 1994 the reckoning was that the film studios would fetch up to twenty times cash flow. This was based in part on the rising popularity of media stocks, evidenced by Viacom's $9.5 billion winning bid for Paramount and the massive, but in the end abortive $33 billion Telecommunications Inc (TCI) – Bell Atlantic deal (called off after a dispute over price). Such valuations would make MCA worth about twice what the Japanese company originally paid for it, not a bad return in a three-year period. Matsushita did have talks with John Malone, chief executive of TCI, but these did not bear fruit.

Then Sony reported on its costly nightmare, and questions were simmering about Matsushita too. Just as these were surfacing publicly, Spielberg stole the Hollywood headlines when he and Jeffrey Katzenberg, who had just resigned as head of the Walt Disney Studio (where he was responsible for *The Lion King*), and David Geffen, the millionaire music and film mogul whose Geffen Records is part of MCA, announced that they were joining forces to create a studio matching the 'big six'* that dominate Hollywood. The announcement brought talk that the three would team up with the MCA management because of Spielberg's past association with Universal and his friendship with MCA's president Sidney Sheinburg. This triggered highly public discontent between MCA and its owner, Matsushita.

MCA's chairman, 81-year-old Lew Wasserman, and the 59-year-old Sheinburg even threatened to leave MCA when their contracts run out at the end of 1995. Their complaint was that Matsushita had not given them the freedom they expected. The two men have worked together for 22 years and expected Matsushita to show deep pockets and take the film studios into exciting new expansion. In day-to-day matters the American managers could have few grumbles, since the Japanese left MCA alone to run the business; but the Osaka bosses vetoed MCA plans to buy Virgin Records and to acquire a majority stake in a US broadcasting network. The MCA duo let it be known that they would press for a management buyback of the film studios from Matsushita.

Unhappiness and rumours of unhappiness were so rife that both president Morishita and chairman Masaharu Matsushita went to San Francisco in October 1994 for an emergency meeting with MCA. According to Tsuzo

---

* Besides Universal and Columbia, these are 20th Century Fox, Disney, Paramount and Warner Bros.

Murase, Matsushita's executive vice president, who was at the meeting, the key question was how much independent authority MCA should have. 'When we acquired MCA, we requested, not in writing but verbally, that Wasserman and Sheinburg manage MCA because we did not understand the software business. But at this last meeting, MCA started to ask for discretion to make M & A [mergers and acquisitions] decisions, which are supposed to be made in consultation with the parent company.'

The Americans were dissatisfied. Wasserman demanded the money to make new investments, claiming that Matsushita managers were on the third floor knowing nothing about 'a big fire raging on the second floor', while Sheinburg, according to Japanese press reports, told his Japanese boss: 'Mr Morishita, you will leave your name in history as a company owner who lost a few billion dollars.' Something of the insensitivity of the situation was captured in a claim by an unnamed Matsushita executive, quoted in the Japanese press, that the five-hour meeting between the MCA managers and Matsushita had been a 'great victory' for the Japanese – in spite of the fact that resignation threats from the American duo were still on the table and that, even if Matsushita insisted on keeping the two, they could legally be out in a year. 'And where would Matsushita's MCA then be without them?' asked a Los Angeles analyst. 'Lost, marooned in a foggy storm, heading for the rocks without a competent captain.' There was certainly anger in the Osaka headquarters that Wasserman and Sheinburg had made millions of dollars from the sale of MCA – Wasserman collected $325 million worth of preferred Matsushita stock, and Sheinburg's share was $92 million – and yet still wanted to make the key decisions in running the company, using Japanese money.

It was a clash of cultures in two ways, not just about who should make expansion decisions. To MCA, both Virgin Records and the controlling stake in a US television network offered great opportunities. To Matsushita, battening down all hatches against the storms of recession, the price tags, including $1 billion for the record concern, were just too high. The Japanese, trying to trim every last yen from spending, used their three to two majority on the MCA executive committee to turn down the proposal. 'I felt that we had been treated as children,' Sheinburg grumbled to *The New York Times* about his reception in Osaka in September, when he suggested investing in US television. Subsequently, there was some recognition that the Japanese owners were being insensitive in handling Americans whose concerns were artistic matters, not the nuts and bolts of turning out millions of bits of electrical and electronic hardware.

Matsushita's president Morishita was almost contrite in a December 1994 interview conducted during the Japanese company's year-end party. He admitted that the discussions could have been handled differently. 'Basically, we have to recognise that there is a slight difference between

Matsushita and MCA on the concept of the entertainment industry,' he claimed. 'It is not a question of who is right or wrong.' He promised a more receptive ear, and 'more involvement' of the MCA top management on important matters. But on the main question of the acquisition of a US television network, he was adamant that a more receptive ear would not have changed the final decision. 'If Japanese were ultimate owners of a major US broadcasting network like CBS, it would have caused problems,' he added. He repeated that Matsushita was not considering selling MCA, or even contemplating reducing its stake. The Japanese company did reconsider and agree to take a 5 per cent stake in the theme park that MCA was building in its home town in partnership with the Osaka municipality. Morishita added that Wasserman and Sheinburg would be in Osaka early in 1995 to take part in the annual Matsushita management meetings – 'like other senior employees,' he added, leaving it uncertain whether he was welcoming them as full members of the Matsushita senior team or letting them know who was boss.

At those management meetings, the tinseltown duo would be in a small minority of non-Japanese. In 1994 only 13 of Matsushita's 158 subsidiaries were headed by *gaijins* (the word for 'outsiders', usually used for foreigners), demonstrating that although Matsushita may be international in its operations, it is far from international in its management and in its understanding of the world.

In the end, in April 1995 Matsushita capitulated and sold 80 per cent of MCA for $5.7 billion to Canadian beverage group Seagram. Though Morishita protested that the 20 per cent stake meant that Matsushita was still pursuing its software ambitions through Seagram, the sale left a hole in the Japanese company's ambitions and in its balance sheet since the price implied a $2 billion loss on the 1990 price paid.

Purchase of MCA was important to Matsushita (as Columbia was to Sony) to help the Japanese prepare for the advent of multimedia. There is increasing general recognition that the wide space called multimedia, involving the huge businesses of information and entertainment, is to be the growth area of the twenty-first century. Lee Iaccoca, former chairman of Chrysler Motors, watched crowds coming from film theatres, saw the amount of new development going on and said, 'I was never at Sutter's Creek during the Gold Rush, but that's what I imagine this was like.'

Business Week magazine calculated that the US entertainment and recreation industries added 200,000 new workers in 1993, or 12 per cent of net employment in a year when Americans spent $340 billion on entertainment. No wonder that the USA is sometimes called a 'Mickey Mouse economy'! Guesstimates of the spending on multimedia by the early years of the twenty-first century go into the trillions of dollars. US companies are spending big bucks to gear themselves up for the future. Time Warner and its telephone partner US West have spent $5 billion on upgrading networks for multimedia.

Nevertheless, the key question is whether the Japanese have the imagination and the flexibility to survive, let alone flourish, in such a fast-moving environment. One handicap is the slow-moving, heavy-regulating hand of the bureaucracy. In the early 1990s, surprisingly, the bureaucrats showed themselves more in tune with the times than their compatriot businessmen involved in the electronics and information industries. A senior official ventured that the future of high-definition television (HDTV) seemed to lie with the digital format being adopted by the rest of the world for all multimedia activities, rather than with the old analogue system. His suggestion that Japan too should switch its HDTV to digital format was greeted with howls of protest from NHK, the BBC of Japan, which had spent large sums of money on developing analogue HDTV, still showing for only eight hours a day. Equally pertinent, and showing the depressing 'pack mentality' of Japanese companies, NHK was joined by all the major manufacturers, including Matsushita. Faced with the united front of industry opposition, the officials dropped their idea, probably until consumer resistance to paying $3,000 a set for analogue HDTV really sinks in. A Matsushita manager pointed out in defence of the analogue system that it had been proven and that HDTV sets existed, whereas it would be several years before digital HDTV was turned from idea into reality.

Matsushita's entry through MCA into the brave new world has been mixed. MCA is in the process of building Universal Studios Japan, an entertainments theme park covering 140 acres in western Osaka and scheduled to open in 1999. The park will follow the model of Universal Studios in Los Angeles and in Orlando, Florida, and will cost $1.5 billion to build. It will rival the Tokyo Disneyland, which has been as successful as Euro-Disney has been a flop. The Osaka venture came as a result of talks between MCA and the city of Osaka, though Matsushita was initially reluctant to contribute its hard-earned money as a partner.

In its attempts to create synergy between MCA and the parent, Matsushita had been clearly struggling. To take one simple example, Matsushita has not been able to use the vast Universal library to build up home video technology. As Reif pointed out, there is only one Matsushita man inside MCA and the Japanese learning process seems to be slow. This point was underlined by American talk-show host Dick Cavott, who got up to welcome guests at US vice president Al Gore's so-called 'Information Superhighway Summit' at Los Angeles in mid-January 1994. He made his opening remarks in Japanese, then stopped in mid-sentence to peer at the audience and say that he hadn't expected so many Americans. In fact, the Japanese were conspicuous by their absence.

Since then, most of the big Japanese electronics concerns and some of the general trading companies have struck a series of deals to get into the information business, but critics sniff that these are for small sums and leave the Japanese as small partners of big American players. This again invites the question of whether the Japanese have missed the bus and may end up – as the New Yorker boasted – at best supplying the hardware, leaving the Americans to walk away with the more profitable products of brain and imagination.

That is not how Tsuzo Murase, one of the two men immediately below president Morishita, sees it. He is in charge of multimedia and also super-vised Matsushita's MCA subsidiary. Critical foreign analysts sometimes compare Matsushita to IBM and say that both are large, old-fashioned and vulnerable to smarter newcomers in a fast-moving market. Murase differs. To him, Matsushita will win because it is highly diversified with a number of different product lines, which, he argues, gives it both flexibility and an ability to flourish in the unpredictable world of the twenty-first century. He contrasts it with single-product companies – naming IBM as basically a computer maker – and asserts that the future will be with those companies diverse enough to operate in several fields at once and to gain the benefit of linking them.

He points to the alliances that Matsushita has made with three American companies, General Magic, 3DO and EO, to give it flexibility and extra punch. Murase admitted the superiority of digital technology, but quoted Malone of TCI that there were still billions of dollars to be spent before any US digital version of HDTV was ready to go on the air. 'You may be right in saying that the Americans are good at software and they may profit from intellectual property rights, but I don't think that the Japanese producers will stick to making hardware. If you think of the coming age of multimedia, the communications terminal will be brought to each home, and we don't think that the image will be a computer image. Some sort of software will be included in the terminal. Since we are human beings, we will have to have some kind of speaker to hear [what is going on], some sort of display to watch . . . We think that the whole architecture [of the multimedia house] is going to change.'

Murase gives his impression of the home of the future. 'When the businessman of the future gets up, he will go to the toilet. While he is there the sensors [in the toilet system] will check many data [like urine, blood pressure, pulse, heartbeat] and transmit them via the central pro-cessing unit [CPU] to the hospital and the computer where his records are stored. The hospital will hold his database over many years and will check the data picked up by the toilet and analyse them and compare them. Having done this, the CPU will communicate with the television terminal in the businessman's house where his wife is preparing his breakfast. In that case she can cook his breakfast based on the information supplied to her about her husband's condition. Maybe if he is hung over, or if his salt content is too high, she can change the ingredients for the breakfast.' (Like the rest of the all-male army of senior corporate executives, Murase assumed that it will always be an essential part of a wife's job to prepare the family breakfast.) This is not innocent star-gazing on Murase's part. Among its wide range of products, Matsushita already includes a 'beauty toilet'.*

According to Murase's picture of life in the home and office of the next century, the biggest changes will be in the extension of computers and electronic wizardry both to existing tasks and to the linking together of jobs. 'For obvious reasons, factories will continue and workers will continue to go to the factories,' he predicted. 'In the case of people like designers, it may be possible for them to work from home. I am not sure whether working at home is a good thing or not.' His point is that jobs will continue to be done where people gather together. This is not just for the advantage depicted in a *New Yorker* cartoon, which showed two businessmen enjoying what was clearly a long and liquid lunch, with the caption, 'Trust me, Mort – no electronic-communications superhighway, no matter how vast and sophisticated, will ever replace the art of the schmooze.' The importance of the workplace as a marketplace for meeting, pressing the flesh, getting to know people and sharing and developing ideas should not be forgotten.

What will change will be computer-aided processing and development of jobs. 'In the future, for example,' added Murase, 'if you are watching some computer data on display and the telephone interrupts, you can get the telephone call on the computer and do many things at the same time.' Computers that can process telephone conversations into facsimile data or screen display are one possibility. For leisure hours, Murase had no single vision. 'Of course, it is up to an individual's hobby. What people enjoy in one sense is very limited, so I don't think that because of multimedia it is going to change very much.'

Nevertheless, Matsushita took a step towards greater involvement in the leisure area of multimedia when it unveiled its 32-bit computer game machine in late 1993 in the USA, and in early 1994 in Japan. But there was a hiccup and a loss of face when Matsushita slashed the intended retail price from 79,800 yen ($752) to 54,800 yen because it feared competition from Sony and Sega, both of which were about to launch cheaper

---

* A number of Japanese manufacturers, compensating for the small size of the typical home, have been developing hi-tech lavatories that have warm seats, can spray warm cleansing water, make a number of health checks including on urine content, and give computer printouts. Westerners are generally lukewarm to most of the ideas – 'I felt that someone had been sitting there before me,' said an Englishman who tested and rejected the warm seat – but Japanese women are proud to show off their new gadgets.

rival products, and because sales in the USA had been sluggish, only 30,000 sets having been sold in the first three months. The Panasonic Real machine can be used to play computer games and can also accommodate music and video compact discs and produce digital graphics. Its format has been developed by Matsushita's partner, the 3DO Company.

President Morishita expressed disappointment with the poor reception of the Real, but did not share the view of critics that this merely proved how backward and poorly tuned-in Matsushita was to the entertainment business. 'We have to look at the longer term,' he said, promising a faster, more sophisticated version by late 1995. 'We will expand the use of the Real machine beyond being a video-game machine into other uses for business, hobbies or education,' he said, offering a wider vision.

The biggest problems from the advance of computers, asserted Murase, are privacy and security of information, and the ticklish question of who is going to pay and how. Take the simple case of the early morning ablutions: the patient would not be best pleased if suspicions that he or she might have warning signs of cancer were also flashed to the workplace or friends. In Japan this may be more of a danger because of special corporate loyalties which tie an employee closely to his or her company for life. Besides the screen of privacy around personal information, manufacturers are also trying to develop systems that will screen out junk messages or faxes, or 'toilet paper' as Murase called them, breaking into English for the occasion.

For all Murase's excitement at the new developments, and his assertion that the Japanese electronics manufacturers are strong and flexible enough to take advantage of the brave new world, Matsushita's skidding profits have the management worried. President Morishita admitted his concern about the 'multiple effects' of worldwide recession and the strong yen, which have caused operating profits as a percentage of sales to drop to 1.4 per cent at the lowest point – 'the lowest in history,' added Morishita grimly. He wants to see profits restored to 5 per cent by 1996.

'Our aim is that 1993 should be the bottom and after that we will work to achieve the revitalisation of Matsushita. We consider profits as a reward for our contribution to society. In order to achieve that goal [of raising profits to 5 per cent of sales] we are choosing a strategy of selecting business areas and concentrating management resources and increasing the productivity of the administration. Research and development will be brought closer to actual business, so that R & D activities will bring direct business results. In addition, we are strengthening product planning to be able to introduce more innovative products that match consumer demands.'

It may prove easier said than done. One of the company's problems is that it has failed to come up with a hit product in recent years, while the cost of sales has continued to increase. Matsushita's manufacturing divisions were recording profits of more than 10 per cent before 1970, but these had slumped below 1 per cent by 1993.

Morishita has adopted a slogan of 'four Ss – simple, small, speedy and strategic', and he slipped into English for the first time to provide the magic words. He also promised that management and headquarters would be the first targets for the renovation. 'The headquarters function has just become too large and we are trying to reduce its staff to 70 per cent of those at present. We have also separated R & D into two divisions, a research division, which will concentrate on long-term basic research, and a product development division to concentrate on current business products. On top of this we have established a corporate-wide research and development council under my direct supervision, so that we can co-ordinate between the three different functions to come up with innovative and imaginative ideas and products, and concentrate resources for investment in promising items. We are giving more authority to each product division to strengthen them and clarify their responsibility. By having a higher headquarters function, some of the product responsibility had become blurred.'

Insiders say Morishita has shown decisiveness and a 'hands-on' approach to his responsibilities, while being willing to allow his managers room to manage. He himself stressed 'the need to empower more authority to each division, so that each management unit will have its own culture and its own spirit. This has been our style traditionally, so we are rejuvenating it. I value the empowerment of each manager by delegation of responsibility, so the business frontline has its own person responsible for that unit. From my position in headquarters I will give them general direction of where the company should be headed, but the actual day-to-day management lies within the businesses themselves. Each manager knows his business and what he is trying to do better than anyone else in the company. I know this from my own experience as a manager.'

On this basis, Konosuke Matsushita can rest peacefully in his grave, assured that his precepts are being faithfully followed. 'Our basic philosophy of the company inherited from our founder has not changed at all. We must contribute to society and contribute to the well-being of the people, and this is immutable and we will follow it eternally. But our founder was a very flexible person, very innovative. I shall be as innovative as he was. Times are changing and the society and economy are changing rapidly, so we must change our management and our products and technology to meet the new challenges. We must constantly maintain our creativity,' Morishita asserted, using the founder's good name to protect himself from critics. Delivering the goods in increasingly competitive times, when Mom 'n' Pop have grown too old and set in their ways, may be more difficult.

8

Next Stop the Stars:
Japan's Aerospace Ambitions

At 7.20 a.m. on Friday, 4 February 1994, on the island of Tanegashima in the south of Japan, cheers resounded that reached Tokyo and beyond. They heralded a historic day. The occasion was the launch of the 50 metre high H-II rocket, the first built entirely with Japanese technology and development. The orange and yellow rocket with NIPPON written on its side that soared into space was the product of ten years' work, 270 billion yen ($2.7 billion) and several setbacks and delays, including two disastrous explosions and one death. 'A 260 ton declaration of independence from US aerospace technology,' declared a Japanese newspaper headline. 'Technically, it puts us into the same league with the big space powers, the US, Russia and Europe,' said a delighted Satsuki Eda, director-general of the Science and Technology Agency and the cabinet minister responsible for science. 'Japan has finally completed a means of transportation in space that we can use at our own free will,' said Kenji Seyama, director of space development at the ministry.

The rocket launch also raised again the ugly fears of the rest of the world about Japan's intentions in entering the space race. Foreign newspapers and political commentators were quick to point to the military potential of being able to put rockets into space. Given that Japan by any statistics is one of the top three military spenders in the world,* given its superior technology, especially in electronics, given the strength of nationalist sentiments, can it be trusted to maintain its commitments to peace in the competitive world of the twenty-first century? After all, a leading Japanese politician, Shintaro Ishihara, boasted that it was only courtesy of Japan's

---

* The US tops world spending on defence with $297.3 billion in 1993, according to the authoritative International Institute for Strategic Studies; Russia came next with $80.7 billion, according to IISS, after trying to give a realistic purchasing value from the rouble; the next highest Nato spender was France, $42.9 billion in 1993, followed by Germany ($36.7 billion) and the UK ($35.1 billion); Japan's Defence Agency requested 4,730 billion yen or $47.3 billion for the fiscal year beginning April 1995, but IISS says Tokyo's budget excludes items that would elsewhere be regarded as defence spending, and it estimates 1993 defence spending as $63.9 billion.

superior electronics that Washington could launch its military weapons.*

In terms of the raw numbers, Japan is certainly an aerospace power of some might, and of course it has a history of putting its muscle to military use. Its aero industry was slower to take off than that of most other countries. It did not emerge until the 1930s, but grew rapidly under military patronage. During the Second World War, Japan's twelve airframe manufacturers and seven engine builders were employing 600,000 people and turning out 25,000 aircraft and 40,000 engines a year. The aircraft included the famous Mitsubishi Zero, one of the best aircraft on any side in the Second World War, used for infamous kamikaze suicide attacks.

Saburo Sakai, by the 1990s the most famous Japanese wartime pilot still alive, with 2,000 hours, 200 air attacks and 64 enemy aircraft 'kills' to his credit, argued that the kamikaze attacks were a mark of the laziness and stupidity of the Imperial military, and came from the desperation of imminent defeat. 'It was the power of the Zero that led to [Japan's] early successes. But later, as the Americans developed newer fighters, the only thing we could do was wrap a 250kg [550lb] bomb on to the plane and dive into targets. This was because the Navy brass were impotent and lazy, still satisfied by our early successes, and forgot to develop better fighters ... The British Spitfire was used for ten years. At first, it was 1,000 horse-power, just like the Zero, but in ten years they had increased the horse-power to 2,500. There were some slight improvements to the Zero, but no increase in power. That's not an improvement.'†

After the war, Japan's aerospace ambitions did not begin again until 1952 in the case of aircraft and 1956 in the case of space development. Because of its enforced idleness during those years, Japan had a lot of catching up to do. In that time the world's aircraft had flown on from piston to jet engines. By the start of the 1990s, Japan was spending 850 billion yen ($8.5 billion) on the aircraft industry, with 30,000 employees, and another 300 billion yen on space development, employing 11,000 people.

For six years after the war, Japan was governed by the US-led occupation forces. Then came the San Francisco Peace Treaty in 1951 (effective from 1952), giving Japan back its independence. When permission was granted in 1952 to resume research and production of aircraft, the country had no established civil airline and no general aviation. Development ironically restarted with the repair and maintenance of the aircraft of US armed forces stationed in Japan – which offered the Japanese industry the oppor-tunity of using advanced American technology to increase its own aero-space development. When the Japan Defence Agency was set up in 1954,

---

* In *The Japan that Can Say 'No'*, co-authored with Sony chairman, Akio Morita.

† Original criticisms in his 1994 book, *Destiny of a Zero Fighter*, repeated in *Tokyo Journal*, December 1994.

On the election stomp. Satsuki Eda is smaller in real life than his electoral image.

LDP trio (left to right): Ryutaro Hashimoto (Miti minister), the maverick Shintaro Ishihara, who believes Japan should stand up to the US, and Yohei Kono (leader of the LDP and deputy prime minister).

Traffic jammed in front of the Diet (Parliament).

One of the chief players in karaoke politics, Tsutomo Hata, who had a nine-week stint as prime minister in 1994.

The PM who fell on his sword, Morihiro Hosokawa.

Kiichi Miyazawa, former prime minister of Japan, who presided over the LDP's loss of power.

Masayoshi Takemura, head of the Sakigake (Harbinger) Party.

Pachinko games are worth $170 billion a year and have gangster connections.

Sex any way you want: Japan has a multi-billion-dollar industry employing Thai and Filipino women.

Monk seeks alms in Tokyo's fashionable Ginza district, still the most expensive piece of real estate in the world.

Advocate of keeping Japan's peace constitution, Nobel literary prizewinner Kenzaburo Oe.

The 'elephant cage', US communications centre in Yomitan, Okinawa.

Korean 'comfort women' protest outside Parliament.

Plea to Russia (with which Japan has no postwar peace treaty) for the return of the disputed northern islands.

A flame burns at the shrine to Atomic Bomb victims in Hiroshima.

its birth brought with it the opportunity for making military aircraft. Again, production of American-designed aircraft under licence has been the mainstay of the Japanese industry.

In terms of value and variety of output, Japan's aircraft industry looks impressive. Japanese manufacturers are involved in building a wide range of aircraft, both military and civil. In 1991 Japan produced 173 aircraft of its own, including 50 fixed-wing and 70 rotary-wing aircraft. It also made 247 engines. Although most modern civilian jets flying international airline colours bear the names of the American Boeing and McDonnell Douglas companies or the European Airbus consortium, Japanese companies have a share of the work and are helping to make Boeing's 747 jumbo jet as well as the same company's 737, 757 and 767 series aircraft. Japan also makes part of the McDonnell Douglas MD-11 and MD-80 aircraft, and is involved in smaller parts of the Airbus A321, Fokker-50 and Gulfstream G-IV.

At the start of the 1990s, Japanese makers boasted that they had taken an important qualitative step forward with their involvement as a subcontracting partner for the 350-seater Boeing 777 aircraft, which began service from 1995. But they are ambitious for greater and more independent production, closer to the cutting edge of modern technology. For civilian use, Japan's manufacturers are pursuing plans for a small airliner carrying fewer than 100 passengers; their military ambitions are to make a twenty-first century fighter jet that can take over from the F-15, the US-designed principal Japanese fighter.

Other major projects include the FSX (new military support fighter), being built jointly by Japan in co-operation with the USA to replace the F-1, and expected to make its first test flight in 1995; the BK117 'fly-by-wire' helicopter; and the V2500 turbo fan jet engine, in which Japan has a 23 per cent share as part of a five-nation consortium. Rolls-Royce has 30 per cent of the project, United Technologies Corporation of the USA 30 per cent, Motoren-und Turbinen-Union of Germany 11 per cent, and Fiat Avio of Italy 6 per cent.

On top of these, Japan is also involved in a broad international study of the future supersonic aircraft – 'a dream concept that will shape the future of international transport aviation in the twenty-first century', according to executives of the Japan Machinery Exporters Association and the Society of Japanese Aerospace Companies. As their project for the next century, the Japanese are also beginning work on both a super/hypersonic aircraft that would be able to fly from Tokyo to New York in up to three hours, against the present twelve or more hours by jumbo jet, and a Mach 5 engine that would power the new craft.

When the evidence is put like this, Japan seems one of the most advanced as well as biggest aircraft industrial powers. It is also feared because it has the capacity to get its big companies working together to achieve national aims in ways that would involve much squabbling in other countries. The Japanese partners in the V2500 engine, for example, include all three big engine makers, Ishikawajima-Harima Heavy Industries (IHI), Kawasaki Heavy Industries and Mitsubishi Heavy Industries. The Japan Society of Aerospace Companies embraces all the 189 domestic companies involved in the business, the biggest of which take it in turns to provide its chairman. However, when the aircraft industry record is examined, total production in value terms is only a thirteenth of that in the United States, a third of the UK's or France's, and half that of Germany. In addition, imports are about six times higher than exports. And although Japan maintains the fiction that it has no armed forces – only self-defence forces – a very high proportion of the aircraft industry's work derives from military demand and has leant heavily on technology licensed from the USA.

Although Japan boasts of its involvement with Boeing, its actual contributions have not been at the forefront, let alone the cutting edge, of technology. On the 747 jumbo jet, for example, Fuji Heavy Industries made the ailerons and spoilers, Kawasaki and Mitsubishi Heavy Industries were involved in wing trailing edge flaps, and other companies made mundane parts like lavatory units. The contribution to the 767 was greater, involving parts of the fuselage and tailwing trailing edges, but still not enough to count Japan as a major, let alone original contributor.

With the latest 777 aircraft, the Japanese manufacturers are claiming that they are coming of age. The Japan Aircraft Development Corporation, a nucleus body of major manufacturers, says that together the Japanese companies will account for 21 per cent of the airframe of the 777, including the majority of the fuselage, making Japan the largest overseas participant and effectively an almost equal partner in the project. More than 30 Japanese parts suppliers are participating. Among the parts of the 777 going from Japan to Boeing's factories in Seattle are cargo and passenger entry doors, landing gear doors, wing body fairings (which help to reduce drag), inspar ribs and pressure dome bulkheads. Mitsubishi Heavy Industries, one of the leading aerospace companies, says that as a result of its work on the 777 it will double its non-military business to 20 per cent of its aerospace operations within five years.

However, the importance of the Boeing 777 work in Japanese manufacturers' eyes is that they are not merely involved in producing and shipping off aircraft parts, but have been brought into design, testing, sales finance and other business aspects. They thus hope to be an even bigger partner in the next generation of civilian aircraft. Isamu Kawai, chairman of Fuji Heavy Industries in 1993, told the Japanese press that he was already looking ahead to the SuperJumbo project for a 600- to 800-seater commercial aircraft on which Japanese manufacturers would join with airlines and the government in helping to shape an aircraft that will suit Japan's needs. One of the reasons is that the development costs of the SuperJumbo are too high even for the world's leading manufacturer, Boeing; the other is that Japan is a potential major market for the new generation of aircraft, and things like the number of seats, speed, flight distance and safety standards have to take Japan's perspective into account if the new aircraft is to be a commercial success. Japan Airlines boasts the world's biggest fleet of Boeing 747 jumbo jets, with 86 in service in November 1994, of which 32 are the latest 400 series.

Japan's government officials and outside experts are not as optimistic as some of the heavy industry manufacturers about how advanced the country is. Kanichiro Kato, professor of aerospace engineering at the University of Tokyo, stripped away the rose-coloured glasses of some of those close to the industry by declaring that the Japanese were still subcontractors. 'Japan's aircraft manufacturing technology lags far behind. The fact that Boeing is willing to co-operate shows that it does not see Japanese companies as rivals,' he said in November 1994. Japan is certainly nowhere near being able to develop aircraft on its own. 'The technology gap between Japan and the US or Europe cannot be closed that easily,' Hideo Suzuki, an official of the aircraft division of the Ministry of International Trade and Industry (Miti), admitted frankly in 1993.

Some of Japan's problems are illustrated by the rows over the FSX military fighter and the YSX and YXX civilian airliners. The FSX development came first. It was originally planned in the late 1980s as the early twenty-first century replacement for Japan's domestically developed F-1 fighter, and was based on technology of the US Air Force's F-16. Like the F-1, the FSX will be built by Mitsubishi Heavy Industries. It is supposed to be superior to the F-16C in several important areas. These include: the increase of the main wing area and the application of composite technology; in its advanced avionics, including active phased array radar; in its improved performance engine; in its use of advanced materials and structural technology in the stretched fuselage; and in a modification to the nose shape. But from the start its progress has been bedevilled by questions of the sharing of technology.

While the original agreements were being drawn up, the US Congress complained that Japan would be getting access to the latest American technology. More recently, the boot has been on the other foot, with the US grumbling that Japan is actually denying it access to technology coming from the development of the advanced fighter. The General Accounting Office (GAO) of the USA said that the 1989 agreement was that the USA would have access to FSX technologies, including those derived from the F-16 and those developed by the Japanese. It complained in 1992 that 'Japan has not always been readily forthcoming with information pertaining to its FSX technologies.' Washington wanted more information about the radar, computer, inertial reference and integrated electronic warfare systems.

Japan had been hopeful of co-operating with Boeing to build the 150-seater YXX aircraft. But Boeing pulled the plug by deciding instead to give a new lease of life to its 737 series with the launch of the 737–700 in November 1993. This was the death-knell for the YXX, and Miti decided to withdraw its backing – almost a *fait accompli*, since with Boeing out the Japanese would be unable to go it alone. But Miti is still determined to go ahead with the YSX, a 75- to 90-seat short-range aircraft which now carries Japan's hopes of turning the aircraft side of aerospace into an important part of the total economy. The problem may be that Miti is ahead of the manufacturers, which were wary of the heavy investment, especially if Japan supplies the engine as well, which is what Miti hopes. Officials at the ministry are determined enough. 'The YSX will definitely be realised. It is the essence of our civil aircraft policy from now on,' said Toshifumi Hirai, director of Miti's aircraft and ordnance division in early 1994. He acknowledged that Japan still has a long way to go. 'We are in a marathon race and our objective is to be able to keep the backs of the first two runners in sight, but not overtake them. Lately, they have been running too fast for us,' he conceded.

Japan's previous attempts to build a civil airliner offer mixed lessons. The YS-11, a twin-engined turbo prop aircraft capable of carrying 64 passengers, was developed in the early 1960s to Japanese design, though using 80 per cent imported parts. In this respect it resembled the early generation of Japanese cars. It made its maiden flight in August 1962, and the first aircraft were delivered from March 1965. But the production line was shut down in February 1974 after 182 had been built, since Tokyo's marketing men could not win more orders and debts had swollen to 36 billion yen. Japanese airlines and government agencies took most of the aircraft; few other countries were interested in the YS-11, in spite of the good rating that it achieved from aviation experts.

The problem with the YS-11 was that Japan had decided to go it alone and had to bear all the costs, but was not experienced enough in marketing to get a share of the most lucrative markets. The subsequent difficulty has been that Japan has tried to find partners, but the already established aircraft makers with contacts and marketing knowledge have been reluctant to take Japan on, except as a junior partner. This will remain a difficulty in getting the YSX from the drawing board on to the airport runways. As the yen rises in value, so will the difficulties of selling abroad, unless Japan at least contracts out essential sections of the work, probably to other Asian countries where labour and manufacturing costs are lower.

In May 1994, the next positive step towards the YSX seemed to have been taken with an announcement from Boeing that it had begun studying joint development of a small passenger jet along with Mitsubishi Heavy

Industries, Kawasaki Heavy Industries and Fuji Heavy Industries, the three heavyweights of the five partners in Japan Aircraft Development Corporation involved in the YSX project. As another important pointer, the announcement said that China National Aero-Technology Import and Export Corporation had joined the project as an observer, offering the prospect of a potential supplier of lower-cost parts.

Interestingly, the name YSX did not appear in the Boeing press release. The move, moreover, brought immediate protests from European aircraft manufacturers, which accused Japan of partiality in the big battle between the USA and Europe for dominance of the world's skies. This is the other dimension of Japan's struggle, that somehow it has to avoid being squeezed between the two giants. Japanese aviation experts admitted in late 1994 that there was a danger that the YSX might be hijacked from them. A senior official, who refused to be quoted by name, said that the plan under consideration was for Boeing to use its marketing clout in selling the YSX abroad, leaving the Japanese partners to concentrate on domestic sales. Such dependence is fraught with dangers for Japan, especially if Boeing brings China in as a partner, with the hope of gaining access to its potentially huge market. That would effectively shut the Japanese out of lucrative China and maroon them in their own backyard.

Japan's domestic market for small airliners is neither as big as China's nor as big as that for wide-bodied intercontinental aircraft. In addition, Tokyo is already facing demands from Europe that it open up its market, and claims that its airlines have unfairly turned their backs on Airbus aircraft and Rolls-Royce aero-engines in an attempt to appease Washington and reduce the $60 billion trade surplus. Sir Leon Brittan, the European Union commissioner and pointman on trade with Japan, has regularly called on Japan to make sure that Airbus and Rolls-Royce face a level playing field. The Japanese official admitted, 'We are in danger of being squeezed. The development costs of the YSX will be $800 million or more, so we need partners.'

Naomi Anesaki, president of the Society of Japanese Aerospace Companies, put the positive view, declaring that in some areas Japan could already teach the Americans and Europeans about modern aircraft development. 'In avionics and materials, Japan is using its own technologies. Composite new materials in aircraft manufacture have been pioneered and developed in Japan.' These advances can be seen in some of the conceptual drawings for the advanced jet fighter of the twenty first century: they show canard wings, fibre-optic fly-by-light controls, radar integrated into the surface of the aircraft, and stealth capability, making the jet difficult to detect by enemy radar. However, Anesaki conceded that Japan's aircraft manufacturers face big difficulties: 'The problem is that the aircraft industry has depended too heavily on the military market and is already being seriously affected by budget cuts.' The extra constraint on military production is that it offers no opportunity for exports because of the strict terms of Japan's peace constitution. All this means that Miti has a lot of work still to do in encouraging the first flight of the YSX – and the new generation military fighter has yet to fly from the drawing board.

These problems have been exacerbated by struggles for dominance between the big Japanese manufacturers. To outsiders, Japan Inc. may seem one seamless cloak of harmony, but under the surface there is cut-throat competition for dominance. Infighting particularly between Mitsubishi Heavy and Kawasaki Heavy, the top two manufacturers, has delayed development work on the next generation fighter until 1996 at least. Mitsubishi thought that, having done so much work on fighter aircraft, it should be the lead contractor, a suggestion which Kawasaki has resisted.

Anesaki asserted that Japan's space programme – unlike that of the USA or Russia, and unlike the country's aircraft industry – has been 'developed and pursued purely by way of non-military research and development, whereas in the US and in Russia space was an arm of competition by military forces.' Japan's attempts to get into space have a long history going back to 1955, when the University of Tokyo started research on solid propellant rockets. The first of these was the 'Pencil' launched in 1955, followed by 'Baby', 'Kappa', 'Lambda' and 'Mu'.

Two government agencies were established with separate mandates to develop the domestic space industry. The Institute of Space and Aeronautical Science (Isas), took over the activities of Tokyo University's institute of the same name, curiously but logically an agency of the Ministry of Education, given its antecedents. It has the charge of overseeing the development and use of Japan's scientific satellites. Meanwhile, the National Space Development Agency of Japan (Nasda) was established to develop application satellites and space utilisation.

It was Isas which in 1970 made Japan the fourth country to lift a satellite into orbit, when it launched an L-4S rocket carrying the 9-kilogram 'Osumi'. Isas continued to launch scientific satellites on M-Series rockets. Nasda launched its first test rocket in 1974 and followed this by the launch of an M-I rocket carrying Japan's first engineering test satellite, 'Kiku' (chrysanthemum), the following year. The agency then developed N-II and H-I rockets to put application satellites, such as for communications and broadcasting, into orbit. The M rocket series use solid propellant and the H series use cryogenic propellant. The development of H-II and M-V rockets was started to accommodate the demand for larger satellite launches.

The H-II that went into orbit in February 1994 was much bigger than anything previous, both in the size of the vehicle and in the 2-ton satellite it is capable of carrying. It required the development of a high-performance liquid hydrogen and liquid oxygen engine for the first stage, and a large-scale solid rocket booster and a laser gyro guidance system. Its creation took ten years, and the launch, originally scheduled for 1992, was delayed by problems with the engine. At one point a Space Agency official complained that budget constraints and a tight schedule made it impossible adequately to test all components. The agency sometimes had as little as ten seconds for each test of the rocket's engine. The worst accident occurred in August 1991, when a prototype of the main engine exploded during a test in a factory. The door of the safety room was blown off and crushed a 23-year-old engineer. His parents were among the people watching the successful lift-off three and a half years later, his mother clutching a large photograph of her dead son.

For its maiden flight, the H-II carried two cargoes. One, known as the orbital re-entry exponent (Orex), was designed to test ceramic tiles and other items that may be useful in future launches. It splashed down into the Pacific Ocean two hours and thirteen minutes after lift-off, after having transmitted data to ground stations about how it endured the 1,600 degrees Centigrade heat and other conditions when it re-entered the Earth's atmosphere. The second cargo was a test satellite which had a life of 100 hours and was used just to supply the proof that the H-II could successfully put a satellite into orbit. It entered an elliptical transfer orbit used to move satellites from low Earth orbit to geosynchronous orbit, almost 36,000 kilometres above the Earth.

Japanese boasts about the completely domestic technology of the H-II were partly a reaction to their previous dependence on the USA, which imposed limitations on their freedom. The rocket's predecessor, the H-I, used an American engine developed by McDonnell Douglas. The portion of Japanese technology had grown from 53 per cent in the M-I rocket in 1975, to 81 per cent for the H-I. Even so, because of the American technology, Washington retained a veto on key questions like what could be exported where, and which foreign payloads could be accepted. So the good news of H-II for Japan was that it at last joined the ranks of the space superpowers in its own right.

Anesaki of the Society of Aerospace Companies said that Chinese rockets could carry a heavier payload. 'But the accuracy and credibility of technology in Japan is much more sophisticated.' The H-II's payload is only slightly less than that of Ariane-IV, produced by Europe's Arianespace, the world's first commercial satellite-launching company, which accounts for 60 per cent of the international market. But Japan evidently still has many problems to solve before its success is assured in breaking into space.

Some of these became embarrassingly apparent not long after the maiden flight of the H-II, when the attempt was made to launch a large engineering test satellite (ETS-VI), again called Kiku, into geostationary orbit. The first effort, in mid-August, fizzled out before the rocket could leave the ground. The main engine fired on schedule six minutes before lift-off, but the two solid-fuel auxiliary boosters failed to start and the main engine then shut down. Nasda officials said that the trouble was not with the rocket, but with the monitoring equipment, which failed to send the correct signals. Another attempt was made ten days later and this time the rocket launch went correctly and got the satellite airborne, but failed to get it into proper orbit. 'We have no choice but to give up,' said Masato Yamano, president of Nasda. 'I deeply apologise.'

Makiko Tanaka, by then the director-general of the Science and Technology Agency, tried to put the best face on the loss of a 69.5 billion yen investment on which Japan had no insurance cover. 'There can't be progress without some waste involved,' she said. 'I still believe the science is trustworthy.' Tanaka hoped to use the satellite in elliptical orbit, even though most of its planned programme could not be carried out at this level. Nasda added that the H-II had still proved sound, and that the fault was in the satellite's engine, not in the rocket itself.

Critics said that Nasda was to blame for taking too much on itself and being too ambitiously experimental. It has revised the procurement process. Previously it selected one company to be main contractor for a satellite and then left it to the winner to order the components and construct the satellite. It changed that to take on the job of master contractor itself, with one of the three companies as adviser. The object was to spread the work around and make sure that all of Japan's companies involved in space and satellite work got business and remained viable. The weakness of this arrangement was that it meant there was no one company to ensure that delivery times and quality controls were met. In the case of the ill-fated Kiku VI, Toshiba was the co-ordinator, but IHI made the engine, which was discovered – too late – to have a faulty valve. An official of another satellite maker accused Nasda of being too eager to try new technology in choosing the more complicated liquid fuel technology for Kiku's engine instead of the tried-and-trusted solid fuels previously used.

But there are other problems holding back Japan's space ambitions. The biggest of these is the cost. To build and launch a single H-II costs about 19 billion yen or $190 million, almost twice as much as its Ariane rival. It is not wholly Japan's fault. During the period of development, the yen rose almost as spectacularly as the H-II, thus raising the costs and deterring Japan from offering commercial terms in the international market. The high costs of developments were also a function of the fact that Japan was doing everything from scratch on its own, from the engines to the fuselage.

The European group is not only cheaper, but is well ahead in cultivating commercial business. Arianespace had orders for 37 satellite launches at the end of 1993. Competition is likely to get tougher, and there are only about 25 commercial satellites launched each year worldwide, a number which experts say may drop to 16 by 2003. The Europeans also have the lead in expertise in launching satellites. Jean-Louis Claudon, Asia-Pacific representative of Arianespace, said that the advanced technology of the H-II is not important to commercial customers, who are looking more for proven reliability and cost. Often, too, customers want two or more satellites launched at the same time – for example, by using a rocket that can carry 2 tons to launch a satellite of 1.5 tons along with another $\frac{1}{2}$-ton brother. Japan clearly cannot claim that amount of expertise.

Indeed, one Japanese space scientist claimed that 'Japan began thinking about what can be done with the H-II rocket after it had actually been built.' There is evidence for this. Some American space experts claim that Japan only opted for the expensive and powerful H-II technology to prove that it could match the USA – although the rocket would have useful space shuttle applications. Hiroshi Harada, general manager of Mitsubishi Heavy Industries' space systems department, said that 'the development of the H-II is designed to advance Japan's technology' rather than to generate new business. If so, it was an expensive way of doing so.

Nobuo Nakatomi, an aerospace analyst who works at the National Aeronautical Space Agency (Nasa), said, 'Japan has to think seriously about which area the H-II can be most useful in. Unfortunately it seems that no one is doing that.' Further evidence is that Miti pointedly declined to forecast the future size of Japan's domestic space industry market, lending credence to the suggestion that the question is politically too controversial. There seems little room to justify the expense of H-II for launches of scientific discovery. 'For scientific purposes, traditional rockets with launching capability one-quarter that of the H-II are adequate,' said Minoru Oda, former head of Isas. In addition, scientists normally prefer frequent launches of small satellites into lower orbits rather than a few heavy satellites.

There is one other problem with frequent launches from Tanegashima station, and that is the opposition from local fishermen. It seems a bit humorous that a hi-tech rocket can be thrown out of its orbit by the opposition of traditional fishermen, but Nasda promised that the rocket would only be launched in a 45-day period during the summer and a similar break in the winter. Conveniently and not coincidentally, these are the periods when the fishermen go on holiday. The point was driven home when the H-II's maiden launch was delayed by twenty minutes because a fishing boat had gone under the rocket's flight path.

Nevertheless Japan is pushing ahead with even more ambitious plans. Nasda is doing research for a winged, unmanned space vehicle, called the H-II orbiting plane or 'Hope', for which the H-II is expected to serve as launch vehicle. The ambition is that Hope will be airborne by the year 2010, but no detailed timetable has been worked out. Clearly the biggest problem is going to be to find the money for the programme. Harada of

Mitsubishi Heavy Industries said that half the money spent on making the H-II was collected by his company. But for further developments, government money will be essential. Artists' impressions of Hope suggest that it will be something like the US space shuttle, a reusable space transport, but the Japanese version will be without any crew on board. It will be perched on top of the rocket for launch.

Isas has also been busy. Its M-V launch vehicle has a solid propellant three-stage booster system and is intended to carry out scientific observation missions from the mid-1990s, and to be able to launch a 2-ton payload into low Earth orbit, or 400 kilograms beyond Earth's gravity pull. The idea is that it will be used for scientific projects, such as exploring comets, the surface of the moon and Mars. Outsiders have criticised the increasing overlap between Isas and Nasda, and have suggested that before too long the two should be merged. With the launch of M-V, the two agencies will be able to lift almost similar payloads, making the distinction under which Isas puts up smaller satellites virtually unnecessary. The H-II's LE-7 uses liquid fuel technology that Mitsubishi Heavy Industries has developed, and then for the second stage uses Nissan solid rocket boosters, incorporating technology developed in working with Isas. In present developments, the distinction between 'research' done by Isas and 'application' done by Nasda seems increasingly artificial. However, there are important bureaucratic turf wars to be fought, which will make any merger hard to achieve. Japan's individual ministries have their own jealously guarded fiefdoms. In days of budgetary cuts, no ministry will be happy to yield any of its power.

Japanese ambitions for space burn brightly as any star. Some Miti officials are talking of explorations of the moon for mineral resources. In mid-1994, indeed, a government advisory panel suggested that the exploration of space, including the establishment of unmanned observatories on the moon, where there is no disturbing atmosphere, and geological expeditions to Mars, should be a major Japanese goal, on which it was worth spending trillions of yen and doubling the space budget to 466 billion yen a year by 2010.

The Lunar and Planetary Society, backed by luminary companies like Fujitsu, Kawasaki Heavy and Mitsubishi Heavy, went further, proposing at the same time that Japan should establish an astronaut colony on the moon, producing its own oxygen from moon dust using fusion technology. The base would be built by robots controlled from Earth, and the astronauts in six-month tours would grow vegetables, examine the use of helium as an energy and perform laboratory experiments. The plan would need 75 launches of the H-II to carry equipment and power plants, and would cost 100 billion yen a year to construct. The society estimated that it would be possible to have the moon base set up by 2017 and manned and operating by 2024. Shiro Mitsumori, a space policy fellow with the society, said that most of the technology already exists for the base, 'except for some telecommunications technology using virtual reality'.

The launch of H-II and some of the jubilant nationalistic comments in the Japanese press triggered alarms abroad that the new range of rockets might be of potential military use. This was immediately denied by then minister, Satsuki Eda, who sang the praises of the new technology for its potential for peace. The advent of H-II, he said poetically, had 'turned space from a theatre for Soviet–US military competition into a sphere of activity for people who want to give wing to peaceful dreams'. He added that the fuel used by the H-II is not really suitable for rockets with military objectives, and the rocket itself is highly dependent on clement weather conditions. 'If there is a thunderstorm in the area, we have to postpone the launch, which is not a luxury that you can afford if you have a war to fight and win,' Eda added. Anesaki also commented that Japan's 'Peace constitution' and the rules governing Nasda both enjoin Japan to use the exploration of space for peaceful purposes. In spite of these assurances, there are many people who would like to explore Japan's aerospace and defence industries fully, and to question their real intentions.

William Webster, former director of the US Central Intelligence Agency, warned the Senate that the engineering required for peaceful and military developments of space was largely the same. He was echoing a 1992 Pentagon report which warned that satellite-launching programmes of Europe, China, Russia and Japan were striving to match or surpass those of the USA within the decade.

It is undoubtedly true that there is a deep nationalistic streak driving much of the research into aerospace. Nobuo Yamaguchi, chairman of Asahi Chemical Industry, in September 1994 called for 'the government's assistance in order to promote domestic production of arms and to accumulate indigenous technology. Before entering joint research with the US, unless Japan has its own unique and superior technology, we have to do everything their way [as in the case of the development of the FSX next generation fighter plane]. The US has built up technology by their willingness to bend budgetary restrictions. Japan's technological level is on a par with the US in a number of fields, including electronic technology, aircraft, tanks and sea vessels. Also, we would like the government to consider employment adjustment subsidies for the industry.'*

Protests that Japan's intentions are peace loving cut little ice with defence experts, who point out that such rockets as the H-II are easily convertible to military use. The decision to build such powerful ones when scientists say that they prefer smaller satellites launched into lower orbits suggests either that the space programme was confused or that it was driven by

---

* Interview in *Mainichi Daily News*, 6 September 1994.

powerful nationalistic determination to be as good as any great power. Moreover, Tokyo only invites questions when it protests that the liquid hydrogen fuel of the H-II lacks quick-firing ability. Many of the inter-continental ballistic missiles in China's and Russia's arsenals use liquid fuels, probably because they are easier to make and maintain, and in any case the M series rockets of Isas are solid fuel launched and are also developing the potential of powerful payloads.

One important worry is the very size of Japan's spending on defence and armaments. Successive Tokyo governments have made much of the fact that Japan only spends 1 per cent of its gross domestic product (GDP) on defence. As the economy has grown, so too has the amount of money spent on arms, so that by 1995 that 1 per cent came to more than 4,700 billion yen, or $47 billion. Admittedly, too, the figure was influenced by the rising yen, which increased the dollar amount of the yen sum spent. But this put Japan far ahead of countries like China and India, which have been accused of major military ambitions. It took Tokyo into a higher spending league than the UK or France, which still have international military and peacekeeping responsibilities. It was also done when Tokyo still sheltered under Washington's nuclear umbrella, with US forces in bases inside the country. This has traditionally meant that Japan does not have to shoulder many of the primary responsibilities which other countries have to bear.*

Digby Waller, defence economist with IISS in London, also claims that the published Japanese defence expenditures understate by 60 per cent its true military spending. He says Tokyo is 'hiding' behind the 1 per cent benchmark figure. Waller wrote in December 1994: 'I believe that [Japanese military spending] is actually some 1.6 per cent of GDP. This is because pensions of retired military and civilian personnel, expenditures on dual use R & D [research and development] and the funding of the para-military Maritime Safety Agency are excluded. Under Nato definitions, I believe that these would constitute military expenditures.' Following his cal-culations, the declared $47.3 billion for the 1995/6 budget would really be military spending of $75.68 billion, almost the same as Russia's. It is also worth noting that, according to the IISS's authoritative figures, Japan is the only major industrial country whose military expenditure has been rising steadily in real terms since 1985. Table 8.1 shows it doubling during a time of falling military spending in the USA, Germany and the UK. Only Turkey of Nato members saw similar growth, but with much lower figures.

---

* Japan budgeted for 135 billion yen in the year beginning in April 1995 as its contribution to the US bases, including paying all the salaries and other allowances of Japanese employees at the bases, and utilities charges. Japanese nationalists were arguing that this was too much to spend.

Table 8.1 *International comparisons of defence expenditure*

Country	$m (1993 prices)			$ per capita (1993 prices)		
	1985	*1992*	*1993*	*1985*	*1992*	*1993*
USA	339,229	312,960	297,300	1,418	1,243	1,156
Russia	n.a.	80,625	80,700	n.a.	545	545
Germany	46,330	42,270	36,654	610	551	460
France	42,918	43,868	42,898	778	771	750
UK	41,891	37,800	35,100	741	667	606
Japan	28,240	60,110	63,946	234	483	513
China	26,083	24,926	27,430	25	22	24
India	8,230	6,873	7,000	11	8	8
Turkey	3,016	6,300	7,073	60	108	119

Source: IISS, extracts from tables prepared for but not printed in *The Military Balance 1994–95*.

There is a legitimate question of how much firepower this military spending buys. Major Atsumasa Yamamoto, seconded from the intelligence division of the Japan Defence Agency to the Institute for International Policy Studies, commented that the league tables of international spending are 'misleading'. 'Comparison with foreign countries is not a wise way since spending is only one aspect and you must look at what the money can actually buy. US estimates of Japanese firepower suggest that it is very low compared with the rest of the world.' In GDP terms, he asserted, Japan's defence spending is at the very bottom, and in terms of personnel, it is slightly smaller than the UK, slightly bigger than Greece. Backing for these protestations of weakness came from a US government study in 1994, which shows that in terms of the 'firepower' commanded by a typical division, the USA comes top, followed by South Korea, with Japan trailing in equal eighth place with the UK.*

Another reason for concern about Japan's spending is the purchase of items that do not seem strictly compatible with mere 'self-defence forces' as opposed to fully fledged armed forces. Although the budgets for 1994 and 1995 promised that the increase in defence spending would be below 1 per cent, the lowest rise for years, among the items planned are purchases of two AWACs reconnaissance aircraft from the USA, four F-15 jet fighters and new radar for Patriot anti-missile defences. When the reconnaissance aircraft enter service before the end of the century, they will give Japan a

* *Report on Allied Contributions to the Common Defence*, May 1994, a report to the United States Congress by the Secretary of Defence.

surveillance capacity for 24 hours a day, well beyond the limits of self-defence. Allied to this were suggestions that the new H-II rocket might be used to put up a spy satellite, so that Japan could keep a close watch on what North Korea was up to without having to rely on the United States.

When in the early 1990s Japan bought a ton of fissile plutonium, reprocessed in France from spent nuclear fuel for use in its fast breeder reactor at Monju, there were howls of protest from more than a dozen countries. One of the loudest to squeal was North Korea. It claimed that the consignment was only the first step towards Japan's 'remilitarisation and nuclear armament'. Tokyo, of course, has strongly protested that its nuclear plants are purely for peaceful purposes. Other suppliers of plutonium, such as the British Thorp plant, have also pointed out that the fuel they supply is not easily usable for military purposes. But the whole plutonium issue is just one of a growing number of areas where civilian technology can be used without much trouble for military purposes.

Admiral Makoto Sakuma, chairman of the joint staff council of the Self-Defence Forces said: 'Before the [Second World] war, the government kept a technical edge as well as investment capability over the private sector in research and development. Today it is the other way around. The civilian private-sector technology is so advanced in most fields that the government has to depend on it. Consequently, the best option is to combine the two sectors so that the private sector's technological strength can be most effectively taken advantage of. Of course, there are fields where the Defence Agency should lead research and development on its own.'

When Nasda launched its thirty-first satellite in February 1992, the 1.34-ton Japan Earth Resource Satellite One (JERS-I) by the H-I, it was specifically for non-military research because Nasda is banned from conducting military missions. But there is general agreement that JERS-I is as good as any military reconnaissance satellite, and it is equipped with a synthetic aperture radar and optical sensor system that can identify and store data for retrieval at any time on anything larger than 18 metres.

Another pathbreaking development in Japanese science which could have immediate military use is the electromagnetic guidance propulsion technology. Japan has developed a system capable of driving a ship at speeds up to 100 knots without conventional propellers. Navies all round the world would love to have propellerless submarines which would be virtually noiseless. The prototype, interestingly called Yamato-I, a name traditionally used for Japan itself by rightists and nationalists, has already started sea trials.

Although American stockbroking analysts have recently been claiming loudly that Japanese technology no longer enjoys the lead it once did, especially in the fields of computers, there are many areas where Japan is at the leading edge of high technology that may have military uses. Some of the scientific efforts of Japan's Self-Defence Forces have been put to civilian use. For example, high-rigidity, lightweight alloy technology has been used for railway rolling stock. The forces' P-11 Doppler field radar was used to monitor lava flows from Mount Unzen, the dormant volcano that suddenly woke up in 1990. Japan and the USA are conducting joint research on military technology projects, including ducted rocket engines for missiles, a hybrid radio wave infra-red sensor, a ceramic engine for armoured vehicles and advanced steel for warships and armoured vehicles.

The Pentagon is one of the biggest customers for Japanese hand-held computers and for Japanese machine tools. It was not an idle boast by Shintaro Ishihara that the US defence systems were highly dependent on essential components supplied by Japan. A number of members of the US Congress have expressed concern about the potential threats to national security because of the Japanese lead in areas like high-grade composite materials, which have immediate potential in aerospace; and avionics, most notably flat-panel display technology. Other Japanese leading edge developments which are causing some concern are the testing of the world's first fly-by-wire helicopter; the tiltrotor, which flies like a fixed-wing aircraft but can take off and land like a helicopter; and projects for mining natural resources on the moon. A Pentagon report in 1991 concluded that Japan was more advanced than the United States in five areas of research: semi-conductors, superconductive technology, robotics, biotechnology and photoelectronic engineering.

In the 1980s, the worry was that Japan was producing leading edge technology with military applications, and might be prepared to export it to countries with hostile intentions. Restrictions imposed by the Co-ordinating Committee on Multilateral Export Controls (Cocom) did not stop a Toshiba group company from exporting key machine tools to the then Soviet Union in the 1980s. By the 1990s, worries that Japan might export its knowledge to potentially hostile interests were only part of the problem. A greater concern was that Japan might use its technology for its own military purposes.

There are pressures from two directions: military tension fed by national-ism in east Asia; and the dangers of budget cuts or isolationism in the USA, which has helped Asia's economic development through the protection of its nuclear umbrella. William Niskanen, chairman of a Republican-affili-ated think tank, the Cato Institute, encouraged a rethinking of traditional relationships. Just after the Republicans gained control of Congress in the 1994 elections, he called for development of an equal partnership between the USA and Japan, which would see the withdrawal of more than 46,000 US troops from their bases in Japan, including Okinawa. The USA, Nis-kanen suggested, should redeploy its naval and marine forces on a smaller scale to bases in Hawaii and the Pacific West Coast.

Yamamoto of the Self-Defence Forces also urged the need for more equality. In a paper published in mid-1994 by the IIPS,* he called for 'a more self-sufficient and well-organised defence capability. In the absence of such a force, it will not be possible to convince other countries that Japan is able or willing to carry out its international obligations fully.' He expressed concern that the USA 'may devote less concern and effort to Japan's national security' and added in any case that 'it will become more necessary for a country to make autonomous efforts to defend its territory without asking allies and other friendly countries for help. Japan, in particular, must adjust to this new reality, given that it is a leading economic power, second only to the United States.'

There are certainly plenty of east Asian regional tensions. Fears of North Korea's nuclear ambitions are far from dead. Pyongyang's progress in rocketry and his ability to hit any part of Japan, and China's continuing nuclear tests, increased military spending and regional, if not international ambitions,† can only encourage Japan to think of its own defences, including keeping abreast of latest nuclear developments, whatever international opinion and the constitution might say. On top of these concerns, Japan fears Russian intentions, not merely because of old hostilities, but also because Moscow is still sitting on four windswept islands off the coast of Hokkaido which Stalin's forces snatched in the dying days of the Second World War, and which Tokyo claims belong to it. The real issues and problems are political.

Politicians and bureaucrats in Japan have been all too happy to adapt the meaning of words, particularly those relating to defence and self-defence, to enhance policies without having to get involved in full-scale debates about changes in the law. The first example was the creation of the Self-Defence Forces in the 1950s. Socialist critics still contend that this was against the famous article 9 of the 'No War' constitution, which forbids a standing army. Most people have now accepted the legitimacy of the Self-Defence Forces. When the Socialist leader, Tomiichi Murayama, became prime minister in mid-1994 of a coalition government – and thus automatically commander-in-chief – he promptly, not quite overnight, threw party dogma out of the window and accepted them.

The 1992 law permitting Self-Defence Forces to join United Nations peacekeeping operations was bitterly opposed by Socialists and others who claimed that it was against the constitution, since the Japanese soldiers might have to take up arms and shoot and kill at the behest of non-Japanese commanders. After an acrimonious debate, the law was passed with a few fudges which asserted Japanese command over the soldiers even on UN duty, and said that the troops could only use their weapons

* *Japan's Future Defence Capability.*

† A leading Chinese general declared in the early 1990s that 'We cannot recognise the Indian Ocean as India's ocean', promising that China would build a blue-water fleet.

in self-defence. The Japanese soldiers are *not* to be used in UN peacekeeping *forces*, but are only allowed to join operations after a ceasefire and the presence of the peacekeepers have been agreed. In this way the Japanese leaders said that they had kept within the strict limits of the constitution. When Japanese soldiers went to refugee camps on the borders of Rwanda in 1994, there was a heated debate about whether they should be armed with light machine guns for self-defence. Finally, they went for a three-month humanitarian stint taking one machine gun, not the two which the forces had requested.

This may all seem too trivial to get excited about, but there is a genuine debate going on about how much the constitution has been subverted by stealth. A number of politicians, prominent among them Ichiro Ozawa, the secretary-general of Shinshinto (New Frontier Party), the jumbo opposition party, and generally believed to have been the real power behind the Morihiro Hosokawa government and later the opposition, wants to see Japan take its place as a 'normal' country: that is, one with political and military influence matching its economic strength in the world. Some right-wing nationalists, who are a small but vocal element in ordinary Japanese life, and who are seen regularly on the streets of Tokyo in their loudspeaker vans blaring nationalist anthems, are anxious that the shame of the war defeat be wiped out. On the other hand, there are other, less politically well-connected people, including Nobel prize-winner Kenzaburo Oe, who believe that Japan's contribution to the peace of the world should be its No-War constitution, and its determination after the atomic bombing of Hiroshima and Nagasaki to outlaw war. The problem is that the issue is too delicate to be debated publicly; instead the danger is that Japan's constitution may be undermined without being rewritten.

In the Japan of the mid-1990s, the danger of militarism seems slight. When he was minister, Satsuki Eda genuinely believed it was Japan's duty and role to see that its space rockets should be used for peaceful purposes, and that this marked an important departure from past practice by other space powers. Executives of Nasda are quick to point to the fact that their constitution prevents them from accepting military missions. The popular mood is anything but jingoistic. Japanese people who have studied history know the terrible price that was paid for the military adventures of the 1930s. Ordinary Japanese are content to explore the world and bring home its goodies with their strong yen.

At the same time there are pressures on Japan. North Korea and its development of nuclear weapons is the obvious one. If North Korea does have the nuclear bomb and the means of delivering it, Japan will increasingly feel the need to respond, possibly not only to match North Korea's technology, but also to develop weapons to forestall Korean madness. Japan's relationship with a rapidly growing China also has many uneasy points, not least because of the unhappy memories of the 1930s when Japanese soldiers raped and plundered in China.

Japanese politicians and public, blinded by their own nationalist rhetoric, have been slow to accept the full extent of Japan's wartime transgressions. Prime minister Hosokawa did apologise in 1993, but in the most general terms, and for this he was sharply criticised not just by ultranationalists, but also by mainstream members of the Liberal Democratic Party suffering a brief spell in opposition. Latent nationalism in Japan must be a constant worry, fed as it is by claims that Japan is populated by unique people descended from a unique sun goddess, racially and linguistically pure. The claims fly in the face of history and common sense, but it is political dynamite to contradict them. The dangers of resurgence of militarism seem far far away. But it would be wise not to underestimate some of the pressures, and it is important to be aware that Japan is already an aerospace power of some force, which could be turned to military use swiftly at any time, whatever the dire consequences.

9

Japan's Miracle Children:
A Hothouse Education

To see them in the early morning, neat and scrubbed and dressed in identical uniform with almost identical heavy backpacks, except for an individual tiny teddy bear or Snoopy or miniature soccer ball, or some other toy to show that they really are still children, they look almost terrifying, the massed advance guard of Japan's economic domination into the twenty-first century. They are the secondary school children of Japan, almost all of whom, whether in private or state schools, wear a uniform modelled on that of the former Prussian state, which at a glance suggests not only rigidity and iron discipline, but also an army on the march. However, closer consideration shows that, although the education system offers the best, it also contains some of the worst aspects of Japan. The system has plenty of virtues, but also a number of serious flaws which undermine Japan's prospects for economic performance and – more important – its potential as an international good neighbour.

Kaisei School in Nishi-Nippori, just a stone's throw from the Yamanote circle line train station, is one of Japan's élite educational institutions. It is an all-boys school with 900 students in the junior high school section, covering the ages twelve or thirteen to fifteen or sixteen, and another 1,200 in the three-year senior high school. Externally, the buildings are nondescript, rather like many other undistinguished glass and concrete blocks. But there is just one attachment that marks the place out. It is a huge device on the wall showing a samurai sword crossed with a quill pen. What does this mean? Inside the satchel of every schoolboy is a fearsome samurai warrior waiting to leap out? No, says deputy headmaster Mineo Fukuchi: 'It actually represents an old English expression – "the pen is mightier than the sword".'

In spite of the tasteless modern buildings, the school owes part of its claim to fame to its foundation in 1871 in the first exciting years of the Meiji Restoration. It continues to flourish because of its terrific academic success rate: of the 400 final-year students, deputy head Fukuchi expects that all will go to university and 200 will get to Tokyo University, the élite institution among Japan's élite, almost like Oxford and Cambridge, Harvard, Yale and Princeton all rolled into one.

Kaisei, which is a day school with no boarding facilities, is not cheap. The boys have to pay an entrance fee of 380,000 yen ($3,800), plus another 200,000 yen which goes to the Construction Fund or, literally, the Institution-Expanding Fund. In addition, there are monthly fees of 32,500 yen, plus 4,000 yen for maintenance, another 4,000 yen for experiments, 2,800 yen for the parent–teachers association and 550 yen for the students fee. In all, this comes to monthly charges of 43,850 yen or $438.50 at early 1995 rates (on top of those hefty entrance charges of 580,000 yen). But there is strong competition to get in, said Fukuchi. About 800 boys take the entrance exam for the 300 places in the junior school. All of the graduating juniors pass through to the senior school, and are joined by another 100 students a year, chosen by examination from about 400 candidates. The school is totally private but like other such schools a third of its costs are paid by the Ministry of Education.

The school's first principal was Korekiyo Takahashi, who went on to become finance minister and later prime minister of Japan in the early twentieth century. He built up the school as his country enthusiastically embraced western ways of education, government and industry in its efforts to catch up after three centuries of near isolation. Fukuchi cannot recall any Kaisei pupils who have become distinguished bureaucrats, politicians or industrialists, though he reels off a list of names of musicians, artists and men who have achieved fame for their cultural activities. 'Basically, we are trying to produce rounded human beings,' he says.

Unusually, there is no general assembly where the Kaisei boys gather to say prayers or sing a school anthem or generally receive a pep talk. 'The most important thing is to teach the students,' said Fukuchi, who in his dedicated but shy schoolmasterly way seemed generally respected and liked by the boys. Classes start at 8.20 each morning and there are four morning classes of 50 minutes each and two in the afternoon, with a 40-minute break for lunch. Most boys stay on for artistic classes in the afternoons.

When you get closer to them, the uniform orderliness of the pupils disappears and they become individuals, some of them rather scruffy and unruly, just like English schoolboys, if not Americans, because they are all wearing the black uniform that is the hallmark of the majority of male Japanese teenagers in school hours. Their black shoes range from scuffed leather to trainers. There have been some small but important changes to the dress. Since April 1994 the junior schoolboys no longer wear the black peaked caps emblazoned with their pen and sword insignia. Fukuchi explained that the senior boys had not had to wear the caps for ten years. 'With modern hairstyles growing longer, it was felt that the caps did not fit.'

Fukuchi, who has more than 43 years' experience as a teacher of mathematics and then deputy headmaster, finds today's students 'more obedient these past few years than they used to be, but they lack in resilience and the strength to continue something. In the past they had more hungry sentiments, always seeking something. Nowadays even if the teachers want to give them some extra learning, it is difficult for them to take it.' He believes that this is not just a feature peculiar to Kaisei or of schools in general, 'but the general atmosphere of affluence which makes it more difficult to educate'.

When he relaxed, Fukuchi put forward in a very gentle voice a number of what he called 'controversial personal opinions'. One of these was to question whether the schools should be churning out so many people for university. 'It is questionable whether or how many did study and understand their textbooks,' he said, adding his view that only 10 per cent of the whole Japanese population should go to university, instead of almost 50 per cent passing on to tertiary education. Japan, he said, was just turning out graduates for companies. These strictures were mixed with affection for his own students. Asked how many of Kaisei's boys would be qualified to take advantage of a university place, he added quietly, 'about 90 per cent'.

In spite of Kaisei's acknowledged excellence, a good number of its students have to go to *juku* or cram school classes to supplement their school learning, in order to pass the examinations to get to university. Exactly how many attend juku is a matter of guesswork, but Fukuchi estimates that between 20 and 30 per cent do – possibly as many as 60 per cent in some grades. Few of the students have experience of foreign countries, and fewer still have lived abroad. 'The major problem is that living abroad hampers the cultural development in our own language,' says the deputy head.

Not surprising to anyone who has lived for any length of time in Japan, when I tried to talk in English to a small group of senior boys aged seventeen, they mostly looked blank. Though they had studied English from textbooks for five years, as one of the key items on the curriculum, this is not the English spoken in England, America or anywhere else in the English-speaking world. It is the dead English of school textbooks, so unimaginative that it would never be reproduced in conversation anywhere. More startlingly, the boys seemed to be taken aback that I should be asking their opinion about anything. This is not Kaisei's fault. Part of the blame lies with Tokyo University, which sets the difficult entrance examinations that are the pinnacle of the hothouse system. Part of the blame lies with Monbusho, the Ministry of Education, Science and Culture, housed in a gloomy redbrick pile in Tokyo's Kasumigaseki bureaucratic heartland.

The mandarins of the Education Ministry have laid down a programme eminently praiseworthy in its outline. Their documents and the officials themselves emphasise the need to develop 'Japanese citizens who will be members of the international community in the twenty-first century'. An English version of the ministry's main aims goes on almost poetically to state that it wants to help 'children grow into people who have rich hearts, as well as healthy minds and bodies'. It promises that 'the Monbusho also aims at securing the content and methods of teaching and learning, in which emphasis is placed on basic knowledge and skills, and in which children can give full play to their individualities'.

Some of Japan's educational achievements expressed in statistics are impressive. Japan has one of the highest literacy rates in the world, at more than 99 per cent. Education is compulsory only until junior high school, which is about the age of fifteen or sixteen, after six years of primary education and three years at junior high school. But compulsion seems hardly necessary. Almost 90 per cent of Japanese pupils go on to senior high school, and 50 per cent, or almost 3 million students at any time, go on to tertiary education. The country has more than 520 universities giving degrees after four-year courses, and almost 600 junior colleges which run two-year courses.*

The thirst for education is great, from kindergarten where there are nearly two million children, right through to university. When the students finally emerge, they are not only literate, but numerate. But they are also handicapped by the methods of teaching, by the very 'textbook' knowledge they have acquired, and by a lot of distracting problems on the way, some of which the ministry refers to in its public texts. In 1993 the ministry said, 'It is striving to strengthen relevant measures for stopping school violence and bullying, for solving other behavioural problems displayed by schoolchildren and for helping children to overcome school maladjustment problems, the symptoms of which include refusal to attend school and dropping out of school at the upper secondary school level.'

For some children, the pressures of the Japanese education system can begin at the age of two. One school for toddlers, Eishin Yoji Kyoiku, recruits two- to five-year-olds with the promise that 'every year more than 80 per cent of our pupils pass the entrance exams for famous elementary schools'. The best elementary schools lead to the best high schools, which lead to the best universities. This school also claims 'to improve the child's capability of expression, the child's intellectual faculties and abstract thinking, the ability to concentrate and memorise accurate and correct

---

* In 1994, the ministry listed 523 universities, 98 national, 41 run by local public bodies and 384 privately owned. In spite of this variety, Tokyo University stands clearly at the top in influence and prestige, followed by Kyoto, another imperial university, then the privately owned Waseda, Keio and Sophia universities, the national Hitotsubashi University and other former imperial universities, Tohoku, Osaka and Hokkaido.

knowledge, learn operative abilities like sense of speed and motion, as well as the ability to play imaginative games using teaching tools'. Eishin Kyoiku charges an entrance fee of 70,000 yen, plus 6,500 yen for each 90-minute lesson.

Some so-called education specialists are trying to start the rat-race even earlier, right back to the child in the womb. Motoo Futamura of the Early Development Association tries to attract pregnant mothers to his classes, claiming, 'Once your child is two or three, it could be far too late. Even if your child is not yet born, you can influence what kind of a child you will raise later on.' The association, established by Sony Corporation's co-founder, Masaru Ibuka, holds maternity classes and devotes itself to 'educating 0-year-olds'. Futamura has special rules. 'In order to show respect for the unborn babies, women address each other using the children's future names,' he said. 'We tell them to talk to the babies in their wombs as much as possible. For example, if they arrange flowers, they should tell their babies which flowers they are using and how they assemble them. Their husbands should participate too, greeting the baby when coming home from work.'

Most Japanese children do get to enjoy a brief childhood, in which they are probably more indulged and pampered than children in the West. The increasing accent on discipline and uniformity begins to take its toll from the junior high school. Many aspects of the Japanese education system in the early years are superb and give it a deserved reputation as the best in the world. American professor Catherine Lewis, who is director of formative research at the Development Studies Center in San Ramon, California, said that at the primary level Japan has a lot to teach the West. The ideal education, she said, would begin in Japanese elementary schools and finish in the American secondary system.

Any casual observer in Japanese cities can see the strength of the system, not just at elementary but also at kindergarten level, in the crocodiles of tiny tots, dressed in identical smocks and funny hats, holding hands and urging each other along. In country areas the children normally take it in turns to be responsible for seeing that a group of classmates is up and ready to catch the bus to school. It is touching to see not only the co-operation, but also the individual and joint responsibilities developed at an early age.

Lewis credited the Japanese elementary system with building skills and problem solving, co-operation and responsibility. 'Japanese elementary schools foster a great deal of self-expression,' she said. She observed a sample of more than fifteen pre-school to first-grade classes in a number of schools, ranging from rich to poor areas of Tokyo. Her conclusion was that the American system is very much based on reward and punishment, but Japanese elementary classrooms foster group co-operation, allowing children the emotional freedom to tackle a problem without worrying about being ridiculed. 'Kids are much more focused on learning and get the intrinsic satisfaction eventually of mastering something, whether or not they get a high grade,' she commented. Each day there are *kaeri no kai* (end of the day meeting) and mandatory *hansei* (self-reflection) periods.

Japan's early school classrooms are in fact very chaotic, and the hand of authority is very light. Even when children begin to fight, teachers will rarely intervene directly, but will encourage other students to solve the problem. This co-operative attitude, commented Lewis, 'changes the way kids look at the world when they see a problem occurring. When two kids are fist-fighting, they don't see that as something that is that child's problem; they see it as something that is their problem.'

In the elementary school years, Japanese education is focused on the whole child. 'Non-academic' subjects, such as art, music, gymnastics, cookery and home-making skills, occupy more than a third of teaching time in the first year and more than 40 per cent of the time by the final year. Children in their first year at school spend as much time studying art and music as they do mathematics. The ministry's official course for the primary schools insists on development of social, emotional and ethical skills as well as on the academic classes. The Monbusho's 'goals' include interest in language, 'affection for our country and its history', 'love of nature', 'love of music', 'richness of sentiment', 'fondness for exercise' and 'reverence for life'.

Besides giving them a good grounding in mathematics and Japanese language, teachers also show their pupils how to brush their teeth, tell them to think about ways of helping their mothers at home, encourage them to 'do their utmost' at the sports days, and check whether everyone in the class is involved in building friendships. Lewis noticed that the schools she looked at often used banners to proclaim the current goals. She counted 94 goals in nineteen classrooms, with the banners written in hiragana phonetic characters so that even the youngest children could understand them. Some of them underlined the ministry's guidelines for moral education, such as friendship and looking after one's own belongings, but others were very much the product of the children's own experiences. 'Let's play dodge without the boys hogging the ball,' read one banner. 'Let's be kind children who easily say, "I am sorry" and "Thank you",' said another.

In addition, Lewis found, teachers were preoccupied with *gakkyuzukuri* – meaning to promote the community of the classroom – exploring doing art projects together, singing and dancing, and even holding group discussions on what sort of class the children wanted to be. The teachers to whom she spoke talked of their aims of creating friendships and encouraging their pupils to look at each other's good points rather than at bad points. As to discipline, the emphasis was on self-discipline, especially through encouraging the *toban* or classroom monitors to take the lead in helping to formulate standards of behaviour.

Lewis noted that Japanese use two words similar to English ones, *wetto* and *dorai* to contrast styles. 'Dorai' or 'dry' means being rational or logical, and sometimes is actually used to mean western ways; 'wetto' or 'wet' is personal and emotional, and sometimes is used to mean Japanese. Even in science or mathematics classes, she commented, 'learning was often an emotional enterprise'. She found that children would spend up to two hours decorating plastic bottle 'boats' that they were going to sink or float as part of a science experiment. They would tell stories about the containers or fruits they brought from home for the day's experiments.

The troubles with the education system begin at the junior high school level. Some of them are built into the system, and others are the bad but incidental products of what develops into a highly regimented approach to education as it reaches senior levels. Among the incidentals are things like hairstyles. The issue came to the fore in 1993 when the new education minister, Ryoko Akamatsu, criticised *marugari*, the close-cropped hairstyle which is mandatory for boys in many schools throughout Japan. The cropping is so close that it looks like the American marine shaven head, with little cover to the skull. Akamatsu commented in response to a letter from a group in the Kansei area, which includes Osaka, that 'marugari sends a chill through my spine with its connotations of the wartime military'. She later apologised for being so outspoken. During the debate that followed, school principals in the Osaka area put forward comments such as 'the purpose of school is group training, not individual education' and 'liberalisation of hairstyles will lower teachers' morale'. After this spotlight had been thrust on the hairstyle, some schools decided to abolish the practice of marugari. In Ehime prefecture, there was an almost uniform decision to do so.

A former member of the board of education in Nakano-ku in Tokyo, Moeko Tawara, pointed out that this abolition was not necessarily progress. She said, 'I find it grotesque that all the schools have decided to stop marugari simultaneously. There is no better example of such thoroughly bureaucratised organisations where top-down order works so effectively as education administration. Ehime is a good example of it. When the prefectural board of education says "revise the marugari rule", schools take it as virtually an order.'

Uniform itself is causing increasing problems. At the extreme, an Osaka group claimed that even wearing a uniform infringed the right of children to be individuals. Most schools, however, retain uniform right through to the age of eighteen. Boys wear stiff black serge trousers and matching jacket, buttoned tightly up to the neck to hide completely the white shirt worn underneath. Jackets can carry school or even class insignia on the buttons or on the collars. For some strange reason, almost all schoolboys wear white socks, which look distinctly odd offset against their black trousers and black shoes. For most girls, the uniform consists of a version of a sailor suit (known as *sera* in a Japanesified abbreviation of the English word), and some schools have a dark blue, heavy-duty uniform for winter and a lighter-fabric, lighter-colour version for spring and summer. Some girls' schools carry the military comparison a step further by having petty officer's stripes and insignia sewn on the sleeves of the blouse or jacket worn by older children.

The girls' uniform has caused even more controversy because of a flourishing underground industry for the benefit of dirty old men. In the early 1990s, shops sprang up selling 'sera' and their *buru* (short for bloomers, originally referring to navy knickers worn underneath, but such shops are not normally choosy about the colour). Japanese newspapers were full of stories of high school girls making 1,000 yen ($10) a pair by bringing their used underwear to such shops, which charged customers 3,000 yen or more for them. Several entrepreneurs offered used underwear from street-side vending machines, with one promising that the goods were fresh because they had been vacuum packed immediately on receipt. 'If I don't, they go mouldy after a few days.' In spite of protests in some areas about the depravity of such practices, the authorities claimed that it was difficult to stop them, although one local government did prosecute a shop for selling used clothes without a licence to deal in antiques.

Few schools have dared to dispense entirely with uniform, although the mixed-sex Fuji High School in Tokyo's Nakano ward is one of them. Its headmaster in 1994, Akira Yamamoto, who was also chairman of the principals of the Tokyo metropolitan high schools, said that his school had abolished uniforms more than 25 years ago. 'There are no uniforms, but standard clothes are supposed to be worn.' Those standard clothes include jeans. At Fuji, as at many other Japanese schools, the children have to take off their outdoor shoes and put on slippers when entering the premises. This creates an incongruous sight of often scruffily dressed teenagers rushing to cast off their dirty outdoor shoes to resume a polite pace inside the school corridors. Headmaster Yamamoto saw the lack of uniform as being a sign that the children could be well behaved and grown up without forcing them into uniform mould.

At high school level, the pressures on schoolchildren increase. The most worrying is the cult of uniformity, which directly and indirectly leads to more than a hundred deaths a year of worried schoolchildren. In one notable case in the early 1990s, a teacher in Hyogo prefecture directly caused the death of a fifteen-year-old girl student by determined application of the school's rules. Ryoko Ishida was rushing to get inside the school gate just before it was closed, but failed to make it. The teacher pushed the gate shut, slamming the girl's skull against a concrete pillar.

The principal of another high school that regularly closed its gate on the dot of time claimed that 'the practice is necessary to teach students the importance of being on time'.

Teachers say that the highly rule-oriented system was introduced in the late 1960s when schools were seeing an outbreak of violence. The attitude was that students' behaviour should be tightly governed by rules and regulations to prevent them stepping out of line. In the Hyogo case, the teacher responsible was sentenced to a year in prison, suspended for three years. Attempts by the defence counsel to suggest that the child's death was caused by the iron code of discipline laid down by the principal, and supported by the rigid educational system, were unsuccessful. A court had ruled in a 1959 case when a student died in a swimming accident that the incident was caused by 'poor class planning' and that the principal himself was responsible.

Such deaths through enforcing adamantine rules are unusual. But each year a number of teenagers succumb to *ijime* or bullying, and some of them commit suicide rather than continue to face torment. The issue came to the fore in late November and December 1994, when Kiyoteru Okouchi gained posthumous nationwide fame because of the letter he left behind, a desperately sad final testament to a thirteen-year life. His mother found him hanging from a tree in the garden. 'I want to die because my schoolmates are demanding money from me,' he wrote. He left behind rudimentary accounts suggesting that he paid out almost 1.2 million yen ($12,000) to school bullies over a two-year period. He wrote that four classmates had demanded sums ranging from 30,000 to 70,000 yen a time. He paid, he said, because 'I was taken to a river, and they forced my head underwater. They did this many times and I was scared because I could not touch the bottom with my feet.' He admitted borrowing the money from home and kept a careful note of the sums, crossing out the old total and writing in the new, with the promise to repay. The money was spent by the bullies on playing in amusement arcades as well as on clothes, food and alcohol. As the sum grew, he recognised the impossibility of repaying it and said farewell to his family.

'Thank you very much for the last fourteen years [Japanese, like Chinese, count themselves as one at their birth]. I am leaving on a trip,' he wrote in the note that his parents released. 'We will surely meet again someday. I am truly sorry about the money. I thought I would be able to repay it by working, but that dream has ended ... Grandmother, I want you to live for a long time; Father, thank you for the trip to Australia; Mother, thank you for the tasty food. Older brother, sorry for being an inconvenience. Why did I not die earlier? because my family was gentle to me. It was easy to forget what happened at school. However, these days they bully me so hard and demand large sums of money although I have none. I can't stand it anymore...'

His death was by no means a rarity. In 1993 Yuhei Kodama, a thirteen-year-old junior high school student in Yamagata, suffocated after classmates placed him upside down in a rolled-up gym mat and stuffed it in a cupboard. He had previously suffered other bullyings. One police officer investigating the death said, 'beating up Kodama seemed to come about as naturally to his classmates as saying "hello".' 'It was fun to watch him react,' according to a classmate of the victim, who accused teachers of watching the bullying and doing nothing to stop it. Other deaths in the 1992–3 school year included a seventeen-year-old who was stabbed, a fourteen-year-old killed by nine classmates for threatening to report bullying of which he was the victim, the murder of classmate by two fourteen-year-old schoolchildren in Osaka, and the suicide of a thirteen-year-old who found several months of bullying too much to bear. In an infamous case in 1986, a thirteen-year-old boy from Nakano-ku in Tokyo had hanged himself in a railway station after suffering constant bullying. Some weeks before, a group of students had staged a mock funeral for him and given him an autographed board full of farewell messages, some from teachers as well as classmates.

Exactly how many deaths result from bullying each year is difficult to tell. The acknowledged number of suicides by schoolchildren is more than 100 a year – and in the two weeks after Kiyoteru Okouchi's death, police reported seven suicides by junior high pupils and two by primary schoolchildren – but the authorities prefer to hide where possible and pretend that bullying does not go on. Kiyoteru Okouchi's headmaster admitted that the school did not take the bullying seriously enough. Even though the boy's grades suffered, the school believed that he was one of the bullying gang rather than its victim. In the 1986 case, a Tokyo court decided years later that the action of the boy's classmates could not be considered a typical case of bullying; it claimed that the boy had probably been flattered by his mock funeral. It was only eight years after their son's death that his parents got partial redress in the form of 11.5 million yen in damages.

The Education Ministry claimed that there had been a reduction in bullying cases from 156,000 in 1985 to just over 24,000 in 1992. It announced the hiring of 14,000 child welfare workers nationwide whose job it would be to monitor bullying, truancy and child abuse – a small number considering the large number of incidents. Elizabeth Yamashita, a school social worker in Saitama, told the *Mainichi Daily News* after Okouchi's death that 'Only the number of reported cases of bullying has decreased, but that's because there are problems in the ways in which bullying is categorised.' Bullying is often difficult to identify, she added, because 'it is often so skilfully executed'. A society which places as much emphasis as Japan on conformity and obedience creates plenty of scope for picking on those who fail to conform.

Typical targets are the brightest children, those who are weak or disabled, and those who have been brought up abroad and have imported different or strange habits, particularly any inability to speak or read or write Japanese fluently. With the increasing sums of Japanese investment going abroad, several hundred thousand employees have been posted to foreign countries. Some mothers prefer to stay in Japan with their children, rather than face the problem of putting them into schools where they will be educated in a language they do not understand. Others take the risk and go together as a family. By 1993 the Ministry of Education estimated that there were 51,000 children of compulsory school age living outside Japan. To cope with these, almost 90 Japanese schools had been established, plus another 150 offering part-time Japanese education. More than 1,200 teachers had been sent abroad from Japan. Even so, only 36 per cent of the Japanese children abroad were getting full-time Japanese education, and another 40 per cent were receiving some.

If anything, the struggle gets worse rather than better when children come home to Japan. Some families who have lived abroad for a long time prefer to keep their children in foreign schools. 'We found our children's Japanese ability to be inadequate for study in Japanese schools,' said one parent, explaining why his daughters remained in an American school. For daughters the decision is sometimes easier than for sons, because if a boy is to have any chance of climbing the career ladder, he has to have had a thorough grounding in Japanese. This also means being able to fit in and not attract attention as someone who is 'different'. It is perhaps truer of Japanese schools than those anywhere else.

The truth of conformity is reinforced by the iron hand of the Ministry of Education in enforcing standards that are the same across the country, from Tokyo to rural Hokkaido in the north and Okinawa in the south. The ministry sets a uniform tone for the school textbooks, a fact which has caused endless argument between authors and bureaucrats, especially on the tricky question of how to describe Japan's behaviour during the 1930s militarism and the Second World War.

One famous professor, Saburo Ienaga, aged 80 in 1994, has conducted an almost 30-year-long battle with the ministry's *Kentei* ministerial guidance system governing textbooks. 'The Kentei system that the Ministry of Education applies to textbooks is violating the freedom of study that the Constitution guarantees, and is a censorship system,' commented the frail, thin Ienaga, who was professor at Tokyo Education University (now called Tsukuba University).

He started his first case against the ministry in 1965, after beginning writing Japanese history textbooks for senior high school students in 1952. Several times he locked horns with the censors in the 1950s. What annoyed him was receiving authorisation for a book subject to his amending 200 passages. He claimed that the guidance in 1963 and 1964 was stricter than ever, and that 'even parts that had been approved in the past were not accepted'. Among the ministry objections that upset Ienaga were that he had written that the descriptions of the *Kojiki* (record of ancient matters) and *Nihon Shoki* (chronicles of Japan) are not fact, and that he had used cover pictures of working-class people and chosen to ignore the ruling class and the samurai in his illustrations. Ienaga grumbled that the ministry supervisors 'disliked questioning the role of the Imperial family in the historical writings; they dislike issues related to invasion by Japan; and they didn't like activist issues. They'd rather ignore issues like sexual discrimination and family problems, which were first being taught in post-war Japan, and all these were issues that I had taken great care to include.'

Ienaga continued to be a thorn in the side of the establishment. He wrote another textbook in 1980, daring to talk about the infamous Nanking Massacre – or 'incident' as the Japanese prefer to call it – in which Japanese soldiers raped, pillaged and murdered in the Chinese city in 1937, and up to 250,000 people were slaughtered by the Japanese Imperial Army; about the medical experiments run by Unit 731; and about the battle of Okinawa, when civilians were induced to commit suicide by Japanese troops defending against the Americans. He thought it was safe because books had been published about these controversies. Instead the censors disapproved 400 passages. Ienaga picked six of them to sue on, 'just to clarify the issue'. In 1993 the Supreme Court dismissed Ienaga's suit, declaring that the screening system was needed to ensure that the content of textbooks was accurate and neutral, and to bring about a standardised level of education for children all over Japan. At that time Ienaga commented that the decision meant 'that the Ministry of Education can do whatever it pleases. The bonds between the judicial system and the bureaucrats are becoming tighter. It's a very frightening situation.'

He admitted that he was reluctant revolutionary. Ienaga was educated in an era when Japanese history textbooks started with the era of the gods and interpreted the mythological account of the Kojiki and Nihon Shoki as if they were historical facts. His father was in the army, although he was of a liberal frame of mind and had retired long before the war. Ienaga himself graduated from Tokyo Imperial University in 1937, did research and then started teaching at high school and on education courses, but he did not protest against the advanced militarisation of education.

As a teacher, Ienaga got deferment from being called up, and then lung problems meant that he was too sickly to fight in the war. 'My non-performance left me with a feeling of war responsibility,' he later confessed about his failure to protest. In fact he was much slower than the mass media to accept the post-war situation and Japan's embrace of democracy. 'I was suspicious of the mass media; the same ones who were promoting the "sacred war" had now suddenly changed their tune and started promoting democracy,' he said in a 1993 interview.

One of the textbook censors in the 1960s accused Ienaga of not being Japanese enough. He complained, 'The Ienaga textbook is one of unknown nationality. I think it has a defect which prevents it from being used in Japanese schools. With respect to the Japanese attitude towards China, when you think of it now, you cannot help but call it an invasion. However, western countries also conducted invasions. Why does he use the word "advance" in the case of western countries' entry to China and use the word "invasion" only for Japan? As a citizen of the Japanese nation he should be considerate enough to use the phrase "invasion of China" in the case of western countries and "advance in China" for our country ... The Korean independence movement, seen from Japan then, was conspiracy and rebellion ... I cannot help but doubt that Mr Ienaga, who writes textbooks, is a historian who looks for the truth, but rather a revolutionary fighter who plans to change our society.'

In October 1993, Ienaga won a partial victory and 300,000 yen when the Tokyo High Court, taking up yet another of his challenges to the system, ruled that the government had abused its authority when it had asked him to rewrite some of the text. But the court again upheld the constitutionality of the Education Ministry's screening of textbooks before they could be used in schools.

The court accepted Ienaga's complaints on three out of eight deletions. One was the account of the Nanking Massacre, which the judge said reviewers were wrong to change, since the account was 'the prevailing view in the academic community' at the time the book was screened. But the court upheld the censors' decision to cut Ienaga's description of Unit 731 – 'the unit established by the Imperial Japanese Army in the suburb of Harbin, [which] used several thousand Chinese people for human experiments for several years until the Soviet Union started its war against Japan.' The ministry had argued that there were no reliable scholarly studies about the unit, which was responsible for the deaths of at least 3,000 people from the late 1930s until 1945.*

Ienaga's challenge has been only the most publicised and stubborn, and

---

* Japan has not admitted the existence of Unit 731 in spite of the growing evidence of its work, including information from America that its head, Lieutenant-General Dr Shiro Ishii, was given immunity from war crimes prosecution in return for supplying the USA with records of his experiments. In 1994 a Chinese historian claimed that between 3,000 and 20,000 refugees were killed in germ warfare experiments in the early 1940s by a southern China offshoot of Unit 731. But Japan continued to try to bury its war misdeeds, and ordered that skeletons excavated from the site of the former head-quarters of the Imperial Army medical School in Tokyo should be cremated, rather than examined to see if they were the remains of victims of Unit 731. Its decision was being challenged in the courts.

was aided by the fact that he drew attention to questions of Japan's international history and present-day global role. His cause was also aided by international protests by China, Korea and other countries against attempts in school textbooks to brush aside Japanese atrocities in their countries before and during the war.

Thanks to these pressures, modern Japanese texts do recognise that the Imperial Army was responsible for brutalities. Junior high school histories in 1994 were critical of the western powers' colonial adventures, but also admitted that in 1937, as one book put it: 'In Nanjing [Nanking] the [Imperial] army massacred large numbers of Chinese people, including not only prisoners of war, but women and children.* The books also mention that civilians, including children, were forced into the defence of Okinawa against the USA by the Imperial Army, and the resentment towards Japan in its colonies.

One issue still causing international controversy concerns what Japan prefers to call 'comfort women' – meaning the young women rounded up from countries under Japanese occupation and forced to serve as prostitutes to provide comfort for Japanese soldiers, sometimes right at the frontline in the sound of guns. Up to 150,000 girls were rounded up, some of them in their very early teens, mostly from Korea, but also including Chinese, Indonesians, Filipinas and Dutch from Indonesia. This issue is even more sensitive because several of the woman involved are still trying to sue the Japanese government for their wartime sufferings at the hands of the soldiers.

The government only admitted official involvement in the army brothels as late as 1993, so the sex slaves made their appearance in the school texts only in April 1995 in carefully screened form. One book included a footnote estimating the number of comfort women at 60,000 to 70,000, but noted that there were no official figures; the ministry ordered a change, and the footnote finally said the number was 'large'. Another publisher put the description '80,000 to 200,000 Korean comfort women' on a map dealing with war compensation issues, but after screening it omitted the number entirely. On the other hand, in the 1995 editions, the ministry did not object to a history textbook saying that the Imperial Army had set up Unit 731, which 'killed many foreigners, including Chinese prisoners of war, by using them as human guinea pigs'.

The process of textbook screening goes on, dealing not only with the obvious sensitive issues, but also with more mundane matters. Even subjects like foreign aid are checked. One author wrote in the original version

* This book, *Chugaku shakai: Rekishiteki bunya*, or *Social Studies for Junior High School: History*, published by Osaka Shoseki, even gives a footnote that 'It has been said that 200,000 people were slaughtered by the Japanese army in this incident, which was condemned internationally as the "Nanjing Massacre".'

of a book on Japanese society and the world: 'Japan's ODA [meaning official development assistance] programmes are criticised on the grounds that they lead to destruction of the environment and of people's lifestyles ... and that they benefit the advancement of Japanese companies into the donor countries more than the donor country itself.' The ministry criticised this as one-sided, and the paragraph was revised to read: 'Japanese ODA is provided to developing countries for the construction of roads, bridges, ports and other public works, and for insurance and medical services. More recently, ODA has also been used for environmental protection programmes and for technical assistance projects. However, compared with other developed countries, the percentage of grant aid that Japan provides to developing countries is small.'

Scholars who have studied the development of Japanese textbooks carefully say that over the past twenty years there has been an increasing assertion of national self-confidence in the writings. In the early 1990s, the ministry 'suggested' that 42 historical figures should be included in textbooks to 'enhance respect for Japanese culture and tradition'. They included Admiral Heihachiro Togo, the man responsible for defeating the Russians in war in the early years of the century, who had been kept out on the grounds that he was a symbol of militarism. When the decision was taken to allow Japanese soldiers to go abroad as part of United Nations peacekeeping operations in 1992, the ministry gently advised publishers to tell their readers about 'the growing acceptance of the Self-Defence Forces'. The forces are themselves a matter of controversy because left-wing politicians believe their existence is an infringement of the Constitution forbidding Japan to keep a standing army.

Critics who look only at the history and economics textbooks sometimes miss the variety of Japan's nationalistic prickliness. Japanese textbook authors sometimes make surprising connections in unusual places. In the late 1980s, for example, one English book for junior high schools discussed 'two visitors' to Japan, called 'Little Boy' and 'Fat Man', the names given to the two atomic bombs dropped on Hiroshima and Nagasaki in August 1945. The treatment in the English books had all the subtlety of a sledgehammer, using the bombs as a warning about giving pleasant names to bad things. 'Some people called the bombs "Little Boy" and "Fat Man". They are charming names, aren't they? They were the names for the atomic bombs dropped on Hiroshima and Nagasaki. A name is a name. It is not a thing. I think it is important to remember this. A thing with a charming name can sometimes do a cruel thing, like "Little Boy" or "Fat Man".'

The vexed textbook question and the subtle changes are symptomatic of wider developments, some of which should be of great concern to the outside world. As it has recovered from the dust and ashes of defeat in the Second World War, so Japan has recovered self-confidence and has sought self-assertion. When the Liberal Democratic Party rule was broken after 38 years in mid-1993, the new prime minister, Morihiro Hosokawa, bowed to foreign sensitivities and apologised for Japanese aggression during and before the Second World War. But immediately he had resigned, the new justice minister, Shigeto Nagano, claimed that the Nanking Massacre was a 'hoax' or 'fabrication', and that Japan was not an aggressor but was merely trying to defeat colonialism. Although he was disowned by the new prime minister, Tsutomu Hata, and was forced to resign because of the public outcry in Japan, the fact that Nagano had been chief of the ground Self-Defence Forces (or army) until entering politics in 1980 suggested that soldiers and some influential politicians were unrepentant.

At the start of the 1990s, Monbusho issued instructions that schools from elementary to senior high must display the *Hinomaru* (Rising Sun) flag and sing the *Kimigayo* anthem at entrance and graduation ceremonies. The ministry declared that it issued the instruction to 'encourage children to learn the significance [of the flag and anthem] and consequently deepen understanding of the nation'. Many teachers, who tend to have left-wing sympathies, object to the edicts because of the historical associations of the flag and anthem with the militarists of the 1930s.

In practice, most schools obeyed the ruling on the flag, but one in five did not sing the Kimigayo. In the early 1990s, between 100 and 300 teachers each year were disciplined for non-compliance – for example, by refusing to stand up during the singing of the anthem. Strictly constitutionally speaking, Japan has *no* national anthem or flag, and Socialists are unhappy about the readoption of the symbols of the militarist years. What might surprise Britons is that the ministry is making such a fuss about the flag (although Americans, who take saluting their flag and singing the anthem more seriously, might understand, if they do not sympathise with the historical associations).

A closer look at the politics of education in Japan shows a complicated system in which some of the outstanding bureaucrats, although sympathetic to Right rather than Left, have been trying for years to reform the system and make education more flexible and responsive to the rapidly changing times. But time after time in the 1970s and the 1980s, they were frustrated by their relative weakness within the overall, supposedly uniform structure of Japan Inc. Conservative forces concerned to preserve right-wing values readily allied with older bureaucrats and the ruling Liberal Democratic Party politicians, who were inspired by a burning wish to obliterate the stigma of wartime defeat – hence their worrying preoccupation with the symbols of flag and anthem.

The other obvious criticism of the Japanese high school education system is that, after at least six years of studying English, the average Japanese student finds it hard to string together a coherent sentence in working English, and virtually impossible to understand ordinary English as spoken by native English speakers. Indeed, Japanese high school English teachers often set a bad example because they cannot speak practical English. Kazuko Uchimura, now working in the World Bank in Washington, and educated in Japan and Singapore, where she learned to speak English fluently as it was spoken in the homes, schools, shops and marketplaces, said that her first visit to Australia years ago was accompanying a party of Japanese English teachers. She was employed as an interpreter, since none of the English teachers was confident about being able to manage speaking the language.

Mineo Suenobu, professor of English at Kobe University of Commerce, traced the problem to the universities, which have the huge number of 7,000 teachers of English, 90 per cent of whom specialise in English and American literature. He questioned whether there was a need for such a number and commented that 'most of the Japanese breed [of university teachers of English] devote their lives to only one novelist, and generally they use Japanese to discuss the plot and background of the fiction and write their impressions in so-called scholarly articles. Although they teach English, they produce almost no articles on teaching methods ... They have nothing but utter scorn for teaching "practical English conversation" ... These are the teachers who make the notorious university English exams, and who give students teaching certificates of English language for junior and senior high schools.'

One small example from a high school English textbook shows how far the English of Japanese schools is removed from the English on the streets of London or New York. This is an excerpt from an exercise for translation: 'The coal or oil to which modern civilisation owes the most is composed of vegetables in which are stored up in another form, light and heat originally derived from the sunshine of distant ages.'* It's hard to imagine many English speakers being able to construct such a complicated, convoluted sentence, which tries so hard to hide the real meaning.

Increasingly, schools are beginning to realise their deficiency, and many schools now have native English speakers who work as teachers or teachers' assistants, trying to inject the essential elements of ordinary English conversation into the classroom. One of them was Bruce S. Feiler, an American.† Feiler's school class quickly gave him a Japanified nickname – 'Curazy boy' – because of his spontaneous enthusiasm in teaching English in ways they had never imagined. He quotes a colleague emphasising that the role of the schools was to be responsible for *shitsuke*, which the colleague defines as 'discipline'. 'We have to teach students how to behave

---

* Suuken Shuppan, *English Structure and its Basis and Application*.
† He wrote an amusing yet highly sympathetic and thoughtful account of his experiences in *Learning to Bow: Inside the Heart of Japan*, Ticknor and Fields, 1991.

properly both in school and out – how to follow rules and develop an honest mind.'

For most Japanese high school teachers, work is not finished either at the end of the school day or with preparation for the next day's classes. A friend, who is a teacher of English and who can with a struggle put together English sentences, complained that she never had an evening and rarely had a weekend to herself because she had to go visiting the homes of students to check with parents why a pupil had not turned up for class, or to try to discover the reason for unruly behaviour. 'My school is in a poor area. Often I have to make several visits before I can find the parents at home. It is a struggle because they don't want to listen, and because their children have given up on school.' Even Japan has its problem children. But in many schools, as Feiler found out, it is the mothers who constantly put pressure on the teachers, sometimes ringing them at home as late as eleven o'clock at night, to urge help in getting their kids through the next round of examination hell.

The examination hell that lies at the end of the school career is also the reason why *juku*, or cram schools, have flourished. The jukus were orig-inally started to help the marginal children whose schoolwork was lagging to improve, so that they could catch up. But in the 1980s came the boom time, a product of greater competition for university places and greater affluence of parents. By the early 1990s seven out of ten children sitting for entrance to senior high schools in Tokyo attended the cram schools. Over the country as a whole, the proportion of primary school students in jukus rose to 44 per cent, and those in secondary schools rose to more than 52 per cent, according to a leading private think-tank. Sometimes, as you travel round Tokyo, it seems that there is a juku on every street and an advertisement for one round every corner. The think-tanks estimate that they had become a business worth 3,000 billion yen by 1994 ($30 billion). The biggest of all, Kumon Kyoiku Kenkyu Kai (literally, the Edu-cation Research Association) began in Okayama in 1978 and grew to a chain of almost 100 jukus, turning in a nice profit.

The industry became so big that it spawned different kinds of juku, mainly *shingaku juku*, meaning academic ascension and catering for stu-dents under fifteen; while *yobiko* or preparatory schools handle up to a million students sitting for university entrance. But there were also other sub-categories, some for difficult students, others, called *keiko goto*, giving sports and cultural activities for younger children, plus *ronin*, named after the masterless samurai of the Edo era, offering tuition for students sitting their examinations for a second or third time.

Or even for a fourth time, such is the lure of Tokyo University, or Todai as it is often known (short for Tokyo Daigaku). A small number of students will try and try again until they can get in. The question is whether, as the twenty-first century approaches and the number of students overall diminishes and the pressures presumably get less, the jukus will get less profitable and the schools will be able to do their teaching jobs better with the smaller numbers, so that the problem fades away. It seems unlikely, at least without major changes in the school curricula, simply because the schools are so examination driven.

The schools that are offering something different and trying to challenge the students seem few and far between. One such is Sakura Junior High School in Miharu, Fukushima prefecture, about 240 kilometres away from Tokyo. The mayor of Miharu, Hiroshi Ito, takes great pride that few students at the school feel it necessary to go to juku. The 'passwords' of the Miharu board of education are: 'to make schools which are full of children's hopes, to make schools which are full of teachers' dreams'. For ten years the Miharu – which means 'three springs', referring to the blossoming of the plum, peach and cherry trees – has tried both to create and to innovate, including involving the townspeople in educational affairs. The school is a modern, but pleasant, concrete edifice designed by Toshio Koyama, a professor of architecture at Tokyo University. But the site is proudly old, denoted by a millennium-old rock at the entrance to the school. Mayor Ito said, 'The clear goal of Sakura is to teach the students how to learn themselves, to find the answers by themselves. We discussed this for more than ten years, considering how education should be.'

The school has peculiar features. Most Japanese junior high school-children have a 'home' classroom with their own desks. Apart from special-ised subjects like science and music, requiring special equipment, teachers will travel to the home classrooms. But at Miharu, it is the children who travel from room to room, not just to the science lab and music room, but also to the geography room or history class or English room, all equipped with their own special facilities and teaching aids. Instead of classrooms, the Miharu students have 'home bases' on the first floor, which contain lockers and notice boards and room for the children to stand and chat or sit and do some work. Another important feature is the open courtyard, *Katarai no Hiroba* (literally, 'a square with a nice chat'), used for gatherings and for lunch when the weather is pleasant.

The school principal, Masaoki Ida, said that there are no bells to order the children to go to classes. They are expected to go there on their own without such commands. There is a loudspeaker system for important announcements to the whole school. On the Saturday morning that I visited Miharu, the atmosphere was clearly relaxed. Some children were dressed in the traditional uniforms, but others were wearing turquoise tracksuits. In one classroom the pupils were actually at the blackboard explaining the lesson. Another I burst in on was an English class, where the pupils struggled at first to understand my accent, but were less embarrassed to have a foreign language thrust at them than the Kaisei boys, who after all were four years older.

Miharu is one of the schools employing foreign teachers; it also, unusually, sends its own teachers to America, to Wisconsin, to learn about foreign education for a year. In the centre of the town, there is a house called Rice Lake built in Wisconsin style and serving as a meeting place and small hotel. The house is kitted out with furniture from Wisconsin, including a table made by the Amish community. This is Mayor Ito's idea, to 'touch a different culture in a meaningful way'.

Principal Ida says, 'The students can't put their feet into the shadow of the teachers; they must stand on their own level as human beings.' This also offers challenges for the principal and for the teachers to exert their leadership and personality in a new way. Ida says that not only are the numbers going to juku down, but also ijime has also virtually stopped. There was one bully at school, but he dropped out and wanted to leave because he could not exert his peculiar brand of leadership in a place where the children were encouraged to develop what the head calls 'their different personalities in a free atmosphere of learning'.

The whole idea of the Sakura school is that there are other things in life than examinations and Tokyo University. But the experiment could still face problems from an unusual quarter, the parents. 'Parents still want to assess the school by what quality senior high school their children can get into, and which university it will lead to,' said Ito, admitting that the school still had some educating to do at home.

That is still one of the problems of the Japanese education system – that it is directed to the universities and particularly to Tokyo University, entrance to which is decided by a very stiff examination, not by anything as subjective as personality interview, or the record of what a pupil has done, or assessments by his or her teachers. Competition for the examinations is very stiff, with more than 10,000 applicants fighting for just over 3,000 places. The numbers might be greater, but for the fact that some children do not apply because they do not think they have much chance; girls form only about 15 per cent of the Tokyo University student population, although Ikuo Amano, professor of education at Tokyo, comments that the 'girl students are more liberated'.

The English paper for the 1993 entrance examination consisted of a series of short essays with demands for sentences to be translated into Japanese or questions answered or précis supplied. Among the sentences to be translated were the following three: 'In fact, the telephone was more of a nuisance than otherwise until local people had satisfied their curiosity by making unprofessional calls.' 'Each individual may have superiors and subordinates, but in such a ranking system any line we draw, to divide an upper from a lower class may be arbitrary.' '(The greater the spread of the terrace and the factory, the office and the suburb,) the more the realities of the countryside receded, until a life governed by unceasing labour and the uncertainties of the weather was transformed into a dreamland of health and happiness.' (The words in brackets were not for translation.)

The passage in English for précis (into Japanese) started off: 'Eight, five, seven, three, one, two. If I asked you now to repeat these numbers, no doubt most of you could. If I asked you again after a long talk, you probably couldn't – you will keep the memory for a short time only . . .' It then goes on to talk about memory systems and the brain. The examiners kindly translated the words epilepsy, concussion, psychiatric, insulin therapy and plastic surgery into Japanese beforehand. Anyone passing the English section of the Tokyo University test clearly needs to have a good grasp of complicated grammatical sentence construction in both English and Japanese, and an acquaintance with science and history would help. Whether a fluent English speaker with an English degree from an English university would pass may be more doubtful.

Once successfully admitted to the university, students can relax. Unlike most western universities, there is no regular system of examinations every term, semester or year. There is no final class list on which a student's future career hangs, as it does in the UK. Many graduates admit that 'my university years were four blissful years of play after the examination rat-race', as one high-flying business executive put it.

Professor Ikuo Amano cautions that things are very different depending on which subject is taken. 'Students who study law work harder than others, such as those studying economics or humanities. Those who want to get into the government or actually to practise law have to work very hard to pass the bar examination or the higher civil service examinations.' Scientists also claim that they have to put in many hours of work in the laboratories, so they cannot just practise having a good time. Some American teachers admit that the work in the best Japanese engineering facilities at under-graduate level is as good as research done at graduate school in the USA. Partly this is because so few Japanese – 5 per cent as against 16 per cent in the USA – go on to graduate school, thanks to the career pressures of getting quickly on to the bureaucratic or corporate treadmill.

Amano notes that 'There's been a lot of criticism, especially from the outside, that there is no education in Japanese universities. Now the universities have started to be conscious and are reorganising the curriculum and re-emphasising postgraduate research.' His own office is a good indication of the poor state of Todai, in spite of its national and international reputation. It is a tiny, narrow room filled with books, but with only room for a basic desk, two flimsy chairs and a telephone. There is a small wash basin in one corner and there is no room to hang a coat except on the bookshelves. By the standards of an Oxbridge fellow's room, this is a slum property.

Other rooms and departments also show a shabbiness that belies Todai's reputation. Once through the fine gateway and inside the actual buildings, you feel you are in a dingy tenement. The university itself realises this. In late 1992, it released a 600-page self-appraisal paper declaring that the university must improve its buildings and equipment to become a world-class educational centre. The dean, Akito Arima, commented, 'This university's education and research is on a par with international standards, but its buildings and equipment fall far short of what's needed to make it a world centre.'

Medical and science facilities in particular are shabby, underfunded and inadequate. In the research laboratories, gas bottles and machines have invaded the labyrinth of basement corridors and passages in clear violation of fire safety regulations. There is a strong lavatorial smell, which suggests that the ventilation is also poor. Scholars have to work almost elbow to elbow using the poorly equipped and cramped facilities. In spite of their academic reputations as the cream of the cream at Tokyo University, a professor in his mid-fifties earns slightly more than 610,000 yen a month ($6,000), far less than his or her peers in industry and even below high-flying bureaucrats' pay.

In spite of this, Todai continues to be the main magnet for the brightest and best of teenagers, far ahead of the second placed. Nevertheless, the very best private universities also have a queue of applicants. Waseda annually attracts about 160,000 students to take its entrance examination and to pay 30,000 yen for the privilege, helping to bring in almost 10 per cent of the university's operating budget. There is even a ranking called *hensachi*, grading the universities by the difficulty of their entrance examinations. A noted economic anthropologist, Shinichiro Kurimoto, who taught at Meiji University before leaving to found his own university, claimed that 'What I have observed is that many students from high hensachi schools are lost causes when it comes to really using their brains.' This is because they tune their brains into learning by rote what is necessary to pass the entrance examinations, and are not encouraged to exercise their imagination or creative thought.

The reason why Tokyo and a handful of other universities are so popular is that they effectively guarantee open doors to the best institutions of the public and private sector, thus giving well-paid jobs for life. Then prime minister, Kiichi Miyazawa, himself a Tokyo graduate, declared in 1992 that 'The hiring of bureaucrats is excessively weighted towards Todai graduates, a situation which must be rectified.' He declared that by 1997 graduates from Tokyo should make up less than half of high-level government workers. In the early 1990s, important ministries like Finance and Home Affairs hired 90 per cent of their new recruits from Tokyo. Of the 23 new recruits to the Finance Ministry in 1993, 19 were from Todai. Officials at the leading ministries protest that they recruit from Todai because it is the best. Kyoto University is also classified as among the 'élite of the élite', and yet 90 per cent of the high school graduates who pass the entrance examinations for both universities chose Tokyo.

The problem with breaking the system is that it is self-reinforcing. It looks for and creates people who obey the rules, not for bright sparks with independent personalities who may seek new or radical solutions. What also happens is that the brightest students go to Tokyo University, and the brightest of them are hired by government, leaving the next tier to go into big banks, trading companies and, just possibly, industry. This guarantees that, apart from self-confident oddballs such as Yoh Kurosawa, president of the Industrial Bank of Japan, most of the Tokyo graduates who go to leading positions in business will remain in awe of their classmates who went into the bureaucracy. During the 1980s and early 1990s, when Japan's financial barriers were just beginning to come down, leading bankers chose to consult the Finance Ministry for permission to do something, even when there was no need to ask for permission, such was the habit of bowing before the all-powerful bureaucrats.

For Japan as a potential international power, the problem is that there is no conception in the educational system of the need for it to be an international player, nor even much perception of the country's place on the world map. This is potentially highly dangerous both for Japan and for the rest of the world. This is not just a simple question of whether Japanese are trained to speak sufficient English to be able to play a full part in an international community which increasingly uses English as a lingua franca. The whole emphasis of the Japanese educational system, the history lessons (even leaving aside the nonsense about the emperor being a direct descendant of Amaterasu, the sun goddess), the emphasis on the flag and on the singing of the anthem, all claim that the Japanese are special and indeed unique. Jose Llompart, a Spanish Jesuit priest who is also professor of law at Sophia University, commented that 'The Japanese put too much emphasis on their uniqueness. But this superficial, fragmentary uniqueness not only fosters a misplaced conception of themselves among the Japanese, but also widens the gap in understanding between Japan and the international community.*

The Ministry of Education is now attempting to reform the university system. Essentially, universities will have more freedom to set their own curricula and will be allowed to dispense with general education core courses. The danger is that this may lead to narrow specialisation – so that

---

* A Japanese banker acquaintance in the late 1980s sent his children to school in England after he saw a television programme about education including a seventeen-year-old girl applicant for Cambridge University arguing with a professor about nuclear physics. 'That would never happen in Japan,' he said with admiration. 'The pupils are taught not to question, but to absorb the teachers' wisdom, like a sponge.'

the only knowledge that students get of the outside world is through parroted high school lessons.

The reform that is most needed is to weaken the all-pervasive influence of the Ministry of Education bureaucrats. Nominally, from 1992 the powerful national universities can set their own courses. But their continuing dependence is neatly symbolised by the fact that their teachers have their pay cheques actually signed not by their university, but by the ministry. The journal *Nature* in a 1993 report complained: 'There are few in Japan, even among academics, who understand the concept of a self-governing public university, a community of scholars with responsibility both for the education of the young and the management of its own affairs which is supported partly by the government on account of the public services it renders. So familiar is the Monbusho's influence that some evidently believe it to be unavoidable and permanent.'

More thoughtful Japanese academics claim that the ministry does not *trust* professors. This does not merely involve questions of management, but goes to the heart of how Japan faces an international world – the overriding value placed on *conformity*. Civil servants, right from Meiji times, have wanted excellence, but not western ideas about the virtues of a university, certainly not the pursuit of knowledge for its own sake, which might lead to criticism. There are some, even leading figures in Japan Inc., who have begun to question whether this is good for Japan.

Former Ministry of International Trade and Industry (Miti) vice minister (permanent secretary) Naohiro Amaya, one of Japan's leading internationalists, wrote in the magazine *Chuo Koron* in 1985: 'Japan's schools, successful in supplying large numbers of homogeneously trained workers, contributed greatly to the nation's economic growth in the second half of the twentieth century. But will what was successful in the twentieth century prove to be successful in the twenty-first? Business must consider such things carefully and plan its strategy. In the pre-war military, a soldier's rank in the army and navy schools determined his place in the military for the length of his career. Japan's defeat in war was linked to this system, which had those who were successful in school manage the battles. I'm afraid that businesses which today remain dependent on an education system which serves primarily as a ranking mechanism are in danger of repeating that mistake.' A former Miti minister was blunter about his criticism, claiming that 'Japan's educational system turns out inferior kinds of robots.'

The system turns out children who are literate and numerate, and have an excellent understanding of their own country's culture and history, though from a very partial and nationalistic point of view. Children are also very aware of the need for harmony and for fitting in. This prepares them well for their later corporate or bureaucratic career. They understand the hierarchy and the importance of the group. This is created at a great price, particularly in individuality and freedom of expression. One tolerant foreign teacher pointed out that 'In feudal times, which are not so long gone, giving one's own opinion was an invitation to death. Even today, it is regarded as immodest for a teenager to announce his or her own opinion, still less to criticise a teacher or writer.'

The costs may rise as even Japan is forced to change by economic circumstances. Leaders of corporate Japan claim that the principle of 'lifetime employment', admittedly only practised by the minority of very big companies, will be sacrificed as growth slows. If they are to survive, companies will need to encourage more creative workers. Bureaucrats may be able to live in their comfortable nationalistic bliss for some years more. But Japan, although twice as big in population terms as the UK, and richer and more advanced than any country before it, is still a small player on the world map and faces economic challenges not only from the USA but also from a bigger awakening China. Narrow nationalism, as still enshrined in the school textbooks, will be a dangerous game to play.

10

The Elite of the Elite:
Mandarins of the Finance Ministry

At first sight it looks like a rather spartan British public school that has fallen on hard times, with a forbidding stone exterior and Stygian echoing corridors built round quadrangles. The floors are made of wooden blocks, some of which have worked loose over the years, so you have to watch your step. The air smells fusty, and the areas of freshly polished floor cannot quite conquer generations of less pleasant smells. Off the corridors there are large rooms cluttered with desks and people, immediately recall-ing schooldays, since there are rows of heads hunched over desks littered with paper, while the occupants scribble furiously. But there are a few clues that this is not a school. The first giveaways are the cigarette machines at the ends of corridors. Others are the posters and girlie calendars stuck to the cupboards in the cluttered rooms, showing far too much flesh for any schoolteacher. And indeed this is a far more august establishment than any school: it is the Kasumigaseki headquarters of the Ministry of Finance in Tokyo.

For all the gloom and forbidding atmosphere, the occupants are the people who, it is frequently said, really rule Japan, the brightest brains, the real planners and overseers of the Japanese economic miracle, who overcame the clumsiness of politicians prone to put their hands in the till and businessmen whose only thought was for their own company's profits without any idea of the country's good. It is often said that Japan is ruled by a trinity or iron triangle of businessmen, politicians and bureaucrats. But bureaucrats have always been regarded as the most powerful, the organisers of the miracle, the guardians of Japan's integrity. And of all the bureaucrats, the Ministry of Finance mandarins are the élite of the élite, especially now that their colleagues in the Ministry of International Trade and Industry (Miti) are trying to increase sales of foreign goods into Japan and have given up their crusading mission.

Nevertheless, of late, there has been a growing tide of criticism from people who question aspects of the rule by bureaucrats. 'It's not just their arrogance and the certainty that they always know best, but the question whether they belong to another age and whether a maturing Japan needs more freedom, more debate, more choice,' said a critic who went to school with many of the best bureaucrats. The question is even more relevant as Japan gets ready to enter the twenty-first century and claims to be a budding international power.

Many aspire, but few are chosen. Like their counterparts in the United Kingdom, the top level of Japanese civil servants are chosen by stiff open competitive examination. There is a common saying that for most Japanese youngsters their university years offer a period of relaxation and fun after years of 'examination hell' and before all the restrictions of joining a corporate regiment. But this is not really true for those who want to take the tough civil service examinations: they have to study hard to pass. In Japan, there is a wider gulf between Finance Ministry men and the rest than between the British Treasury mandarins and those who go to other departments, such as the Foreign Office, Trade and Industry, or Education.

It is fair to talk of Japanese finance 'men' because they are predominantly men. No woman has yet made it to be vice minister, director-general or head of a department, or even to be deputy director-general. 'We only get one woman entering at executive level every three or four years,' said a senior official. 'Apart from passing the competitive civil service examination, they then have to go through interviews with the individual ministries. I don't think the Finance Ministry is so popular among girls. They tend to prefer the Health Ministry or Education or Labour, or perhaps the Economic Planning Agency. We've only been taking women at the highest grade for just over 25 years or so. The highest-ranking woman was head of a regional tax office and we find they tend to leave to get married or to look after their children.'

If anything, Japan's finance officials are more dedicated than their British counterparts. A senior British government official served for a time his ministry's personnel department and reflected, 'It was a most depressing experience. I had access to the files and records of all my colleagues, and could see the very bright class A brains who lost their enthusiasm or suffered cancer or divorce, or just decided to put their family first and so didn't make it to the top ranks. And I could also see the class B brains who got to the top by hard work and observing the rules. Also, worse still, I could see the class C brains who got to the top by – what shall I say? – buttering up the right people who were making the vital career reports.'

Isao Kubota, senior deputy director-general of the International Finance Bureau and thus the second in command of the bureau, said, 'Finance Ministry bureaucrats tend not to put their family first. That sort of person would not choose to become a bureaucrat in the first place. The job comes first and the private life is left behind.' Not quite abandoned though: Kubota himself resisted being posted abroad when his wife was not very well and he did not want to be separated from her.

*   *   *

Kubota says he had few doubts about wanting to join the Ministry of Finance (MoF). 'Perhaps I was influenced by my father, who was a civil servant working in the Fukuoka customs house. Fortunately at the university my academic report was not so bad, so I got several offers from first-class institutions, both public and private, including the Bank of Japan, Yahata Steel, now part of Nippon Steel, and Sumitomo Bank. I wanted to know what kind of job I was best fitted for. I was also offered a job by Miti. But when I had my interview at the Ministry of Finance, I thought that I could do the job without changing my character, my way of thinking or approach to matters. I later found that my father did want me to join this ministry, though he never said anything. But in fact, my father's character is emotional and good natured, and many of his friends told him he was much more suited to be a private lawyer, which is what my brother became, so he must have inherited my father's characteristics. My friends say that I am much more influenced by my mother, who is rather calm and neutral and such things as make a cold civil servant.'

Having graduated from the law faculty of the University of Tokyo, the almost ubiquitous alma mater for budding bureaucrats, Kubota entered the MoF in 1966 or Showa 41* with 25 other similar high-fliers. He was posted to the international organisations division in the ministry's grim Kasumigaseki headquarters, and allotted one of the tiny desks in the huge schoolroom-like department. Even today, when computers have made some inroads, the fledgling bureaucrats have precious little room to put their elbows on their tiny desks, heaped with files and other documents. You might think you were back in the time of Dickens, apart from the fact that the furniture is gunmetal coloured, not dark wood, and the posters and pin-ups are glaringly late twentieth-century Technicolor.

Kubota only had to serve for one year before he got a foreign posting by winning a coveted scholarship to Oxford University, offered by the trading firm of John Swire and Sons to mark its centenary. Years after the event, Kubota recalled with gentle laughter how he was selected by a distinguished panel of representatives from Swire and Oxford: 'I was asked what is the image of an English gentleman. I thought carefully and replied "An English gentleman is someone who thinks seriously about his jokes." Everyone laughed.' Kubota became the first MoF bureaucrat to go to Oxford.

It is very much a Japanese tradition for frontline ministries and com-

---

* In the forty-first year of the reign of the Showa Emperor (known in the West by his given name of Hirohito rather than the name he chose for his reign). The Japanese official calendar starts on 1 January as in the West, but uses the year of the emperor, so 1995 is Heisei 7 or the seventh year of Emperor Akihito. Showa means enlightened peace; Heisei means the attainment of peace in Heaven and on Earth, at home and abroad.

panies to send their brightest people abroad for further study, mainly to the USA or the UK. Unlike in the West, a person will normally join the ministry or company with only an undergraduate degree. It is very unusual for someone to enter having achieved a second or graduate degree because that would mean losing precious time that could be devoted to the career. Kubota emerged from St Antony's College, Oxford, in 1969 with a Bachelor of Philosophy degree in economics.

Then it was back to the MoF schoolroom for another two years, before he was sent to be head of the Wakamatsu district tax office for a year, a position of large responsibility for somebody so young. Toyoo Gyohten, now chairman of Bank of Tokyo, but before that a career MoF official who became 'Mr International', or vice minister for international affairs (equivalent to second permanent secretary in the UK), recalled how 'one of the attractions of being a Finance Ministry official rather than going to business or industry was that responsibilities and power to take important decisions came early, within a few years of joining.' Nevertheless, the career escalator of a young MoF official moves slowly if surely, and it is a long time – unless he gets a foreign posting or secondment to the minister's or prime minister's office – before he can get some privacy outside the schoolroom. The successive steps lead from *kakari-in*, or section officer, to *kakari-cho*, section chief, and then to *kacho-hosa*, deputy director, and *kacho*, director, a post not reached until the official is in his forties.

In Kubota's case, his next step was to return to one of the Kasumigaseki schoolrooms as deputy director in the Tax Bureau, successively in charge of research, indirect taxes and corporate income tax. These are the times, at deputy director level, when the young official has to forget about family and outside life and put his career first, last and everything in between. Kubota remembered working 'four nights a week until either midnight or 1 a.m.', working on the vital tax proposals. (During the weeks of preparing the annual budget, MoF officials say that it is common for Budget Bureau executives to clock 200 hours of overtime a month.) Outsiders say that 'The deputy directors, men in their thirties, are the backbone of the MoF.' One foreign banker went so far as to say, 'About 80 per cent of the thinking through of policy is done by them, especially tracking things through and the number crunching.'

There's something of a dispute about this. Makoto Utsumi, who succeeded Gyohten as international vice minister in 1989, thought that in the MoF the decision-making process was somewhere between the Ministry of Foreign Affairs, 'where decisions tend to be made on a top-down basis', and Miti, 'where the deputy director is most influential, since all administrative services are divided into small sectors of business'.

Gyohten's view was that the deputy director had a key role because 'the original plan [for any decision or law] is usually prepared by the deputy director with the help of his junior colleagues. This is probably the hardest working group in the MoF. Almost all new ideas and plans will be implemented from this layer. Sometimes the director-general will instruct staff to study a particular aspect or programme, but the actual original plan is made by the deputy director and he will lead his group discussion. When the plan is approved, it will be put to a bureau meeting attended by the director-general and his deputy and directors.' Sure enough, if you linger long enough round the offices of the director-general, you will see steady migrations of platoons of up to fourteen people moving from the cluttered big rooms to a much better furnished office, far too big for one man. Each director-general has a large table for these work sessions with his juniors, and about a dozen hard seats around it.

With quiet satisfaction, Kubota recounted the lessons of his young years in the 1970s as a deputy director at the Tax Bureau, and the knowledge and understanding it gave him of the internal workings of the MoF's gloomy corridors of power. 'When things develop into turmoil, it is very interesting. When things are quiet and the war has not started, the opinions of the senior officials prevail. But when the negotiations start, and everyone is quarrelling, then, if your choice is right and your judgement is correct, you can push your ideas through ... When I was in the Tax Bureau, with a really excellent director, I was the first person to negotiate with the different bureaux to reduce substantially the special taxation concessions. I had to fight with thirteen different ministries and agencies of this government. In another year I succeeded in doubling the motor vehicle tax and increasing by 20 per cent the gasoline tax at the same time. I think this was a great achievement.'

There was nothing special about his technique, apart from hard work in studying the facts and tough negotiating. He added, 'You have to listen to them very carefully and try to understand what they mean. Then you have to study what they said very deeply, enough to know more than your counterparts. And then you start to negotiate. Being with the Tax Bureau doesn't give you any advantage or power. The Budget Bureau is different because it controls the purse strings and unless the budget official says yes, they are powerless; but in the Tax Bureau you have no such easy weapon and have to negotiate and to cut favours.'

The young official will usually stay at deputy director level for a decade or more. Kubota spent four years in the Tax Bureau, and a year in the Minister's Secretariat, a good sign of a high-flyer. He then went to the second fund division of the Finance Bureau, in charge of the fiscal development and loan programme, the counterpart of the budget. This was followed by two years as deputy director of the short-term capital division of the International Finance Bureau, in charge of Japan's foreign exchange policy, where he helped prepare defence measures for the yen. This was the kind of responsibility which somebody in business or industry would not have until well into his forties or even fifties, and even there, what could be more important than playing the key role in managing the country's foreign exchange policy!

After that, Kubota went back to the Minister's Secretariat as special officer for research and planning. Then he was made director of the office of the International Vice Minister of Finance. That was only a one-year appointment before Kubota moved for a year to the planning division of the National Tax Administration Agency and then back to the International Finance Bureau as director of the international organisations division, where he was also responsible for planning the 1986 Tokyo summit meeting of the Group of Seven industrial nations (Canada, France, Germany, Italy, Japan, the UK and the USA).

All this time, Kubota was sitting in one of the cluttered big rooms, though at director level he got his own desk in a good spot close to the window, with a view over his junior charges. By the time a young finance bureaucrat reaches his early forties, it is becoming clear which of the 25 officials who joined in the same year is going to make it to the higher levels and especially to the job of director-general, the legal head of the bureau, the man who deals with parliament and has the actual authority for policies.

Not all nine bureaux are equal, of course. In the Japanese system, the power of the director-general of the Budget Bureau is paramount. The Budget Bureau bureaucrats have some slightly old-fashioned sayings which underline their importance, including 'Shukei-kyoku atte sho nashi' ('There is only a Budget Bureau, no ministry') and 'Shukei ni arazunba' ('If you are not in the Budget Bureau, you are nowhere'). The Tax Bureau might be regarded as second-best, but the positions of director-general of the Mint or Printing Bureaux are given to the people who are not destined for the very top. The head of the International Finance Bureau and the international vice minister – crucially for Japan's international reputation – occupy ambivalent positions. Any foreigner would think that these are key people, since they are responsible for how Japan is seen in the outside world. But in Kasumigaseki, the international vice ministers not only of MoF but also of Miti have often been described as 'the Barbarian tamers', possessors of specialist skills undoubtedly, but viewed with suspicion and somehow tainted on the domestic career ladder.

MoF officials themselves are guarded about revealing the arcane processes by which some of them become vice minister, others become bureau chief and others fail to make these high grades. Perhaps an outsider can never really understand. 'Sir Nigel Wicks [second permanent secretary at the British Treasury] asked me to explain how the promotion system works,' laughed a deputy vice minister. 'I tried my best, but I think he went away even more confused than when he started.' The opinion of the peer group is certainly vitally important. The high-flier will be a good steady worker who fits in well. Seigo Nozaki, who left the MoF in 1986 as director-general of the Printing Bureau, said that a top bureaucrat, as opposed to a good one, 'has to be a man of integrity, well balanced in two ways: in terms of knowledge and as an emotional human being'.

Although the bureaucrats might all look the same, dressed in their neat dark blue suits and pastel shirts, with only their ties marking out their individuality, deep down they have different hearts and souls and very varying personalities. One high-flyer has a reputation for losing his temper, especially with secretarial staff when they do not understand his instructions immediately, which will probably be a black mark against him for higher office.

Gyohten was outstanding for his ability to speak, joke and even think in English, which marked him out for years as a future 'Mr International', but even he was careful to maintain good relations with his domestic peers. According to one of his juniors, Gyohten had a special talent for 'listening and weighing the evidence before reaching a decision, but on the other hand he was a short-term planner'.

Yoshihiko Yoshino, administrative vice minister – the very top of the MoF – in the late 1980s, was regarded as powerful, hard working, intelligent and a good administrator, and even attracted a widely used nickname. He was known as 'Waru-waru'. The word *waru* means bad, an affectionate counterpoint to the 'Yoshi' of both his family names (*yoshi* means good).

Gyohten's predecessor as international vice minister, Tomomitsu Oba, from an old moneyed family, according to one of his juniors 'was autocratic, but mostly he knew what he was talking about'. On the other hand, Utsumi, vice minister after Gyohten, 'was autocratic and sometimes doesn't know what he's talking about, but mostly gets away with it publicly because he's an accomplished diplomat'. Tsuneo Fujita, who was director-general of the Securities Bureau and is now president of Bank of Hokkaido, had a reputation for liking French wines and karaoke, and was perhaps too outspoken to make it to be vice minister.

On the domestic side, it is perhaps easier to tell who will gain promotion to the very top. Some Kasumigaseki-watchers can even provide the names of the next seven or eight administrative vice ministers through to the year 2003. That is because the essential qualification is to have made a mark in the Budget Bureau. The career of Jiro Saito, the first man in six years to get a second term as vice minister, is instructive. He took more than a decade of quietly working and studying the mechanics of the MoF before anyone really noticed him. Then he got his break as budget examiner responsible for construction and public works, before taking a series of jobs in the Budget Bureau mixed with high-flying posts in the Secretariat, then heading the Budget Bureau before becoming vice minister.

Saito is described by a colleague as 'the kind of man who comes along once or if we are lucky twice in a generation'. He is the master of the art of budget making, so confident that he dared to *lower* the ceiling for budget requests, which came as a nasty shock to ministries used to getting slightly higher requests each year. He also stands out in being abrasive and not suffering people whom he regards as fools.

On the international side, personality and connections count for more. There have even been Japanese officials who have climbed to a very high rank by buttering up the right people. 'One man won golden opinions and promotion over his equally qualified peers by making sure that the finance minister on a visit to the US was fed only the best sushi. He even persuaded his grown-up daughter to go over to look after the minister's wife,' said a junior who was unhappy that blatant sucking-up should have paid such dividends. In this case, the vice minister regarded a promotion as deserved because feeding the finance minister well kept him good-tempered and made the senior's job easier. The junior did add deferentially that 'buttering up alone, without ability, will not win promotions'. Normally, the minister is not involved in decisions about who moves up the career ladder – in fact, unlike in the UK, there would be an outcry in Japan if any minister interfered in the selection for senior jobs.

Such interference happened in late 1993 in Miti when its minister, Hiroshi Kumagai, ordered the dismissal of Masahisa Naito, the director-general of the Industrial Policy Bureau, one of Miti's most powerful posts, because he had promoted a young official who was retiring to stand in general elections as a Liberal Democratic Party candidate. The young official lost and the LDP lost power for the first time for 38 years. Naito claimed that he was merely following precedent, and there was a feeling of outrage within Miti at this political interference, even though the minister did clearly have the legal power over his officials. Naito quit, but said he was resigning 'to avoid further confusion'. He then read from Psalm 64 from the Bible, in which King David asks God to protect him from the enemy.

A year later, the LDP was back in power and Hideaki Kumano, the Miti vice minister, and Sozaburo Okamatsu, the international vice minister, both resigned, victims of a mixture of political revenge and lack of confidence within Miti for failing to protect Naito. On the same day, a senior official at the Science and Technology Agency was fired for tangling with his political boss, Makiko Tanaka, daughter of a former prime minister. MoF officials were not exactly trembling in their boots at this assertion of political will, regarding themselves as above the battle. 'It is a sign of Miti's modern weakness,' claimed one MoF man.

There are several major differences between the Japanese and the British career bureaucrat systems. Most important, Japanese civil servants have much more power than their British counterparts: ministers are expected to accept the policy of the bureaucrats, not to set their own agenda.

Bureaucratic control became easier in the early 1990s when the MoF had a rapid succession of weak ministers. On top of this, Japanese civil servants differ from those in Britain in that they never stay in any particular post for more than a couple of years; they help to lobby legislation through parliament; and they retire up to five years earlier.

Kubota's career demonstrates the fact that the escalator is always moving and the bureaucrat never stays very long in one particular job or, except for the budget men and the internationalists, even in one particular bureau.* After his year in charge of the international organisations, Kubota became assistant vice minister for international affairs for two years, then did a year as director of the foreign exchange and money markets division, before being seconded for two years as managing director to the Overseas Economic Co-operation Fund, one of Japan's two aid-giving organisations. Then he came back to Kasumigaseki headquarters and got a room of his own (plus a chauffeur-driven car, in-car telephone and first-class air travel abroad, on which he can keep his air miles)† as deputy director-general of the International Finance Bureau, in charge of aid policy. After two years he was promoted to senior deputy director-general.

If Kubota fulfils his promise, he will win promotion to director-general and then to vice minister, and will then retire at the age of 56 or 57. He refused to be presumptuous about his chances of getting the top international job, but colleagues say that there is just one challenger, Eisuke Sakakibara, who is one year senior to Kubota. He is much surer of himself and more assertive, and is respected by Americans because he can stand head to toe arguing with them. Kubota is quieter, more thoughtful, and weighs matters carefully before speaking, and Japanese colleagues say that he 'knows economics and Japan better'. The decision on promotions to the highest ranks is taken by the current vice minister, but he will consult with the élite club of former vice ministers.

The fact that legal power resides in each of the bureaux and not with

---

* To recap, young MoF bureaucrats start their career with two or three years training in a division. Those who pass the entrance exam with the highest marks will get the secretarial division of the Minister's Secretariat, or the overall co-ordination division, or the Budget Bureau co-ordination division. In their third year, they will be sent abroad for further training, then come back to head office. In the seventh year, most will be sent into the wilderness to head a local tax office, before coming back as a deputy director of a division. Reaching this by year 10 is a mark of someone heading for the top. The next decade will be spent as deputy director, possibly with a spell in a Japanese embassy abroad, before promotion to director. What is equally important is *which* bureau and *which* division the official joins. He or she will have another stint outside MoF headquarters before promotion to deputy director-general of a bureau and finally director-general.

† Unlike equivalent US Treasury officials who fly economy class and are not allowed to keep the air miles.

the vice ministers has important implications for policy and for the attitudes of officials. MoF executives sometimes boast that 'A man may be in, let's say, the Banking Bureau, pressing hard for liberalisation and for the banks to be able to tread on the turf of the securities companies; then he could be posted to the Securities Bureau, and expected to espouse the position of his new bureau, favouring the securities companies over the banks by demanding liberalisation of the banking system.'

The power held by the bureaux is illustrated by a story told by Tsuneo Fujita. In the late 1960s and early 1970s, Yusuke Kashiwagi was Japan's most internationally renowned civil servant. He became director-general of the International Finance Bureau, then the post of international vice minister was specially recreated for him (it had existed before the war). Fujita remembered, 'Kashiwagi was very very influential and was known as "the Emperor" of the International Finance Bureau. But when he became vice minister and asked directors of other bureaux to visit *his* office, the director-general was very dissatisfied with his behaviour and firmly reminded Kashiwagi-san that *he* represented the International Finance Bureau.' Even a man of Kashiwagi's stature cannot exercise influence over the Budget Bureau or the Minister's Secretariat.

Former vice minister Oba explained the practice of the rapidly moving career posts by saying, 'The American bureaucratic system relies on the personal memory, but ours is an institutional memory. Policy does not change as the new incumbent gets into power, but there is continuity.' Fujita added, 'If one person stays in the same position for too long, his influence would be too strong.'

This system also means that a Japanese MoF official does not get a long period in the top job, compared with, for example, Sir Robin Butler, Britain's cabinet secretary and head of the civil service, or Sir Terry Burns, Treasury permanent secretary. They were appointed to their positions in their late forties and thus could look forward to more than a decade in the job, time enough to mould or remould the institution to their view of the changing times. The Japanese administrative vice minister, the head of the MoF, does not get that luxury, not least because the legal responsibility lies with the director-general of each bureau, not with the vice minister.

However, a senior MoF official cautioned that a strong character like Jiro Saito can usually get his way through force of personality, integrity and seniority. Reiterating the view that there is an institutional memory, one MoF man added, 'Yes, I suppose you could say that we are a rather splendid club, or perhaps a cosy family is a better expression, since some officials marry the daughters of former MoF officials. There is even an informal introduction service inside the ministry, useful for young officials who have to work long hours.'

Another important way in which the Japanese practice differs substantially from other parliamentary bureaucracies is that, from the director level upwards, MoF officials help to lobby legislation through parliament. A former senior British Treasury official remarked that 'Under our system, junior and middle-ranking bureaucrats would hardly see the politicians. The theory is that ministers make the political decisions and the bureaucrats implement them, so a healthy distance is maintained.' But in Japan, MoF bureau chiefs are responsible for attending parliament and answering questions directly. Kubota, in his new 1994 job as senior deputy director-general of the International Finance Bureau, said that besides going abroad as Japan's principal negotiator on tricky international financial issues, he would have to spend time in the office looking after the bureau, while the director-general was answering questions in parliament.

Directors in addition spend many hours a month arguing for legislation and generally urging MPs to accept their plans. In 1987 when the MoF was pushing for tax reform through the introduction of a sales tax, the main protagonists were the Tax Bureau and the prime minister, Noboru Takeshita. The then finance minister, Kiichi Miyazawa, who would have been expected in any other country to be in the vanguard of the struggle, stayed on the sidelines. Several times, MoF officials whom I wanted to interview fixed provisional times but warned, 'We may have to rearrange this if I am called at short notice to parliament.'

No one should make the mistake of thinking that the Japanese civil servants are any less bright than their counterparts in Europe or the USA. One senior European official who met Kubota for the first time commented after an hour's conversation 'That is one bright man with a mind like a razor, an old-fashioned sharp cut-throat job. Negotiating with him would be tough.' Defenders of the Japanese system assert that the continuity of the bureaucracy means that they do not make the American mistake of having to rethink everything and make all the same old mistakes when a new administration comes into power. There are position papers ready on any conceivable policy, and a well-researched and argued Finance Ministry point of view. There is, of course, a dissident stream of thinking even within the ministry itself, which argues that the bureau system and the Japanese emphasis on consensus, rather than a majority vote or direction from the top, is a handicap. 'Consensus means that we're always getting partial answers, and we're always getting them too late,' grumbled one senior official.

Curiously too, given the predominance of the brightest brains heading for the MoF, the ministry is not able to exercise influence by sending out its best graduates to lead other ministries, although the Economic Planning Agency and the Self-Defence Agency have become colonised by Finance. One insider says that the post of administrative vice minister at defence is reserved for the Budget Bureau man who comes second or third in his class, who will go via the Financial Bureau. With these exceptions, there is not the flexibility of other civil services, which have a measure of integration and loyalty to the service as a whole rather than to a fiefdom within it.

The MoF's control over the rest of the government machine is exercised powerfully, however, through the budget process. This can be seen when the annual budget is being prepared and officials of other ministries go to the MoF with their requests. You only have to see the long queue of petitioners outside the Budget Bureau, waiting like nervous schoolchildren clutching their test papers outside the headmaster's room, to realise just how mighty the MoF is.*

Although finance officials routinely retire much earlier than in the West from their bureaucratic jobs, there is a sense in which Japanese bureaucrats never retire at all until they die. 'Yes it's true, we see ourselves as a family, and once you join the ministry you never leave,' said the director-general of a bureau in another powerful ministry. Some officials leave early at director or deputy director level to enter politics. Kiichi Miyazawa was perhaps the most famous ex-MoF politician in recent times, although his intelligent and independent spirit meant that, when he came back as minister in 1986, he gave his bureaucrats an uncomfortable time and they did not really regard him as 'one of us'.

They were much more comfortable with Hirohisa Fujii, who became finance minister in the Morihiro Hosokawa government of August 1993, and even flattered him by saying that he had been 'a high-flyer who might have become vice minister', a tribute to someone who was never known to assert any view independent of what was fed to him by his bureaucrats. The ministry seems to welcome the fact that some of its bright young men defect into politics because they can be used as the spearhead of the finance *zoku*, or tribe, in parliament, who will help make their parliamentary colleagues more receptive to the MoF viewpoint.

But for most officials, retirement comes at the latest in their mid-fifties and sometimes earlier. This is because of a tradition, when an official becomes administrative vice minister, that all other officials who entered the ministry in the same year must retire, almost symbolically bowing to his superiority. The crucial factor is not age, but year of entry to the ministry, denoted of course by the year of the emperor on the throne at the time.

None of the Finance Ministry bureaucrats will have to worry about eking out a living on a meagre pension. The ministry will look after them and

* Budget time is when about 2,000 officials from Japan's 47 prefectures descend on the capital to lobby ministries with their case for projects, many of them bearing gifts, including mandarins, persimmon leaf sushi, rice gruel, sweet dough crackers, trout and wine, not to mention the more portable beer coupons.

even provide them with a more lucrative retirement job. The process, widespread through the bureaucracy, is known as *amakudari*, which literally means 'descent from Heaven', and sees the civil servants taking up top positions in the private sector after a decent but short interval. Certain posts, including those of chief executives of the Export–Import Bank of Japan, the Japan Development Bank, the Overseas Economic Co-operation Fund (OECF) and the Tokyo Stock Exchange are regarded as MoF posts to be occupied by amakudari officials. Some officials who reach the vice minister level may be able to have a whole amakudari career and not retire until their late seventies, unless death takes them away beforehand.

Mitsuhide Yamaguchi, for example, retired as administrative vice minister in June 1986, went on to become president of OECF that year, then skipped over nimbly to become head of the Ex–Im Bank in May 1990. After four years there he moved on again to become president of the Tokyo Stock Exchange. At OECF he was getting about 1.2 million yen a month, about the same as at the MoF, but at Ex–Im he picked up 1.6 million yen a month, plus a 27 million yen lump sum on retirement. A Japanese magazine reporter commented that Yamaguchi is likely to have received 260 million yen ($2.6 million) in the eight years after he retired from the MoF until mid-1994.

Yasuo Matsushita, another administrative vice minister, crossed over to the private sector in 1986 to the (probably even better-paid) job of director of Taiyo Kobe Bank, became president the following year and then took over in 1990 as chairman of the merged Taiyo Kobe Mitsui Bank (renamed Sakura Bank in 1992). He retired as chairman in mid-1994, but was not out of a job. He remained as director of the bank until December, when he took over as governor of the Bank of Japan just two weeks from his sixty-ninth birthday and with a five-year term ahead.

In spite of the oddity of having someone move from being head of a bank struggling with problem loans to lead the central bank, one of whose main preoccupations is the potential financial crisis caused by problem loans at all commercial banks, the MoF insisted on its prerogative of having its old boys take turns as governor of the Bank of Japan. As for longevity, Takashi Hosomi, who retired as international vice minister in 1972, was still going strong in 1994 on his amakudari career. He joked that he doubled, then tripled his pay when he set off on his new lease of life after retirement.

It is not just the very top superbureaucrats who get comfortable soft landings when they quit the ministry. The top jobs at a large number of Japanese banks, including Bank of Tokyo, Yokohama Bank, Hyogo Bank, Tomato Bank, Tokuyo City Bank and Nippon Credit Bank, were held in 1994 by MoF 'migratory birds', as a leading Japanese magazine, *Shukan Gendai*, called them. It counted up to 100 companies, including brokerage houses and insurance concerns, where MoF 'birds' were perched comfortably. The magazine said waspishly: 'On the surface it is said that the MoF sent its old boys in response to requests from the banks, but this is not correct ... Though it seems the MoF is sending its people to help reconstruction of the troubled banks, if you look at it from the other side, it seems that the ministry is taking advantage of the management crisis of banks in difficulties to keep seats warm for its amakudari ... It sends its former officials by using a candy of financial support to banks whose managements are weak, and a whip, the threat of investigating the bank's management, to grab the initiative of management.'

Few people even among the critics suggest that this creation of comfortable retirement jobs is corruption, although it smacks unhealthily of the arrogance of the institution that it always knows best. An official of the ministry confirmed this when he said rather smugly, 'The reason the number of amakudari from the Ministry of Finance is large is just that we have capable persons.' The MoF men are the model of rectitude, but it is not healthy that so many comfortable perches are preserved for them, and that they resist giving them up.

A trade union study in 1994 found that there were 820 people working for 92 special government corporations, more than 47 per cent of them amakudari former bureaucrats. These are in jobs where a ministry has the power to place its old boys, as distinct from private companies where it may have to twist arms (and excluding the 200 ex-Home Ministry bureaucrats at the head of local governments).

For all the heady talk from politicians about the 1990s being the era of deregulation, two facts emerged. One was the good pay and handsome lump sums that former bureaucrats got on retirement from the corporations. The lump sums averaged 20 million yen ($200,000) after three years and 40 million yen after five, with pensions of 36 per cent of regular salaries to top up a happy retirement. The other fact was the uniform resistance by ministries to the idea of getting rid or privatising corporations under their charge. The Ministry of Agriculture protested that the Japan Raw Silk and Sugar Price Stabilisation Board was needed to ensure price stability on international markets, even though protection of Japan's diminishing number of silk farmers has driven the price of their cocoons to four times the international level and there is little that Japan can do to influence sugar prices.*

There are more doubts about amakudari as practised outside the MoF. The ministries of Construction, Transport, and Posts and Tele-

---

* The Ministry of Posts and Telecommunications was all set to extend its empire in defiance of a cabinet request. *Asahi Shimbun*, a leading daily newspaper, claimed that the ministry had bought about 40,000 square yards of prime land formerly belonging to the (now privatised) Japan National Railways to build ministry-run hotels and convention halls in competition with the private sector.

communications in particular have had an uncomfortable spotlight thrust upon them for their practices. Ministry of Construction officials are divided into two streams, administrative and technical. Administrative officials tend when they retire to go to public service- or government-related organisations or foundations. The problem occurs with technical officials who find their cosy retirement nests in the general construction companies that they have been supervising.

Public disquiet was only increased by recent scandals showing that almost all the big construction companies were busy handing out money liberally and illegally to leading politicians. When *Shukan Gendai* checked which Construction Ministry officials went on retirement to construction companies, it found that most of them had been in charge of regional constructional bureaux. For example, a member of the board of Kajima had been director-general of the Tohoku regional bureau, a managing director at Taisei Kensetsu had been director-general in Chugoku, a director of Obayashi had been in charge of Hokuriku, and the vice president of Tobishima had been director-general in Kanto.

'Common to the positions is that they had authority to order public works,' charged the magazine. 'For example, the director-general of regional construction is in charge of ordering regional public works, the person who considers bids and nominates construction companies which have been accused of bid-rigging. After retirement, these officials joined the construction companies, so there is little point in saying "no more *dango*" [bid-rigging consultations] in these circumstances.'

The gist of the complaint is that the officials move to marketing jobs at the construction companies, where it is easy for them to use the natural deference towards seniors to lean on their juniors still working at the ministry. They can then get critical information about public work schedules and long-term projects in the pipeline to make sure that their new employers always know about the juiciest public works programmes before they have been published.

According to the magazine, construction companies also hire ministry people from the less high-flying ranks to make sure they have constant access to privileged inside information. One construction company even had the wit to go outside the Construction Ministry to pick up an official of the Ministry of Agriculture, from the bureau dealing with public works budgets involving villages, rivers and dams. It was, said the critics, an amakudari which paid off a billionfold for his new employer. No wonder that cynical Japanese talk not of the iron triangle of bureaucrats, businessmen and politicians, but 'the devil's triangle'.

Amakudari is most destructive when it is combined with the other great bureaucratic power, control over licenses, permits and discretionary rules and regulations. Unlike in the West, Japanese laws are written in such a way that they leave plenty of room for discretion by the bureaucrats. In all, at the end of the fiscal year ending March 1993, Japan had 11,402 regulatory permits and approvals in force. Surprisingly, for a country which has talked a lot about opening up its government and getting rid of regulations, this number was 460 more than in the previous year, and 1992/3 was the seventh year in succession in which red tape had increased. No wonder Shoichiro Toyoda, the chairman of the motor giant Toyota, who became chairman of the influential Keidanren (Federation of Economic Organisations) in June 1994, immediately called upon the government to 'break the wall of vested interests' damaging Japan's economic development. Baring Securities estimated that regulations cover industries representing 40 per cent of Japan's gross national product.

To put matters into perspective, during his eight months of supposedly reformist government, Morihiro Hosokawa produced a hit list of precisely 94 areas for deregulation. The consensus of opinion outside the bureaucracy was that the bureaucrats were doing their best to undermine the drive to get rid of the rules and regulations. The directors of the American Chamber of Commerce in Japan noted sceptically, while Hosokawa was still in power, that the government 'has set out a policy of promoting deregulation, but we are doubtful as to how much progress will be made. Previous Japanese governments have established a policy of deregulation several times in the past, yet there has been virtually no progress to date.'

Japanese officials can pride themselves on their efficiency. Not only are there 45,000 fewer public employees than there were in the late 1960s, but the government payroll is only 6.5 per cent of total employment, well below the 15 per cent average for all the industrialised countries making up the Organisation for Economic Co-operation and Development, the rich nations' club. But Japanese bureaucrats obviously use their powers more than most.

Stories are legion and legendary. When the president of the Japanese subsidiary of a foreign company made critical remarks about a government office in a newspaper, one of his colleagues promptly received a phone call from a bureaucrat in the department concerned suggesting that, if the president continued to be critical, the company would encounter delays of a year or more in getting permission to market its product in Japan.

Nagami Kishi, president of the HIR Company, said, 'The extent of bureaucratic interference in Japanese life is mind-boggling. In some cases it is clearly designed to keep foreign firms out of the domestic market; in other cases, its only purpose is to preserve bureaucrats' jobs; and in some cases it has no visible purpose whatsoever.' The bureaucrats can also count on the obedience of most Japanese companies. After all, the top bureaucrats were superior students at the best universities, so they are naturally looked up to. And if they are not, business executives know the powers that bureaucrats have.

The British concern the Body Shop opened in Japan in 1990 through an agreement with a subsidiary of a Japanese supermarket chain. It quickly built up a good reputation, especially in its shops in the trendy areas of Tokyo, where young Japanese liked its 'green' environmentally friendly attitude. It was therefore surprised when it tried to bring its popular banana hair products into Japan and was promptly told that it could not because banana skins, from which it was made, contained substances that were not permitted in Japan. It took the Body Shop three years of tough negotiation before it succeeded in getting the line accepted.

Another bright idea, of refilling the Body Shop's simple plastic containers, also fell foul of the Health Ministry on the grounds that refilling bottles was manufacturing, which is tightly controlled under the Pharmaceutical Law. After a barrage of protests from customers and two and a half years of negotiation, the ministry changed the interpretation of refilling containers from manufacturing to sales and allowed it. Mitsu Kimata, president of Aeon Forest, which operates the Body Shops, expressed surprise at the pettiness of the regulations, even though she is a former Labour Ministry bureaucrat. But she added that 'Basically their intentions are good.'

Another company tried to import an internationally popular brand of vitamins into Japan, but they were banned by the Health and Welfare Ministry, not because the vitamins were judged unsafe, but because the pigment used in colouring the top of the bottle contained something that was not licensed in Japan. When a journalist challenged the ministry, the official simply pulled out a list of pigments officially permitted and responded that it was not on the list. He was not prepared to argue whether the pigment was safe or not, but simply to check that the rules had been followed.

Regulations have often been used to keep out foreign products. The persuasive power of bureaucrats to bend and twist the rules almost at will was demonstrated over beef imports. Under pressure from the General Agreement on Tariffs and Trade, Japan moved away from a blanket ban or quota restrictions on imports, towards protection of its own industry by tariffs. These started off at an extremely high level and then came down to 60 per cent. Even at this high level, Australian and US beef was cheaper than Japanese-produced beef and – in spite of comments by Tsutomo Hata when he was agriculture minister that Japanese intestines were different from everyone else's and so could not digest foreign meat – the imported product was selling well. Too well in fact, as far as Japanese officials were concerned. A senior official at the Agriculture Ministry had an easy solution: he suggested that importers should reduce the volumes of foreign beef they were bringing in. It was done as easily as that.

Several ministries do seem to have given themselves the extra task of protecting the Japanese against barbarians. In 1992, the Health and

Welfare Ministry at long last approved a drug by a foreign pharmaceutical company to treat obesity. The product had been used safely for up to 30 years in Europe and America, and had passed all the normal health tests. But it took ten years to get permission to sell the product in Japan. At first the ministry's tactic was simply to shelve the application, claiming that 'obesity is not a disease'. When the product was finally approved for sale in Japan, several newspapers highlighted its long struggle to get into the country. It seemed a good example of the foreign pressure for a 'level playing field', and the Ministry of Health and Welfare ran into some criticism. The bureaucrats did not apologise or try to explain the delay. Unembarrassed, civil servants rang up the magazines and newspapers that had told the story to warn them that they were 'giving [this foreign firm] too much free publicity'.

Some foreign firms, however, have benefited from the regulations. Coca-Cola is almost as well known in Japan as it is in the USA. The company has seventeen bottling plants in the country, including the biggest in the world, in Tokyo. It controls 90 per cent of Japan's cola market at 110 yen a can, equivalent to more than $1 and thus more expensive than in its home country. This happy existence had gone on for years until Isao Nakauchi, head of the Daiei supermarket chain, the largest domestic retailer with sales of 5,000 billion yen, in 1994 got bolder in the discounting business and started to import cola from Canada, pasting on his own labels and selling it for 39 yen a can.

Coca-Cola hit back, deciding to import Coca-Cola classic from North America to compete with its own high-cost Japanese product, but selling for 70 yen a can through supermarkets and large retailers, rather than through vending machines that accounted for most of its sales before the battle began. All the signs were that Japanese consumers welcomed the freedom to make their own choices and were opting for cheap products without too many frills. The cola battle was hotting up so much that some vending machine owners were trying to shortcircuit the established distribution and price-fixing chain so that they could knock 30 yen off the prices of drinks.

In terms of power measured by numbers of regulations, the Ministry of Transport comes top with about 2,000 regulations under its wing, followed by Miti with almost the same number, then the Agriculture Ministry, Finance, and Health and Welfare, all with more than 1,000 each, and Construction with about 850. The Transport Ministry's role is extensive. It has complete authority over land, sea and air transport, including new entrants to those businesses, shipping charges and other matters. Altogether it has more than 870 regulations concerning safety and the environment, 600 for business and almost 500 lumped together under miscellaneous.

One of the annoying but amusing aspects of Japanese life concerns times of flights from Japanese airports. Regular commuters between Tokyo and Osaka say that timetables governing the daily shuttles between Japan's two biggest cities are subject to frequent change, although often it is only a matter of five minutes or so. The reason is that the Ministry of Transport insists on approving all schedules of aircraft departures and arrivals each month, and if the flights were allowed to leave at the same time, all the time, there would be no work for the bureaucrats to do in giving the approvals.

More seriously, to the annoyance of car owners, the Transport Ministry has decreed, through administrative guidance not through law, that cars must be tested under a regime that is entirely peculiar to Japan. The test is called the *shaken*, short for *jidosha kensa*, or auto inspection. One special complication is that even new cars must undergo a pre-shaken check-up in which 102 technical items are examined, at a cost for a new car of 70,000 yen, before going on to the formal shaken. The shaken itself costs only 1,300 yen, but with the charges of using a garage rather than facing the hassle of driving to the inspection, it usually costs 150,000 yen for a new car. Subsequently, cars have to be tested every three years, which helps to ensure that few Japanese have a car more than six or seven years old. Cynics say that the scheme is a racket run by the ministry to keep 80,000 car maintenance companies in business.

Among the products not allowed in Japan are motorised skateboards and roller skates, which are becoming a big hit in the USA selling at between $500 and $1000 each, a comparatively cheap price for quick mobile transport in Japan. Another product banned by the National Safety Commission is tandem bicycles, except, strangely, in Nagano prefecture. Sometimes Japan's concern for safety goes further than that of most other countries. Popular convenience stores which stay open round the clock in many cities are not allowed to sell aspirins or basic medicines like eyedrops or cold remedies. This is because Japanese law requires a licensed pharmacist to be on duty at all times where such medicines are on sale. Japan also has no self-service petrol filling stations and very expensive petrol because under Japanese law such a station must have at least two people qualified to handle hazardous substances and supervise tank-filling operations. Food and other retail services are two areas where the regulations have worked with vested political interests to prevent competition which might bring prices down.*

Japanese grumble that it is not only foreigners who have to face the plethora of rules. Opening a restaurant, for example, requires passing a national chef's examination, plus getting nine licences and a sewage

---

* Japanese costs for food and basic everyday necessities tend to be 20 to 100 per cent or more higher than in the West, except, strangely, for tissue and toilet paper, which is cheaper in Japan.

licence (for the dirty dish water). Big supermarkets face a particularly tough time, partly because of political protection to traditional 'mom and pop stores' by zoning laws. Getting permission to open a large supermarket requires approval under the large-scale retail store law from small shop owners in the area. After that, which might take a decade, Nakauchi of retail leader Daiei estimated that a big supermarket needed 40 licences under 19 different laws. The cost of getting all these permits just for a single store comes to about 160 million yen, according to Nakauchi.

In 1994 a major breakthrough was made when supermarkets were allowed to stay open until 8 p.m. Even Tokyo Disneyland got caught in this law on opening hours because of its size. A manager grumbled, 'Just because of our size, our business hours come under the control of the law, even though we serve only visitors to the theme park and are unlikely to take business away from local shop owners.'

Some of the big chains have tried to get round the rules only to run into other obstacles. FamilyMart, Japan's third biggest convenience store chain, joined up with local cleaners to offer drycleaning services. By making these joint ventures, it satisfied the Small and Midsize Business Promotion Law, but ran into the Food Sanitation Law, preventing laundry and food products being handled from the same place. Another concern wanted to offer package tours through convenience stores, but ran into the Travel Service Law, requiring every agency offering travel services to be overseen by a qualified manager to prevent fraud.

Some Japanese companies have experienced problems at home but not abroad. For example, Seiko, the electronics company, has made a Dick Tracy message-flashing wristwatch. The watch has a small display that can flash messages and information like stock market prices, weather reports, results of sports games, plus paging and information services, using standard FM radio frequencies. It has test-marketed the device on the US West Coast and has had some success there, and it also has plans to sell it in Europe. Japan's FM radio broadcasters say that a paging service like this requires very little investment and that it can be operated simply. But Japanese who want the fancy communicating watch have to go to the USA, since the Ministry of Posts and Telecommunications in Tokyo declared that the market was already overcrowded, so there was no need for Seiko to bother to apply for permission.

Bureaucracies everywhere work according to rules and precedents. But the Japanese system is worse because of its insistence on consensus and harmony to squeeze out dissenting views or mavericks. This at least is the view of one of the rebels within the system, Masao Miyamoto. He came to the bureaucracy with the clear vision of an outsider, having qualified as a medical doctor and then gone to the USA, where he studied psychiatry. He was assistant professor of psychiatry and psychoanalysis at Cornell

Medical College. When he came back to Japan, you might have thought that the ministry would have been anxious to use his experience, but this was not the case.

Admittedly, Miyamoto made life more difficult for himself. He has a touchingly naive view that does not understand the need for a bureaucracy to operate by rules and precedents. He has compounded his unpopularity by deliberately flouting the rules, and has tried to operate a crusade for individualism. He asserted that the unwritten code of the Ministry of Health and Welfare for which he works is 'Don't take holidays. Don't work. Don't compete. Don't display initiative.' He even brought the issue into the public eye by writing a best-selling book, *Oyakusho no Okite* (*Government Office Rules*).*

He was annoyed when he asked for a two-week holiday to Europe, using some of his 23 days of paid holiday, and was bombarded with comments such as 'how could someone in your position dare to take a long vacation? ... You should be too busy to take a vacation ... Don't disturb group harmony.' In the end he lied and said he was going to attend a Buddhist ceremony, in order to get his days off.

'It is so ironic. The ministry, the organisation supposedly working for the betterment of individual basic human rights, forces its workers to give them up,' Miyamoto claimed. 'By writing the book using a social and psychological perspective, I wanted to point out the problems of Japan, where people sacrifice their individuality for the sake of the expansion of Japan Inc. The contempt for individualism must be corrected if Japan wants to be a world leader.' Further to flaunt his individuality, he wears well-tailored suits, drives a champagne-pink-coloured Porsche, eats French food and goes to classical music concerts.

According to Miyamoto, 'Good bureaucrats have to be masochists, because there is too much self-sacrifice involved. Because selfless devotion to the organisation is considered the most important code in the government, having one's own way, even in trivial matters such as dress, is considered disruptive to the unity of bureaucrats. Athletic meetings, cherry blossom viewing parties and annual office trips are all intended to reinforce sameness. Government workers share the grand illusion that those who belong to the same organisation should look alike, behave alike and think alike. But this is possible only when you give up your private life, and I will not do that.'

He refused to stay late when he discovered that there was no work to do. His colleagues stayed late in the office, he claimed, or went out drinking until midnight, just to give a sense of unity and to keep company the few who were still working. A Japanese worker, he said, is only admitted to

* It sold 350,000 copies and was later published in English as *Straitjacket Society: An Insider's Irreverent View of Bureaucratic Japan.*

the group when 'he becomes an efficient human robot'.

Ministry bureaucrats admitted that 'Miyamoto made a stinging indict-ment of government customs which his colleagues followed diligently without complaint. Some of us are very angry and disturbed. Miyamoto belongs to the inner circle of government and should not have made this matter public.' The ministry had its revenge. Apart from calling him a heretic, renegade and alien, and treating him as such, as only Japanese can, it posted him from headquarters to be director of quarantine at Yokohama port.

This may sound a grand title, but it is more pompous than grand, and a far cry from helping to formulate policy matters, which is what he hoped to do when he came back to Japan in 1986 with his American qualifications and experience. He himself pointed out that not only is the quarantine job, involving inspecting ships and their cargoes, minor in the ministry's hierarchy, but it is also the classical burial ground for officials. In 1994 the ministry responded to his considerable public acclaim, both domestically and abroad, by posting Miyamoto from Yokohama, close to his Tokyo home, where he still has to look after a sick mother, to Kobe in the alien Osaka hinterland.

But Miyamoto continued his assault. On 8 February 1994 he wrote an open letter in the *Japan Times* to president Bill Clinton, detailing some of the problems in relations between the two countries and congratulating Clinton for his remark to Russian president Boris Yeltsin that 'when the Japanese say "yes", they actually mean "no" '. He advised the US president on the peculiarities of the Japanese language, an important but often neglected consideration in international relations. Americans and others should long ago have learned from the time when president Richard Nixon tackled Japan's Eisaku Sato about booming synthetic textile sales to the USA. Sato promised to 'take care' of the issue, meaning to American ears that he accepted the US complaint; but what Sato was doing in Japanese was merely stalling and trying to say that he had heard enough of the matter.

Miyamoto compared agreements made in July 1993 between Clinton and then Japanese prime minister Kiichi Miyazawa, by looking at the English and Japanese texts. One sentence committed Japan 'substantially to increase access and sales'. Miyamoto wrote: 'When I read this in English I get the feeling that there will be a significant increase. But when I read the Japanese, it does not have to mean a significant increase.' 'From the moment they enter the bureaucracy, Japanese bureaucrats learn not to be explicit,' Miyamoto complained to Clinton. 'This is due to their instinct for self-preservation, which means they do not want to take responsibility, and to their desire to maintain their hold on power.' He helpfully offered a child's guide to some of the most frequently used Japanese words, their apparent meanings and their true meanings to any savvy bureaucrat.

'When the word *maemuki*, which means positively or constructively, is used, it brings hope to the other person, but nothing has to be done. The word *eii*, which means eagerly or zealously, is used when there is no positive outlook, but you want to impress on the other person that you are trying. The word *kento*, which means investigation or scrutiny, means that while bureaucrats may look into a matter, in reality no formal action is going to take place. The same holds true for the word *shincho*, discretion; nothing is going to be done. The word *jubun* or thoroughly means that the matter will probably be delayed indefinitely. The word *tsutomeru*, to make an effort, means that in the end nothing will be done. When the word *hairyo*, consideration, is used, it means that the matter will stay at the bottom of your in-box.'

He then offered a test for a budding bureaucrat. 'How would you respond when you hear, "We will constructively and eagerly investigate this matter" or "We will try hard to consider this matter with discretion"?' Miyamoto supplied the answer: 'From the bureaucrats' point of view, the answer is very simple: they won't do anything.' In spite of all his travails, Miyamoto vowed that he would take advantage of the system and not be pushed out of his job, even claiming that he was enjoying it. But in early 1995 he angered his masters by visiting the USA on holiday, talking at the press club in Washington DC without permission, and not rushing back to earthquake-stricken Kobe. He was sacked.

The Ministry of International Trade and Industry, which used to be every foreign critic's *bête noire* because of its alleged role at the centre of Japan Inc., plotting to make the country the industrial master of the world, has changed direction. This was evident even a couple of years ago, with jolly colourful posters in the Miti headquarters lobby extolling the joys of importing. Some bureaucrats within Miti even lament that their ministry has lost its way. 'Miti's power has declined considerably,' said Kozo Watanabe, former Miti minister and a leading figure in Shinseito (Renewal Party). 'The oil crises [of the 1970s] were probably its last chance to impress people with its presence.'

Immediately after the end of the Second World War, the ministry had the clear goal of catching up with the West. It exercised great influence, especially over heavy and chemical industries, such as coal mining, steel, electric power and petrochemicals. When recession hit Japan in the mid-1960s, Miti ordered steelmakers to form 'depression' cartels, and lowered the individual companies' production levels until demand recovered. The ministry targeted key industries in which Japan should excel, promoted them heavily and protected them from competition until they could stand firmly on their own feet. It was responsible for bans on imports of colour televisions until 1964, cars until 1965, semi-conductors until 1974 and computers until 1975.

Miti had an advisory panel called the Industrial Structure Council which drew up key policy recommendations. In the 1970s the aim was to promote knowledge-intensive industries, like computers, semi-conductors and energy-saving technologies. In the 1980s it shifted the target to creativity-intensive industries, especially computer software and environmental protection. For the 1990s, it has been searching for economic reforms, emphasising a higher quality of life in accord with former prime minister Kiichi Miyazawa's promise of 1992 to make Japan a 'Lifestyle SuperPower'.

Some Japanese industrialists, of course, complain that Miti never deserved foreign plaudits for its masterful manoeuvring of Japan's industrial policy. It also had its failures. If Miti had had its way, the Japanese motor industry would not have had as many players, and aluminium was a failure. Something of the end of an era was marked in April 1994 when the Semiconductor Industry Research Institute Japan was born, a product of ten leading chip makers with Miti playing only a minor role. 'This is an experiment to form industrial policy through private initiatives,' said a Miti bureaucrat. 'It is no longer appropriate that bureaucrats draw up industrial policy on a desk inside our ministry.'

Modern industries and the new ambition to promote social infrastructure and a better quality of life would anyway have been more difficult to direct. But the modern irony is that Miti is now calling for deregulation and the dismantling of controls which its says are handicapping Japan's economy. Some of those controls were the direct result of Miti's previous policies; if it wants to dismantle others, it will have to trespass on the territory and tread on the toes of other ministries, a difficult task which is likely to call into question Miti's own existence. At the finance ministry, for example, some bureaucrats are furious at Miti for demanding deregulation of financial markets. 'That's our turf; they should not trespass,' said a fuming finance official. Chalmers Johnson, author of the landmark account *Miti and the Japanese Miracle*, agreed that Japan's switch from being a producer-driven to a consumer-driven society will mean Miti's new role is to draft economic blueprints. 'Japan will increasingly have to replace the US as the major market for manufactured goods made in south-east Asia and China. So Miti will inevitably have to become more internationalist and less protectionist.'

Naohiro Amaya, formerly Miti vice minister and then president of the Dentsu Institute for Human Studies, commented in early 1994 that 'while bureaucrats are adept at working toward clearly defined goals, they are poor at creating or discovering them. This is the role for government. But no recent government has been able to come up with new national objectives. The bureaucracy has thus been left rudderless.' He also criticised bureaucrats for pursuing the goals of their own particular ministries.

Amaya noted that after the Meiji emperor was restored in the nineteenth century and a modern constitution written, 'the constitution stipulated that ministers were the emperor's advisers, so the bureaucrats developed a sense of being directly responsible to the emperor ... After losing the Second World War, Japan was occupied by the US and received a new constitution. Militarist bureaucrats disappeared along with Japan's empire, while the feared Home Ministry was abolished and economic bureaucrats rose to the top. Superficially at least the bureaucrats became public servants. But the traditional sense of serving the emperor did not vanish. The bureaucrats to this day take pride in their belief that their role is to steer the nation, unswayed by partisan political interests.'*

The relative demise of Miti leaves the Ministry of Finance as the sole powerful national guardian. The accusation against the MoF is nothing as trivial as petty peculation in favouring a particular firm in contracts, or being in league with crooked politicians and helping them to feather their nests. The MoF officials give the impression of being above such sordid money matters. There is a finance zoku or tribe of MPs dedicated to Finance Ministry matters, but they are very much subservient to the bureaucrats and not their masters. This is very much the reverse of what happened when former prime minister Kakuei Tanaka built his political base from control of the Construction Ministry. 'MoF officials go to great lengths to try to keep the politicians out of the budget making, which is a prime political preserve in other countries,' said a respected British economist. 'To let the politicians decide the budget would be – to the MoF – like letting the rats into the granary.'

There is an argument that, by dividing Japan's banking system into a maze of specialised layers, the MoF has been too much concerned with providing amakudari jobs for its boys, and has exacerbated the crisis of bad loans to the extent that it may yet cause a full-blooded crisis. Few people seriously predict anything as dramatic as a collapse of Japan's financial system. As a leading London banker said, 'You *know* that the Japanese government won't let a big bank go bust, let alone contemplate the collapse of the whole financial system. That would be impossible.' But prolonged difficulties over problem loans are making banks reluctant to lend, leading to an inefficient use of capital and slowing down the rate of growth of the economy. There is also a serious charge that cosy relations between MoF officials and their charges through the bureau system have led to them turning a blind eye to potential abuses. (Relations between the MoF, the banks and the financial system are examined in Chapter 2.)

---

* Amaya, who died of cancer in autumn 1994, was himself controversial. He was among the most internationally aware of Japan's leading figures, but remarks such as 'If we want to sustain Japan's prosperity, we can't attract envy and hostility from abroad' won him enemies. Such people derided him by saying that he was so pro-Washington that he was referred to in Miti as president Ronald Reagan's 'mistress'.

The charges against the MoF are in many ways more serious, and are directly related to its international perceptions and role. Foreign economists, plus a number of Japanese bankers and businessmen, claim that the finance bureaucrats have been slow to take measures to help the economy out of recession. They should have been more prepared to cut taxes, and even to encourage the Bank of Japan to reduce interest rates further below the record 1.75 per cent discount rate of 1994.

Foreigners have been quick to complain that Japan by 1993 and 1994 was experiencing the longest recession since the Second World War. 'In classical economic theory Japan could have combated the recession by using fiscal policy,' said a European economist based in Tokyo. 'The theory is simple: you reduce taxes at time of recession to encourage growth and increase them when the economy picks up again.' This theory would have seemed particularly valid in 1993, when unusually cool and wet summer weather reduced the rice harvest, depressed the popular mood and contributed greatly to creating an economy which had run out of confidence. Tax cuts would have helped to restore that confidence and perhaps got the economy moving again.

Senior MoF officials put up a spirited refusal to cut taxes, based on the medium-term view that Japan's society is rapidly ageing and by the year 2020 will be the first industrialised country with more than 25 per cent of its people over 65. With this prospect in mind, bureaucrats argue that they cannot afford to reduce the burden of taxation. Although Japan's government deficit according to the OECD is 1.9 per cent of gross domestic product, far lower than the 2.6 per cent of the USA, MoF officials claim that this figure is misleading. It excludes a 3.8 per cent of GDP surplus on its social security budget, artificially large because the system is young and has not started to pay out big sums. Vice minister Saito and his officials argue that it is not right to plunder the social security budget, since that is robbing future pensioners. Therefore, if income taxes are to be reduced, they claim, there must be a compensating increase in the consumption tax, or Japan will run into permanent deficit problems.

After a protracted debate, income taxes were cut, with a commitment to raise the general consumption tax from 3 to 5 per cent in April 1997. But MoF officials warned that the consumption tax would soon have to be raised again, and some would like to see a 10 per cent tax. Evidently the bureaucrats so distrust the politicians on tax matters that they were putting forward the problems of an elderly society in a decade's time as a reason for not loosening taxes to tackle the immediate tasks of a sluggish economy, with all its difficult national and international implications.

Kubota made a spirited defence of this status quo in spring 1994. The Bank of Japan was saying that the economy was still bumping along the bottom, and Kubota asked for proof of the claims that Japan was experiencing the worst recession since the war. He asked what was the definition of recession, pointing out that in the classical American terms – a drop in growth of GDP for two successive quarters – Japan was not experiencing a recession. On an annual basis, growth was still positive.

Kubota contrasted Japan's practice with what he thought the sad British experience of using tax cuts for political ends. 'In the case of Britain, frankly, economic policy, especially taxation matters, has been used too often for the sake of short-term political battles. There are different priorities in economic policies, such as price stability, growth, unemployment, and you don't expect the demand of the people as to what priority to place on each of these policy aims will suddenly change. It is not the case. Look at Germany, they are very keen on price stability, whereas in the US they want growth and don't worry too much about the balance of payments.'

But Japan has been fortunate enough to enjoy rapid growth, low inflation and full employment all together. The question which the MoF may reluctantly have to face up to is a potentially devastating major structural change where it can no longer have everything together. The good old days have come to an end.

The Economic Planning Agency, the government's own ministry responsible for tracking economic growth, claimed in mid-1994 that the country was going through the worst recession since the war, in terms of the gap between the average growth rate and the actual rate. By the end of 1993 it calculated that 6.4 per cent of output had been forgone. It is easy to play with statistics, difficult to estimate the real potential growth rate and still more difficult to achieve it, but this was a big gap, enough to alarm people at the front end, business executives and workers confronted with rising yen, falling profits and limited employment opportunities. Such critics argued that the MoF's complacency may have been acceptable when Japan was growing in double digits or even at 5 per cent. But in the late twentieth century, the potential growth rate of the economy had fallen to 3 or maybe even 2.5 per cent a year, so it called for a more flexible hand on the tiller.

Kasumigaseki's mandarins showed much less concern than alarmed business managers about the continuing rise in the value of the yen, along with the high levels of Japanese trade and current account surpluses. At times of floating exchange rates, determining the 'correct' value of a currency is particularly hard. In one sense, the rate on the foreign exchange markets, day by day, minute by minute, is *the* rate because that is what the free market has decided. But in the late twentieth century, the money playing on the world's foreign exchange markets is much greater than even the biggest government can command. On a typical day in London, the biggest forex market, $300 billion and more is traded, or three times Japan's total foreign exchange reserves. At busy times, the speculative flows can become a tidal wave that will swamp any government foolish enough to think it can tell the market which way to go.

'We are talking of $500 billion to a trillion and more dollars on the forex markets, whereas the best that governments can do is put up a few billion if they can agree on concerted action – a big if,' said a forex dealer at a big US bank. 'So the best they can do is nudge the market in a direction it was already going or try to squeeze positions, or sometimes a single government can signal its own intentions to a confused or unsure market.' Comments of the US treasury secretary are always closely scrutinised to see if they contain any hints of discord between Washington and Tokyo, or suggestions that the yen should appreciate as a way of eroding the trade surplus.

The forex market dealers have no concern about what should be the 'correct' value of any currency. 'I can't even tell you what the rate will be at the end of the week,' confessed the same dealer, 'as I am concerned to stay ahead in the first five minutes of the market tomorrow.' What was certainly clear in the 1990s was that the forex markets were driving the yen too high for the comfort of Japan's industrialists. In terms of purchasing power parity against the dollar – the exchange rate at which the two currencies could buy similar goods – they argued that the yen should be somewhere between 140 and 180 or even 190 against the dollar, while boasting that they had so squeezed their costs that they could still be competitive on world markets with the currency traded at 115 to 120 against the dollar.

When western currency analysts in Tokyo were predicting that the yen would weaken to 115, it rose, touching 100.40 very briefly in 1993, then breaking the 100 barrier the following year and threatening to rise above 95. By the end of 1994 it was still hovering around 100 in spite of higher US interest rates. Its strength was partly a mark of the perceived weakness of the US dollar, partly the price of Washington's treasury policy of sometimes benign, sometimes malign neglect, and partly the result of speculative daring in the markets. Meanwhile Japan's trade surplus reached an all-time record for any country of $142 billion in the year to March 1994.

Superficially, the strong yen and the soaring surpluses might seem evidence of Japan's economic superiority; in reality, they were signs of weakness and were hurting the economy. The strength of the yen in particular was helping to trap Japan in a vicious circle: profits of manufacturers were squeezed, overtime was cut, and spending was reduced, leading to an increase in unemployment to 2.9 per cent by mid-1994. Although this is not high for western countries, some of which were suffering unemployment of 10 per cent or more, it was unprecedentedly bad for Japan. In addition, many workers who in the West would have been laid off were kept on only because of Japanese traditions against sacking. Some economists calculated that the real unemployment rate in 1994 was as high as 7 per cent, with between one and two million workers surplus to requirements.

Prospects for fresh graduates were poorer than ever, with household-name companies slashing their recruitment; young women were finding it particularly hard to get jobs. This poor performance was further depressing confidence, holding back spending, reducing output further, and further tightening the screw on recruitment and raising questions about how long the 'lifetime employment' system could survive. Even though only the biggest firms guarantee jobs for life, getting rid of the system would have major social as well as economic implications.

The strong yen was not only cutting deeply into the profits of Japanese industry, but also reducing the value of investments in US Treasury and other foreign instruments held by the big Japanese pension funds and other investors. If they had put money into America, whether in stocks, bonds or land, when the yen was at 150 or 125 or 120 to the dollar, it meant that when they came to redeem the investment and were given only 100 yen for each dollar, they took a huge loss – perhaps much more significant in terms of loss of future income for an ageing society than the losses that the MoF's Tax and Budget Bureaux were expecting if they reduced income taxes. By some accounts, 25 to 30 per cent of the value of Japanese dollar pension investments was lost with the rising yen. When belatedly they learned their lesson, refrained from investing abroad and kept their money at home in yen, that exacerbated the supply–demand imbalance between yen and dollars, and pushed the yen still higher.

The tragedy for Japan's manufacturers is that they are caught in a time-trap. Over time they have been restructuring, moving to more sophisticated production at home, while shifting labour-intensive operations offshore. But the rise in the yen has caught them without notice. As one director of a large manufacturer put it: 'We adjusted to the yen's rapid rise from 250 to 150. We developed leaner production to cope with a yen of 125 to the dollar and still sell internationally. But the rise in 1993 and 1994 has been swift and damaging and, added to the recession, has forced so many companies into three or four years of losses.'

Meanwhile, the trade surplus was slow to turn because of a combination of the normal delay of the J-curve effect,* the recession in Japan, which meant reduced demand for goods whether domestic or foreign, and rapid recovery in the USA, increasing Japan's exports. By the end of 1994, the

---

* As the yen rises, Japanese exports invoiced in yen automatically become more expensive in dollar terms, while exporters who sell their goods in a foreign currency will be forced to price goods higher to maintain their earnings, with both factors raising the dollar surplus.

surplus had begun to fall quite rapidly in yen terms, although more slowly expressed in terms of the weakening dollar, as recovering Japan began to import again, and as consumers saw the attraction of falling prices of imports. Unfortunately, the surplus with the USA rose rapidly pre-Christmas as Americans turned to Japan for electronics and other products 'that only the Japanese now make'.

The danger now is that strident Americans in a more critical, Republican-led Congress will continue to keep pressure on the yen, slow Japan's recovery and the growth of exports, and set up pressures for manufacturers to move offshore, with all the consequent risks of 'hollowing out' Japanese industry or starting a trade war.

How much of the blame for these gloomy prospects can be laid at the MoF's door is disputable. It cannot, of course, be blamed for its failure to control forex markets, at least not directly. However, the ministry's complacency over recession hurt everyone. Encouraging growth would have helped to bring down the massive trade surplus, taken the pressure off the yen, reduced foreign political grumbles and fostered Japan's growth as a good international neighbour. Deregulation and the cutting of red tape would also have stilled some of the threats from the USA about opening Japan's closed markets. It would have helped Japanese consumers to the tune of between $75 and $100 billion a year, or almost $900 per person per year, according to a study by three Japanese economists in late 1994.* The study, the first to look at the impact of non-tariff barriers as well as tariffs, said that in some cases prices were 400 per cent higher than they would have been without the regulations.

One of the biggest shortcomings of MoF officials in the early 1990s was their lack of international vision. Of course, in some ways the bureaucrats have come a long way. Toyoo Gyohten, perhaps the MoF's most distinguished 'Mr International' ever, told the story of a trip abroad with a colleague, whose whole life had been spent within the gloomy Kasumigaseki headquarters. 'When we got in the air, and out over the sea, away from Japan, he called the stewardess over and said to her, "It's rather stuffy in here; can you please open a window." He had never even travelled outside Japan and knew nothing of aircraft pressurisation,' Gyohten laughed, amused at this evidence of an insular mind.

Today Japan has many bureaucrats who can speak foreign languages and are much more internationally minded than their counterparts in the USA or Europe, who tend to be monocultural. But when it comes to exercising their influence internationally, the Japanese have a long way to go. At the start of the 1980s, a Japanese based in Washington admitted

* *Measuring the Costs of Protection in Japan*, by Yoko Sazanami, Shujiro Urata and Hiroki Kawai, published by the Institute for International Economics, Washington, DC.

that at international gatherings he and his colleagues followed what he called the four Ss: 'silence, sleep, sometimes snoring'.

Nowadays the MoF is much keener to get its message across, but it has not learned the art of diplomacy or convincing others. A western delegate at an international gathering in 1994 said, only a trifle cruelly, 'It's easy to handle the Japanese. On any issue they have only one thing they want. If you satisfy them on this, they will go along with everything. But in terms of their contribution to the discussion, the Japanese play like a broken gramophone record.'

The real problem lies not in the failure of the international bureaucrats like Kubota, who has clearly thought a lot about burning international issues. In mid-1994, he said that he had two immediate questions he thought should be studied. 'One important issue is how to secure the efficient transfer of capital across the border of this country and examine whether the Tokyo market is efficient and competitive as a financial centre. There are many opinions on this critical issue. There is a popular argument that Tokyo is losing its competitiveness as a financial centre partly because of the taxation system, partly because of regulations, partly because of labour costs and partly because of rent. Tokyo is not Singapore, which lives from its financial services, and we should not artificially create incentives to make Tokyo an international financial centre, but at least the system should be neutral in the transfer of resources out of or into the economy. I suspect that for various reasons our system might penalise this neutral transfer and we should look at it.

'The other thing I want to do is look at the market itself, especially the foreign currency market. The present system is established on the theory that completely free market forces do secure a stable exchange rate regime. Again, supporters of this assumption say that foreign currency markets are similar to other markets such as bond markets, stock markets and markets for cotton, coffee, beans and eggs and so on. But if you look at the cotton market, even if prices go down dramatically, it doesn't affect the whole economy too seriously in the way that the currency does. If there is a big fluctuation in the currency, you might have to change fiscal and monetary policy, increase taxes or spending and change the whole economy to the extent that you might have a depression. The malfunction of this market has more serious effects on many areas of the economy, so we should consider more seriously its stability and the desired level of exchange rates.'

Kubota is even more interesting in the longer-term project he thinks it is important to examine – 'A reflection on the events of the long years which ended in 1945. I don't think that we have studied the implications properly. So many people died in this country and in Asia. What brought our ancestors to these wars? This has a very important bearing on our policies in the future. One might look on the process towards war as the failure on the part of Japan to adjust our systems to a changing world environment and circumstances.' Exactly, but is anyone listening, most of all within Kubota's own powerhouse, and will he get a chance to help avoid a repetition of old history?

Japan's real failure is of the domestic mandarins in Kasumigaseki, and in the structural failure of the MoF's organisation. Its policies are dictated at the bureau level and mostly by a Budget Bureau which is thinking entirely of domestic problems and in a very blinkered way. Of course, to an extent this is true of all treasury departments anywhere in the world. But an aspiring power like Japan with great ambitions, but without, as Miyazawa put it, 'military might to back up the yen', must take international factors into consideration. In Japan's case, some of the cost will have to be borne by the rest of the world, deprived of Japan's contribution to questions of international development and capital flows. But much more of the price will have to be paid by Japan, suffering unpleasant fluctuations in the value of its yen because of its failure to get its message across.

In 1994 the recently arrived US ambassador to Tokyo, former vice president Walter Mondale, asked to see Jiro Saito. The first response was that foreigners were not allowed to see Saito, but had to see the international vice minister. Mondale persisted and eventually met Saito. But the story illustrates the dichotomy that the bureaucrats have created. The international vice minister is still seen as 'the barbarian tamer', somebody who will keep the barbarians at bay, away from the real decision makers.

This brings with it another problem. When a true internationalist like Gyohten is appointed to the top international job, he is a participant and partner in international discussions; his voice and opinions are listened to. But at home he is disregarded as tainted by foreigners. Safely out of office, Gyohten lamented that at international gatherings, even when he was vice minister, he was never sure whether his proposals would be accepted back home, and he had to wait for the pronouncements from Tokyo of a junior director of the Budget Bureau to give an imprimatur for his plans.

When a basically domestic man such as the vice minister from 1993 to 1995, Kosuke Nakahira, is chosen, he is trusted at home for his obedience, but does not carry any weight abroad. 'Can't think of any major contribution that Nakahira has made on any question,' commented his western contemporaries from round the international negotiating tables. Japan's performance at the key 1993 annual meetings of the International Monetary Fund and the World Bank, attended by Nakahira and minister Hirohisa Fujii, a faithful alumnus of the ministry, was summed up in the newspaper headline: 'Shiny shoes and dim policy'.

A mature MoF would have abolished the international/domestic dichotomy. It would at least have been prepared to appoint an 'internationalist' to the top post of administrative vice minister, on the way to abolishing the distinction. But that would be only a first step. The ministry should also consider giving longer terms in office, say four or five years instead of one or two, to its top people, so that they have an opportunity really to consider modern inputs and adjustments to the accumulated institutional memory. It is an indictment of the bureaucracy that its officials serve faithfully, but then leave well before the age of 60 to make their real money outside its gloomy corridors.

11

Karaoke Politics:
Anyone Can Be Prime Minister

An old man was pushed into court in a wheelchair. He looked vulnerable, fragile, alone, in spite of the hordes of newspaper reporters, photographers and television cameras all jostling with each other to get his picture. It was hard to imagine that the man, 78-year-old Shin Kanemaru, had only a few months before been the most powerful person in Japanese politics, called 'The Godfather', 'the kingmaker', and other such epithets of power. This was July 1993, fittingly just after Kanemaru's downfall had brought about the fracturing of the government and the collapse of the Liberal Democratic Party, which had ruled for 38 uninterrupted years.

It was also a matter of days before parliament was to elect a new, 'clean' prime minister, heading a multiparty rainbow coalition government. Its supporters rejoiced, promising that Japan would soon see a new era of reforms that would sweep away the cobwebs, the dirt, the distrust, the corruption that gave the country's politics – deservedly – such a bad reputation for grubby, self-seeking rulers concerned only about feathering their own nests. Now, more than a year later, the reforming zeal has gone and no one is sure of the political future. 'It is like a sumo match, with the two wrestlers locked on the edge of the *dohyo* [ring] and no one is sure how the result will go,' said former prime minister Kiichi Miyazawa. 'Swimming in the Japanese political waters is a dangerous and unpredictable business,' commented Satsuki Eda, one of the reformers.

Superficially, Japan has all the trappings of a modern democracy in which the politicians are rulers of the land. It has free and regular elections, every five years for the more powerful lower house, the House of Representatives, whose members are all elected together; and every three years for half the membership of the upper house, the House of Counsellors, whose members enjoy six-year terms. The elections are on the basis of one person, one vote, and are attended by fanfare, and boisterous and completely free press and television coverage.

The politicians have to go out and meet the people, and many of them are still old-fashioned enough to wear white gloves and huge rosettes as they climb on board their campaign buses to wave, smile and promise the earth to their voters, as politicians do everywhere. Profusions of campaign posters; armies of cheerleaders and election workers who stand on the street bowing to passers-by and offering leaflets; a constant cacophany of campaign music and tinkly signature tunes from the more imaginative candidates as their buses blare round the constituency, their occupants waving and urging everyone in sight that voting day is near and that they should get out and vote; all make Japanese elections affairs to remember.

To make sure that the elections are fair and clean, there are strict rules governing how much candidates can spend and what types of behaviour are allowed. Door-to-door canvassing, for example, is prohibited, in case candidates might try to give or to accept bribes. There are limits on when canvassing can be done, so that no unfair advantages are taken, including a ban on using the noisy campaign vehicles after 8 p.m., a precaution to let people get a peaceful evening's rest.

For decades, this framework gave Japan a stable conservatively inclined government, provided by the Liberal Democratic Party, which ruled from its foundation in 1955 to 1993. The head of the party became the prime minister, and presided over a cabinet of ministers whom he chose from elected MPs from the two houses. The ministers are responsible to parliament, which passes laws on the basis of bills drawn up by the government with the help of a permanent civil service, again similar to the British one, selected by open competitive examination and offering a career for life. The points of difference seem unimportant, such as the shape of the parliamentary chambers, semi-circular like the American Congress, with members going up to a rostrum to make their speeches, rather than standing at their regular places in a rectangular chamber, as is the British practice.

The system has created some distinguished figures, such as Shigeru Yoshida, the single most influential immediately post-war politician, Hayato Ikeda, author of the famous and successful 'income-doubling' plan, which laid the foundations for Japan to become a modern great economic power, and the brothers Nobusuke Kishi and Eisaku Sato, both of whom became prime minister. Later Yasuhiro Nakasone made the most of Japan's presence at international economic summits, rejoiced in his friendship with then US president Ronald Reagan, and loved their popular 'Ron–Yasu' nicknames.

When Kiichi Miyazawa was chosen to take over as prime minister in 1991, Japan had a leader who was as intelligent as any politician anywhere in the world. He was skilled in economics, had been involved in the negotiations leading to the San Francisco Peace Treaty, which effectively gave Japan back its post-war independence, and was also a key figure supporting Ikeda in the income-doubling plan. As a bonus, Miyazawa could speak fluent English. 'If you heard him speaking English without seeing his face or being told his name, you would think he was a native English speaker,' said an admiring Japanese bureaucrat. When he took over, many people, both Japanese and non-Japanese, hoped that under his leadership Japan could assume a position of political stature and maturity in the world, commensurate with its standing as the second largest economy in absolute terms (after the USA), but the strongest in financial muscle.

But appearances are deceptive. It was Miyazawa who presided over the break-up and almost the dissolution of the LDP. The mighty façade of Japan's single-party rule was revealed to be rotten underneath. And in spite of its great economic strength, Japan was seen for all the world to be a country of greedy political pygmies. Ichiro Ozawa, one of the key up-and-coming leaders of the LDP, wrote that 'the prime minister ... is in theory all but omnipotent ... [but] the prime minister is nothing more than master of ceremonies for the ritual at hand'.*

One reason was that, for all its years in power, the LDP had no strong centralised party machine, like the British Conservative or Labour parties. Instead it became an unruly collection of fiefdoms or tribes, called factions, each headed by an ambitious chief. The factions were based not on principles or policy differences, but on greed for power and the spoils which it could bring. Like the tribes of Israel, chiefs could trace the ancestry of their faction back for many years to the foundation of the LDP and beyond. Miyazawa, for example, took over the faction previously headed by prime minister Zenko Suzuki, and before that by former prime minister Masayoshi Ohira and originally by Hayato Ikeda. Ohira had once said that, whenever you had three LDP members, there were two factions.

The biggest of six major factions by mid-1992, with 111 of the more than 380 LDP members of both houses of parliament, was that nominally headed by former prime minister Noboru Takeshita, but controlled by Kanemaru. It has previously been run by Kakuei Tanaka and before that by Eisaku Sato. The party and factional structures meant that at general elections there was as much of a contest between the factions of the LDP as between the ruling party and its opponents – in-fighting that the electoral system encouraged. Sometimes there was bitter squabbling within a single faction as rivals tussled to choose their own candidate for a seat. All this meant that Japanese prime ministers never had the freedom of choice of a British or other prime minister in choosing their own ministers. Cabinet-making time offered another chance for the tribal leaders to test their strength and get as many of their own people as possible into office. Once in power, even the prime minister was beholden to the factional bosses, who operated from behind the scenes, but controlled the powerful pursestrings. Kanemaru, from a family of sake-brewers, boasted that he had 'created' successive prime ministers, Sosuke Uno, Toshiki Kaifu and indeed Miyazawa himself.

*   *   *

* Ichiro Ozawa, *Blueprint for a New Japan*, Kodansha, 1994.

The key event in triggering the political earthquake of 1993 which saw the LDP's departure from power was Kanemaru's admission the previous year that he had received an illegal 'gift' of 500 million yen ($5 million) from Tokyo Sagawa Kyubin, a controversial parcel delivery firm. There was an outcry from a previously docile public. When Kanemaru was prosecuted under the Political Funds Law, which limited donations from a single company to 1.5 million yen a year, and was fined a paltry 200,000 yen, the storm grew. The fine was, one ex-prosecutor claimed, the political equivalent of a parking ticket. Kanemaru had refused repeated requests to appear before prosecutors and merely submitted a written statement. More than 31,000 people wrote to the prosecutors' office claiming that there had been a whitewash.

Eventually Kanemaru gave up first his position as deputy president of the LDP, then his parliamentary seat, which he had held for 34 years. Miyazawa pleaded with him not to do it, but the old man in the end saw the avalanche of popular discontent being heaped on his head. 'There was much to blame myself about for this,' Kanemaru mumbled in his raspy voice, doing a good Japanese impression of Marlon Brando's Godfather. 'It is natural for me to take responsibility.' When giving up his MP's seat, he said, 'I have caused too much trouble for the people, and I sincerely apologise for it.' At that stage, few people inside or outside politics could have any idea of the consequences that were to follow, though Miyazawa immediately felt the repercussions of the loss of his godfather. Plans to pass a 10,700 billion yen economy-boosting package were halted as the opposition played their pantomime games, demanding that Kanemaru and other leading figures testify before parliament about their involvement.

Remarkably, given the forests of newsprint and the hours of parliamentary time given to discussing it, much less is known about what became known as the Sagawa scandal (named obviously after the lorry and parcel delivery group) than about other scandals that have regularly hit Japan. Equally remarkably, this scandal was an earthquake that did not just shake but brought down the government.

Sagawa was a relative newcomer to the complicated and competitive world of parcel deliveries, an area full of trip wires of permits and licences to operate. It was founded by Kiyoshi Sagawa, an ambitious man from Kyoto, who started by using bicycles to transport packages between his hometown and the nearby city of Osaka in the 1960s. He adopted the symbol of a *hikyaku*, the swift letter carrier of old Japan. His business quickly began to flourish, graduating from bicycles to lorries. But on the way, the impatient Sagawa encountered the inevitable problems of a newcomer breaking into a business with a maze of rules and regulations and roadblocks. He decided that the best way to get into the big time was to cultivate links with politicians and give liberal donations to smooth both their and his paths.

In 1974 Sagawa absorbed a Tokyo-based delivery firm, founded by Hiroy-asu Watanabe. This became the Tokyo Sagawa Kyubin offshoot of the group. Watanabe had similar views that the best way to speed development was through politicians. Watanabe reportedly told friends that support for the politicians was similar to the backing of sumo wrestlers or geisha by their patrons, something known as *tanimachi*. 'After all, politicians are the ultimate geisha,' he said. The Sagawa group grew into a loosely structured concern of 235 companies, 15,000 vehicles, 22,000 employees and esti-mated revenues of 900 billion yen in 1991, when it was Japan's second or third biggest surface parcel delivery service. (The group did not have to publish its annual accounts.)

The first public evidence of Sagawa's dubious methods of delivering success came in February 1992 with the arrest of Watanabe and three other executives on suspicion of criminal breach of trust, involving a massive sum of 530 billion yen in questionable payments, loans and loan guaran-tees. What followed, as the prosecutors examined the books and docu-ments, was a remarkably complicated and twisted tale of a big corporate group's attempts to buy influence not just with politicians, but with shady underworld and gangland figures.

The sums mentioned climbed higher and higher. Some of the inspired leaks coming from the prosecutors' office whispered of up to 100 billion yen ($1 billion) being given to 100 or more politicians. 'Sagawa certainly threw its money around,' said one of the investigators in a casual remark. 'Its bosses didn't just confine themselves to the top leaders of the LDP, but gave money to leading figures from other parties.' Later attention was concentrated on a group of about a dozen prominent Liberal Democratic Party politicians, including former prime ministers, who – stories from the prosecutors' office said – were handed a total of 2.15 billion yen by Sagawa, mainly from the Tokyo offshoot run by Watanabe. Lists of names actually circulated widely in Tokyo in 1992. Some politicians denied that they had received money – or that they had received it illegitimately – while others were said to be aggrieved that they were not thought import-ant enough to be named in the latest round of rumours.

The furore over the scandal was not just because of the huge sums supposedly handed out, but also because of Sagawa's links with criminal gangs. Besides the money handed out to politicians, Sagawa had made loan guarantees worth 115 billion yen to the firms controlled by Susumu Ishii, head of the Inagawa-kai, Japan's second biggest *boryokudan* (yakuza), or criminal gang. The most interesting connection of all was that Sagawa was evidently playing the role of helpful intermediary between the poli-ticians on the one hand and gangsters on the other, so Sagawa quickly became known as the 'money and mobsters' scandal.

Watanabe of Tokyo Sagawa Kyubin alleged to prosecutors that Kanemaru had asked his help in trying to stop a public loudspeaker campaign by the rightist Nihon Kominto (literally, Japan Party of the Emperor's Subjects) group, which was threatening to spoil his protégé Noboru Takeshita's bid to be prime minister in 1987. The rightists' methods were unusual: instead of attacking him directly, the message coming from their loudspeakers was 'Let's make Mr Takeshita prime minister because he is good at making money.' Watanabe claimed he had sought the help of Susumu Ishii successfully to stop the rightists. To assist in this task, Watanabe suggested that Takeshita should visit the ailing Kakuei Tanaka, whose faction he had grabbed, or stolen according to the Tanakas.

Takeshita himself, in sworn testimony to parliament, denied that he knew anything about negotiations going on on his behalf with gangsters. He dismissed demands that he should resign as an MP, saying, 'If I were to resign, it would be an admission that I became president of the Liberal Democratic Party and prime minister through gang intervention.' He admitted meeting Watanabe and that the Tokyo Sagawa chief had urged him to visit Tanaka, which he did the next day, but said that his visit had nothing to do with the rightist campaign. It was merely that he wanted 'to greet my mentor [before announcing my candidature]'. Takeshita also admitted thanking Watanabe when he had got the prime minister's job, but said that 'At that time I was in such a state [over becoming prime minister] that I thanked almost everyone I met.'

In dramatic testimony in November 1992, from a hospital bed where he was undergoing treatment for glaucoma, Kanemaru told the chairman of the Budget Committee and six other MPs that he could not remember what had happened at the crucial meeting with Watanabe because he was drunk. In an account offering comic relief, Kanemaru said, 'I remember there was Takeshita, myself, [Ichiro] Ozawa, [Takeshita's political secretary Isao] Aoki and Watanabe. I drank three glasses of *mizuwari* [whisky and water] at the party. Later, at the meeting on the 16th floor, I had a few more. Under these circumstances, and because I was not really interested in the discussion, I really don't remember the discussion very well.'

Ozawa, who gave testimony to parliament in February 1993, also suffered convenient memory lapses about the crucial meeting claiming ignorance of the purposes of the meeting and adding that he was only 'in and out of the room to serve drinks and change ashtrays'. Kanemaru agreed that he had had dealings with the gang boss Susumu Ishii. When asked to give more details, he said Ishii had helped in 'smear campaigns'. He even defended thanking Ishii for his help: 'If your child falls in the river and nearly drowns and someone helps that child and you later learn that that person was a yakuza gang member, you are still indebted to that yakuza gang member.'

It was certainly true that the right-wing groups had mounted a vigorous public campaign against Takeshita, that Takeshita had visited Tanaka's home (where he was snubbed and not allowed entry), that this campaign had suddenly stopped, and that Takeshita became prime minister (only to lose the job through implication in another scandal nineteen months later). Why Kominto chose to attack Takeshita and whether there was another payoff are matters for argument. Eight key figures, including the founding Sagawa and gangster Ishii, who might have been able to throw light on a mysterious subject, were dead by the time of the investigation. But most of the Japanese public surveyed about the hearings thought that Takeshita had told lies in his evidence to parliament.

The Sagawa affair thus ended with Kanemaru the only national politician prosecuted. The only other political victim was Niigata governor Koyoshi Kaneko, to whom Sagawa gave 200 million yen, but he had to face a full-blooded prosecution, not the summary trial and paltry fine that Kanemaru received. Nevertheless, there was surprise that 'the Godfather' was the scapegoat. 'It was only Shin Kanemaru who was wrong,' he had said after resigning from parliament. 'There was no other bad guy.' He used one excuse after another in refusing to say to whom he had passed shares of the money, thus protecting others from prosecution. His sense of honour may have been admirable, but no one believed him.

But Kanemaru's troubles with the investigators were not over. Perhaps stung by the criticism of their failure over Sagawa and helped by the fact that he no longer had an MP's immunity, the prosecutors stepped up their investigation of Kanemaru and made some surprising discoveries. On the surface the old godfather was an austere figure, not known for high living. He kept tough control of his faction of the ruling party, and was clearly not a man to tangle with. He lived in a spacious house in a good area of Tokyo, but it was not palatial or flashy in the style of politicians obviously on the take.

After his second wife Etsuko died in December 1991, it was said that Kanemaru was lost. He was so dependent on her that 'he didn't know where his underwear was or what to wear each day; his wife did everything for him,' according to Takao Toshikawa, editor of *Tokyo Insideline* monthly. But when the investigators raided Kanemaru's homes and offices in Tokyo and outside, they discovered billions and billions of yen in hidden income, kept in the form of bank debentures, stocks and even gold bars. The Japanese media kept their readers and viewers fascinated day after day with pictures of hidden wealth being pulled out of Kanemaru's closets. His lawyers told the court that he had amassed the money to help realise his 'dream' of realigning Japan's political forces.

Kanemaru was charged with evading 1.04 billion yen in income tax on about 1.84 billion yen in undeclared income during a three-year period from 1987. His aide, Masahisa Haibara, was also charged with evading 310 million yen in taxes on 610 million yen. The two men were additionally charged with conspiracy to evade taxes. Most of Kanemaru's political contributions came from big construction companies in Tokyo and Osaka, as well as from builders in his home area of Yamanishi prefecture.

This was hardly the first time that Japan's political life had been hit by scandal reaching to the very top. There had always been dark rumours about political leaders and how they got their money, but for most of the post-war period the Japanese media, enjoying a cosy relationship with politicians, did not bother to investigate or turned a blind eye. However, denials of dirty deeds could not be covered up when Kakuei Tanaka was driven out of office in December 1974, chased by allegations of corrupt financial dealings. Only after he stepped down as prime minister was he convicted of taking a bribe to ensure that All Nippon Airways bought Lockheed TriStar aircraft. His appeal against that conviction was still wending its slow way through Japan's courts when he died in 1993.*

Perhaps the remarkable thing was the toleration shown towards Tanaka. Though he nominally left the LDP, he continued to be in absolute control of his faction – and thus reigned as Japan's real kingmaker from behind the scenes – until just a few days before his crippling stroke in 1985, when Takeshita made a pre-emptive strike effectively to snatch control away from him. The family blamed Takeshita for causing the stroke by his action. Tanaka was commonly called *Yami Shogun*, the Shogun of Darkness, carrying implications not merely of connections with black money, meaning money that was illegal and coming from nefarious sources, but also of control from behind the scenes by dark forces.

Tanaka was the archetype of the successful money politician. Miyazawa said, 'Tanaka did not multiply the money involved in politics twofold or threefold, but changed the digit, increasing it tenfold, and that became the new norm in politics.' He was a man in a hurry, in every sense. He left school at 15 to get a job and prop up the family finances. Even before entering politics, he had already made his money in the construction business, a foundation for future fund-raising. He became an MP at 29 and a cabinet minister in 1957 at the age of 39. This was unusually young in Japanese politics, where leaders generally only arrive on the national scene after serving six terms as an MP, in their fifties or sixties.

Tanaka said in 1969, when he was secretary-general of the LDP, 'I eat in a hurry and work in a hurry – I am a rationalist, you could say. But think about it, people do not live a hundred or two hundred years. I am already 51 years old, and assuming that I live to age 70, that means I have just 7,000 days left. I hate lifestyles where an ideal conclusion is never reached during the person's lifetime. In everything I do, I am the type that strives

---

* In February 1995, Japan's supreme court finally decided, 19 years after the case opened, that bribes had been made. But the book against Tanaka was closed by his death.

to do what is possible within the time limits available.' He was nicknamed the 'computerised bulldozer' because of his energy and motto of 'decide quickly and implement'.

Tanaka's greatest achievement was probably to raise his hometown of Niigata from an obscure centre to a city that was really on the map, served by the *Shinkansen* (Bullet train), an airport, trunk roads and bridges, schools and community centres. Even when he was in deepest disgrace, convicted of corruption and sentenced to four years in prison in 1983 (which of course he never served), his home supporters not only sent him back to parliament to represent them, but also gave him 220,700 votes in the election of that year, a record for Japan. Just before he died, his daughter Makiko, with no previous political experience, won her father's old parliamentary seat with a landslide majority.

But Tanaka's most lasting contribution to Japanese politics was to cement the 'iron triangle' of politicians, businessmen and bureaucrats, using the construction industry as the foundation. As a former construction boss, he milked the industry and turned it into one of the main funding sources for the LDP. There was an identity of interest between the industry and selected LDP politicians, especially those belonging to Tanaka's favoured camp. At election time, big companies put their staff to work in the campaign offices of 'friendly' politicians; their salaries were paid as usual by the company. 'Paying off local politicians is much like committing a traffic offence,' said one political expert. 'You know it's against the law, but it's not seen as unethical.'

The political history of the 1980s and 1990s in Japan is littered with scandals that proved the point of that contention. One of the most spectacular was the Recruit Cosmos scandal. When most of the truth was finally revealed in 1989, Japan's political and business stage had more casualties than a Wild West shoot-out. The prime minister announced that he would step down, but only after he had lied to parliament, three cabinet ministers had been forced ignominiously to resign, the head of the world's biggest company (Nippon Telegraph and Telephone) and twelve other top businessmen and bureaucrats had been arrested and charged with bribery, parliament had been brought to a complete standstill by an opposition boycott and the prime minister's popularity in opinion polls had plummeted to an all-time low of 3.9 per cent.*

Like Sagawa, Recruit was a company founded by an ambitious new-

---

* Just for good measure Japan enjoyed 'the year of three prime ministers' because Takeshita's successor, Sosuke Uno, was discovered to have had an affair with a minor geisha who broke the cardinal rule: she blabbed of their relationship, accusing him of the mortal sin of not paying her enough. He had to step down because a cheapskate womaniser was not qualified to be Japan's prime minister. Toshiki Kaifu took over.

comer, Hiromasa Ezoe, who was anxious to break into the world of publishing and politics. He did not have the right connections, so he decided
to make some of his own. Between 1984 and 1987 Ezoe handed out shares
in Recruit Cosmos, a property subsidiary, at cheap prices to dozens of
highly placed politicians, businessmen and bureaucrats. When the
company went public, the recipients made a killing.

When news of Recruit and Ezoe's adventures first became public, it got
little attention. 'This is small beer: it happens all the time,' a senior
Ministry of Finance official said to me dismissively at the time. Later the
same official admitted he was impressed 'because Ezoe has been spreading
his money around to all and sundry'. The investigations continued, and
the headlines got bigger and bigger, with revelations of murkier and
murkier details.

Ezoe cultivated a veritable who's who of the Japanese establishment,
and minister after minister quickly took refuge in claims that *he* had
not bought shares, but his secretary had. Kiichi Miyazawa, then finance
minister, was the first to be caught out, either unlucky or foolish
enough to have his name, not the secretary's, on the docket, so he was
forced to resign late in 1988. Shintaro Abe, secretary-general of the
LDP, the following April admitted that Recruit had given 8 million yen
in consultative fees in the name of his wife over a two-year period,
although he quickly claimed that neither he nor his wife had been aware
of the money because, conveniently, his secretary handled all his financial
affairs.

The then prime minister, Noboru Takeshita, reluctantly admitted that
he had been one of the biggest recipients – taking 150 million yen in all,
although he accepted personal responsibility only for 95 million – and
some of the money had not been declared, as was legally required. Takeshita's predecessor as prime minister, Yasuhiro Nakasone, was also a major
beneficiary, making profits of 130 million yen on the sale of Recruit
Cosmos shares.

Prosecutors looked into allegations that, in return, the then prime
minister had assisted Recruit to get into the telecommunications business
with the help of Nippon Telegraph and Telephone, at that time a state-
owned monopoly running Japan's domestic telephone services. One
suggestion was that, at a summit meeting with president Ronald Reagan
in 1987, Naksone mentioned that NTT might be interested in buying a
$8 million Cray supercomputer. The company duly bought one and passed
it on to Recruit.

But the scrutiny of Nakasone's involvement came to an abrupt halt with
the official end of the investigation in spring 1989. By then the scandal
had also brought the downfall of 78-year-old Hishashi Shinto, chairman
of NTT and one of Japan's most respected business leaders, who had
had a distinguished career as president of Ishikawajima-Harima Heavy

Industries and as a director of the influential Keidanren (Federation of Economic Organisations).

In addition, Ezoe made inroads into Japan's education and labour industries at a high level. When all this evidence had come out, the same Ministry of Finance official had to revise his verdict. He concluded, 'All of the major parties have leading figures who were given Recruit money – except for the Communists, and they were probably too stupid not to grab a share.' Former prime minister Takeo Fukuda, by then in his eighties, expressed his astonishment at the corruption. 'The ruling party is completely devoid of ethics. Political corruption has become more normal than abnormal in our party.'

Takeshita had pledged in 1989 that he would 'make every effort, in a humble manner, to wipe out distrust in politicians'. This was the same man who told parliament a few months previously that he had 'accepted no money at all from Recruit'. By April he was conveniently saying that when he made his October statement, 'my memory had been unclear'. He was forced to resign. But some politicians made spirited defences of their necessity to get money wherever they could. An LDP official crudely called Eiji Suzuki, president of Nikkeiren (the Employers' Association), 'a political jerk' because he advocated reforms. 'We cannot always handle politics with the gloves off.' Younger LDP members of parliament complained that reforms to clean up politics 'would chop our heads off'.

A more eloquent defence of the system was made by Michio Watanabe, at that time chairman of the LDP Policy Affairs Research Council, one of the top jobs in the party. 'We must make efforts to cleanse Japanese political circles,' he admitted. 'But if we created distilled water, no fish would be able to live in it.' Apologists like Watanabe claimed that it was an expensive business being an MP, about 100 million yen a year, or several times the official salary, and 500 million yen upwards for an ambitious minister. Watanabe added, 'If the electorate wants clean politicians, it has to stop expecting us to give them gifts at every turn.'

He did a quick estimate of the costs of surviving in politics: he claimed that a busy political leader needed a payroll of between ten and twenty assistants and secretaries to manage the office, costing 40 to 90 million yen a year; 'donations' to shrines and temples in the constituency; condolence payments of 50,000 yen each 'almost daily' for funerals and wedding presents; and gifts of between 10,000 and 20,000 yen for each of several hundred *bonenkai* (year-end) and *shin-nenkai* (new year) gatherings. He joked that a conscientious MP who wanted to stay on top of things in his constituency should at all times carry a black tie (for funerals) and a white one (for weddings).

Politicians got these sums from a variety of sources. Contributions from big business and industrial organisations were important, and respectable big business organisations like Keidanren and the Iron and Steel Federation as well as leading individual companies were significant contributors to LDP coffers. But it was common knowledge in the stockbroking industry that an event like Recruit Cosmos was really only remarkable because of the scale of operations and the large number of beneficiaries. 'It's quite common for a politician to get a call from a chum in a big brokerage house tipping him off when a particular stock is about to be traded heavily,' said an American working as a stockbroker in Tokyo at the time. 'That way they can trade early and make a killing.' At the time, the stock market was roaring ahead on its way to new records every month.

The last sullied word should perhaps go to Isao Aoki, Takeshita's political secretary for 30 years, who tried and failed to commit suicide by slashing his wrists, then hanged himself in April 1989, the day after Takeshita finally said he was stepping down. Aoki left a note that he could no longer stand the dirty politics. He had written: 'Behind the scenes of this peaceful democracy are the same bloody struggles to the death that were waged time after time by medieval warlords.' He was of course privy to the Sagawa scandal, which did not come into the public arena for another three years.

Unlike characters in Wild West films or novels, however, politicians caught out in political corruption neither died nor faded away, but came back to life and some of them to power. The supreme example was Tanaka. Shintaro Abe still hoped to become prime minister until his cancer caught up with him. Miyazawa did become prime minister. Takeshita hoped to be prime minister again until he was caught in the backwash of Sagawa. And in the political jostling that occurred in 1993 and 1994, it was even said that Nakasone fancied his chances again.

New scandals meanwhile surfaced. Just before Sagawa hit the headlines, there was the Kyowa scandal, involving claims that Fumio Abe, former director-general of the Hokkaido and Okinawa Development Agencies, a cabinet post, had taken bribes from the Kyowa steel frame-making company to push its case for building a leisure resort and golf complex in Hokkaido. Embarrassingly for prime minister Miyazawa, Abe was a close aide. The affair also forced former prime minister Zenko Suzuki to parliamentary testimony to admit receiving 10 million yen from Kyowa via Abe, although he claimed that it was not a bribe and that he did not even keep the money, but returned it after a while. He denied claims that he had taken another 100 million yen from Kyowa after agreeing to become honorary chairman of its planned club.

The *Japan Times* of 28 February 1992 scathingly noted that the statements of Suzuki 'indicated that it is almost routine for politicians to serve as an influential intermediary for specific firms and to receive questionable money in return. Such activity may not always be illegal, but using political influence in the interest of a specific business concern evidently strengthens the roots of the money-oriented politics of the Liberal Democratic Party'.

Next came a rather curious interlude involving former prime minister Takeshita again, this time over the sale of an overpriced gold leaf screen in 1985, when Takeshita was finance minister. It was claimed that Takeshita's influence was sought on behalf of struggling Heiwa Sogo Bank, so that it could put itself together again and avoid being swallowed by Sumitomo Bank, and that 300 million yen of the 4 billion yen price tag was to have been channelled to him. (Later Heiwa was absorbed by Sumitomo Bank rather than allowed to go bankrupt.) Summoned yet again before parliament, Takeshita denied that he had received any money.

The years 1993 and 1994 brought more scandal revelations, as one construction company after another was in the headlines for handing out money to provincial politicians. Almost all of the top construction companies, Hazama, Kajima, Mitsui Construction, Nishimatsu, Shimizu, Taisei and Tobishima were named in a series of cases involving governors of Ibaraki and Miyagi prefectures and the mayor of nearby Sendai city. These were not just small fry, but the top executives of the construction firms, also holding leading positions in the industry association. Leaks also filtered out of regular donations from the construction giants to national politicians, with former finance minister Ryutaro Hashimoto (who became Miti minister in 1994), Kanemaru, Miyazawa, Nakasone, Ozawa and Takeshita among the names. Where the politicians admitted they had received the money, all claimed that it had been handled 'properly'.

The revelations threw light on the shady connections between the partners in the increasingly unholy trinity of bureaucrats, businessmen and politicians that has helped the Japanese economy to grow. One executive of a contractor revealed, 'If you have one of the big alumni of the Construction Ministry, then it makes it easier for you to win a large-scale works project like the construction of a dam. The access to information that this provides adds an extra dimension to the company. It's completely a give-and-take situation.' He explained also how the relations with politicians worked. 'You generate money with the slush fund from your own company, of course, and you get subcontractors to create a slush fund. It's common knowledge that general contractors use under-the-table funds.' He admitted that, since the general contracting work was hardly hi-tech, 'There is a lot of space for politicians to intervene. Sometimes the politicians even make their demands publicly.'

While those cases were still creating fresh scandal headlines daily, another one overtook them. Kishiro Nakamura, a 45-year-old member of parliament, was arrested in March 1994, the first national politician for 26 years to be arrested while parliament was actually in session. Parliament voted to strip him of his immunity, and he was indicted on charges of having accepted 10 million yen ($100,000) in bribes from Shinji Kiyoyama, the then deputy president of Kajima Construction.

In court, Nakamura admitted that he had accepted the money in January 1992, but said that it was a political donation, not a bribe, and that he had not been asked for any favours. The Kajima executive backed up this story, also claiming that he had not asked Nakamura for anything when he had handed over the cash. The investigators, however, claimed that the money was given in return for helping to prevent Japan's Fair Trade Commission from filing a criminal complaint against a local contractors' association in Saitama prefecture, which was suspected of violating the anti-monopoly law through bid-rigging. The commission decided in May 1992 not to file a complaint, and merely told the association to stop unfair business practices, which are commonly regarded as widespread in the construction industry. It said that it lacked hard evidence for a formal complaint.

At the time of the incident, Nakamura was head of the LDP lobby of MPs concerned with revising the anti-monopoly law. (He later became construction minister.) Kajima was the head of the Saitama contractors' association. Kiyoyama was also the executive indicted in the case of money given to the Ibaraki governor. In court, Nakamura claimed that the dropping of the bid-rigging accusation was part of a backroom deal between Kanemaru, then prime minister Miyazawa and the chairman of the Fair Trade Commission, in exchange for higher fines for violations of the anti-monopoly law.

The case highlighted the role of the LDP's *zoku* – tribes of MP-lobbyists who had strong influence over industries and ministries in which they specialised. Whatever the truth of the Nakamura case, the incident drew attention to another shady aspect of the co-operation between the trinity. Politicians came to believe that it was a proper part of their role to exert pressure on bureaucrats, local government and private companies. Some political experts say that, in construction and some other industries, the zoku were the most powerful influence on policy – more powerful than the bureaucrats. On one notable occasion when the FTC was considering the abolition of resale price maintenance, the LDP zoku covering the health care area opposed the plan and put sustained pressure to get cosmetics and medical goods exempted. Over the years, the zoku politicians got to know their areas inside out, and traded their expertise and influence for contributions from the industries they were involved in. The bureaucrats also found them useful to put pressure through the LDP for special funds for their ministries.

The other murky aspect was the involvement of gangsters. Kenji Ino, author of books about rightists and gangsters, said that it was inevitable for LDP politicians to make ties with the underworld as they climbed the greasy pole to power, simply because the need for vast amounts of dirty money attracted extortionists and spongers. 'If tens of billions of yen are needed to win an LDP presidential election, candidates and their chief supporters go to extraordinary lengths to raise funds without writing receipts. Information on such activities is bound to leak,' Ino told the leading newspaper *Asahi Shimbun* on 12 November 1992.

'Gangs are a parasitic existence in society. But those in power have always exploited them. When a company asks a gang boss to secure for it the required status to tender bids on local government works, the boss goes to a politician indebted to him. When the vote count in the final stages of an election campaign falls short of expectations, what most secretaries to politicians do is ask gang bosses to help. Mobsters in Japan total about 90,000, according to the National Police Agency. But they control 30 to 40 times as many votes in mob-operated businesses, including family members ... It costs a factional leader hundreds of millions of yen to get a newcomer elected, so he has no choice but to reach out for dirty money, and when he does that he makes himself vulnerable to extortion and sponging.'

Before Nakamura was arrested, the radical repercussions of the downfall of Kanemaru occurred. These factors left the LDP leaderless, and let loose instead a whirling kaleidoscope of ambitious men chasing after power. The immediate consequence of Kanemaru giving up politics was that the biggest faction had to find a new boss, and a bitter personal quarrel took place over who should run it. The most ambitious man was the young Ichiro Ozawa, who had already been secretary-general of the LDP. Still only 50, Ozawa was bitterly opposed for his youth, arrogance and naked ambition by a number of 'old guard' members in the faction. Ozawa had a majority among the faction in the lower house, but the old guard had the support of almost all the members in the upper house.

Attempts to find a compromise candidate went on for a while, then the old guard tried to pre-empt the battle by snatching the leadership in a coup, but in the end the faction split. The mainstream leadership formed under Keizo Obuchi, a rather colourless, but reputedly pliant figure whose main claim to fame was that briefly as chief cabinet secretary* he had announced that the new reign of Emperor Akihito would be known as *Heisei*, or 'striving for peace on Earth and in Heaven'.

Reformers in the Kanemaru faction set up a study group under the chairmanship of Tsutomu Hata, the minister of finance, but Ozawa was their mastermind. In December, the Hata–Ozawa group took the extreme step of splitting and forming its own faction within the LDP, called Reform

* The chief cabinet secretary is a member of the cabinet, normally someone close to the prime minister, who serves as the government's regular spokesman for press and public.

Forum 21, promising 'reform to lay foundations for Japan of the twenty-first century'. The assets of the formerly united Kanemaru faction were split 60:40 in favour of Obuchi's group.

There was an uneasy interlude for six months while Miyazawa tried to assert his authority and to push political reform measures. He swore solemnly that he would commit all his energies to cleaning up the dirty political system. But he failed. The departure of Kanemaru from the political scene did not free Miyazawa to play the role of prime minister in the western sense. Instead it released other factions from Kanemaru's controlling hand, so that they could resume their infighting against each other and against Miyazawa. He was left, as Ozawa correctly wrote, as the master of ceremonies of rituals that had been decided in advance.

Since the factions could not agree, Miyazawa's solemn promises of reform were empty air. His claims to fame in office were as the host of the ill-fated banquet for visiting US president George Bush, who vomited in Miyazawa's lap in early 1992, as the lame-duck host of the summit of industrialised nations in July 1993, and finally as the master of ceremonies for the LDP's loss of power. By that time the reform pledges had been defeated by the LDP old guard, with the Obuchi faction members prominent. Ozawa struck. When the opposition called a motion of no-confidence for Miyazawa's failure to fulfil his reform promises, he took his faction into the lobby against the LDP, which was defeated and had to call fresh elections for the lower house.

The vast gulf between a western democracy and the Japanese system became evident. Tsutomo Hata – showing extreme charity – claimed that Kanemaru was the victim of a corrupt system. He complained that the political system itself encouraged corruption. Unlike in the West, where one person uses his or her vote to elect a single member, Japan's sprawling constituencies were represented by anything from two to six members. The individual has just a single vote, but up to six members will be chosen to represent the constituency. According to Hata and other reformers, this meant that 'Candidates from the same party must fight against each other to get the electorate's support. It means it's impossible to discuss serious issues.' If a candidate were brave – or – stupid – enough to suggest examining the merits of opening Japan's rice market, he or she would be stabbed in the back by rivals from the same side. To succeed, candidates must show that they have money and influence and vested interests on their side, to deliver the very best pork barrel goodies for the constituency.

Hata added, 'Instead of serious matters, the election turns on how many roads, how many concert halls, the political candidate can bring to the constituency. We have to attend marriages and funerals of people in the constituency. The most important requirement is servicing individuals. If we deal with serious national or world matters, we will never be elected.' The system encouraged a never-ending cycle of infighting and corruption, breeding still more. It was this that led the freshman MP Masayoshi Takemura in 1989 to complain that 'Our country has a first-rate economy, second-rate standard of living and third-rate political system.'

The other distortion in the electoral system was the over-representation of rural voters and under-representation of densely populated urban areas. In some lower house constituencies, a single rural vote was worth almost four urban ones, and in the upper house the disparity was wider still. The Osaka high court ruled in late 1993 that, in the 1992 upper house election, one vote in sparsely populated Tottori was worth 6.59 votes in heavily populated Kanagawa, and that a disparity of more than six to one was unconstitutional. But it would not nullify the election, claiming that such a move would cause social and political 'inconvenience'. The Supreme Court had earlier set a ceiling of three to one on lower house disparities. Failure of the courts to set aside any election meant that rural and farming interests enjoyed disproportionate influence and protection on vital issues like opening Japan's expensive rice and other agricultural markets.

The election campaign of July 1993 was exciting because of the entry of Hata and Ozawa's new political party, called Shinseito (Renewal Party), as well as two other new parties, Sakigake (Harbinger), founded by Masayoshi Takemura, who had also defected from the LDP with a smaller number of supporters, and Nihon Shinto (Japan New Party), led by a former LDP prefectural governor with film star looks, Morihiro Hosokawa. Nihon Shinto had made its debut in the 1982 upper house elections, where it had won four seats and created a stir because Hosokawa's promises of clean politics and reforms had clearly caught a popular mood, although overall the LDP triumphed because of its mastery of the arts of *kuroi kiri*, the black mist of election money. Conveniently, Kanemaru's fall from grace and the public outcry came just after the upper house election, not before it.

In the 1993 elections, Nihon Shinto continued to capture the imagination, thanks to its cheerful, young, well-turned out supporters, many of whom were dressed in neat green tee shirts. 'Even the colour looks fresh and spring-like, the promise of something new,' said an ever impressionable and hopeful Japanese voter in the Hyogo constituency of Yoriko Koike. A former television personality in her early forties, fluent in English and Arabic, she was typical of the new wave of Nihon Shinto candidates – young, bright, with professional qualifications.

Out in Okayama, south-west of Tokyo, Satsuki Eda was finding it tough being a leader of one of the smaller parties. Like many Japanese MPs – especially in the LDP, where seats were handed down from father to son – politics had become a reluctant family business for him. 'I never intended to get involved in politics,' he said. He graduated from Tokyo University in law, then unlike most of his bright university colleagues decided not to go into the mainstream bureaucracy, but to take the tough law exams to become a practising lawyer and judge. In 1977 his father, Saburo, died and the 36-year-old Judge Eda thought it was a matter of honour to take up the political banner.

His father was one of the old Socialist leaders, imprisoned by the militarists before the war, became secretary-general of the Socialists,* but was then booted out of the party by left-wing critics. He formed a small party, Shaminren (United Social Democratic Party), hoping ultimately to heal the Socialist divisions and reunite them as a single party. The fact that his father's reputation had been hurt by the Socialists, and the filial desire to attempt the *rapprochement* that his father had not had time to accomplish, were the factors leading Eda to enter the political lists.

Even after sixteen years in parliament and with a growing reputation for being honest and bright, Eda lacked political muscle. Several people on the streets of Okayama said similar things. 'That Mr Eda is one of the brightest people in politics, probably too bright, but he lacks a big party supporting him and that's no good for us,' said the driver of a local bus. In the LDP, where more than a third of the 276 outgoing MPs were sons or grandsons of MPs or cabinet members, the family inheritance brought three assets, *jiban*, a political machine, *kanban*, a signboard, meaning the family name, and *kaban*, a war chest; but for a small party man like Eda, there was only the family name.

For Eda, the election campaign was life constantly on the move, typically starting before dawn and going on until the early hours of the next morning. The candidate-leader moved rapidly from Tokyo and a rally with other like-minded reformers, including the Socialist leader Sadao Yamahana, to Tohoku in the north of the country to speak in support of a Shaminren candidate, then back to his constituency for a whirlwind of six speaking appointments in and around the sprawl of Okayama city – in a school, at a women's meeting, a stand-up appearance on the top of a bus in front of the main railway station, a visit to farmers' groups, and another two appearances in front of alfresco crowds doing their Sunday afternoon shopping. Then it was back to Tokyo for an all-important television appearance, to wave the party flag and tell the electorate that Eda had national views and ambitions too.

The defeat of the LDP had given him a vision of a new government formed round the unity of the opposition parties and stiffened by the arrival of Shinseito. 'The new alliance is just like a tiny bird breaking out

---

* Shakaito, the Socialist Party, for most of the post-war period the leading opposition party to the Liberal Democratic government, changed the English version of its name to Social Democratic Party of Japan, but kept the Japanese Shakaito. Since this was merely cosmetic and the policies did not change, I have continued to use Socialist as the party's name.

of its egg, and it can't even walk, let alone fly,' Eda said. 'People may say that they don't like the look of the fledgling creature. But we should understand that this is newly born and we should help it to grow and fly.'

Besides trying to be 'the glue encouraging the opposition alliance to stick together', Eda had formed a study group among 100 MPs of different parties, called Sirius, a name that was a tribute to his father's career. 'When he was in prison before the war, he tried to cheer up my mother by telling her to look for Sirius, the brightest star which always appeared in the darkest part of the sky,' Eda explained.

Life on the run was tough for Eda's family. 'When he leaves the house, I am not sure whether it will be one, two or three days before I see him again,' said his wife, Kyoko. She also played her part in his election campaign, helping to run the small office, working with women's groups and selling posters and telephone cards with Eda's picture on them. The smoothly smiling picture on the telephone cards and in the posters did not quite match the rushed look of the man on the hustings.

For women, the elections did not offer much joy. Mariko Mitsui was pessimistic about her chances as she stood at 7.30 a.m., dressed in a shocking-pink suit and white running shoes, outside a suburban Tokyo railway station, trying to interest the people going to work and school. Westerners who were worried about the formidable fine-tuned Japanese industrial machine might have calmed down had they witnessed this early morning display of economic muscle: children creeping like snails, unwillingly to school; *sararimen* (salarymen, as Japanese white-collar workers are usually called, using an adapted English word) puffing desperately on their cigarettes to wake themselves up as they wait for the Tokyo train.

Mitsui was having only a one in ten success rate even in persuading them to take her election leaflet. She and her young women attendants, all wearing shocking-pink tee shirts bearing the legend in English 'We can', yelled 'Good morning' to all and sundry, and bowed low like supercharged toy dolls, but few people looked up on their trudge for the sardine salaryman train. 'Less than 10 per cent of the candidates are women,' Mitsui grumbled, 'and this time there are a record number of women standing.'*

Mitsui was standing as an independent, having previously been a Socialist member of the Tokyo metropolitan assembly. She had resigned from the party, claiming sexual harassment by her colleagues. She was clearly struggling to organise her campaign, since it was fifteen minutes before an assistant arrived with a glossy white sash bearing her name, and a further ten minutes before she was brought a loudhailer.

---

* In fact, women were only 7.3 per cent of the candidates, with just two out of 285 LDP candidates and ten out of 142 Socialists.

The extra volume seemed to give her fresh inspiration and she launched into publicising her twin programme: 'With the right hand, equality for women; with the left, electoral reform.' Several times she used a few words of English, especially stressing the word 'clean'. She herself claimed to be so clean that the election campaign would leave her broke. She calculated it would cost 30 million yen to run, of which a third came from her savings, another third from supporters, and the rest would have to be borrowed. Mitsui lamented that, in spite of the Equal Opportunities Law, Japanese women were far from equal. According to a survey of 1,700 large companies, 87.6 per cent of the supposedly equal women had to make and serve tea for their male colleagues, 70 per cent of them had to clean the men's desks and only 33 per cent of women were allowed into policy meetings.

At a rally in the upmarket Tokyo area of Shibuya, three LDP heavyweight friends, chief cabinet secretary Yohei Kono, maverick author MP Shintaro Ishihara and heartthrob former finance minister Ryutaro Hashimoto, addressed a crowd for an hour under the broiling sun. They each clutched five microphones bundled together, like overgrown schoolboys greedy for lollipops. So inspiring was the address that one man went to sleep standing up, using a book to shield his head from the sun. Another complained that the electric power made it impossible for anyone to heckle or ask questions. But the women swooned when addressed by Hashimoto, who received sacks of fan mail from schoolgirls and grandmothers alike.

When the votes were counted in July 1993, the Japanese electorate had delivered a mixed verdict. There was a clear swing in the votes away from the Liberal Democrats, who emerged with 223 seats, far short of a majority in the 511-seat house. The problem was that the next best party was the Socialists, whose support also plummeted from 136 seats to 70. The main gainers were Hata and Ozawa's Shinseito, which picked up almost 60 seats, Hosokawa's Nihon Shinto, which took 35, and Sakigake, which came away with 15. After much argument over personalities and policies, a seven-party rainbow coalition was formed, comprising the Socialists, Shinseito, Nihon Shinto, Komeito (the Buddhist-backed Clean Government Party, which had 51 seats), Sakigake, the Democratic Socialists and Shaminren. Together they had 261 seats, or 38 more than the LDP. It was a barely working majority, especially given that the partners were prone to quarrel within their own ranks as well as with government colleagues.

As master of ceremonies of this motley collection, the power brokers decided on 'Mr Clean', Morihiro Hosokawa, who was 55 at the time of his appointment in August 1993. For his chief cabinet secretary he chose Masayoshi Takemura of Sakigake. Normally the chief cabinet secretary comes from the same faction as the prime minister, but at this stage Nihon Shinto and Sakigake planned to merge. Hata was appointed deputy prime minister and also foreign minister, and Shinseito took most of the other important jobs, like those of finance, defence, and trade and industry. Eda took one of the lower-ranking of the 21 cabinet jobs, as director-general of the science and technology agency. Ozawa stayed in the wings, remaining secretary-general of Shinseito, but with no government post.

The new prime minister, Hosokawa, seemed born to rule. 'He was born as a boss,' laughed Eda, pointing to Hosokawa's use of the word *tenmei*, meaning 'God's order' or more loosely 'fate', when he accepted the job of leading the coalition. Politics and ruling ran deep in Hosokawa's blood. He came from a line of warlords and feudal rulers of Kumamoto in southern Japan going back six centuries. One of his ancestors, Gracia (or Tama) Hosokawa (1563–1600), was the virtuous Christian samurai wife who provided the inspiration for Mariko in the James Clavell's novel *Shogun*. His maternal grandfather, Prince Fumimaro Konoe, was prime minister from 1937 to 1939 and again from 1940 until just before the attack on Pearl Harbor in 1941; he committed suicide by taking cyanide rather than face the victorious Allied powers in judgement after the war.

After being educated at the Jesuit Sophia University, Hosokawa joined *Asahi Shimbun*, one of the leading Japanese daily newspapers. Colleagues recalled that when he was posted to Kagoshima in the far south of Japan, Hosokawa used to receive messages from a butler telling him to beware of local girls. For all his recent foundation of Nihon Shinto, the new prime minister was no political neophyte. He had originally been an LDP politician, the youngest member of the upper house in 1971 at the age of 33, when he was in the Tanaka faction. Disillusioned with national politics, he then became governor of his home prefecture of Kumamoto for eight years from 1983. There he was renowned for his lordly bearing and his frequent attacks on national government for stamping on local initiative. He once grumbled that, in order to relocate a bus stop by 100 metres, he had to get permission from Tokyo.

These attacks on the central bureaucracy's interference greatly enhanced Hosokawa's local popularity. Thus strengthened, he was able to return to national politics, launch his own party dedicated to clean up politics, while preserving his reputation as a grand aristocratic figure, still frequently called 'Lord Hosokawa', even though Japan had abolished such titles decades before.

The rainbow government started off well, and not just in the high popularity ratings of Hosokawa and his cabinet, which were consistently in the high 70s and sometimes 80 per cent range. There was something new and clean and refreshing about the government, especially in its determination to reform the corrupt political system. Almost the first thing that Hosokawa did as prime minister was to apologise for Japan's wartime conduct and the suffering that its troops had inflicted on neighbouring Asian countries. He admitted that Japan had waged 'a war of aggression, a war that was wrong' and offered 'our profound remorse and apologies for the fact that past Japanese actions, including aggression and colonial rule, caused unbearable suffering and sorrow for so many people'. This was something totally unexpected. The LDP had long resisted making an apology for colonial or wartime rule, and had only begrudgingly recognised just before going out of office that the Imperial Army had forced 150,000 Korean, Chinese, Dutch, Filipina, Indonesian and Taiwanese women to serve as frontline prostitutes for its troops.

Next, Hosokawa's government quickly drew up reform bills, to cut out corruption both directly and also indirectly, by changing the electoral system from the complicated multi-constituency arrangements to a mixture of single-seat constituencies and proportional representation. Then the arguments began over precisely what the mixture should be.

Smaller parties feared that single-seat constituencies would benefit the big, rich and powerful parties. Some Socialists worried for their own seats. The LDP old guard saw their reign coming to an end and fomented opposition. Personality differences also began to emerge in the government ranks. These were exacerbated because the government also had to give attention to a sickly economy facing the uncomfortable repercussions of the bursting of the 'bubble' of the late 1980s, protracted recession and a rising yen. If members of the Hosokawa cabinet had several different opinions about the nuts and bolts of political reforms, they were also sometimes bitterly divided over how to tackle the recession and especially over what taxation measures to take.

It is not quite true to say that discussion and debate on the political reforms were long and drawn out, since the opposition LDP tactic was to stall and prevent discussion at all. The four reform bills eventually passed the lower house in November 1993, but then parliament came to a halt as the upper house, ironically not affected by the reforms, refused to discuss them. When they did finally come before the upper house, an unholy alliance of the LDP and Socialist renegades defeated them. One of the prominent Socialist dissidents, Masao Kunihiro, claimed that the changes were being sprung on members undemocratically and they had not had enough time to discuss them.

Defeat created a constitutional crisis. But the government did not act decisively by challenging the upper house decision. One excuse was that, if Hosokawa had called an election, it would have been held under the old rules. Instead he parleyed with the new LDP opposition leader, Yohei Kono, who had been elected to take over when Miyazawa had resigned to take responsibility for the election defeat. The reforms were further watered down and passed with LDP help just before the drop-dead deadline of the end of the parliamentary year.

Under the new laws, 300 MPs will be chosen through single-seat constituencies and the remaining 200 by proportional representation, with each person having a vote for the constituency and another for PR. Political parties will get public subsidies. Companies will be allowed to make donations to only one fund-raising body per politician, and corporate donations to individuals will be phased out after five years, although corporate gifts are allowed in various indirect ways. In all, the anticorruption measures may prove as watertight as a leaky colander. The bills passed, but the government's problems began anew.

The next crisis was the budget. There was already dissension in the ranks of the coalition when chief cabinet secretary Takemura took issue publicly with the finance minister over crucial tax questions. Bankers, businessmen and industrialists were pressing for tax cuts to jumpstart the sickly economy. Yoh Kurosawa, for example, the respected president of Industrial Bank of Japan, told Hosokawa in August 1993 that there should be an immediate reduction in income tax, to be offset three years later by an increase in the 3 per cent general consumption tax.

Given the government's preoccupation with the reform measures, the question of boosting the economy drifted and was not tackled until 1994. Ministry of Finance bureaucrats, concerned about falling revenue and an ageing population which would reduce revenues in the years to come, were anxious that any tax cuts should be matched by tax increases. The minister, Hirohisa Fujii, himself a former finance bureaucrat, was according to a cabinet colleague 'personally opposed to tax cuts, so the issue didn't get the attention it deserved'. The Socialists were unhappy with any increases in indirect taxation, which would fall hardest on poorly paid people, who would hardly benefit from any fall in income tax. The argument became public when chief cabinet secretary Takemura challenged the view that the increases in the consumption tax, reputedly to 7 per cent, should go hand in hand with the income tax reductions. For this he was swiftly rebuked by both Fujii and Ozawa.

The issue by then was not just tax rates or how the sickly economy should be boosted, but had become a much more serious one of friction within the coalition. Takemura, according to some of his sympathetic colleagues, was out of line when he made public his antipathy towards Ozawa. But it was perhaps understandable given that Ozawa had clearly played a clever political game and had manipulated himself, not the chief cabinet secretary, to be the main confidant of prime minister Hosokawa. Dates for a merger of the prime minister's Nihon Shinto with Takemura's Sakigake were postponed and then quietly dropped.

Eda had some sympathy with Ozawa, in spite of not being naturally sympathetic to Ozawa's machinations: 'Ozawa is almost the only person to put forward new ideas,' he told me at the time. 'The Socialists have been asked, pressed for their views to make a contribution, but time after time they have nothing to say, except criticise suggestions by someone else, mainly Ozawa.' Meanwhile, prime minister Hosokawa had clearly exhausted his reform ideas and had little to offer in terms of leadership initiative which might have maintained the government's claims to govern. 'Soon it will be seen that Hosokawa is the emperor without any clothes,' said a cabinet minister over a private dinner in early 1994, suggesting that Japan was simply waiting for a young innocent to come along and reveal the truth.

The challenge came in an unexpected way, with an attack on Hosokawa for alleged shady deals with the Sagawa group when he was governor of Kumamoto, and over shares in the privatising Nippon Telegraph and Telephone. Hosokawa denied any wrongdoing and insisted that 100 million yen he had borrowed from Sagawa for repairs to a family house had been paid back legitimately and on time. The NTT shares had been bought by his father-in-law.

But the case did not go away. The LDP again used the same simple but effective tactic of obstructing parliamentary business: the party refused to attend parliament to discuss the budget until Hosokawa promised to appear before it and answer questions about his alleged shady dealings. In typical Japanese style, parliament did not go ahead and meet without the LDP, but was at a standstill for weeks. It resumed only to pass a temporary emergency budget, so that money was still available for the conduct of government when the new financial year started on 1 April.

Then on 8 April, prime minister Hosokawa surprised everyone, including his own cabinet, by announcing that he was stepping down because he had discovered at 'the last minute' that there were irregularities in the handling of his personal financial affairs by an old friend. Apparently, interest payments on the money loaned had gone into Hosokawa's personal account and no tax had been paid. Thus 'Lord Clean' fell on his own sword and the government was left casting around for someone to replace him.

The account by Kyodo News Agency showed the consternation in the coalition immediately after Hosokawa's bombshell. There was ten minutes' silence before Socialist chairman Tomiichi Murayama and Keigo Ouchi told the prime minister they wanted time to discuss things together. After this, Kyodo recounted the following:

'Wataru Kubo, Socialist secretary-general to Ichiro Ozawa, co-leader of Shinseito: "WHAT SHOULD WE DO?"

'Ozawa: "Yes, WHAT SHOULD WE DO?"

'Kubo (to Yuichi Ichikawa, chief of Komeito, or Clean Government Party): "WHAT SHOULD WE DO?"

'Ichikawa: "It's useless to say WHAT SHOULD WE DO? And it looks like we can't ask him to take back the decision now that the prime minister has made his announcement."

'All: "Let's all meet at about 5 p.m. To decide WHAT to DO next." '

*   *   *

It took them three weeks of haggling before Hata took over in a most unusual way. For a time, Ozawa was trying to tempt Michio Watanabe to defect from the LDP, so that a new coalition might be able to detach the tiresome Socialists, but Watanabe saw that he did not have the support to swing it. Then the partners in the rainbow coalition patched up their differences and cobbled together a common platform on ticklish questions of tax reform, deregulation, defence and North Korea's recalcitrance on nuclear issues.

On Sunday, 24 April, Eda assumed that he would still hold the science and technology portfolio in a Hata cabinet showing few personality changes. The next day parliament chose Hata as prime minister with Socialist support. Then it became known that Ozawa had been working to form a group within the government, comprising his own party, Nihon Shinto, the Democratic Socialists and a few more LDP defectors. The group was somewhat provocatively called Kaishin, after a seventh-century coup designed to eliminate a group of powerful mandarins and restore the emperor of the day.

Outraged, the Socialists stamped out. Hata protested that even he had not known what was being planned by Ozawa. He urged the Socialists to rejoin, but in vain. The Socialists said they would support the government until the budget was passed. So Hata formed a minority government with only about 200 supporters, fewer than the LDP (depleted by defections but still numbering 206 members).

Hata lasted for precisely nine weeks, and his period in power was noted for two things. First, the budget was passed with income tax cuts valid for one year and comprehensive tax reforms shelved. Second, there was a storm over Japan's wartime activities. Immediately after taking over, Hata went to Europe during the 'Golden Week' holidays (so called because there are four holidays in the space of seven days). While he was absent, the justice minister, Shigeto Nagano, gave his views about the war, in which he had served as a junior officer. He declared that the 'Rape of Nanking' (in which 200,000–300,000 Chinese were slaughtered by the invading Japanese army) was 'a fabrication' and 'a hoax', and that Japan had acted during the war as a liberator of Asia from western colonialism, rather than as an aggressor.

The fact that Nagano was a late entry to politics and had been a career army officer who rose to be a general and head the Ground Self-Defence Forces made the interview all the more dramatic. He was first reprimanded via Hata then, ten days after the interview, he was sacked. But the damage was done. With the budget passed, the opposition drew up a no-confidence motion. The kaleidoscope then shook furiously as all players assessed their chances. When it was clear that the Socialists were not going to rejoin the coalition, Hata resigned at the start of July to avoid being defeated formally.

What followed was a week of pure farce, which should have been played in a pantomime theatre rather than on the stage of an important country with pretensions to great-power status. One key question was whom the Socialists would support. With 74 seats, they were the deciding block between the LDP and the remains of the coalition. They were wooed both by Hata and by the Liberal Democrats, and until the last minute it looked as if they would rejoin the coalition, perhaps with the prime minister's job.

But the other key question was what Ozawa was up to. He had been busy. Hours before the parliamentary vote was due, he scored a coup and tempted over former prime minister Toshiki Kaifu, who had been sitting as the leader of the reform camp in the LDP. Two other veteran LDP leaders, former prime minister Nakasone and ever-hopeful prime ministerial candidate Michio Watanabe, announced that they were backing Kaifu, although they would stay within the LDP. The Socialists then promptly did a quick about-turn and marched into the arms of the LDP, which had been their hated enemy for 38 years.

The LDP swallowed its pride and put forward 70-year-old Murayama, the Socialist chairman, nicknamed 'Grandpa', as its candidate for prime minister. 'What a choice, between a man who is only known for his collection of 600 polka dot ties [Kaifu] and another whose reputation is in his bushy eyebrows [Murayama],' scoffed a dissident Socialist. With defections on all sides, Murayama was chosen and announced a government that was one-third Socialist and two-thirds LDP, with Sakigake in support and its leader, Takemura, taking the finance minister's job. It was the second time that Japan had had three prime ministers in a calendar year, and Murayama was the fourth prime minister in thirteen months.

Surprisingly, having fought so long for their principles, given a touch of power the Socialists quickly abandoned the most cherished of them. In decades of opposition to the LDP, they had been sympathetic to the Soviet Union rather than to the USA, to such an extent that their opposition to the 1960 Security Treaty with the USA led to riots and the cancellation of a visit to Japan by then president Dwight Eisenhower. They had sided with Communist North Korea, and until recently refused to recognise South Korea as a sovereign state. Above all, they declared that article 9 of Japan's constitution made the Self-Defence Forces illegal.

That article, covering 'Renunciation of War', declared that: 'Aspiring sincerely to an international peace based on justice and order, the Japanese people forever renounce war as a sovereign right of the nation and the threat or use of force as a means of settling international disputes. (2) In order to accomplish the aim of the preceding paragraph, land, sea and air forces, as well as other war potential, will never be maintained. The right of belligerency of the state will not be recognised.'

Intrusion of ugly realities, starting with the Korean War, led to the establishment of the National Police Reserve in 1950, which then became the National Safety Forces in 1952 and the Self-Defence Forces in 1954, with Ground, Air and Maritime Self-Defence Forces under the command of the prime minister. But the Socialists did not recognise them as constitutional. Their intense hostility led the Socialists to oppose the 1992 Peacekeeping Law, allowing Japanese soldiers to join United Nations' peacekeeping operations, and on the final vote they did their infamous 'cow walk', delaying the approval by taking up to five minutes each to cast their ballot, as they meandered and ruminated to the rostrum.

Clearly, however, it was embarrassing to have commander-in-chief, prime minister Murayama doubting the legitimacy of the forces under his command. He duly removed the doubts and accepted the US Security Treaty, the Self-Defence Forces and, for good measure, the Hinomaru (Rising Sun) as Japan's national flag and the 'Kimigayo' as the country's anthem. The Socialists had long objected to the last two because of their association with the militarists of the 1930s.

Yohei Kono, LDP leader, deputy prime minister and foreign minister, one of a group of three close associates commonly known as 'Sanfrecce' (three arrows), declared that there were now three new arrows: himself, Murayama and the Sakigake leader, Takemura. 'When you bind three arrows together, they will not break,' declared Kono, promising that the alliance would be more than a nine-week wonder and would endure.

Some previous supporters of the coalition government declared that they would rather support the LDP–Socialist alliance. 'If the LDP can get rid of its really corrupt old guard, junk dangerous rightists like Nakasone, make some compromises with the Socialists, then it seems to me preferable to a coalition which is dominated by Ozawa,' said one prominent public figure. But Satsuki Eda, who had dissolved his Shaminren 'because it had served its purpose and we were chasing a big dream with a tiny organisation', and who had joined Hosokawa's Nihon Shinto as deputy leader, put the opposite view: 'For years the Socialists opposed the LDP in public, while joining hands under the table. Now they have proved they are the old unreformed guard.' The coalition, he asserted, comprised 'the reformers'.

The games continued. The unlikely coalition government of old enemies supervised the passage of the final touches of the political reforms, involving new constituency boundaries. Under the reformed system, votes in rural areas will be worth only twice the value of urban ones, showing that the old rural interests have had their influence trimmed but not removed. The coalition also agreed that income tax reductions passed for a single year earlier in 1994 would continue, and to pay for them the consumption tax would be raised from 3 to 5 per cent in April 1997. There were grumbles from the Finance Ministry that this would not be sufficient. However, the Socialists were already unhappy that the income tax reductions would benefit middle-income and rich people, whereas any rise in consumption tax would immediately hurt the poor.

More worrying to the cause of clean politics, in September 1994 former chief cabinet secretary Takao Fujinami was found not guilty in the Tokyo district court of accepting bribes from Recruit Cosmos as part of the scandal of 1989. The defence accepted that Fujinami received 20 million yen from Recruit as well as buying shares in the Recruit affiliate before their listing at well below market prices, but the court naively claimed that 'there remains doubt that the defendant knew that the money offered was a bribe'. Later a Komeito (Clean Government) MP was convicted of similar charges, but escaped a prison term. In all, the Recruit case was wrapped up, with only Ezoe himself being sentenced to prison and none of the politicians having to suffer imprisonment for having benefited from his favours.

Ozawa was busy behind the scenes, and by December 1994 he had managed to persuade most of the big opposition parties apart from the Communists to combine into one. In all, nine parties came together with 179 members of the lower house, 21 fewer than the LDP. With much razzmatazz and showmanship, the public was invited to give a name to the new party. Some imaginative ideas came in, including 'Ozawa's Black Party', but such scurrilous suggestions were rejected by a distinguished panel, including a university professor, music composer and young woman *tarento* (talent) who had been photographed topless and had had a celebrated affair with another Japanese television celebrity. They whittled a list of several thousand names down to five, from which the party itself voted to choose Shinshinto as its name.

There was a minor drama in selecting the English translation for the party's name, which is comprised of three kanji or Chinese characters. The first 'shin' is the character for 'new'. The second 'shin' is written differently and means 'progressive', and 'to' is the character for 'party', so the initial English name was new Progressive Party. But after a couple of hours the leaders decided that this did not sound radical enough, so they revised the English first to New Frontiers Party, then to new Frontier Party (dropping the plural), supposed to carry echoes of John F. Kennedy's new policies in the USA.

As president of the new party, its members elected Kaifu over Hata. Ozawa was chosen unopposed as Shinshinto's secretary-general. The urge to form the new party was partly so that the opposition could contest the next election efficiently. Money politics was also involved because of public subsidies of 30.5 billion yen on offer to the parties according to their popularity, measured by lower house seats and financial turnover. Together the LDP and Socialists or the jumbo opposition might be able to collar 15 billion yen, whereas a party the size of Nihon Shinto with a shoestring budget would get only 200 million yen or so.

Neither the government nor the opposition looked fully comfortable with its new bulging membership. Arguments continued especially in the Socialist ranks, with dissent being sparked by the right 'democratic' wing of the party. Former leader Sadao Yamahana, who had been minister responsible for reforms in the Hosokawa government, and Wataru Kubo, secretary-general and number two in the party, urged the creation of a new party or the Socialists would lose their identity inside the coalition, wither and die. 'The Socialist Party is now making big strides towards the formation of a new party, or break-up,' declared Kubo. Ironically, left-wing members of the party resented this as an attack on leader Murayama, and there was the prospect of a Socialist split.

But Shinshinto also had its tensions. Not every prominent opposition leader joined it. Keigo Ouchi, former chairman of the Democratic Social-ists, refused, saying that there was a lack of agreement over political philosophy and fundamental policy matters. He was also unhappy about the influence of the lay Buddhist Soka Gakkai movement within Shin-shinto. Soka Gakkai claims 17 million members and provided the funding base for Komeito, which joined Shinshinto. Ouchi claimed that 'The new party is destined to be a party of Soka Gakkai.'

In part this was a personal worry because Ouchi was supported by a rival Buddhist group, but he was also reflecting a more widely held fear of the powerful financial muscle of Soka Gakkai and its disciplined body of supporters. A vice president of the Buddhist group, Hiroshi Nishiguchi, admitted to bigger ambitions: 'Since Komeito is relatively small, it has been limited in what it could accomplish. In this sense, the possibility of achieving our own goals will increase' within Shinshinto.

Another group of members of Shinshinto were unhappy about the all-pervasive influence of Ichiro Ozawa. They insisted on elections for the leadership, rather than let the choice be made in the smoke-filled back rooms as Ozawa wanted. The final choice of top leaders offered a curious *déjà vu*, since Kaifu was LDP prime minister and Ozawa the party secretary-general back at the start of the 1990s, until Ozawa resigned for bungling the Tokyo gubernatorial election and Kaifu fell for advocating a political clean-up.

Kaifu claimed that he had joined the opposition rather than stay with the LDP because 'The LDP lost all the honour of the past by choosing a prime minister from the Socialist Party. It is my responsibility, as the one who started reform, to say this was wrong.' In spite of leaving, however, when he made a courtesy call to LDP headquarters after being chosen as Shinshinto leader, he demanded that his picture, dropped from the halls of past LDP presidents, should be restored to its rightful place.

Clearly there had been something of a falling out between Hata and Ozawa, formerly close colleagues-in-arms in breaking from the LDP, since Ozawa backed Kaifu and resented the entry to the lists of Hata for Shinshinto leadership. Party insiders said the rift started when Hata allowed himself to be put forward for prime minister in April, 'when Ozawa was still negotiating with Watanabe, and Hata did not ask Ozawa, "Mother, may I?"' Goodnaturedly, Hata in December hid any feelings of hostility that Ozawa had backed Kaifu. 'There may be an instance, when arriving at different paths, that I may take a different route. But I bet we'd still go drinking together.' He added that he would 'go hand-in-hand with the devil' for the sake of the country, before quickly claiming, 'I'm not necessarily calling Ozawa a devil.'

Although Shinshinto presented itself as a new party dedicated to reform, the top jobs were doled out according to the old party strengths. Ozawa and his lieutenants did well, but Hosokawa and Nihon Shinto were visible by their absence. Eda, joining his third political party in a year, was given responsibility for the party's public relations. He claimed that this was an era of 'new politics and the new politics can't be led by old parties'.

What happens now is in the unpredictable hands of the electorate, who will have to vote under a new system. Smaller constituencies, with only one person representing them, may perk up interest in the electoral process and who represents people, and in due course may make policy rather than pork what really matters in casting a ballot. Last time round, in summer 1993, the abiding impression was that voters were fed up with corruption, but felt they count not directly influence politics.

In Iwate, Ozawa's constituency, the fishermen complained about the din politicians were making: 'The ayu [Japanese river trout] are not coming like they should,' chuntered one fisherman. 'The noise must have disturbed them. Blasted politicians, ruining everything.' In Nakano in outer Tokyo, a newspaper seller complained, ' A quarter of a million people pass by our stall every day, so it is a major target for the political campaigners. They make such a noise with their electrical microphones that my ears are still ringing when I go home at night.' In the countryside, a farmer grumbled, 'All politicians are out to line their own pockets. All the politicians make promises, but they are never interested in keeping them.' Author Shusaku Endo complained, 'I find it very strange that I pay more tax than the politicians who live so well; there is something wrong there, somewhere.'

One problem is that it may be a new electoral system, but it is the same old political faces behind it. One view by Takashi Inoguchi, a professor of political science at Tokyo University, was that Japan had become a 'karaoke'* democracy: anyone can participate, and that stirs the feeling that anyone can become prime minister ... To enable anyone to present at least a so-so performance as prime minister, the bureaucracy appears to

---

* *Karaoke* literally means 'empty orchestra'.

be waiting in the wings to provide the background music.'

In one respect, the creation of the opposition jumbo party meant that instead of one LDP conglomerate party there were two, both containing awkward bedfellows from Left and Right. The reform credentials of LDP leader Yohei Kono are at least as good as most Shinshinto members, who originally came from the LDP. On the other hand, Miti minister Hashimoto played with fire in October 1994 by declaring that it was a question of 'delicate definition' whether Japan was guilty of aggression against its Asian neighbours. It showed that neither big party could claim a monopoly of right-wing apologists for wartime Japan.

In spite of the protests of government and opposition that they were pro-reform, there were signs that money politics was making a comeback. Both major parties began reaching out again for corporate donations, and banks, trading companies, steelmakers and car companies were planning to give money to the LDP and Shinshinto. Political sources said that no money would be given to the Socialists because they had not asked for any. To get matters into perspective, in 1992 corporate donations to political parties came to 332 billion yen – or ten times the public funds available under the reforms.

In another respect, Japanese politics almost boiled down to Ozawa v. the rest. To his credit, Ozawa did have ideas and had set out his political stall in a best-selling book called *Nihon Kaizo Keikaku.** In this he advocates the need for Japan to become a 'normal' nation. He complains that Japan accounts for 16 per cent of the world's gross national product, second only to the USA, so that 'Japan's slightest move has an impact that reaches every corner of the globe'; but Japanese politics have been concerned only with sharing out the spoils of economic growth. He rails against consensus politics, which, he claims, have prevented Japan from growing up politically. Ozawa backed up Eda's contention that the LDP and the opposition were part of the same political game. Writing before the 1993 election, he asserted, 'both the LDP and the opposition preferred to stay in their comfortable tubs rather than get out of the water to change baths and risk catching a cold'.

Ozawa urged sweeping reform, envisaging the creation of a two-party system, in which power actually changes hands from time to time; enhanced powers for the prime minister; and a parliament which actually works, takes decisions and governs the country in co-operation with a bureaucracy that is there to serve and be co-ordinated by politicians, rather than dominating them. Abroad, he is full of admiration for the American president, who can actually take decisions.

* Published in English in 1994 as *Blueprint for a New Japan: The Rethinking of a Nation*, the book was important enough for the US Central Intelligence Agency to translate privately.

He opens his book with a description of the vastness of the Grand Canyon, with its 'truly awesome' 1,200-metre depth, 'more than four times the 70-storey height of Japan's tallest building. To my surprise, I didn't see any fences. Multitudes of tourists come to the park annually, but no fences!' Ozawa marvelled, 'I saw a young couple playing on one of the great boulders but no park official was telling them to be careful. There wasn't even a sign to that effect. In Japan, there would be fences, "No Entry" signs, and park attendants who'd come running to warn people away.' This, Ozawa thought, demonstrated American freedom and expectations of self-responsibility.

Ozawa's prescription would have the Self-Defence Forces recognised as a proper army and Japan playing its part in international peacekeeping operations. Ozawa was strongly affected by the Gulf War, following the Iraqi invasion of Kuwait. As secretary-general of the ruling LDP on the day of the invasion, he rushed to the prime minister's residence, but found there was nobody on duty, an incident which caused him to explode with fury. Only after many requests and much time did Japan put together a huge $13 billion contribution to pay for the western war effort, but not a single soldier was involved. Because of this, he laments, Japan failed to get credit for what was a considerable financial involvement.

Ozawa's history, as well as his personality, causes not only opponents but rational Japanese to fear him, not least because he was the disciple of Kakuei Tanaka and chosen heir of crooked Kanemaru. Indeed, allegations of corruption against Ozawa himself have never satisfactorily been answered. He has little to say about the damaging effects of corruption in his book, although his supporters would argue that the reformed system, with power concentrated in party headquarters rather than around factional barons, will make the political system both less corrupt and more accountable.

What is surprising in Ozawa's conduct is that, for a man who wants responsible leadership, his own track record is of continuously undermining people from behind the scenes. He did it when as LDP secretary-general he put up his own candidate to run against the party choice for governor of Tokyo. During the coalition government, he machinated furiously both to undermine the Socialists and to cause defections from the LDP, and he did not particularly care who had to pay the price – even if it was Hata, who had to sacrifice the prime minister's job. In one memorable off-the-cuff remark, Ozawa turned on critics attacking his lack of principle. 'I can sleep with any woman I choose,' he said in one version; 'Whom I sleep with is my business alone' was another.

Ozawa played this leading role without any formal – or accountable – position in the government. Hata openly admitted that he was the actor and Ozawa was the playwright. The harshest critics contend that Ozawa is principally motivated by spite towards the LDP for not allowing him to take over as Kanemaru's crown prince. Satsuki Eda, however, gives Ozawa credit for being a genuine reformer, and adds in his defence, 'Very often he is blamed for too many things; he is painted worse than he is.'

Leaving aside these important personal and personality questions, there are also plenty of Japanese who dispute Ozawa's key aims, not just his methods. As a central point, to many Japanese article 9 is sacred, even a saving grace for the first, and so far the only, country to have suffered nuclear bombing. It is a sacred pledge that Japan would show a new way, show other countries that a world without war is a worthwhile deal. Realists, of course, claim that this is a hopeless illusion in a hard world.

There's no doubt that the first essential for Japan becoming Ozawa's 'normal nation' is that article 9 should be removed, that Japan should have proper armed forces able to participate in UN peacekeeping forces, not just peacekeeping operations. The distinction may look insignificant, but it is important: under the Peacekeeping Law of 1992, Japanese troops can join UN operations, but not those where they are liable to take part in military operations or shooting. For example Cambodia was acceptable, but Bosnia, still less the Gulf War, would not be.

The question of whether the US Security Ttreaty makes Japan less than a 'normal nation' is complicated by history. Any attempt to scrap that treaty would still raise all sorts of questions in neighbouring Asia, especially if Ozawa's colleague Nagano is still sitting as an MP, and presumably reflecting not only a strand in influential political opinion, but also the view of the armed forces which he once commanded. It is also important to repeat that Ozawa's methods have been effectively to undermine the constitution by subterfuge, rather than facing the issue, having a debate and letting the Japanese people have their say.

Ozawa makes much of the 'tyranny of the minority', and claims that Japan's emphasis on consensus prevents decisions from being taken swiftly enough, and sometimes from being taken at all. This has sometimes been true, but other modern states also have reason to worry about the tyranny of the majority, especially when it is a tyranny supported only by an election result of four or five years previously. British governments do not hesitate to ram through legislation supported only by 'the mandate' of having put the measure in the previous election manifesto. The quality of debate is often poor, especially when the whips employ their powers to speed up legislation; the flaws, loopholes and unintended consequences are apparent only much later.

Many of Ozawa's proposals for allowing more initiative, restoring political control and reforming the system generally, would be widely applauded, but they are almost all *political*, and therefore should be debated and approved before being passed. He has an unfortunate tendency autocratically to assert his own opinions: for example, he wrote in his book that schoolteachers are providing an essential service and therefore should be forbidden by law ever to strike.

And in the end, for all his claims that the politicians must have control over the bureaucracy, Ozawa in practice has relied heavily on the bureaucrats. Shijuro Ogata, former deputy president of Bank of Japan and of Japan Development Bank (who is married to UN High Commissioner for Refugees, Sadako Ogata), commented that 'Unfortunately too many of Japan's politicians are on-riders tending to accept the advice of bureaucrats without question, when what Japan needs is politicians who are prepared to override their bureaucrats' advice.' A combination of autocratic bureaucrats and autocratic politicians would not only be a disaster for Japan, but could threaten the rest of the world. The good thing to emerge is that the Japanese people will now have a better chance of making their voices heard. It is to be hoped that they will use them.

Eda is optimistic: 'The period of the LDP–Socialist confrontation was a reflection of the cold war. Now the cold war is over, both parties should dissolve.' Rare among Japanese politicians, Eda is thoughtful, concerned about ideas and has a few principles of his own. 'If I forget the importance of the improvement of citizens' daily life, not only in the material sense, but also in real satisfaction of mind, it would be a waste of time for me to stay in politics.' Unfortunately, so far few other prominent figures have been prepared to stand up for the same views, and the old guard of both Left and Right regard Eda as a wimp for having such ideals.

12

Conclusion:
Japan, Victim of its Own Delusions

Almost 50 years ago, at 8.15 a.m. on 6 August 1945, the Enola Gay, a B-29 Superfortress aircraft in US military colours, dropped a single bomb on the port city of Hiroshima, south-west of Tokyo. This first atomic weapon of war in an instant created the infamous mushroom cloud of fire, smoke and ash – the 'black rain' of radiation and devastation which killed about 200,000 people, wiped out the centre of the city, brought Japan to the brink of defeat, and scarred the country's history so that even today its own victimised image prevents Japan from taking its rightful place as one of the leaders and shapers of the world of the twenty-first century. Unless Japan can come to grips with its past and accept its own responsibilities, the rest of the world will be poorer, but Japan will suffer most. The attempts of successive governments in Tokyo to whitewash the country's colonial past stir up anger in a wide area of Asia. More damaging, Japan's pretence to be an innocent victim of the war means that it cannot see itself as the world does, and cannot understand the resentment, hurt and suspicion that lingers. In the year of the fiftieth anniversary of defeat, it is vital for Japan – for its own sake – to understand, apologise and go forward.

This glimpse at the powerhouses of Japan's modern miracle reveals that in sheer industrial muscle many of the big Japanese companies have shown the rest of the world a superior way to produce goods, from the everyday to the hi-tech. Toyota rescued the motor industry from the mere drudgery of the assembly line and became a by-word for refined, quality production techniques. Working on the assembly line is still hard, but thoughtful production processes have tried to take away much of the backbreaking effort and to give workers an incentive as part of the team. Where would the world have been if driven by General Motors and Ford – which belatedly have had to copy the lean techniques of Toyota and the other Japanese manufacturers? Procedures which the Japanese pioneered, such as just-in-time production, *kanban* and *kaizen*, have now become part of the language not just of the motor industry, but of modern management methods.

In electronics and consumer goods industries, the Japanese have also set new world standards. It is hardly possible to buy quality consumer electronics goods anywhere that do not have a Japanese label. Americans are virtually out of it. Philips of the Netherlands lags laps behind, and only a few other highly specialist niche players remain from Europe. The main challenge to Japan's dominance of consumer electronics comes from its neighbouring South Koreans, who alone have the vision, the audacity, the determination and commitment to the long-term funding to make the chase.

Of course, it is often objected that the Japanese are merely copycats and have stolen other people's ideas – as it used to be said of the Americans who developed British ideas for new cutting edge products like radar and the jet engine. But, as the British found out, unless you can transform an idea into a commercially viable product, you cannot make the money to provide the seed capital for your next new idea. Admittedly, the Japanese have had some expensive learning experiences, such as the H-II rocket, which is proving twice as expensive in putting satellites into orbit as its European competitor's version; the 'flying' Maglev train, which may never be commercially viable; and the nuclear-powered merchant ship whose reactor sprang a leak on its maiden voyage, leaving a hole to be plugged with boiled rice. But they are working hard to show how creative and inventive they are.

'Flash' memories, the next generation of semiconductor products, originated in Japan, as did the commercial application of liquid crystal displays, where Intel, the leading semiconductor maker, had to team up with Sharp of Japan in order to get back into the business. In Osaka Bay in April 1994, the prototype of a new generation cargo ship, capable of travelling twice as fast as existing vessels at speeds of up to 50 knots, successfully completed its trials. Meanwhile, all sorts of quirky, crazy inventions are being developed, such as shirts, hats, socks and underwear that not only do not need ironing, but can 'remember' and mould themselves to the shape of their wearer; the world's first building 1,000 metres (3,400 feet) high, possibly able to house 500,000 people; a suitcase that can be turned instantly into a crude version of a motor car; 'beauty toilets' that can analyse and report on the state of your health; on-line karaoke machines with a choice of 14,000 tracks at the press of a button; artificial merkins; and – for something completely different, the ultimate in recycling – a burger that is made from human sewage (though it has not yet been passed fit for consumption).

The growth of Japan's industry is something of a miraculous success, remembering the utter devastation of war. Robert Oppenheimer, often called 'the father of the atomic bomb', recalled the Sanscrit *Bhagavad-Gita* when he saw the test of the bomb in the desert at Los Alamos – 'I am become Death, the shatterer of worlds.' Hiroshima was selected as target partly because it was the home of important military installations, but also partly because it was one of the few major cities not already laid waste by fire bombs. A look at the comparative progress of the USA and Europe, the victors of the Second World War, merely shows the measure of Japan's achievement.

The success is tinged with lingering doubts about some of the ways it was achieved. After all, the Tokyo bureaucrats did twist the rules to make sure that foreigners could not intrude into their cherished industrial preserves, until their own companies were fully matured and making a success of exporting. But sympathy for the foreign grumblers must be limited. To take motor cars as the obvious contentious example of complaints, recent strident American demands for a greater share of the car and auto parts market have smacked of extremely special pleading and very much of an attempt to produce managed trade, the very antithesis of an open and free international market.

The Japanese car makers, led by the adventurous Honda, with the others following cautiously after Toyota's early fanfare and failure to sell in the USA in the 1950s, earned their share of the US market through their pioneering, painstaking efforts to understand what drives the American car buyer, and through their great expenditure in setting up their own distribution systems, all on top of producing the right kind of cars at the right kind of prices for the American pocket. The Americans had laughed at the Japanese for years, but Honda, Nissan and Toyota did their homework and produced the cars that silenced the scorn of the US 'big three' car makers in the most effective way.

The Japanese can legitimately ask if any of the American companies even tried to make the same kind of effort or spend the same kind of money in investigating the Japanese market. Ford bought 24.5 per cent of Mazda, one of the sicklier Japanese car makers, but until 1994 did not have the wit to use this alliance to try to tap into Mazda's dealership network. The dealership system is very much the clue to success in the Japanese market (just as building a strong dealership network was vital to the Japanese infiltration of the American market). Another small but significant example of US demands that the trade and economic playing fields should all be level, but levelled to American standards, is the refusal of the big American makers until 1993 to offer cars to Japan with the steering wheel on the right. An aggrieved Japanese manager said, 'They did not even notice that we drive on the left-hand side of the road and prefer cars with the steering column on the right, that's how much they take us for granted.'

Western companies in general and Americans in particular can also be criticised for allowing themselves to be deflected from the main task of manufacturing quality products. Pressures from a stock market greedy for instant gratification played an important part. So too did the rise of accountants – 'bean counters', as they have rudely been called – to leading management positions. Keeping proper control of costs is, of course, a vital aspect of good management – and Japanese companies in the service and construction sectors could have done with western-trained accountants to trim their excesses and make them leaner and more efficient, if not less prone to the corrupting influence of cosy relationships with politicians. But in some sectors of US and Western industry, bean counting became obsessive and led to the neglect of the quality and marketability of the product.

In other sectors, megalomaniac managers got their heads, seeking swift expansion through takeovers and mergers, building castles of commerce on shaky foundations, and hang the product. This worse fault, the quest for bigness, was the undoing of the homegrown British motor car industry when Donald Stokes, later ennobled as Lord Stokes for his efforts, in the 1970s put together a monster combining almost all the mass production car and lorry makers not foreign owned. Bit by bit, the giant crumbled until the last piece, the Rover Car Company, was bought by BMW of Germany in 1994.

Japanese have not been exempt from the temptation to worship money. Indeed, the bubble economy of the late 1980s was inflated by the quest for *zaiteku*, or financial hi-tech engineering, as companies tried new kinds of fund and played and the ever-booming stock market, or bought into land developments that were – on paper – making hundreds of millions of yen each day before anything was built. When the bubble burst, some well-known companies were badly burned, and the biggest banks are still counting the cost in write-offs. But at least in the case of the Japanese industrial giants, zaiteku was the icing on the cake, not the cake itself. Toyota, Toshiba and Matsushita never let the financial whiz-kids control the company, or allowed their production excellence to be threatened.

In another tribute to the industrial miracle, some British economists and trade unions were by the early 1990s singing the praises of the Japanese for rescuing what was left of British industry. Britain has won the biggest share of growing Japanese investment into Europe, thus helping to preserve skills and create new jobs, as Matsushita, NEC, Nissan, Sony, Toshiba, Toyota and other Japanese household names set up considerable factories in the UK, and Fujitsu even took over the computer maker ICL. Not quite in parentheses, it is worth asking whether Japan would contemplate doing what the UK has effectively done in allowing foreign interests to take over huge chunks of its manufacturing industry.

These questions became most obvious in the motor car industry when the government of John Major ignored protests and refused to stop the German company BMW from buying Rover, the last major British-owned auto manufacturer. Critics claimed that this meant that key decisions concerning investment and research and development in the British car-making industry were now being taken in Bavaria, BMW's headquarters, Tokyo (for Honda and Nissan) or Toyoda City. If it came to the crunch, these critics challenged, would Bavaria allow BMW to build a valuable new car plant or switch key research to be done outside Bavaria, let alone outside Germany?

Honda Motor Company president Nobuhiko Kawamoto made it plain that Japan would not have permitted such hollowing out of its industry in a key area. Admittedly, he had a vested interest. Honda had been a partner of Rover for fifteen years and had played a big role in revitalising the company both with its technology and with its management techniques. By 1994 Honda and Rover had 20 per cent cross-shareholdings in each other's operations. So when it was announced that BMW was buying Rover, Honda's outrage was barely concealed. Honda and Rover, the Japanese manufacturer said, had enjoyed special 'synergy', indeed 'a symbiotic relationship, Honda benefiting from Rover's tradition in British car manufacturing and Rover from Honda's technical, engineering and design skills'. Kawamoto explained that he was disappointed not only on Honda's behalf, but also for Britain. He pointedly said that Honda had been given a chance to buy the whole of Rover, but had declined, believing that it was not right to buy the country's last mass production company. It had instead offered to increase its stake up to a maximum of 47.5 per cent (which, of course, would have been much cheaper for Honda).

'Car manufacturing has a very big social responsibility in terms of employment and resources, not just towards the current generation but towards future generations as well,' claimed Kawamoto to the *Financial Times* on 7 February 1994. Speaking with the passion of a jilted lover, he added, 'It is not possible to manage a car manufacturer without taking that into consideration. That is our belief. Rover was the last original UK car company. I think it is acceptable to take a 100 per cent stake in a company if there are a lot of other car companies and if it is not the last one to be controlled by the people of that country and if doing so does not have such a crucial impact on the country's car industry. Because Rover was the last, and the only, car company that is British, we judged that it should be left British. This is not out of sympathy. We think it is too simple to judge everything in terms of value for shareholders and customers alone.'

The Honda president pleaded that the nationality of capital was vitally important, and not something that could be left to markets to decide. 'The British view is that it is not necessary to be concerned about the nationality of capital ... What I don't understand is, if you take the case of Japan, industry is the only way to survive. I wonder how the British people expect to make a living in future. The money game is fine and there must be a business logic to it all, but how do people expect to make a living in future? I would like to know.' A Japanese economist claimed that 'especially in the light of the sale of Rover, it is evident that the really key decisions on the future of Britain's economy are now taken by the foreigners who are responsible for much of the investment, by the unpredictable financial markets in the City of London and by tourists whose spending contributes significantly to earnings and jobs. Japan would never permit its economy to be so vulnerable to outside forces beyond its control.' But the test of Japan's commitment to its own industry may now be coming.

One of the glaring failures of the modern Japanese miracle is the very flip side of the success: it has been such a success that it has come under fire from the rest of the world, with an increasing number of countries protesting that Japan is not a fair trader, that its markets are protected and closed to foreign competition. Remarks of the US administration also helped to increase the strength of the yen, which has put most of Japan's big manufacturing companies under great pressure.

The stage is now set for a fascinating but potentially dangerous struggle, which could lead to world trade and economic war. The USA under president Bill Clinton and his aggressive team, with trade representative Mickey Kantor noticeably in the vanguard, have been playing a dangerous game, stepping up the hectoring decibels. They claim that Japan's markets are closed and should be opened up, with the openness to be determined by targeting some particularly closed areas and demanding barriers be removed through performance criteria. Washington honed in on cars and car parts, telecommunications, medical equipment and insurance. With the Republicans in control of the Congress from 1995, the chances are that the White House and Congress will vie with each other in suggesting ways of opening Japan up.

The Japanese have thrown their own mud back at the USA, claiming that in the kingdom of unfair trading practices, the Americans are the real emperors and empire-builders. Washington's trade practices, retorted the Ministry of International Trade and Industry in its first world trade report card in 1992, are full of unilateral actions infringing not just the rules but the spirit of international fair play. It awarded the USA nine black marks out of a possible ten, more than Europe, which got only six, and Hong Kong, a single one for failing to protect intellectual property.

Lest anyone should think he is a wimp or that this is just a childish game of name calling, Clinton in March 1994 called up a big gun by reviving the Super 301 provisions of the Omnibus Trade Act, allowing the USA to take a battery of retaliatory actions against countries deemed to be offending. Worse, the USA threatened to fire the Super 301 artillery against Japan if it did not take urgent action to open its markets. Miti pointed out that Super 301 itself is 'against the letter and the spirit of the Gatt [General Agreement on Tariffs and Trade] and Uruguay Round accords'.

In free trade terms, these exchanges amount to playing with fire. Supporters and opponents of Japan traded accusations freely. Miti pointed out that its average tariff rates on manufactured and mining goods are lower than anyone else's (2.2 per cent on average, against 5.4 per cent for the USA and 5.7 per cent for the European Union), and that few items are subject to quotas. The USA responded that customs and practices, such as hidden rules, regulations, definitions, inspections, health checks, certification requirements and corporate ties of Japan Inc., as well as the plain hostility of Japanese to foreigners and their goods, all made Japan impossible.

As an example of the acrimony and the fruitlessness of some of the exchanges, Glen Fukushima, former director for Japanese affairs in the Office of the US Trade Representative, recounted a conversation with a leading Japanese businessman, who, he said, claimed: 'I will concede to you that the US market is much more open than the Japanese market. The Japanese market is much more closed. But your market is open *not* [italics in the original] because we Japanese asked you to have it open; it's open because you Americans *like* it that way – it's your way of life. So don't blame *us* for taking advantage of your openness. If you don't like us selling so much into your market and destroying your producers, you should *do* something about it!' And Fukushima added darkly, 'A valid point. And one being pondered by a growing number of Americans.'*

There are philosophical as well as practical problems over the booming Japanese trade and current account surpluses. One question is whether the surpluses, which reached $142 billion for trade and $131 billion on the current account in the fiscal year ending in March 1994, are a mark of success or of failure. In the view of some American commentators, there is nothing particularly virtuous in running a trade surplus, since it means that you are sacrificing goods that you have produced to the importing country, and in return are getting money in the bank; the importer gets goods which it would not otherwise be able to afford.

Such a view perhaps neatly sums up different prevailing attitudes in the USA and Japan: in the USA, there is rejoicing at the thought of getting something for nothing; in Japan, economic managers and businesspeople are more concerned with the underlying strength of the economy and the industrial superiority that the trade surplus proves. By the early 1990s, as its deficit on trade with Japan alone soared to $60 billion a year, however, even the USA had realised that there was a price to pay in the hollowing out of its industry and the consequent loss of jobs. Hence it was fighting back.

Paradoxically, the failure on Japan's part is greater. Indeed, by 1995 it added up to a monumental case of international stupidity, which reflects on the structural faults of both the bureaucratic and political systems, and

* Fukushima's column in *Tokyo Business Today*, May 1992.

which demands urgent reforms. In the first case, Tokyo was the butt of international hostility that potentially threatened not just trade between Japan and the USA, but the very principles of the international trading system. Sir Leon Brittan, the European trade supremo, described Clinton's revival of Super 301 as 'disappointing'. Peter Sutherland, head of Gatt and then of its successor, the World Trade Organisation, said it was 'misguided and dangerous'. In spite of Washington's claims to the contrary, the new US path amounted to attempts to impose managed trade. More damaging, it opened the door for conducting international trade by the principles of bullying.

The British trade minister, Richard Needham, more or less conceded the point when he was asked about the contrasting approaches of the Americans, and the British and other Europeans, over Scotch whisky and other liquors whose sales in Japan are subjected to higher duties than are faced by competing domestic spirits. The foreign liquor makers won a ruling by an international trade panel in the 1980s, but as of 1994 the Japanese had only partially reduced the difference in duty rates. Needham admitted that when you are a big power, like the USA, you can use different negotiating methods. 'You can't play the part of the bully unless you are the bigger guy. If you do, you are likely to end up on your back. Needham was in Japan trying the friendly approach to boost British exports. He claimed success, in that British sales to Japan had risen to a record £2.65 billion in 1993. But perhaps the measure of the friendly approach is that Japan's trade surplus with the UK had also risen to a record of almost £6 billion.

There were signs that the bullying US policy was having its effects. The British minister complained on behalf of Rolls-Royce that the British aero-engine maker had won orders all round the world, but not a single one in Japan for twenty years. 'No matter whether we have the best price or technology,' he grumbled, the 'big ticket orders' have all gone to the USA. Part of the reason may be that the American engine makers have paid more attention to the lucrative Japanese market – Pratt and Whitney has a team more or less permanently attached to Japan Airlines, so that they are considered part of the JAL family. But another explanation is that the Japanese have from time to time found it an easy way to assuage American grumbles by placing big ticket aircraft orders.

More striking was the way that trade representative Kantor took up the specific case of Motorola for better access to the Japanese mobile telephone market. After arguing for weeks that Motorola had to stand on its own feet in a competitive market, Japan gave in on the eve of the summit meeting between Hosokawa and Clinton to sweeten Motorola's access. Professor Jagdish Bhagwati of Columbia University described the concession: 'Japan ended the dispute by bribing Motorola with investment outlays while affirming the dispute's uniqueness and reiterating the policy

USA. The prospects of a fall in the Japanese surplus with the US are more remote.

It would be the most savage irony if the most productive and efficient part of Japan's economy, its competitive manufacturing industry, is badly damaged because of the combined incompetence of bureaucrats and politicians, while the inefficient, overmanned and expensive service and distribution sectors and the protected farmers escape. But this is the danger for Japan because of the rapid rise in the value of the yen. In the face of the crisis of the early 1990s, leading bureaucrats remained incredibly complacent, while politicians were too busy squabbling over their petty shares in the spoils of power. Toyoo Gyohten, Bank of Tokyo chairman and formerly international vice minister at the Ministry of Finance, was relaxed in mid-1993 as the yen climbed to 110 against the dollar, claiming that Japanese industry would have to adjust to the appreciating currency, go into more and more hi-tech, sophisticated products at home, and invest more abroad. He pointed out that Japanese industry had only 7 per cent of its total investments outside the country, against about 15 per cent by Germany and as much as 25 per cent by the USA.

Leaders of Japanese industry all said that they were in favour of additional investment abroad to take advantage of cheaper labour costs, especially investments close to the markets to which they were selling. Consequently, investment has been moving factories abroad. In 1990 Malaysia overtook Japan as a producer of air-conditioners, thanks to NEC's factory there. By 1994 Japan was a net importer of colour televisions, most of them made in Japanese factories abroad. But industrialists pointed out that it was not possible to shift a factory abroad in the short time that the yen had taken to appreciate from 120 to 98 against the dollar.

And there is the central point made by Honda president Kawamoto, as to how many of its key industries a country can sacrifice abroad without losing control over its own destiny. Almost without exception, the captains of industry are keen that the central, core production operations and research and development must remain in Japan, so that head office can see and regulate it, provide the most skilled and vital jobs to Japanese, and retain the industrial heart that keeps the economy alive and healthy.

By 1994, the rise and rise of the yen was happening so fast that it was badly damaging Japanese industry, which had neither the time nor the opportunity to make an orderly retreat and to increase investment abroad. Such decisions take several years depending on the industry and how long it takes to find a suitable site, negotiate the deal, build a factory and get it on stream. They could not be taken in the hurly burly of the yen's rapid rise, especially when all the economists were predicting in 1993 and early 1994 that 'on the fundamentals' the currency should be weaker against the dollar. Instead the rise of the yen wiped out large chunks of profits and left whole industries financially hard-pressed.

Peter Drucker,* the management guru, claimed that Japan, rather than the USA, benefited from a weak dollar. The falling dollar meant that Japanese imports, of all its industrial raw materials, 80 per cent of its fuel and energy and a third of its food, were all cheaper and would lead to reduced prices. This is true, but unfortunately such benefits leak out through the inefficient distribution system and do not have their full effect on final prices. Drucker is right that a strong yen has deterred Americans from investing in the world's second biggest consumer market, Japan, while making it cheaper for Japanese to invest in the USA. (This refers to physical investment, to make goods that will bring profits to Japanese manufacturers, not to real estate or art or Treasury instruments, where yen put into dollars have brought diminishing returns in yen.) But the question remains of whether the yen has risen too fast or too far for the future of Japanese industry.

A Japanese think-tank claimed in mid-1994 that, if the yen stayed at 95 to the dollar, only semiconductor chips and liquid crystal displays could survive, profitably manufactured in Japan. For video games and ships, the Japan Society for the Promotion of Machine Industry put the break-even point at 110 yen to the dollar; for personal computers, copiers, fax machines, machine tools and construction machinery, it said the rate was 115; for passenger cars and video cassette recorders, it rose to 120 yen to the dollar; and for radio cassette recorders and paper and pulp products, the point of profit was 125. Even allowing for the proven ability of Japanese exporters to cut costs and improve quality, these are big gaps between the ideal and prevailing foreign exchange rates.

Some commentators rejoiced, declaring that Japan after all has to obey normal economic laws, and predicting that Japanese companies will and should become more and more like western companies, governed by the profit motive and responsive to the stock market, rather than following arcane Japanese practices like the pursuit of market share and lifetime employment. However, there are legitimate questions. As William Miller of the English Agency in Tokyo pointed out, 'If the measure of a successful economy is to provide a job and a nest for people, then Japan has done rather well.' Equally pertinent, if the price of becoming western is unemployment at 10 per cent or more, with all the incumbent social costs of dislocation and disruption of community life, not to speak of the strains on the government budget from having to make welfare payments to the unemployed, it is not clear whether the sacrifices are worth making.

'Should we really become more and more like New York or even London,' asked a rising Japanese manager just back from a posting in the UK, 'with their deprived underclass, growing gap between the rich and poor and

* Professor of Social Science at the Claremont Graduate School in California, writing in the *Asian Wall Street Journal* in December 1994.

between the poor and those just kicked off the bottom rung of society, and the decaying social fabric? It is not a prospect I relish. Yes, Japan need changes, opening up, more awareness of the rest of the world, more flexibility, better use of the talents of women and those who don't fit in easily. But I don't see a lot worth copying in the US, and the UK's best assets have begun to fray badly under Margaret Thatcher's assaults.'

Of all the culprits, Japan's Finance Ministry mandarins must take the main prize for complacency. The could have done more to lift confidence and boost the economy in 1993 and 1994 by lowering taxes. But the MoF is the prisoner of the shortsighted budget and tax bureaux, which can only see the problems from a shortfall in tax revenues, and are already beginning to fret about the consequences of an ageing society. They wonder where the money is going to come from to pay for the pensions of the 25 per cent of Japanese who will be beyond retirement age by the year 2020. This is well and good. But a slow-growing economy, or one stopped in its tracks, will yield fewer profits to be taxed.

Most people who are thrown out of work do not have much income on which to pay taxes. By 1994, the official unemployment rate had reached a record 2.9 per cent. That may not seem much by the standards of western countries used to double-digit rates, but the figures hide a large army of underemployed, somewhere between one and two million, kept on company payrolls doing odd jobs because of the abiding social traditions. Counting these in, the true unemployment rate was about 6 or 7 per cent. With the recession continuing, more and more bosses were talking of ending traditions of lifetime employment because they can no longer afford it. Equally significant, by 1994 the ratio of jobs for jobseekers among new graduates and school-leavers was hovering at about 64 to 100. On top of that, the rising yen has wiped out huge sums from the value of Japan's assets, part of its income for the future.

It was – is – time for someone to restore Japan's self-confidence, but the finance mandarins locked in their spartan public school rooms had little imagination. A more internationally aware and internationally respected MoF might have been able to convince other industrialised countries' leaders of the folly of trying to force the opening of Japan's economy by punishing it with a soaring yen, and might have explained how everyone's growth would be hurt. 'The fundamentals, respective interest rates in the US and Japan, the differing growth rates, all point to a weakening yen,' said a senior MoF official in 1993, just before the yen climbed the post-war mountain face again. Hardly anyone in foreign treasuries was listening, and almost no one in the foreign exchange dealing rooms.

The MoF should not be allowed to shoulder the blame exclusively. Another way forward would have been to carry out widespread deregulation measures to remove restrictions, reduce prices, open up new areas of Japan to the grumbling foreigners and release the pent-up energies of its own people. A series of opinion polls showed strong public support for such measures. Morihiro Hosokawa took office as prime minister in August 1993 pledging political reform followed by sweeping deregulation. But he never even completed his political reforms before leaving office. Deregulation measures that were proposed were few, wishy-washy and further watered down by the opposition of self-interested bureaucrats in time-honoured ways.

Essential change is now blocked by structural factors, involving all aspects of the government machine, bureaucratic and political. Although on the surface Japan is a western-style parliamentary bureaucracy in which the politicians take the final decisions, in practice most real power is in the hands of the civil servants. But it is widely dispersed power, residing in the hands of individual ministries rather than a powerful and centrally controlled 'Government' machine. Indeed, to take the maligned Finance Ministry as an example, the legal powers are in the hands of the various heads of bureaux, while the actual decision making on the main issues of the day is widely dispersed through the directors and deputy directors, bright young men in their thirties and forties. The Dutch journalist Karel van Wolferen, in his seminal work *The Enigma of Japanese Power*, pointed out that Japan was unlike the USA where the sign in front of President Harry Truman's desk – 'The buck stops here' – exemplified the power equation; in Japan the buck does not stop, but simply goes whizzing round and round.

Some thoughtful and knowledgeable bureaucrats claim that this view is an oversimplification. There is undoubtedly a tendency for the buck to whiz round and round, and that is certainly the impression – probably intentionally – given to any outsider confronting the system, particularly a foreign one. But the personalities and the decision-making framework within any ministry mean that one person or one bureau may be able to pull the machine together and get a decision. In the Finance Ministry, for example, the Budget Bureau officials reign supreme because of their control over the money, but a clever vice minister is often the most important person guiding and shaping the decisions of the ministry. The vice minister commands not by rules, but by a mixture of personality, detailed knowledge of the leading issues of the time, the natural defence to seniority, understanding of the machine, and command over juniors' next jobs – all part of the subtle art of bureaucracy. Jiro Saito, vice minister of the MoF in 1993–5, was a natural commander. The fact that vice ministers do only one or sometimes two years in the job means that the focus of power within any one ministry is constantly changing, like a shaken kaleidoscope.

There is also the extra problem of relations between ministries – that Japan has no regular mechanism for reaching agreement in arguments involving several ministries. Again bureaucrats say that there is an 'old boy' network, just as there is in the UK's Whitehall, in which the vice ministers and bureau chiefs know each other, probably rather better than senior British civil servants know each other. Virtually all the top Japanese will have come from the same class at Tokyo University – or from a band of three or four years if vice ministers and bureau chiefs are taken together – all sat the same civil service examination at more or less the same time, and all know each other's places in that exam and reputations within their ministries.

Students of the Japanese government machine also assert that, although ministers are not expected to interfere or countermand their own bureaucrats' decisions, they can be useful in conveying the ministerial view to their cabinet colleagues and helping to reach a consensus on contentious questions. Toyoo Gyohten, formerly the MoF international vice minister, lamented the extended political crisis that followed the downfall of Shin Kanemaru and the upheaval in the then ruling Liberal Democratic Party. His claim was that the Japanese bureaucratic machine was quite able to tackle normal issues of the day, 'but it needs political leadership to sort out the tricky and critical issues, and that is not possible when domestic politics is in turmoil'.

Sometimes, of course, bureaucrats experience an unwelcome taste of political leadership, as happened in July 1993 when the 'lame duck' prime minister Kiichi Miyazawa sat down to a sushi dinner with president Bill Clinton after the economic summit of industrialised nations in Tokyo, and made a framework agreement on trade issues. The bureaucrats had to accept this, while doing their best to redefine and generally undermine it to conform to their own views – something that is more difficult on international matters when there is a foreign party checking on the deal. Curiously, a prime minister has more freedom to exert his leadership on international issues than on domestic ones. That was certainly Miyazawa's unhappy experience. He could strike deals with the so-called most powerful man in the world, the US president, but he was not in control of his own party and lacked any sort of government mandate since he had been defeated in a no-confidence vote and was awaiting the election.

It is clear what the arguments are against this Japanese bureaucratic system: it is confused; has no proper focus of authority; lacks transparency; has little concern for the national view, let alone for international considerations, in reaching decisions; and, above all, is not accountable. Few people would accuse MoF or Miti mandarins of being venal. Indeed, they are imbued with a sense of rectitude, which inspires them even in their *amakudari* jobs in retirement. 'I suppose you could say that we see ourselves as the guardians of the institutions we are sent to, seeing that the rules of the MoF are kept,' said one ex-bureaucrat turned banker, loftily. The argument against the MoF and Miti is that they have a narrow and blinkered view from their own bunkers.

The same declaration of integrity cannot be made about all other ministries. Indeed, it is clear from the spate of political and construction scandals that the problem in some ministries is that, although the buck whizzes round and round, it does not keep some officials busy enough to prevent them pilfering and passing on benefits to their political friends. The amakudari system is abused to give bureaucrats cushy jobs where they can feather their own nests and those of political chums with whom they have struck up a cosy relationship.

In the final analysis, however, Japan's problems are political. And the prime political facts are that Japan in 1995 has only a limited awareness of its true place in the modern world, and apparently cannot reconcile conflicting domestic interests to improve its understanding. This was shown glaringly over the negotiations for the Uruguay Round of trade talks in the early 1990s, from which Japan stood to be a major beneficiary. Protection of the domestic rice market stood in the way.

All countries pay special heed to their agriculture as it is the main source of their food, but none more so than Japan, which by the start of the 1990s was controlling agriculture and rice in ways reminiscent of a backward third world country. Since the 1930s, the government has strictly supervised rice production, controlling its planting and sale, both at the farm gate and at the retail level. The government sets the price, obliges farmers to sell most of their crop to it, and distributes the grain through authorised shops. The law was intended to guarantee essential food supplies, but it has been a steady drain on the budget. In 1993, when a cool wet summer hit, Japan was exposed as a failure even in assuring enough rice. Ironically, the government stood to make a cool $2 billion by importing cheaper rice and selling the imports at its higher prices.

Over the years, the policy has brought grumbles from the people whom it was supposed to benefit: both the farmers, who were told to take more and more land out of production as rice consumption fell from almost 13 million tons in the early 1960s to about 10 million tons 30 years later, and the Japanese consumers, who had to pay prices six times those on the international market for their staple food. The profusion of controls and the high prices guaranteed to farmers encouraged inefficiency. The average rice plot is less than one hectare, and farmers are increasingly in their sixties and seventies, old-timers constantly grumbling that 'youngsters cannot take the life of the rice cycle, which is rather tough and too boring for them', as one 76-year-old put it. Youngsters have increasingly deserted the farms for the bright lights of the city.

Yet in the spring and early summer, it seems as if all of Japan is afloat on a green sea of rice, as if every family has its own tiny outdoor swimming pool into which it has thrown rice seedlings. This is evidence of the problem because most of these plots are too small to offer regular work or income. They are 'Sunday farms'. In fact, only 90,000 of Japan's 3.83 million farms offer income and work equivalent to those of non-farming industries. By 1993 some of the younger farmers, especially those with bigger lots, were beginning to rebel against the restrictions. 'If you could get farmers to speak honestly, you would have a lot of them say that we are prepared to give up controls for the freedom to make our own decisions,' said a farmer in the rice heartland of Miyagi, counting the cost of the poor weather. 'But people will not speak because they are afraid of the bureaucrats who control the policy.' 'We are facing an age of imports, but we have no freedom to grow what we know best,' grumbled another 'young' 55-year-old, picking up withered, sunless grain from his muddy field.

Increasingly, rice was escaping the controls on to the black market. Defender of the status quo said that rice was more than a food; it was the backbone of Japan's sacred tradition, essential to the country's religion, culture and society. 'Rice growing may be said to have determined the very contours of Japanese society,' declared one authority, 'because of the communal co-operation needed to grow the crop. Our villages are built round and on rice.' The Ministry of Agriculture claimed that protection of rice was needed for food self-sufficiency. Then in the next breath it boasted that Japan was the biggest importer of food in the world, and was only 30 per cent self-sufficient in overall grain production, 8 per cent in beans, 63 per cent in vegetables, 78 per cent in dairy products and 70 per cent in meat, as reasons why it should be excused from importing barbarian foreign rice. The chorus of protests was very similar to that in Britain in the 1840s over Corn Law repeal, perhaps an indication of how far behind the times Japan's agriculture was – and is.

The wet, sunless summer of 1993 brought such a bad harvest that the government was forced to import rice. Only a year previously, an official US agency had been threatened with prosecution if it did not withdraw a tiny bowl of rice – for demonstration only – from an agricultural show; Australian exhibitors were permitted as a special indulgence to show pictures of their ripening rice fields. When the rice did come in, it was subjected to orchestrated scare stories that the barbarian grain contained forbidden chemicals, mould, rats, cockroaches, chalk, cigarette butts, bird bones, wire, elastic bands and string, although in blind tastings most Japanese could not tell the difference between home- and foreign-produced Japonica rice, the short-grain, sticky variety used in sushi and Japanese cooking.

More powerful than all these bogus claims in keeping out foreign rice were the arcane political and bureaucratic practices that were growing well even in a year of poor harvest. High rice prices allowed the Liberal Democratic Party, which ruled uninterruptedly from 1955 until 1993 in effect to buy the farmers' votes. Given that many rural constituencies were half or a third the size of the urban ones, it paid healthy political profits. Bureaucrats also did well out of it by getting jobs not only for life, but after retirement too. One farmer noticed this: 'The Ministry of Trade and Industry helped Japan to become a great industrial, trading and economic power with only 8,000 civil servants; but the Ministry of Agriculture with its 38,000 bureaucrats and hangers on has undermined rice farming.'

When push finally came to shove in December 1993, Japan had to make a difficult choice. The clock on the Uruguay Round international trade talks had reached five minutes to midnight before Tokyo made up its mind. The choice was whether to allow minimal rice imports, costing at most a few hundred million dollars, or to sacrifice industrial free trade, out of which it makes hundreds of billions of dollars a year. Begrudgingly, Japan said that it would allow imports of 4 per cent of its rice, rising to 8 per cent after the turn of the century, after which discussions would start on lifting the controls and putting tariffs in their place, possibly as high as 700 per cent.

Some sacrifice: there was no mature political discussion of how the country's agriculture could be reformed to make farmers competitive, no attempt to see the perspective of the industrial, employment and economic gains from free trade, no sense of any international obligations, just hurt expressions of the sacrifice of poor Japan bullied by the rest of the world. It was an example of Japan's failure as an international player at its worst.

There was an unseemly sequel a year later, when the government voted to increase rice subsidies by 11.7 billion yen to 28.5 billion, and then decided to give the massive sum of 6,000 billion yen ($60 billion) over a six-year period to help farmers face the impending foreign competition. But there was no talk of a comprehensive reform plan to make Japan's farmers more competitive and thus stand on their feet against competition.

Not only bureaucrats, but many people who know Japan throw their hands up in horror at the prospect of politicians having the effective powers of decision. The whole political system has proved corrupt and pernicious, focused on individuals and factions and grabbing the shares of the pork barrel, rather than on policies or even on rational discussion of issues which come up for urgent decision. In addition, there is much that is wrong with the way parliament itself functions. Most of the time, members of the Japanese parliament organise and conduct debates like spoilt children playing hooligan games.

One culmination was the 1992 bill on whether Japanese armed forces should be allowed to join United Nations peacekeeping operations. The outnumbered Socialists and other opponents made themselves look like fools as they conducted their infamous 'cow walk', meandering to the podium to cast their final votes on the bill, and delaying its passage by a matter of hours. But it was possible to sympathise with their frustration:

the quality of the debate was poor and the government managers shrugged aside all the most important questions of what implications the bill had for the constitution.

When Morihiro Hosokawa was prime minister, the by then opposition Liberal Democratic Party had its revenge in full and got to play the fool more effectively by stalling discussions on the budget, not by opposing or filibustering clauses it did not like, but by blankly refusing to attend parliament and stopping the discussions from getting under way at all.

A parliament of adults would have a proper timetable, so that business would be conducted every day during the session at regular hours, with time allotted to questions, debates on important national and international issues, and the passage of legislation. Even when Japan's parliament is in session, if a committee is meeting to discuss the budget or an important bill, the plenary does not sit. Indeed, normally if a committee of one house is meeting, there is no plenary session of either house. Other parliaments have managed to arrange schedules so that committees meet regularly in the morning and the main house in the afternoon; some manage to plan things so that the two houses of bicameral parliaments can meet at the same time, and sometimes so that committees and plenary sessions can be held simultaneously. The only saving grace of the Japanese system, and the freedom which it gives to the opposition to confound and hold up debate, is that it affords some protection against the tyranny of the majority.

The crying need for reform, both of the electoral system to end corruption and of the actual functioning of parties and parliament, has led to immense interest in the behaviour and work and writings of Ichiro Ozawa, probably the single most powerful – and controversial – politician in Japan today. Heir to the corrupt and long-dominant faction in the LDP built to prosperity twenty years ago by Kakuei Tanaka, the 'Shogun of Darkness' – the name in Japanese conveys menacing and even evil undertones – Ozawa split with his faction, split the party, cost it its majority and then turned up as kingmaker of Hosokawa and the multiparty rainbow coalition. He was dished by the unexpected alliance of old enemies, the LDP and Socialists, in mid-1994, but continues to exert both fascination and interest as a practical politician and as the leading theorist of reform. Ozawa's book, *Nihon Kaizo Keikaku*, published in English as *Blueprint for a New Japan: The Rethinking of a Nation*, has been widely praised, especially in the West. Former US secretary of state James Baker wrote: 'His arguments are compelling and his recommendations wise. He shows conclusively that for Japan to thrive in the 21st century, it must work to reform and open both its political and economic systems.'

In spite of such resounding praise, controversy still surrounds Ozawa as a politician as well as a propagator of reform. As a politician concerned about Japan's use of power and its place in the modern world, Ozawa wants to see it established as one of the leading countries, ably led and therefore able to take a lead in international counsels. He advocated reform of the electoral system – some of which has been accomplished, although the first elections have not taken place under the new system – to help create a two-party system and more open government. He favoured stronger leadership by the prime minister, with civil servants following the directions of their political masters, a more limited remit of central government, and Japan becoming a responsible member of the international community, sharing the burden of its costs of peace and freedom.

Like motherhood and apple pie, it sounds wonderful. But Ozawa tarnished his case by his past, as a key member of the political faction that did more than any other to make corruption a by-word. True, Japan also has a history of Damascene conversions: the Meiji reformers who started the country on its path to catch up with the West experienced such conversions. But even after Ozawa broke the LDP and was the driving force behind the Hosokawa coalition, he showed he predilection for operating behind the scenes – elected to parliament, yes, but unaccountable for his actions as puppet master of the government.

In opposition after the LDP and Socialists joined hands in unholy coalition, Ozawa orchestrated the creation of Shinshinto, the jumbo opposition comprising nine previously independent parties, but opted to stay behind the scenes as its secretary-general and manipulator. It was the same kind of role that his mentor, Shin Kanemaru, relished. Like the disgraced Kanemaru, too, Ozawa was welcomed by his new colleagues as the man who could pull in the funds to help them win election. The reform of Ozawa himself still has a long way to go.

Nevertheless, his demands that Japan should become a 'normal nation' found an echo both at home and abroad. Surely 50 years after the end of the war would be a good time for Japan to be given a seat at the world's 'top table', the United Nations Security Council, to mark its remarkable prowess and the fact that it is the second biggest economic power in the world and the second biggest paymaster?

However, these demands pose particular problems for Japan and for the rest of the world. The most important one is that, 50 years after it finished, Japan has still not come to terms with the Second World War, which makes it difficult for Japan to come to terms with the rest of the world, still less understand itself as other countries see it. In the space of four months in 1994, two cabinet ministers made controversial comments trying to absolve Japan from blame for the war.

Shigeto Nagano's views were the more challenging. As we have seen, he claimed that the 1937 'Rape of Nanking', when Japanese Imperial Army troops marched into the Chinese city and slaughtered between 200,000 and 300,000 citizens (by western and Chinese estimates respectively) was 'a hoax' and 'a fabrication'. He went on to assert that Japan was not the aggressor in wartime: 'It's a mistake to call the [Pacific War] a war of aggression. It's not true that [the war] was carried out with invasion as an objective. We sincerely believed ... in liberating the [European] colonies.' The fact that Nagano occupied the sensitive post of justice minister, and that he had been a serving army officer, general and chief of staff of the Self-Defence Forces before becoming a politician, compounded the revulsion towards Japan that quickly echoed round Asia.

Shin Sakurai held the less important cabinet job of director-general of the Environment Agency when he declared that Japan did not intend to wage a war of aggression and should publicise internationally that its wartime actions had a good and a bad side. 'Although we caused trouble for Asian nations, it was thanks to that that they were able to become independent [after the war] ... Because of [Japanese] education, [former Japanese colonies] have far higher literacy rates than in African countries ruled by Europe.'

The two men had been colleagues as MPs in the once united LDP, but Nagano left and was minister in Tsutomu Hata's short-lived cabinet as a member of Ozawa's party, Shinseito; Sakurai stayed with the LDP and was minister in the coalition it formed with the Socialists. It proved that no party had a monopoly on such views. Both men quit their cabinet jobs, but only after plenty of damage had been done through an outcry in China and Korea, two countries which suffered under Japanese occupation – Korea from 1910 and China from the 1930s. Their apologies for causing problems merely added insult to injury, suggesting that they still thought the same way but regretted the fuss.

Both men's prime ministers disowned their views. Indeed, the rebel ministers' statements caused anger in neighbouring countries precisely because Tsutomu Hata, who took over from Hosokawa, and Socialist Tomiichi Murayama, who succeeded Hata, had both expressed apologies and repentance for the injury that Japan had caused during its colonial and wartime occupation. The early 1990s had shown a new attitude of acknowledgement of Japan's responsibilities. In its closing days, the Miyazawa government had acknowledged that Korean, Chinese, Dutch, Indonesian and Filipina 'comfort women' or sex slaves – had indeed been forced, many at bayonet point, to serve the Imperial Army as wartime prostitutes close to the frontline.

But evidently several senior colleagues could not see Japan's history or role outside their blinkered nationalistic view, did not understand the sensitivities of their neighbours, and were crassly prepared to defy the leadership to boast their unique Japaneseness. It is difficult to assess how many other Japanese, especially leading politicians and bureaucrats, share the views of the two ministers. Miti minister Ryutaro Hashimoto was not deterred by the experience of Nagano or Sakurai, and caused an uproar by claiming that Japan tried to fight the USA and Britain, not other Asian countries, and that it was thus a matter of subtle definition as to whether it waged wars or invaded Asian nations. But he escaped with a rebuke and survived to be a popular candidate for the prime ministership in a full-blooded LDP government.

Each year on Memorial Day, the anniversary of Japan's surrender, some cabinet ministers visit the Yasukuni Shrine in central Tokyo, a hallowed place for Japanese nationalists because the spirits of war heroes like former prime minister General Hideki Tojo, hanged for war crimes in 1948, are enshrined there as gods. Visiting the shrine to worship is a special assertion of Japanese nationalism. In 1994 eight cabinet ministers, all from the LDP, visited the shrine, although most claimed they were going there in 'unofficial' capacities. In 1994, too, Emperor Akihito and Empress Michiko paid a state visit to the USA, including Hawaii. When the programme was originally drafted, it was suggested that they should visit Pearl Harbor and the Arizona Memorial (to the sunken USS *Arizona*) to the Japanese attack. But the Japanese government withdrew the idea days before the Imperial visit started because it feared trouble from rightists.

The most unequivocal statement about Japan's wartime behaviour came not from a politician or bureaucrat, but from a member of the Imperial family, Prince Mikasa, younger brother of Emperor Hirohito and uncle of the present Emperor Akihito. In an interview with *Yomiuri Shimbun*, Japan's biggest daily newspaper, he unequivocally condemned the conduct of the Imperial Army in China. Mikasa, fourth in line for the Chrysanthemum throne, lashed out at the Japanese military's 'policy of aggression' and atrocities against the Chinese. He spent 1943 on assignment with the army in China, and recalled a young officer saying he got his young recruits to do bayonet practice on Chinese prisoners of war to instil 'guts' into the men. Mikasa wrote his views in a memorandum in 1944, but the army headquarters decreed it to be a 'dangerous' document and ordered all copies destroyed (one turned up in 1994 in the archives of parliament). He noted a tendency in Japan to hold Chinese in contempt, and told of the Japanese army's widespread 'looting, rape and arson'. Claims that Japan was helping China to build a unified nation were self-serving lies. He also quoted a Japanese military doctor as saying that League of Nations delegates visiting Manchuria in the early 1930s to investigate Japan's aggression there had been served 'fruit laced with cholera germs', although they failed to do their work.

This is part of the background to Ozawa's pressure for Japan to become a 'normal nation'. The one particular factor that makes Japan less 'normal' than other nations is its commitment against war as an instrument of policy, and its promise to maintain no armed forces. Spending on its defences has been limited by fiddling the books to 1 per cent of gross domestic product, although its Self Defence Forces pack a greater punch, with better and more modern technology, than all but a handful of other countries' armed forces. It has been able to do this thanks to the American security umbrella. This has increasingly caused tensions on both sides: US politicians resentful of Japan's economic muscle claim that is has been able to build its economy thanks to the 'free ride' of US defence protection; Japanese hawks claim that Japan is less of a true nation because its defence is not in its own hands.

The way forward is not easy, and pressures will grow for Japan and the USA to become more equal partners in defence. So will the risks. The solution that Tokyo should make a bigger financial contribution to the costs of the US defence umbrella is probably unworkable. Not only would the hawks say that this made Japan even less of a nation, but the Finance Ministry would object. Even under the present arrangements, tensions were growing between Japanese and Americans, and not just over routine matters like the low rents paid for the bases and accidents involving Japanese and US military personnel. Budget Bureau pressures in 1994 led the Self-Defence Agency into difficulties over paying the wages of Japanese workers on the US military bases in the country. Civilians living near the biggest bases were also become increasingly vocal, and were instituting court cases against the noise of late-flying US aircraft. And in Okinawa, where 70 per cent of the American forces are stationed, the local government was demanding the return of land on which the US bases were housed.

Normality for some Japanese politicians is the creation of fully fledged armed forces which will play a bigger and bigger part in Japan's defence, lessening the dependence on the USA, 'since we are in Asia and the US is across the world and quite naturally our interests will diverge from time to time', as one of them said. However, few politicians, even on the Right, would be bold enough to suggest dispensing with the treaty with the USA.

Ozawa, ingeniously, does not go down this road either, but sees Japan's international role cast within the United Nations. Normality for Ozawa is not to disown the US Security Treaty, which he regards as a vital pillar of Japan's future, since 'Japan does not have the capability to assume the defence of the nation independently', but to expand the role of the Self-Defence Forces. He wants to 'develop an SDF centred on the United Nations ... We must make the leap from our passive "exclusive defence strategy" to a dynamic "peace-building strategy".' Ozawa embraces secretary-general Boutros Boutros-Ghali's idea of a UN reserve force for peacekeeping activities, and is prepared to commit Japanese troops to it (rushing in where angels fear to tread, while other politicians and countries experienced in UN peacekeeping can only see difficulties in having such a force). Even this will require a big expansion in the range of skills and roles of the Japanese military.

'The future SDF will require a wide range of knowledge in fields like industry, distribution, and other civilian needs,' he writes in his book. 'We will have to maintain a level of knowledge and technological ability that fulfils the spirit of the expression "a nation's military capability depends on its human resources".' It would also require an addition to the constitution, by adding a paragraph to article 9, or a new fundamental law for peace and security. Ozawa's ambitions are heady stuff, and he also concedes that the greater role for the soldiers would mean the need for greater control – by politicians, he emphasises. But who can trust the present Japanese politicians?

Bluntly, the question is whether Japan can be trusted as an international player. No one who knows Japan can suggest that anyone in Tokyo's ruling circles, bureaucratic, political or even military, harbours the sorts of ambition that led to aggression and war 50 years ago. The present generation in command hardly remembers the war, but can remember the devastation and hardship of defeat. Anyone with any passing acquaintance with the media can see that countries that get involved in wars suffer. Japan's own experiences are proof enough of the happiness that pursuit of economic success unencumbered by military ambitions brings.

But there are pressures, such as the suspicions about North Korea's nuclear programme and the potential of China's military expansion, either of which might lead a Tokyo government to take extra steps outside the US umbrella to improve its independent capability for action. Tokyo has its own reasons, too, to worry about Russia, especially as Moscow is still sitting on four small misty and windswept islands just off Japan's Hokkaido coast, which both countries claim. The leaks of nuclear technology from Russia and the former Soviet Union territories are consequently a matter of concern, although no one in Tokyo is yet suggesting that Japan should abandon its pledge not to make, possess or introduce nuclear weapons into Japan.

Economic tensions, particularly with the USA, add another excuse for being properly prepared. Indeed, one of the real dangers of the trade squabbles between Tokyo and Washington is that they could undermine political trust. China, flexing its potential economic superpower muscles and threatening to challenge Japan's domination in the Asian backyard, is already causing some concern.

The most worrying pressure of all is Japan's own view of itself as the wounded misunderstood victim, especially as there are signs that it is an increasingly arrogant one. A Foreign Ministry official, for example, saw Japan getting a permanent UN Security Council place as inevitable, with little thought for the claims of other countries that are big, such as India, or from regions of the world that are unrepresented, like Africa or Latin America. If there was a slight problem, it was the financial one: 'It is really a question of money. When we raise our contribution to 15 per cent of the UN's budget [from 12.4 per cent], we will be in.'

Leading Japanese politicians and officials are aware of their money, and indeed one of the worries when prime minister Hosokawa apologised for his country's past actions was that it might trigger a spate of fresh demands for compensation from freshly acknowledged victims. Tokyo has also been quite prepared to use its aid budget – and Japan is the world's largest donor, providing $11 billion a year – as a source of largesse to quieten neighbours, rather than as part of a vision of developing a new world order in which other peoples can learn from and share Japan's economic successes.

It is a standing joke in some neighbouring countries that, whenever a Japanese leader turns up, he will bring a new packet of a billion yen of aid, 'almost as a not very subtle bribe,' commented a minister in one of the recipient countries. 'But they never listen to our real feelings or share with us their view of Asia and the world. I don't think they have one except as it impinges on Japan's selfish immediate interests.'

Critics have noted Tokyo's general refusal to stand up for principles. Japan hastened to reopen ties with China after the Tienanmen Square massacre of the democracy movement – but that was excused because of Japan's economic interests in China and its fears about chaos on its doorstep. When the Thai military in February 1992 carried out a coup in which soldiers shot unarmed civilians, Tokyo quickly justified it as a need to restore law and order – but obviously it was concerned about Japanese commercial interests there. Now Japan is trying its best to resume aid and commercial links with the military junta in Burma, which stamped on the results of democratic elections and put the elected leader under house arrest. Clearly Japan is afraid that smaller Asian countries such as Singapore are going to beat it to investment opportunities, never mind any principles.

At least one prominent former bureaucrat is worried about similarities between now and the 1930s, in that Japan is refusing to face the big questions of its national interest and use of justice and power. 'The state is walking along a dark road at night,' wrote Naohiro Amaya, former Miti vice minister, just before he died. 'Most of Japan's politicians and political parties of today resemble the pre-war leaders in their perceptions of Japan's national interest, justice and power. Their attention is not attuned to the world. They do not look squarely at history. They are solely concerned with calculating their own gains or losses in a little teacup called Nagatacho [where parliament is], in Kasumigaseki [the bureaucratic district] and in their electoral constituencies. They conduct no serious debate on the just cause that Japan should boldly raise in international society. They talk about liberalism and democracy, peace, a 'normal nation' or a 'small but brilliantly shining nation'. These are only words with no substance. It is all shallow talk. Take Japan's power, for example. It is either overrated or underrated. So long as this situation continues, no country will see Japan as dependable in an emergency or a country that can and will fulfil its responsibilities to the global community. In that event, the prosperity in the teacup will be fleeting.'*

Kenzaburo Oe, the Nobel literature prize-winner in 1994, was surely right when he said in his Nobel lecture that 'to obliterate from the constitution the principle of eternal peace will be nothing but a betrayal against the peoples of Asia and the victims of the atom bombs in Hiroshima and Nagasaki. It is not difficult for me as a writer to imagine what would be the outcome of that betrayal.' In an interview, Oe lamented that 'When the war ended, we believed that a new democratic society would begin in Japan. This was a period of very bright hope that we could create a genuine democratic society. Now conservative critics claim that was a dream or phantom, only illusory.'

Oe refused the government's offer of the Order of Culture, saying that such a government-sponsored award was an affront to the ideal of democracy. He also complained that the emperor was being used and Japan's culture and politics were still 'under the shadow of the very great emperor system, even though in the new constitution our emperor hasn't any power in politics ... Every day on television you can judge the social feeling by watching how the newscasters talk about scandals of Japanese actresses and singers using harsh words. But when the same person speaks about the Imperial family it is with warm words.'

One of the biggest problems is that Japan is still a tribal society. Loyalty is owed to one's family – and a Japanese does not officially exist until he or she is listed in the family register kept in local government offices – one's company, one's ministry and above all one's country, which is presented as the ultimate family. Big Brother has power to reach to all corners of the country, not just through the police who know their neighbourhoods thoroughly, but through a loudspeaker system from the local government offices to every corner of Japan. Every day at 5 p.m., for example, in Tokyo's Nakano ward the chimes for the end of the working day echo to every corner of the ward. Higher ideals of citizenship or human rights or the good of the government – other than the view of the particular bureau of the particular ministry – are in short supply, which means that when there are no clear rules or loyalties, controls can break down. This can be seen daily on the footpaths of Tokyo, where cyclists ride merrily ringing their bells and expecting everyone, able-bodied or sick, young or old, to make way.

The fiftieth anniversary of the atomic bombings of Hiroshima and Nagasaki could afford an opportunity for a thoughtful reassessment of how and why Japan suffered, and what the lessons are for the world now and into the twenty-first century. That would mean painfully re-examining

* *Tokyo Shimbun*, 29 May 1994.

relations with China and neighbouring Asia as well as with the USA, being honest about some of the achievements of colonialism and also about the excesses, the mistakes, the brutalities and indignities, the damage that Japan did to its own people, its own responsibility for Hiroshima and Nagasaki, and for the hundreds of thousands more who died in American firebombing attacks on Japanese cities. In all, Japan suffered 2.6 million war dead, but the mushroom clouds of Hiroshima and Nagasaki summed up the folly of Japan's colonialism in Korea, its invasion and massacres in China, and its attack on Malaya (which came before the attack on Pearl Harbor) and Pearl Harbor itself.

Sadly, judging by the performance of politicians and the strength of nationalist campaigns, the prospects are gloomy. A Japanese psychologist said, 'If westerners are defeated, say in battle, their immediate reaction is to go over what happened to try to learn their mistakes and to learn from them. Japanese are different: they will make a plan of action and follow it, and if they are defeated, follow it again and again, believing that it is not a mistake in their strategy, but failure of spirit. If they have the right spirit, Japanese believe they can conquer anything. We find it hard to face the truth.'

It is possible to sketch in a programme of action. A first step would be apologies backed by compensation payments to those individuals who suffered at the hands of Japanese aggression. This is something that successive governments have resisted, fiercely claiming that Japan's obligations were satisfied by the San Francisco Peace Treaty and other bilateral treaties (signed decades before Japan recognised most of its victims). But the sight of the Tokyo government making belated payments to elderly men and women who had waited and pleaded patiently for years would do wonders for Japan's image abroad – human after all. It might also shame Washington into apologising to the victims of the atomic bombs, since after all there is a vigorous debate going on in the USA as to whether the bombs really had to be dropped to end the war. Whether or not the atomic bomb was essential, it would be a good gesture for the USA to recognise and apologise for the suffering caused.

After that, Japan could begin to think about revising its governmental system to create a central cabinet secretariat, and could look at centralising the bureaucracy rather than dispersing the power to many different ministries. This would carry the obligation of making government more transparent and accountable. The education system should be revamped and teaching revised to accommodate the demands of Japan as an international good neighbour and world citizen in the twenty-first century. In these ways, politicians and bureaucrats might belatedly catch up with Japan's other powerhouses, which have long recognised that the demands of an international world mean it is no longer possible to pursue a narrow nationalistic road. The political leaders might then better appreciate how their shortsighted economic policies are making life difficult for the business powerhouses and ultimately for Japan.

If it is too much to expect action as part of genuine repentance for the excesses of the past, then Japan's leaders might do it from consideration of their country's vulnerability: 123 million people in an Asian region of 2.5 billion and a world of 6 billion are a small number who would be wise not to flaunt their pretence to being special and unique. Without pushing the comparison too far, Japan is much like Britain, a small offshore island kingdom, which has to survive by trade and good relations with its larger continental neighbours. It would be better if it helped establish the ground rules of openness, democracy, human rights and respect for neighbours before China grows up from its present awkward adolescence.

But it is not possible to be too hopeful. All the signs point to the prospect of an orgy of remembrances of Japan as a victim of the atomic bombings. In this case, Japan will be victimising itself, spoiling the prospects of a new beginning, and leaving itself a small and increasingly vulnerable player in a rough world.

Index

See Page 269-70 re Translations.

Violence - Page 244

SWIRE PROPERTIES.   Page 87.